THE BOYS FROM THE BLUE STUFF

THE BOYS FROM THE BLUE STUFF

Everton's rise to 1980s glory

GAVIN BUCKLAND

First published as a hardback by deCoubertin Books Ltd in 2021.

First Edition

deCoubertin Books, 49 Jamaica Street, Baltic Triangle, Liverpool, L1 0AH.

www.decoubertin.co.uk

ISBN: 978-1-9162784-6-2

A CIP catalogue record for this book is available from the British Library.

Cover design by Thomas Regan | MilkyOne.

Typeset by Leslie Priestley.

Printed and bound by Melita Press.

Contents

Preface

ALTHOUGH THEY COULD NEVER REALISE, THERE IS A LINE AT THE end of the second verse of *Jet Airliner*, a US hit for the Steve Miller Band in 1977, which sums up the journey Evertonians were on at the time: '*You know you got to go through hell before you get to heaven*'. Even more appropriately, the song originated in 1973, the year when Billy Bingham replaced Harry Catterick in the Goodison hot-seat, which is where this book, the follow up to *Money Can't Buy Us Love,* begins. The story finishes in the spring of 1985, a time and a place that needs no introduction if you are of the blue persuasion.

Like the preceding decade, the 1970s is a curiously under-recorded part of Goodison history. During the 1960s, Everton and their neighbours contested the game's big prizes, but in the next ten years the gap between the two clubs was, figuratively speaking, as wide as the nation's trousers. If that decade was known as 'the age of beige', on Merseyside it was the age of red as Liverpool, under Bill Shankly and Bob Paisley, carried all before them. While Evertonians watched on in anguish, at Goodison the very characteristics that had driven previous achievement, like a strong boardroom and naked ambition, were now counter-productive, as a new generation of independent, self-sufficient managers gave the manager's role the widest of berths. Outsiders saw the club lacking in both soul and warmth. Less, indeed, was Moores.

Consequently, instead of Don Revie, Brian Clough, Bobby Robson or Ron Saunders, after Harry Catterick departed Billy Bingham and Gordon Lee subsequently filled one the biggest – and most unloved – jobs in football. The two men contrasted hugely. Bingham was the personable, charming Irishman while Lee was a dyed-in-the-wool football-obsessive whose rich black-country brogue accompanied occasional mystifying utterances about the game. Both had things in common, believing success was largely down to hard work while eschewing those with real skill that all champions require. But there was also contrasting approaches in the most boiling of hot-seats: Bingham had dour 'robots' while Lee's free-scoring 1977/78 side is still the favourite campaign of many of that era, thanks to a national newspaper. Elsewhere, they both fell victim at times to the rising power of players. Yet supporters see that period as a time when Everton were very unlucky. But this book shows that if history is written by the victors, then it can certainly be rewritten by the losers too.

Meanwhile, as both managers struggled to wrest control from across Stanley Park, the city itself was now entering an extended period of economic and social decline that seemed to have no end, or a solution. 'Liverpool is a disaster zone,' a *Guardian* article commented in 1981, 'a recent study described Liverpool as the Bermuda triangle of British capitalism.' The economic downturn plus collapsing interest in the game similarly impacted the Goodison purse-strings. A decade after John Moores gave the 'Mersey Millionaires' access to the unlimited funds of his Littlewoods empire, Everton were now selling bingo tickets as a means of making ends meet.

By the summer of 1981, as the city burned and Liverpool celebrated a third European Cup in five seasons, former player Howard Kendall was now handling this most poisoned of chalices. Kendall was later fond of describing his relationship with the club as like a marriage, but the appointment of the rookie boss was a reminder of Samuel Johnson's famous line about matrimony being the triumph of hope over experience. One thing was clear though, with talk of super leagues and clubs becoming more commercially aware, Everton probably had one last opportunity to hang on to the coattails of the elite. Get it wrong and there was a real possibility of joining the fallen giants of English football.

However, by the end of 1983 the pressure on Kendall and empty seats at Goodison were rising at the same rate as a group of talented, but wildly inconsistent, players were failing to fire. But one of the most miraculous turnarounds in football history followed, as relegation candidates became the best team in Europe within the space of eighteen months.

Immediately before talking about travelling from hell to heaven, Steve Miller sang '*Riding high, I got tears in my eyes*' and that was the feeling of many Everton fans as that twelve-year journey reached its thrilling conclusion in the spring of 1985.

CHAPTER 1

Greece is the word

THE TROPHYLESS YEARS WERE OVER AT LONG LAST. AFTER WHAT seemed an eternity, the multitude of fans lined the streets of Liverpool to welcome home their all-conquering heroes. Their open-top bus carried precious cargo: the league championship trophy, won for an eighth time, plus a first European trophy, acquired in thrilling style on the continent.

Yet the team returning to the summit of the domestic game, following a shift in power across Stanley Park, was admired more for their classic English characteristics of teamwork and resilience than free-flowing football. With one or two exceptions, here was an outfit lacking in star quality according to the critics. Hugely successful? Yes. Easy on the eye? Perhaps not. However, the feeling was this was a team set to dominate in the years ahead.

But when Bill Shankly's side crawled around the city on that warm Friday evening in May 1973 the gap between Liverpool and Everton was as wide as any time in recent history. While the Anfield club was celebrating winning silverware for the first time in seven years, their bitter rivals were involved in what was becoming a farcical search for a new manager, after the sacking of Harry Catterick seven weeks earlier.

However, there was no doubting which club was pre-eminent when chairman John Moores appointed Catterick twelve years before. With Liverpool in the Second Division, a combination of Moores' financial backing and some shrewd purchases by Catterick's predecessor Johnny Carey had taken Everton to fifth position, their highest since the title-winning campaign 22 years before.

The merciless Moores was still not satisfied and infamously sacked Carey during a trip to London in April 1961 and, after Wolves boss Stan Cullis had earlier turned down the job, Catterick took over. Twelve months later Everton climbed to fourth and, with Liverpool returning to the top-flight, the following season brought a sixth league championship to Goodison. But there was hardly universal acclaim. Many felt that the 'Mersey Millionaires' had 'bought' the title and their physical style and fanatical fans reflected the chairman's ruthless edge. 'Everton have made sure of winning at least one distinction this season. They will become as unpopular beyond Merseyside as Arsenal were outside London,' *Daily Mail* columnist J.L. Manning predicted.

By the following spring Catterick's side were well-placed to defend their crown but allegations in the *People* over Tony Kay's unwitting involvement in a betting conspiracy when at Sheffield Wednesday disturbed the equilibrium, as did the late-season signing of striker Fred Pickering, and they handed the title across Stanley Park. With the team failing, in January 1966 there was an unsavoury incident between the manager and supporters following a 2-0 defeat at Blackpool which summed up their broken relations. Given a vote of confidence by his chairman, Catterick badly needed a cup run and got one, resulting in a comeback victory against Sheffield Wednesday at Wembley four months later. Within twelve months, the manager had acquired Alan Ball and Howard Kendall and capitalising on a wealth of local talent, in 1970 Catterick won a second title, with a club record 66 points.

Talk of the club dominating English football was optimistic. Some players were past their peak and the side was reaching the end of a natural cycle for any team that lasts, at most, five years. That said, the decline over the next three years was far too steep to explain simply and there were several other reasons covered in *Money Can't Buy Us Love*. One was Catterick's motivation to rebuild again after the pressures of a twenty-year managerial career, while having the security of a contract that had the best part of a decade still to run. Those pressures undoubtedly contributed to health problems, including a heart-attack in early 1972, but the manager hung on until a bad run of form in front of falling crowds led to his sacking in April 1973. However, Moores in resolving one problem had merely caused another.

The job nobody wanted

There should have been a queue of interested parties, but several potential candidates turned down the role. Bobby Robson rejected the job[1] while Jimmy Armfield, who had taken Bolton to the Division Three title, later told BBC Five

---

[1] After an anonymous contact Robson termed 'Deep Throat' had telephoned him to arrange a meeting with Moores. It is not the last time the mysterious man appears in this story.

Live what happened when Moores called. 'I went to his house and we never talked about football, he was talking about his paintings,' Armfield recalled, 'and then he says "do you fancy the job at Everton?" I think you can do this job here.' Given 24 hours to respond, the great man phoned Moores and explained that he was not ready yet: 'He said "okay" and put the phone down.' Chelsea's Dave Sexton also turned down £12,000 a year to take charge at Goodison. Also attracting interest was the promising Grimsby boss Lawrie McMenemy. 'I was one of the men recommended to their chairman John Moores,' he told the *Liverpool Echo* in 1985, 'I had an informal interview for the Goodison job.'

Moores was becoming increasingly frustrated as another target, Leeds' manager Don Revie, led him a merry dance from his Greek holiday hideaway. Eventually, on the morning of Liverpool's triumphant homecoming, Revie phoned Elland Road to confirm his intention to remain in west Yorkshire. The Leeds manager said there were 'personal reasons' for staying. Given recent questions in the House of Commons over his supposed annual contract of £30,000, on the basis it breached Pay Board rules, the initial feeling was Revie pulled out over the legitimacy of the deal.

However, three weeks later, Revie explained to James Mossop of the *Sunday Express* the real reason. While he was pondering the offer, the Elland Road side played in the European Cup Winners' Cup final in Athens and the manager, who had nurtured the majority of the team since they were youngsters, became emotional when he explained the dilemma: 'I shed a few tears in Greece,' he admitted. Before the final, the Leeds boss was leaving but changed his mind after receiving a telegram from Jack Charlton that said, 'Stick together and you will win everything.' The emotional ties to Leeds proved impossible to break and he was staying. Charlton's plea had worked. 'That telegram really struck home,' Revie recalled, 'Big Jack doesn't do things like that.'

All this was no use to Moores and Everton, who now appeared to be back to square one. 'The reputation of the club has suffered greatly,' wrote Michael Charters in the *Liverpool Echo* about the fruitless search. But then there was an unexpected development.

Bing search

After a varied managerial career, former Everton winger Billy Bingham became manager of the Greek national team in September 1971, on a two-year contract.

By May 1973, after a 3-1 defeat to Spain virtually ended hopes of World Cup finals qualification, Bingham was mulling over deals from Panathinaikos and AEK Athens. Nevertheless, there were rumours on Merseyside within 24 hours of Catterick's sacking that Bingham was on the shortlist and the well-connected Belfast journalist Malcolm Brodie was reporting that the club's former player had backing within the boardroom, believed to be director Jack Sharp.

Any rumoured Everton interest in Bingham faded but when Revie pulled out he was back in the frame, on a shortlist of two with Wolves' Bill McGarry. 'Everton are determined to fill the vacancy that has become an embarrassment before their next board meeting on June 4,' reported John Roberts in the *Daily Express*. 'So far Everton have not been in touch with me,' Bingham said evasively, 'I have an excellent contract here [in Greece] but that's not to say I wouldn't be interested in the job if it was offered.'

Moores, with no other viable option, contacted Bingham with an attractive offer: a five-year contract worth £50,000 and a £20,000 signing-on fee. Having not hidden his ambition to manage in the top-flight, unsurprisingly Bingham agreed terms swiftly. For all the money on the table, like his immediate predecessor the emotional attachment to the club held sway. 'I've still blue blood in my veins from my Everton days. I've a sentimental attachment to the club and this should help too,' Bingham admitted, 'Everton expect me to bring them success and the pressures will be great.' Although a surprise appointment, the chairman subsequently explained the rationale:

We have been very impressed in Bingham. He is full of enthusiasm and the big factor in his favour is although he has not managed a First Division team before this, he has handled both the Northern Ireland and Greek national teams. He has so much experience at international level. He is used to dealing with players of the highest class and this was one of the key features in our bringing him to Everton. This national experience will be invaluable to him.

While there was logic to Moores' argument – none of Bingham's rivals for the role had experienced international football – the words sounded like somebody trying to convince himself that appointing a manager with no top-flight experience was the correct one. With supporters cognisant that the Ulsterman was, at best, fourth choice then Bingham also had to persuade the doubters. The new manager took umbrage at suggestions over his unsuitability, maintaining contact was made two weeks before Moores spoke to Revie, which was probably news to Robson and Armfield, who had also been offered the job in that timeframe. That said, there were two factors in the new manager's favour: firstly, being a former player; and secondly not being Revie, an appointment that would have tested the loyalty of many fans, given Leeds' unpopularity. As Bingham said, 'I'm sure I start with a major advantage over any "outsider" who might have got the job – I know Everton, I know the politics of the place, the people, the fans.'

Moores was canny enough to also manage the expectations of supporters at Bingham's welcoming press conference. Twelve years before, when asked what would happen if Harry Catterick repeated Johnny Carey's fifth-place finish that resulted in the sack, Moores replied that the new manager would be invited to look for gainful employment elsewhere. However, when probed about his target for Bingham's first campaign, the chairman's response indicated how far Everton's stock had fallen. 'If Everton could get back in the top half of the First Division next season it would be a foundation on which to build for the future,' Moores declared. Those comments acknowledged that the club was decaying rapidly, having just finished seventeenth.

Moores found another aspect of Bingham's appointment attractive. The Catterick years had been characterised by the club's poor image, not helped by the manager's distrust of the press. By the early-1970s, this attitude was outmoded. The rise of television and the crossover of the game into popular culture made a media-savvy figurehead essential in the era of the 'good for a quote' boss. Moores' problem was the brand leader was across Stanley Park. Any new appointment was always going to draw comparisons with Bill Shankly, of which Moores was only too aware. 'He [Bingham] is a personality and I'm quite sure that he will do a great public relations job for us,' said the Everton chairman, 'He is an outward-looking man and this is what we want at Everton. I'm certain he will create a very fine atmosphere at Everton in that respect.'

For supporters, this was a welcome antidote to the dour secrecy of the Catterick years, but one of Bingham's issues on his return to the club was that his

---

[2] Rob Sawyer described Catterick's job in his superb biography of the great man: 'The role agreed on for the deposed manager was "consultant"; in effect this entailed attending matches filing scouting reports.' That arrangement was never going to be permanent and Catterick took the Preston manager's role in September 1975.

predecessor was still on the payroll.[2] But as the Ulsterman charmed the press on his unveiling in the first week of June, what part the former manager had to play was just one of the many items in his Bellefield in-tray.

CHAPTER 2

King Billy

'THE KING IS DEAD, LONG LIVE THE KING,' PROCLAIMED JOHN Moores at Harry Catterick's unveiling in April 1961. Twelve years later the chairman showed he was as consistent in introducing managers as he was in sacking them. 'The king is dead long live the king,' he told the club's AGM, before adding, 'And I think we have a good king in Billy Bingham.' So who was the man on whom Moores had staked his reputation?

'W.L. Bingham, Manager'

William Laurence Bingham was born in Belfast in 1931. He was a Glentoran regular as a teenager and, after a starring performance for the Irish League against the Football League in October 1950, he lay in the bath as rumours about his future gathered speed. Out of the blue, a stranger held his hand out and muttered, 'Congratulations, you've been transferred to Sunderland.' As a right winger, there were eight years at Roker Park before a further two seasons at Luton Town.

The Hatters were relegated to the Second Division in 1960 and later that year Bingham scored from 35 yards at Anfield, described as one of the finest goals scored on the ground. Suitably impressed were Johnny Carey and the Liverpool chairman, T.V. Williams, seated together in the Main Stand. Both clubs contacted Luton immediately, but Carey got his man after a proposed move to Arsenal collapsed. The *Liverpool Daily Post's* Horace Yates interviewed Bingham and described the natural charm that Moores found so compelling. 'Here was a personality. A fluent flow of words, a ready wit and sound thinking, convinced me that here was a footballer extraordinaire.'

Bingham settled in seamlessly as a player, forming effective partnerships on the right with Alex Parker and Bobby Collins. Parker later said that Bingham was 'probably the best right winger I've played with.' But Harry Catterick's arrival in April 1961 promised a new broom and Bingham, now into his fourth decade, was more vulnerable than most. But the winger provided two more years of sterling service before Alex Scott's arrival in February 1963 hastened his departure to Port Vale, although 23 appearances in the title-winning campaign was enough for a winner's medal. A broken leg in early 1964 ended his career.

Bingham had taken his coaching badges and, after joining Fourth Division Southport as trainer-coach in June 1965, he became manager six months later. Promotion followed at the end of the following season before Bingham became part-time Northern Ireland manager. Inevitably, the good progress at Haig Avenue made Bingham a target and, in February 1968, the attraction of a larger salary and the directors' assurance that they were 'a big club' took Bingham to Second Division Plymouth Argyle. The south coast side was actually close to bankruptcy and by the end of the campaign Bingham was back in the third tier of English football.

The following season was steady: the side were in mid-table in January 1969 when Bingham turned down the Ipswich Town manager's post, a decision that ironically had a significant influence on the future of English football, providing an opportunity for Bobby Robson to flourish in East Anglia. Twelve months later when Bingham refused the Plymouth board's instructions not to take charge of a Northern Ireland under-23 side in Wrexham, they sacked him for a breach of contract – although he later won an out-of-court settlement.

In August 1970, Bingham returned home to take charge of Linfield, leading them to the league title in the following spring, when he also vacated the national team manager's role. At the time the Greek FA were keen to expand the British influence in their homeland and, because of his previous international experience, there was a successful approach to Bingham to become national team manager. Two years later John Moores came calling. One of the new appointee's first actions after taking the Everton role was to change the sign on his Bellefield office door, from 'Manager' to 'W.L. Bingham, Manager'.

All in the family

Bingham was inheriting a side that had been in decline, with the seventeenth finish being the lowest in the top-flight since the relegation campaign of 1950/51. Bingham subsequently had a tough job in reinvigorating the fortunes of the squad. 'The club went through a traumatic period,' he later admitted, 'and when I came in I had to motivate the players again.'

Off the pitch, there was also the fractured relationship with supporters to heal. A shareholder asked Moores at the AGM what 'the directors were doing to end the image of aloofness which had existed between the club, shareholders, supporters and the press.' Moores reacted strongly, saying, 'I reject that. Everton do not have a poor image. When clubs are winning, they have a good image; when they are losing they have a bad one.' That may have been true but the club needed to improve its reputation. As one shareholder had said several years before, 'Why do Everton have to be anti everything?' Not only were Everton perceived as being old-fashioned, but the fanatical and public demands for success since the early days of the Moores regime did not sit well with many. In Catterick's latter days, the chairman had promised on television that if Everton 'didn't pick up before the end of the season' he would 'do something about it.' One journalist commented: 'I conjured up a vision of a masked executioner, axe poised high above his head ready to crash down on the condemned man.' Indeed, Moores as the fearful dictator perhaps added difficulty to filling the manager's role. But Bingham was keen to remedy this reputation:

I like people. I like to mix with them and I like talking to them. But I'm not a blarney merchant. I don't have to force myself to get on with people. It is part of my character and personality and I intend to get to know our Everton supporters. I want them to feel that they are part of a great club once again. Wherever possible I want to keep them informed, through the press, of my hopes and intentions.

Bingham also wanted to build a rapport with players, using lessons learned from his own experiences. 'When I was with Everton in the early sixties, all the players felt a love for the club. It was perfectly genuine,' he explained, 'But they also felt that feeling was not returned. They felt they were all right while they were doing their stuff on the field but once it was over they were discarded and forgotten. I want that at Everton – now. I want the players to feel they are appreciated while they are on the staff and that the club is prepared to do something for them.' One of his first actions was to remove the dreaded 'clocking in' book at Bellefield, a legacy of the overbearing discipline. Unlike Catterick,

Bingham aimed to name the starting XI in advance rather than 'perming eleven from sixteen' in his words. However, like his predecessor he had to speak to several players about their hirsute appearance. 'They will look as Everton footballers should look,' Bingham said after instructing them to trim their long hair and beards.

Although Bingham desired an *esprit de corps* at Goodison there was not going to be a lax regime. 'Don't imagine I'm going to be a softie,' he told the *People* in his first summer, 'I mean to have the players' respect, and already I've issued an open warning that anyone stepping out of line will be hammered hard in any way I think appropriate, even by being fined or dropped.' The Irishman was as good as his word. When Joe Harper, Mick Bernard and Roger Kenyon were 45 minutes late after a night out on the pre-season tour to Sweden, he fined all three a week's wages. 'It has been an expensive tour for them but they must learn to do as I say,' Bingham said afterwards, 'Club discipline must be maintained and I intend that it will be.'[3]

Bingham may have wanted warmth but the nice guy act did not extend to pre-season training. The new manager had developed a reputation for pragmatism and discipline – the latter characterised by a fierce fitness regime, reflecting his own. The Plymouth players had staged a near mutiny over his methods, which included a summer trip with the Royal Marines, which baffled some. 'No matter how long you spent on the training ground… it wasn't going to make you a better player,' one remarked, 'The training with the marines didn't make us better players, it didn't make any of us better soldiers or commandos either.'

His fearsome, almost cruel, reputation had been born in Southport. After a hard training session on the beach, the manager would force players to run up a sand dune they nicknamed 'Bingham's Hill'. He gave players forty seconds to climb to the top and back and even if they were close to the finish after, say, thirty seconds, Bingham would shout 'thirty-six, thirty-seven…' to get that extra effort. Local journalist Brian Caven witnessed the torture at close hand and wrote that if the players 'had been horses the RSPCA would have had a field day.' Before pre-season started Bingham declared, 'Power is no substitute for skill but if we can

---

[3] Harper in his autobiography *Joe Harper: Upfront and Personal* claimed that a club director in their restaurant said, because of the slow service, that if they returned late he would explain why to the manager. Ten minutes late back at their hotel (not 45), Bingham ignored the director's mitigating explanation and fined the players. Harper also claimed that details of the disciplinary meeting were leaked to the press.

add a little extra zest and fitness to the players, that will be good for us next season.' Bingham was as good as his word and the Everton squad suffered the ordeal described by Caven with their first full week's training on Ainsdale beach, including his eponymous dune.

The Bingham style

'I like good defensive football,' Bingham once said at Plymouth, 'but I always like my players to be positive and adventurous when we are in possession.' But like most managers who had spent their career in charge of a largely moderate playing staff, Bingham placed great emphasis on sound organisation and fitness to counter more skilful teams. 'Billy preferred discipline and strategy to creativity. He has a passion for physical fitness and for tall and strong strikers,' the Greek forward Antonis Antoniadis told Bingham's biographer Robert Allen.

Bingham was therefore a strong believer in method and getting players to fit into a system, rather than buying players and finding one to make the most of their collective abilities. 'It is a hard game to learn,' he later told the *Observer's* Peter Corrigan, 'but you have to learn within the team framework. It is the vogue to cry out for the aesthetic, for the individual skills, but football is a team game after all and the only freedom comes from being in a good team.' The new manager was also conscious that one thing lacking in the modern game was patience. Bingham had taken a step back in Greece and looked at domestic football with a fresh set of eyes. 'I could look at the English game objectively,' he told Corrigan, 'and see how it is conditioned by the environment and our impatience for action.'

Whether Everton supporters, who had watched their bitter rivals become the country's best team, had patience was a moot point. Also, Bingham faced the challenge of convincing fans that fitness, defensive stability and organisation was a priority over good football synonymous with the School of Science. Although he said, 'I also know all about the club's tradition of classical, attractive football. Goodison crowds have been brought up on skill and style,' to meet those demands Bingham's teams would need to show far greater imagination and verve than previously seen.

Changing of the championship guard

'The most difficult problem will be to pick the team up again and get them going once more,' Bingham said before the start of the 1973/74 season. 'The Everton fans are naturally impatient for success and I think that good training methods will come first and then organisation and, if they are needed, I shall add players.' On that basis the Ulsterman, surprisingly, did little in the transfer market during his first summer.

Bingham had inherited three distinct groups of players. The first were those senior professionals who had appeared in the 1970 title-winning campaign, several of whom had been or were battling long-term injuries. Roger Kenyon and John Hurst formed a decent central defensive partnership following the retirement of Brian Labone but neither possessed his confidence and leadership qualities. The second group were those signed after 1970, of these only John Connolly, a Scottish winger bought eighteen months before, showed promise. Record-signing, striker Joe Harper, brought down from Aberdeen for £180,000 in December 1972, had scored eight times in 22 games but required a forward partner. Goalkeeper David Lawson had enjoyed a decent first season but there appeared to be no future for striker Rod Belfitt and the perennially injured midfielder, Henry Newton.

The final group were those who had come through the youth system. With ample opportunities to shine, they were clearly below the class of their immediate predecessors. However, a small number had promising futures. Of these, Mick Lyons had shown the greatest potential. Originally a goalkeeper, Lyons was a centre-forward when Everton signed him as an apprentice in 1968. The club believed his lack of pace would ultimately mean a role at centre-half but Joe Royle's injury meant that Catterick largely deployed the 21-year-old as a forward.

Manchester-born Mick Buckley was a feisty midfielder also brought to Everton during the Catterick years. The former England schoolboy international had been the target of several clubs, but chose Everton only after Sir Matt Busby – based on his experiences with a fifteen-year-old George Best – convinced a doubting Catterick that the 5ft 4in Buckley's slight build would change with age. Although the ever-optimistic Bingham claimed Buckley could be the new Alan Ball, there were still concerns over his strength. 'The lad's frame could always prove his personal handicap and prevent him from being able to reveal his skill in full flow,' Michael Charters wrote in the *Liverpool Echo,* 'In midfield, skill, pace and the ability to win the ball are essential: Buckley is short of the last attribute.'

The last of the promising Bellefield triumvirate was winger Gary Jones, the closest Everton had to the infamous group of 1970s mavericks like Stan Bowles and Rodney Marsh who entertained fans royally – as well as infuriating their managers. Jones had shown dazzling skills as a right-winger of rare potential but eventually became the resident *enfant terrible* under Bingham and their spiky relationship was always going to end in bitter separation.

Consequently, by the summer of 1973, there was only one player capable of consistently satisfying the demanding Goodison crowd. The *Daily Express* had just voted Howard Kendall as their Footballer of the Year, some achievement whilst playing for a side who finished just above the relegation zone. The club captain appeared to be the player around which Bingham would build his side, but a visit to a ground where two fellow club legends ended their Everton careers put paid to that.

Howard's away?

The Baseball Ground, Derby was undoubtedly the worst pitch in the top-flight during the era. Bizarrely, the stadium also acted as a graveyard for two of Everton's greatest sons. Alan Ball played his last game for the Toffees there in December 1971, when a dressing room row with Harry Catterick put the final nail into his Goodison coffin. Catterick left after effectively his final game as manager there in April 1973 and five months later came the fixture that ultimately led to Howard Kendall's departure.

Scepticism regarding Bingham's appointment had resulted in poor season-ticket sales and the gate for the first home game against Leicester City was 33,000 – against a post-war average of 52,000 for the opener. On the pitch, Everton had taken four points from four games without producing anything in the way of good football to attract the fans. One supporter's letter to the *Liverpool Echo* summed up the frustrations of many. 'I looked to Mr Bingham to return to the Everton traditional forward play' he complained, 'But this team selection of eight defenders and three marked forwards is doomed to failure before the start.'

The Baseball Ground encounter was controversial. 'It was a highly unsatisfactory afternoon all round,' Michael Carey wrote in the *Guardian*, 'Everton, reduced to ten men and then beaten by two controversial goals, may be forgiven if, with that kind of luck, they ask their manager to produce his Irish birth certificate.' The drama started after 27 minutes when Colin Harvey fell awkwardly and Jimmy Husband came on. Five minutes later Howard Kendall stretched for a ball and strained his knee ligaments. Remarkably while the skipper lay on the ground in agony, Husband put the visitors ahead with his first league goal for two years. A man down, the visitors heroically defended their lead only to concede two goals that looked suspiciously offside. Bingham had to step onto the pitch to stop Roger Kenyon from protesting to the linesman after Derby's winner, while a young supporter crossed the width of the playing area to confront the mistaken official. The usually mild-mannered trainer Stuart Imlach was so frustrated he told the referee, 'How does it feel to be a cheat?'

With both of his experienced midfielders out of action, Bingham entered the transfer market but, to the surprise of many, the Everton manager went to Sheffield Wednesday and acquired fellow countryman Dave Clements for a fee of £60,000. The 28-year-old brought intelligence both on and off the pitch – at a time when players owned family saloon cars, the Irishman drove a Jaguar XJ6. With Bingham clearly intent on bringing in his own men some players were vulnerable – a feeling that gathered speed when Henry Newton went to Derby County for a fee of £100,000. 'Clements will give the side composure,' Bingham said, 'Newton? He might be able to do a job for Derby. I hope he does. But I didn't feel that he could do one for me.' As for Kendall, in his autobiography, *Love Affairs and Marriage,* he revealed that the local press tipped him off that Bingham did not rate him as a player. In fact, as soon as the Northern Irishman took over there were rumoured bids from Derby County and Manchester United, which the manager naturally denied.

With Kendall injured, Clements's arrival brought an upturn in form – five wins and a draw from six games took Everton second at the end of October. Bingham told Harry Miller of the *Daily Mirror* the sudden renaissance was largely due to 'more emphasis on pressure work and building up stamina. Everton have always had this reputation for playing skilful football. I want us to retain that reputation. But I also wanted a bit more power to our game.' An encouraging gate of more than 41,000 witnessed the 1-0 victory over Burnley, with Tom Jack in the *Guardian* proclaiming, 'Everton are finding the confidence, the cash and cheers surging back.' However, with the club skipper's recovery taking longer than expected, there were rumours that Bingham was keen to offload his star player. When Sunderland striker Dennis Tueart was a £225,000 target, the manager denied speculation the skipper was bait in a swap deal.

With Kendall fit before Christmas after three months on the sidelines, supporters expected a return to the team. However, the midfield trio of Clements,

Mick Bernard and Mick Buckley had gelled well, with the youngest impressing. 'And then there's Mick Buckley,' Bingham told Harry Miller, 'I don't want to sound like Bill Shankly, but what a player this is. He's nineteen, a midfield man who makes magnificent runs. He's powerful and wants to score goals.' To the annoyance of fans, Kendall consequently remained in the second string. 'At the start of this season, an Everton team without Kendall seemed unthinkable,' opined Michael Charters in the *Liverpool Echo*, 'But Mr Bingham feels his current midfield trio cannot be disturbed on their present form.' But as one supporter noted in the same paper: 'The fact that Howard Kendall... has had to waste two months in the reserves waiting for one of the inferior midfield men to be injured, means that I will join the growing ranks of Evertonians who have given up their tickets in disgust over the last few years.'

Then there was an extraordinary development. At 1pm on 22 January, Charters spoke with Bingham to clarify Kendall's position and informed him 'of the number of letters the *Echo* had received from angry Everton fans protesting at the idea of Kendall leaving the club'. The following day Bingham told Charters what happened next. 'At 2pm, after I had spoken to you and had other inquiries about Kendall,' the manager revealed, 'I decided we should end the speculation once and for all. I telephoned the chairman, Mr Waterworth, and suggested we should meet Kendall during the afternoon. Mr Waterworth came to Bellefield and we had a chat. We have offered Howard a new contract which he will sign later... I am tired of saying it that Howard is an Everton player.' Incredibly, the intervention of the local press forced the club into action.

But the contract remained unsigned. Birmingham City manager Freddie Goodwin had previously registered an interest, which had far-reaching complications, but the Everton manager responded vigorously to stories of his captain's imminent departure to the Midlands. 'I am tired of denying all these rumours,' said Bingham, 'We want him as long as he wants us.' In reality, that proved to be about three weeks.

Goodbye Joe

Midway through the 1973/74 campaign, Bingham had clearly engineered if not a revolution, then an encouraging rehabilitation of the club. Reviewing progress, Michael Charters wrote Bingham's changes 'have all been on the credit side. And the most important has been the remarkable uplift he has created in spirit, atmosphere, optimism and the general well-being of the club.' Although there were positive signs, Bingham knew the biggest weakness. 'Along with most other clubs this season our problem has been up front... if we had scored a few more goals our current League position [seventh] would be so much better.' In 28 league games thus far, the team had scored just 29 goals.

Consequently, with Joe Royle short of full fitness, Bingham needed a striker. Having offloaded Rod Belfitt to Sunderland for £70,000, the Everton boss was also open to offers for Joe Harper. The thickset Scot was the antithesis of Royle in some respects, a predator with razor sharp instincts in the penalty box. When Royle returned to training, hopes were high that the little and large forward pairing could form a profitable partnership. However, there were teething problems. 'When Harper came back from his summer break, he was probably the most unfit player on the books,' Bingham claimed, 'He had put on a lot of weight.' The Scot would consequently fall victim to Bingham's fitness regime. 'He brought in a programme of weight training and rather than tone us up he had us lifting heavy weights, I was bench pressing about 250 pounds,' the Scot admitted later. 'All that did was make me bigger and stronger, but my game was about speed and sharpness. If you asked me to sprint all day I'd do it but lifting weights wasn't good for me.'

By the end of January, Aberdeen had been in negotiations for two months and made a third cash offer of £110,000. But Everton had also been speaking to Hibernian and when the Easter Road club upped their offer to £120,000, a Scottish record, Harper's former club angrily withdrew. Bingham spoke with the Scot and personal terms were swiftly agreed. 'My wife and I never really settled in England,' Harper admitted, 'And when this deal came up I could not turn it down. It was too good to miss.' In truth, Harper was a victim of the changing priorities of the game. It was the era of work-rate and keeping it tight at the back, of goalless draws on the road and 1-0 victories at home. The Scot, as a specialist penalty-box striker, was never going to thrive in England. In a struggling team, a record of fourteen goals in 51 appearances bears testimony to a talented player in the wrong place at the wrong time.

Welcome Bob

Having received nearly £400,000 in fees and laid out only £60,000, Bingham could spend big. After tightening up the defence and creating an effective, if slightly one-dimensional midfield, Bingham was finding the same problem as Harry Catterick – the purchasing of a top-class forward. However, with primary targets Mick Channon and John Richards out of bounds, Bingham was not going to panic. 'I am not going to be stampeded into buying people,' he declared, 'We do not want other people's castoffs at Goodison. I want to sign players I want. I am only interested in top-class men.'

Bingham had apparently identified the top-class striker needed shortly after taking over. Birmingham City's Bob Latchford had been a prolific scorer since making his debut five years before. After helping the Midlands side back into the top-flight, Latchford had scored twenty goals in 1972/73 and added seventeen in the current campaign, excellent figures for a struggling team in a largely defensive era. It is largely unknown that Harry Catterick had been a massive fan of Latchford and made several approaches. Journalist John Moxley had bumped into the now former Everton boss at Goodison at the start of the season and later recalled the conversation: 'The first thing he asked me was: "How is the big fellow playing?" I told him that to date Bob Latchford seemed to have lost the dash and power of the previous season. I added that Trevor Francis was continuing to broaden his game. "Ah," said Catterick. "Francis is the cream on the cake but Latchford the cake."' Catterick had spoken to Goodwin several times but the Birmingham manager would turn a deaf ear when it came to money. The nearest Everton came to a breakthrough was in late 1972 when they made a British record offer for the England under-23 international, but any chance of a deal fell through after talks between John Moores and his Birmingham opposite number, Clifford Coombs, collapsed. Coombs later recalled the final conversation, which took place at Goodison on Boxing Day: 'We were at Goodison for a match when Mr John Moores approached me and said "Mr Coombs there must be a price for him. Everyone has a price." I thought for a while and said, "It's a deal if you offer one of your mail order businesses and four or five of your stores."'

So after rejecting Freddie Goodwin's approach in early January for Kendall, the Everton manager sensed an opportunity and, after both parties met at a secret rendezvous in Manchester, details of a complicated three-way deal emerged: to meet Birmingham's demand for a British record fee of £350,000, Everton would have to transfer Howard Kendall (valued at £180,000), full-back Archie Styles (valued at £90,000) plus £80,000 cash.[4] With Birmingham refusing a cash-only deal for Latchford and Everton not prepared to do the same for Kendall, then the skipper was the key figure and he saw the writing on the wall. 'When your manager asks if you are prepared to join another club,' the midfielder admitted, 'then you begin to realise that there is not much room for you and that it is time to sort things out quickly.' Bingham elaborated: 'The only way out, therefore, was a compromise and we reluctantly decided to offer Kendall in an exchange deal. If you want a player who can score goals you have to pay the asking price. I didn't want Howard to go but I had no option if I wanted to sign Bob.' Michael Charters described the challenge facing the new signing. 'This large young man, described with awe by manager Billy Bingham as a "tank" and a "powerhouse" carries a big burden on shoulders broad enough to cope with it,' he wrote, 'It is simply to produce the goals for Everton which strikers Joe Royle, Joe Harper and Mike Lyons have been unable to do.'

Latchford's departure also disappointed a section of Birmingham supporters for whom the 23-year-old meant more than just scoring goals. 'Latchford has a certain charisma,' said the *Birmingham Daily Post,* 'His handsome bearded features and his athletic frame appealed to female supporters who went into raptures every time we scored.' On the evening of the announcement, calls from upset girls jammed the newspaper's switchboard. Although Everton were gaining a striker who would become a hero to an entire generation of fans, his arrival raised questions over the future of one of his illustrious predecessors.

Goodbye Joe

For Joe Royle, by late 1972 the years of leading the line against hard-tackling defenders and inadequate protection from referees were taking their toll. After starring and scoring for England against Yugoslavia in October of that year, the big striker suffered a career-threatening back injury shortly afterwards. Two operations meant the rest of the campaign was a write-off. During recovery, Royle discovered he had lost all power in his left leg, his 'jumping leg'. This was the most painful part of his rehabilitation, as he explained: 'It was a crutch to me, because if everything else was wrong with my game I was still winning balls in the air, and

---

4 The 'fees' for Kendall and Styles can be regarded with cynicism. Everton offered Styles to several lower-division clubs in the preceding months for just £15,000, with no takers. Although the future Everton boss was still a fine player, a notional 'fee' of £180,000 (one of the highest paid for a midfielder in England) meant the club were surprisingly doubling their money on someone nearing 28 years of age and who had been out injured for three months.

it's a horrible thing to know you've lost your left leg.' Royle then suffered a series of ankle injuries in Bingham's first season and form and confidence suffered. 'It's almost like learning to play again, the things you do naturally – you've got to think about it, and time is space in football,' the striker told Brian Glanville in the *Sunday Times* of his return. 'The whole of the 1973/74 campaign was a waste of time for me,' Royle said in his autobiography. Dropped from the team before Latchford's signing, the future Everton boss was out for three months before a surprise return in April.

However, the arrival of Scotland Under-23 striker Jim Pearson for a fee of £100,000 indicated that Bingham was looking for further options. With Everton willing to sell and with Royle out of contract, Manchester City and Nottingham Forest were circling as was Tommy Docherty at Manchester United, who was rumoured to want a swap deal involving Brian Kidd. Royle's stance was clear when D-Day arrived. 'I have been offered a new contract by Everton but have refused to sign it for several reasons,' the 25-year-old said, 'The main reason is that Mr Bingham has made it obvious by his signings of strikers that there is no place for me anymore.'

With Royle's Goodison career seemingly over, there was a lifeline. Although still out of contract, the striker showed greater fitness in the summer of 1974 and struck up a promising partnership with Latchford on the tour of West Germany. Such was Bingham's confidence he selected both for the opening three league games and the pair rewarded him with four goals. 'Probably the most threatening striking duo in football just now,' mused Horace Yates in the *Liverpool Daily Post* after a 3-2 win at West Ham, 'their understanding is growing all the time. They are playing for each other as well as themselves and the Royle transformation seems complete.' But it was a false dawn. After six goalless games, Royle was out of the side for reasons he later expanded upon in the *Liverpool Echo*:

I played with Bob Latchford up front for Everton and it was going quite well. I was fit again after two and a half seasons with back trouble. Early on that season I felt I was in better form than Bob, but we lost at home to Villa in a League Cup replay at Goodison. One of the TV commentators made a point of saying that he couldn't see the Royle-Latchford partnership working. I only played one game after that. My relationship with the manager, Billy Bingham, grew worse. His obsession to sell me to Birmingham didn't help.

Having taken an option out on Royle following the Latchford transfer, Birmingham made a move in early October and, although the clubs agreed a fee of £220,000, the striker turned it down due to family ties on Merseyside. However, both parties inevitably found a convenient exit door and on Christmas Eve 1974, Royle joined Manchester City for £200,000. The move was a low-key end to the Everton career of a Goodison giant and, in many ways, one unfulfilled because of the crippling back injury – a record of 119 goals would surely have been substantially higher otherwise.

Farewell to the White Pele

Like his former manager and fellow members of the Holy Trinity, the Baseball Ground played a key role in the fortunes of Colin Harvey. Injured in the same game as Howard Kendall, he played just one league match in the following five months – during which time Dave Clements had taken up his favoured role on the left-hand side of midfield.

Like Royle, there was transfer speculation involving Harvey, and he too was rumoured to be part of a deal involving Manchester United's Brian Kidd. Although the Toffees legend regained his place, he was some way below his brilliant best and Bingham attempted to offload him, as part of a deal involving Aston Villa's full-back John Gidman, but the Midlands club rejected an exchange of Harvey plus £200,000 cash.

Although the elegant midfielder was back at the start of the 1974/75 campaign when Martin Dobson arrived for £300,000 at the end of August, Harvey's days at Goodison were numbered. Within a fortnight one of the club's greatest-ever servants moved to Sheffield Wednesday with some fine words from the Goodison hierarchy: 'We wish to place on record our grateful thanks and appreciation to him for twelve years' wonderful service. He is a model professional and a credit to himself, his club and the game.' If anything, the sale of Harvey provoked more of an adverse reaction than that of Howard Kendall. The following home game against Wolves featured the famous banner draped over the side of one of the stands: '£70,000 is an insult to Colin Harvey, the White Pele'. With the greater emphasis on work-rate, Harvey was a player whose sublime skills were somehow obsolete because of a changing game. The opening sentences of one letter to the *Liverpool Echo* summed up the views of many:

As a dedicated fan of 'the White Pele,' my initial reaction to the news of Colin Harvey's transfer to Sheffield Wednesday was one of disgust. My disgust was at Billy Bingham for even thinking about selling him and disgust at the paltry £70,000 transfer fee. On reflection, however, it became clear to me just why it had to be so. Colin Harvey was, and still is, a luxury to the modern game of football. He was a pure footballer, a man who knew no other way than skill. Like George Best (I can now understand why he quit) and Pele, he was always three steps ahead of the opposition. He made the hard things in football look easy and the easy things even easier. He thought football and not tactics; he knew what to do, when to do it, and how to do it without being told.

Harvey would, of course, return to the club within two years as youth coach, ironically under the man who deemed him surplus to requirements. While, Bingham now had a team capable of challenging for honours, the failure to land a player who was up for sale in the same week as Dobson was to prove costly for the rest of the decade.

Any given Sunday

By the end of 1973 the country was in the midst of what the Chancellor of the Exchequer, Anthony Barber, admitted was the biggest economic crisis since the war. There had been a quadruple increase in the price of oil, after the Gulf states drastically cut supplies to the West following Israel's victory over Egypt in the Yom Kippur war. At home, the National Union of Miners implemented an overtime ban after the government rejected their thirteen percent pay claim. The country could cope with one of the scenarios but both occurring simultaneously caused an energy crisis, forcing desperate measures. In November, Prime Minister Edward Heath declared a state of emergency with the use of electricity banned for floodlighting and the heating of shops and offices. In January 1974, to help preserve energy, Heath brought in the Three Day Work Order, which limited the use of electricity by firms to three consecutive days in a single week. The infamous 'three day week' brought chaos initially to Merseyside. Major users of electricity like Ford at Halewood and Cammell Laird had to negotiate with power suppliers to establish the days on which they could operate, to ensure the biggest companies would not overload the grid.

The effects on football were wide-ranging. Due to the floodlit ban, midweek fixtures moved to afternoons, which affected attendances. Saturday working was commonplace so, with concerns over a further drop in gates, there were demands to play fixtures on the Sabbath. Consequently, before Christmas, clubs were permitted to play their forthcoming FA Cup third round matches on a Sunday. Although many in the game welcomed the move, others did not. Harold Legerton, general secretary of the Lord's Day Observation Society, described the FA's move as 'the thin end of the wedge'. Events would prove him correct.

Reaction was mixed on Merseyside. The Liverpool secretary, Peter Robinson, claimed they would not be playing any matches on a Sunday and a survey in the *Liverpool Echo* found two-thirds were against the proposed plan, primarily for religious or family reasons. Everton were more open-minded. 'Transport problems are worse on a Sunday than in midweek,' said secretary Chris Hassell, 'In future years it might be a good thing, but I don't think it will work now.' However, he added a caveat: 'I have my doubts over whether it would work, but we would certainly talk about the idea.'

The experiment, in attendance terms, proved to be an enormous success for the quartet of third round ties played on the first Sunday of 1974. More than 39,000 watched Bolton against Stoke City at Burnden Park – three times their league average and a bigger gate than any Saturday tie. With both Merseyside teams drawn at home in the fourth round and electricity suppliers unable to guarantee power for the floodlights at both grounds simultaneously, Everton moved their tie against West Brom for the final Sunday in January. 'This does not mean to say we are now in favour of Sunday football,' Chris Hassell said about the historic decision, 'We do think though that this is an opportune moment to experiment and test the reaction.'

There was an unusual payment method to get into Goodison. The Sunday Observance Act prohibited the charging of admission for entertainment, so clubs circumvented this by making admission free but only allowing entry if supporters paid for a programme – or in Everton's case a team-sheet, which later became a sought-after piece of memorabilia. There may have been opposition but the experiment was a huge success: a crowd of more than 53,000 against the Second Division side was 20,000 more than the third-round tie against Blackburn. Nevertheless, the game was an appalling spectacle of 'feuds and personal subplots within the play,' according to Gerry Harrison of *The Times*. He added that 'by the time the players had scrambled their way through a tattered ninety minutes, which included forty-five fouls as well as a heavy spicing of other stoppages, there were thousands who felt their journey, and experiment, had been wasted.' Apart from a Mick Buckley effort that struck the bar, the match provided dismal fare for the spectators who paid receipts of £30,600 – but 'that was before anyone asked for his money back,' according to the *Guardian's* Eric Todd. One spectator summed up the prevailing mood, labelling it 'Scars on Sunday'.

Like many FA Cup replays, if the original match was bad-tempered then feuds continued and, at a rain-soaked Hawthorns, the game was described as a 'smouldering volcano' by the *Daily Mirror's* Chris James. Typically, the only goal of the tie was full of controversy. The Baggies' centre-forward David Shaw had continually obstructed goalkeeper David Lawson by holding the latter's jersey at corners, so the Everton stopper warned the linesman beforehand. But just before the break, Shaw appeared to impede Lawson and the prolific Baggies marksman Tony Brown headed home at the far post. However, the tie's major flashpoint occurred fifteen minutes from time when West Brom winger Willie Johnston lunged at Archie Styles with studs showing and caught him just below the knee. Styles understandably retaliated and both players rolled around in the mud exchanging punches before the referee sent them off, although the Everton man could consider himself unfortunate.

Afterwards Bingham blasted the Welsh referee, John Williams, 'He let the game go at Goodison on Sunday and the same thing happened again. He just lost control and neither side benefited,' before bitterly adding, 'he was a junior referee in charge of a professional game.' With little to play for, there was frustration amongst the supporters. One fired off an angry missive to the *Liverpool Echo*:

Everton under Billy Bingham are no better off than they have been for the last three seasons... He criticises defensive football, yet Everton still play 4-3-3 at home and are fast becoming the most boring away team in the country because of dull defensive tactics. The only way Everton are better off than last season is that they are higher up the league, but that's only because the teams below them are playing so badly. Once again we have been knocked out of the FA Cup by a Second Division team, after having a home draw.

Although the arrival of Latchford improved the firepower of team – the big striker netting seven times in thirteen games before the end of the season – Bingham's side had no momentum and failed to record consecutive league victories for the rest of the campaign. 'Mr Bingham has created a strong, capable, and efficient formation,' wrote Michael Charters in the *Liverpool Echo*, 'But strength at the back and in the middle can only make a team difficult to beat: it cannot make a team win consistently.' That said, there was still time for the Toffees to cause damage to their two closest rivals before the end of the campaign.

Reducing the red menace

By the penultimate weekend of April 1974 when Everton travelled to Anfield, Liverpool lay second in the table, four points behind Leeds United but having played two games less. Therefore, Bingham's side could dash the home side's title hopes and avenge an unlucky defeat at Goodison four months earlier. On that occasion, the home supporters in the 56,000 crowd leapt to their feet when Mick Lyons headed in off the post from Joe Harper's cross on the hour mark. Referee Mr Homewood signalled a goal, only to change his mind after consulting his linesman, who had flagged for offside. Ten minutes later the visitors' Ian Callaghan crossed and reserve striker Alan Waddle (a cousin of Chris) poked out a foot for the winner. After the game, Emlyn Hughes – never one to miss an opportunity to rub dirt in the face of the city's senior club – admitted 'If I had been an Everton player and got beaten, I would have felt sick.'

The visitors were far more resolute at Anfield and rode their luck in Everton's best derby performance since their last title-winning season. Latchford, George Telfer and Gary Jones all had good opportunities to score as Everton fully deserved a hard-earned point in front of their massed ranks of supporters at the Anfield Road end. A small battalion of away fans at the other end of the pitch who, although only 'an embarrassingly small fraction of the Kop's thousands,' according to the *Liverpool Daily Post,* 'soundly trounced them for most of the afternoon.' Bingham claimed afterwards: 'The quietness of the Kop reflected Liverpool's play, they played across us. They did not penetrate us.' However, Shankly was scornful. 'When Everton forced a corner they were so pleased I thought they were going to do a lap of honour,' he sarcastically remarked. Bingham had the final word: 'Liverpool are supposed to have enormous stamina, I thought Everton finished the fitter and more composed team.' Tom German of *The Times* was suitably impressed: 'Everton are a side to look for next season.'

Bingham's side severely damaged Liverpool's championship hopes and they eventually failed to catch Revie's outfit. Equally significantly, the Toffees also had a role in Manchester United's fight to remain in the top-flight. Tommy Docherty's side were three points from safety with five games left, two of which were against Everton. United won the first 3-0 at Old Trafford on Easter Monday which gave hope, but they were still in the relegation zone when travelling to Goodison with three games left. 'The Doc' was in bullish mood: 'I always thought we would get out of it and we will start by murdering Everton.'

The crucial encounter proved to be an ugly no-contest, with several years of poor management at Old Trafford manifesting itself in a lacklustre performance as Everton triumphed 1-0, the crucial goal arriving five minutes after half-time when a George Telfer mishit fell kindly for Mick Lyons to score from close in. 'This was not a narrow defeat. Everton, superior almost without raising a bead of sweat, might have had four as United's recent stylish co-ordination sadly evaporated,' opined David Miller in the *Daily Express*, 'They were not even beaten by an outstanding side.' Also playing that night were Birmingham City, a point ahead of United at the start of the evening. The Midlands side hammered QPR 4-0 and the Goodison PA announced the result to the 46,093 spectators before the game finished. Dejected United understandably lost the will to fight thereafter.

Docherty went on the offensive afterwards about the home club's behaviour. 'The announcement was made in bad taste,' he complained. 'It came when the players were still on the pitch. We wouldn't have told them the Birmingham score because we were in with a chance of winning our own match and we wouldn't want to dampen their spirits.' The Scot may have had a point but his promise to 'murder' Everton had not gone unnoticed within the Goodison hierarchy, and perhaps this was a case of revenge is a dish best served cold. Significantly, although Denis Law is often erroneously credited with sending United down when scoring the winner for Manchester City at Old Trafford four days later,[5] the result that ultimately relegated Docherty's side was the defeat at Goodison, as it took matters out of their own hands.

The final position of seventh was respectable, with average home attendances

---

[5] After the midweek results, Birmingham City's victory against Norwich City on the same day as the Manchester derby made the result at Old Trafford irrelevant.

slightly higher than the previous campaign. A further achievement of Bingham was to banish memories of his predecessor's brooding presence. 'There's definitely a different atmosphere now,' Mick Buckley told Brian Glanville in the *Sunday Times,* 'The new manager is a tracksuit manager, you can laugh and joke with him and play with him in five-a-sides. Harry Catterick was always in the office.' 'I think I've been lucky,' Dave Clements said during the campaign, 'in joining a team who are not playing up to their ability yet. I see a hell of a lot of reserve.'

That said, the improvement did not impress those supporters who told chairman Alan Waterworth at the summer AGM that the city was 'a one-horse town' with the Anfield side having lifted three trophies in two seasons. 'Rome wasn't built in a day,' the Everton supremo argued back, 'If we improve our League position as much as we did last (ten places) we'll finish top.' Ambitious words but, with champions Leeds United and Liverpool both needing new managers, a championship challenge was surely not out of the question.

CHAPTER 3

Fear is the key

BILLY BINGHAM MAY NOT HAVE BEEN THE MOST POPULAR OF Everton managers, but there is no doubt about his impressive early work in the transfer market. The former winger had smoothly engineered the departure of championship stalwarts and fans' favourites like Howard Kendall, Colin Harvey and Joe Royle for a collective sum of more than £400,000 and offloaded others for very decent fees. One, sadly, was the injury-prone Jimmy Husband, after a Goodison career of 55 goals from 199 games. His words on departure to Luton Town were a bitter reminder of the moment which cruelly defines his time there: heading over when well placed to net the winner late on in the 1968 FA Cup final. 'I'll never forget the chance I had to make it my Cup Final and it passed me by,' he admitted. The sale of one player though still rankled Bingham. 'We have to sell and buy and this is probably the hardest part of a manager's job,' he told shareholders at the end of the 1973/74 campaign, 'Most players transferred were surplus to the needs of the club, but the one involving Howard Kendall gave us pain.'

Bingham had largely kept his powder dry with regards to incoming players – even after bringing in Dave Clements and Bob Latchford for more than £400,000 he was showing a profit of £300,000 on player trading. The manager had admitted Duncan McKenzie was on his radar but with Nottingham Forest still in the FA Cup, they rejected any overtures and the skilful ball-player eventually went to Leeds United before a memorable spell at Goodison later in the decade.

Dobson's choice

Elsewhere there were the usual rumours of bids and near misses. A functional midfield that lacked poise and creativity needed reinforcing. 'Individually, they are all talented,' the *Liverpool Echo's* Alex Goodman said, 'Buckley with his youthful enthusiasm, Harvey with his cool football brain, and Clements with his deadly accurate left foot. But collectively they seem to lack a dominant figure.'

Needing a playmaker, Bingham unsuccessfully attempted to hijack the deal that took gifted Scottish midfielder Asa Hartford from West Brom to Manchester City. That rejection took him to Burnley and their gifted craftsman Martin Dobson. Having tried to buy the player in the previous autumn, Bingham made a £200,000 bid but with other clubs interested, the Everton boss moved quickly. Dobson wished to remain in the area for family reasons, so matching a Spurs offer of £300,000 was enough to clinch the biggest cash-only transfer in British football history.

The money appeared well spent. Having started his career as a centre-forward with Bolton, Dobson went on to play at centre-half before finding his natural role in the middle, where he had scored 41 league goals in 120 appearances, as well as winning four international caps. 'I have always regarded Dobson as one of the greatest midfield players in the game,' Bingham proclaimed, 'He has all the qualities of leadership and outstanding ability, especially the quality of being able to score goals from midfield.' Asked by the press whether that completed his spending, Bingham vowed: 'I've not finished yet.'

The Everton manager was clearly talking about the pursuit of the transfer-listed Leicester City goalkeeper Peter Shilton, the problem was seven other clubs also wanted to sign the England international. The Everton boss surprisingly pulled out of any deal. 'I was told they wanted players in part exchange or £350,000 in cash, but they would prefer players,' he explained, 'I have no intention of paying £350,000 for a goalkeeper and I do not have the players to sell whom Leicester want. The matter rests there.'

Bingham's thinking had no logic. Players of Shilton's quality, never mind goalkeepers, rarely came onto the market. Although the asking price was high, the manager had just paid a similar amount for someone who was not a regular starter for England, while Shilton was approaching world-class with his best years ahead. Bingham's skilful manipulation of the transfer market in his first twelve months ensured the fee would not stretch club finances. Nevertheless, like others, the manager was underplaying the importance of a strong, top-class goalkeeper. One who eventually did was Brian Clough's sidekick, the shrewd Peter Taylor. Asked after their momentous 1977/78 campaign what Forest's aspirations had been initially, Taylor said, 'I thought we could challenge for Europe, but when we bought Shilton I knew we could win the championship.' Like others, Bingham was not as perceptive, and the failure to land the goalkeeper would haunt Everton for the rest of the decade.

Challenging for the title

With Everton's traditional rivals in transition or decline, the 1974/75 season was clearly going to provide the most open title chase in the post-war era. Brian Clough and Bob Paisley had replaced Don Revie and Bill Shankly respectively during the preceding summer, while the big London clubs were in freefall. By October, Bill Nicholson (Spurs) and Dave Sexton (Chelsea) had lost their jobs and Arsenal were bottom. Manchester United, of course, were not even in the top-flight, although as expected their stay in the second tier was short-lived.

In their place were a number of provincial clubs, led by men whose strengths lay in their ability to reinvigorate the careers of players regarded as either being difficult to manage, or had left their best days behind, combined with an eye for identifying undervalued young talent. Brian Clough had started this trend at Derby County, and was then followed by Bobby Robson at Ipswich Town, Tony Waddington (Stoke City), Jimmy Adamson (Burnley) and later Lawrie McMenemy (Southampton). Jack Charlton, who had romped to the Second Division title with Middlesbrough in his first season, had now joined them in the top-flight. Included in his squad was a young Graeme Souness, bought from Spurs for a fee of £30,000.

These new challengers may have been a threat to the cabal of big-city clubs but for some the increase in potential title-winners indicated a drop in standards. 'In terms of skill and organisation British teams are being left behind in Europe,' David Lacey claimed in the *Guardian*, before adding, 'A frequent retort to this view is that no country can match the Football League's depth of strength, but this is rapidly becoming an excuse for mediocrity. Mere quantity has never been a satisfactory substitute for quality.' With a levelling off in standards and a third relegation place added in the previous campaign, Lacey presciently concluded that 'the First Division will adopt a more cautious approach this time, with managers thinking more in terms of forty points and security than sixty-plus and celebrations.' With two points for a victory and one for a draw, the latter was becoming a mutually agreeable outcome for both teams, as supporters – especially those at Goodison – witnessed more and more stalemates. Whatever the outcome, the 1974/75 season was not going to produce vintage champions.

Early days

Bingham was optimistic about the new season. The Irishman's scientific and robust training program was bearing fruit. 'I was delighted to find the boys were 25 per cent fitter on the opening day of our programme than they were at the corresponding stage last year,' he proudly proclaimed. The bookmakers shared that optimism, 50/1 for the title in his first season, Everton were now fourth in the betting at 16/1, with Liverpool favourites at 3/1. Although the opening day goalless draw against Derby County at Goodison was disappointing, four days later there were early signs of promise when highly-fancied Stoke City were dispatched 2-1 at Goodison, with Joe Royle reaching a century of league goals.

By the time Everton defeated Arsenal 2-1 in an excellent display at Goodison on the final day of August they stood third in the table, with eight points from an unbeaten five games. Liverpool were top under rookie manager Bob Paisley, with Horace Yates in the *Liverpool Daily Post* warning that it could be a two-horse race:

> *Undoubtedly it is too early to suggest that the League Championship will be a Merseyside carve up, with the title bound for Anfield or Goodison. But there are all the signs of a Merseyside monopoly that must cause concern everywhere. Billy Bingham's remorseless build up of Everton strength is clear enough indication that his team are back in business... Those who maintain that Everton's rise means that the pendulum is swinging their way after years in the wilderness are only half right. Without doubt their prospects are brighter than ever, but there is no sign of any Liverpool slide.*

The bright start faded like the summer sunshine in September. The visitors suffered their first league defeat of the season at a windswept Portman Road, 1-0 to Bobby Robson's fast-improving Ipswich team. Significantly, the bad press after the game was a harbinger for the rest of the campaign. 'Everton meant business right from the start,' the Ipswich skipper Mick Mills claimed, 'Perhaps they thought that if they roughed us up a bit, we would crack. Well, they know differently now.' James Wilson in the *Sunday Times* was more brutal. Describing

Bingham's outfit as 'a poor man's Liverpool,' he added, 'One hopes that Everton, and their manager Mr Bingham, in particular, will think long and hard about the kind of team they want to be before it is too late. On their form yesterday, they are already down the wrong road.'

Eleven days later Bingham's team took on Second Division Aston Villa at Goodison, in a League Cup replay after a 1-1 draw in the Midlands. Heavily fancied to move into the third round, Everton were comprehensively defeated 3-0. 'Everton were out-thought, out-run and out-played,' pondered Yates in the aftermath. Such was the manner of the defeat, Bingham held an emergency meeting with the players 24 hours later.

Lyons made

'This is a dedicated, enthusiastic lad who gives everything for Everton,' Harry Catterick commented about Mick Lyons in 1972, 'He is a wonderful header of the ball, a powerful tackler and is big enough (6ft. 1ins.) and strong enough (12st. 7lb.) to make opposing forwards think about tangling with him.' Therein was the problem, where to best deploy the versatile youngster?

Lyons' adaptability was highly-prized by other clubs and Bingham rejected a bid from Coventry City at the start of the 1974/75 campaign but, with skipper Roger Kenyon out with injury, he made his first appearance of the season at centre-half for the 3-2 victory over West Ham United at the end of August, performing heroically with a cut head after clashing with Bobby Gould. The 22-year-old then added to his growing reputation during the 3-2 home victory over Leeds United five weeks later. The Elland Road outfit had already sacked Brian Clough and with caretaker Maurice Lindley in charge, they were uncharacteristically vulnerable at Goodison Park. Goalkeeper David Harvey exacerbated their problems when allowing full-back Steve Seargeant's speculative shot from 35 yards to slip through his hands. Although Allan Clarke equalised shortly afterwards, the Toffees went ahead before the break when Harvey allowed a corner to cross his six-yard box and Lyons scored with a typically brave diving header, when there was a 50:50 chance of meeting Norman Hunter's boot. Harvey's largesse continued after the break, the goalkeeper failing to collect John Connolly's cross and Dave Clements scored from close range. Although Terry Yorath netted a late consolation, the 41,000 crowd gave the teams a standing ovation at the end. 'I cannot praise Everton highly enough for both their spirit and ability,' commented Alan Thompson in the *Daily Express*. Bingham was in a prickly mood after a first victory in six games. Asked by the press afterwards whether his side had turned a corner, the Ulsterman replied brusquely: 'Turned the corner? There was never any corner to turn.'

Two weeks later, Lyons was on the mark again in a 2-2 draw at Sheffield United. Two goals down at the break, the centre-half pulled one back with a fierce left-footed shot and caused havoc after replacing the injured Bob Latchford as centre-forward. Lyons went close with a diving header and then set up Mick Buckley for a well-deserved equaliser. Three days later the defender scored again in a further 1-1 stalemate at home to West Ham. 'Mick Lyons revitalised Everton against West Ham at Goodison last night with a goal which typified this lad's tenacity, spirit, effort and never-give-in approach to the game,' proclaimed Michael Charters in the *Liverpool Echo*. Another interested party was former Liverpool manager Bill Shankly, who told the same newspaper:

Mick – the Lion of Goodison. I think Everton's Mick Lyons should have his name spelt LION. If ever there was a lion-hearted player, this is the boy. His courage and enthusiasm is a delight to see, and don't let anyone say there isn't ability there as well. He has the ability all right. I was very impressed with him in the game against West Ham on Tuesday night. He keeps getting goals whether he is played as a defender or attacker.

Yates gets rowdy at Goodison

With Bob Latchford still injured, Lyons filled the centre forward void against Chelsea four days later during a feisty encounter memorable for an erratic performance by referee John Yates.

The opening half was a moribund affair that gave few clues to the later theatrics. The visitors went ahead on six minutes when Chris Garland headed John Hollins' cross into the goalmouth but Dai Davies fumbled the ball and moustachioed Scottish winger Charlie Cooke pounced to score. The home team seemed destined for a frustrating afternoon before referee Yates took matters into his own hands after 56 minutes. The official appeared to allow the Chelsea trainer, Norman Medhurst, onto the pitch to treat the injured John Dempsey but, to the bemusement of those present, Yates then booked Medhurst for tending a player without permission.

Four minutes later the referee escalated proceedings by awarding the home team a free-kick outside the Chelsea penalty area but then booked Hollins, Cooke, Peter Houseman and Tommy Baldwin for not retreating ten yards. 'The referee had rolled the ball a couple of yards nearer to the defensive wall seconds before, he could not be said to have given them that much time to comply with his demand,' suggested the *Guardian's* Paul Wilcox. Yates then harshly booked Chelsea midfielder Chris Garland for a foul, before six minutes from time awarding Everton a baffling penalty. Gary Jones' tame cross floated into touch but Yates had noted a coming-together of John Hurst and burly Chelsea centre-half Mickey Droy. Although the Everton player maintained the defender had 'grabbed him round the neck and tripped him,' Droy replied: 'The geezer ran into me and fell down.' Substitute Gary Jones netted with aplomb, for a first goal after four years and 36 first-team games.

There was more drama when Yates booked Droy for a foul on Buckley and then appeared to caution Dempsey for verbal abuse as the players left the pitch – although it was more serious as the referee revealed: 'Although he was not technically sent-off, it will be reported as a sending-off offence as if it had happened during the game.' Dempsey responded: 'As we came off all I said to the referee was that a player could have broken a leg, and he wouldn't let the trainer on.' The Chelsea player was charged with bringing the game into disrepute[6] while eight bookings and a sending-off were a Football League record for one side. It was not a dirty game – even Droy was 'less intimidating than usual' according to the *Daily Telegraph*. Remarkably, there were no home players in the referee's now historic notebook, which Yates proudly displayed in the Monday morning newspapers, earning him a three-game ban, not because of his performance (which earned a 1/10 rating from the *Daily Mail*) but a referee allowing publication of his notes was illegal.

Two weeks later the Toffees defeated a strong Manchester City 2-0 at Goodison, in probably their best performance thus far under Bingham. Martin Dobson was outstanding in the mauling of the Maine Road outfit, so much so that his tripartite partnership with Dave Clements and Mick Buckley drew comparisons with a trio of Goodison gods of recent vintage. After watching

---

[6] On the same day as QPR's Terry Mancini, who infamously took his shorts off and 'mooned' in front of the directors' box after a home victory over Ipswich Town.

the midfield completely outperform players of quality like Colin Bell and Asa Hartford, the *Liverpool Daily Post's* Ken Lawrence was effusive in his praise:

Connoisseurs will say that one of the finest midfield trios of the modern game was that of Harvey, Kendall and Ball; and that would be correct. Saturday, at Goodison, however, proved that, remarkably, only four years since those famous players combined to produce midfield artistry and genius and help Everton to their last Championship, Everton have been gifted by another set of midfielders who have the potential to not only emulate, but surpass their famous predecessors.

The trio were reasonably well balanced. Clements sat in, could put his foot on the ball and was able to control the tempo and direction of the play. Buckley, an energetic midfielder with no little skill, provided the brawn and mobility. The midfield was completed by Dobson, who could create and carry the ball to drive at defences. Nevertheless, Bingham's side reverted to type in their next two games, drawing both, the latter a hard-fought goalless first derby of the season at Goodison. The home side were inventive in the opening period – 'Everton, at times, looked close to their magnificent side of the mid-1960's,' declared Chris Lightbown in the *Sunday Times* – but failed to capitalise and the visitors' second-half renaissance ensured the goalless draw was probably a fair result. Consequently, those forecasting a tightly-fought contest for the title could settle back with some comfort that evening. Everton were one of four teams tied with 22 points at the top, the Toffees having reached the summit with just five victories in eighteen games, a ludicrous position that justified David Lacey's pre-season prediction that caution would be the *modus operandi*. But Everton's robust, negative style was now subject to bitter criticism from their rivals.

A question of mechanics

On face value, there was some merit to the condemnation. Bingham's strategy aggravated both opposition and neutrals. As Lacey noted: 'Everton's tendency is to break up an attack by fouling the man in possession, stifle the free kick, and repeat this process so many times that opponents retire, disgruntled, to no-man's land, whence high centres and through balls are lobbed into the penalty area – easy stuff to defend.'

The week before the derby game, Everton had gone to White Hart Lane and returned with the fashionable result of the time, a 1-1 draw – their eleventh overall in seventeen league games. 'It is unthinkable a team as negative as Billy Bingham's should outstrip the positive, entertaining assets of Manchester City, Liverpool, Derby, Ipswich and others,' David Miller claimed in the *Daily Express*. Yet, for all the criticism of their strategy at White Hart Lane, after the game the Everton manager could point out that their eleven away goals was the joint-highest in the division. Nevertheless, sterile tactics drew fierce comments from the Tottenham side. Speaking to the *Daily Mirror*, defender Phil Beal pulled no punches. 'If they carry on like this, it will kill football,' he said, 'Everton came for a draw. Once they got their equaliser they blocked the middle, sat back and showed absolutely no interest in coming forward... The League ought to step in and do something about teams who go away and play like that.' But Roger Kenyon, the Everton skipper, hit back: 'It's utter rubbish to say we're a defensive side. Every other week at our ground, we face the problem Tottenham are talking about. It was up to them to break us down. Anyway they are a bad side. We'll murder them at Goodison.'

So why was Bingham deploying these tactics? Firstly he was not the only manager interested in gathering points more than friends. Brian Clough in his *TV Times* column wrote:

> It is more difficult to play attacking football because managers are close to perfecting sound defensive systems. Why? Because it is the easy thing to do. We have so much pressure in our jobs that we take the easy way out. We know that it is easier to get a no-score draw than go out and win 5-0. Today, clubs fear losing and this is why the game has deteriorated so much as entertainment.

Secondly, there was the additional pressure facing any Everton boss who had John Moores at his shoulder. The Littlewoods boss may have resigned as chairman but his desire for success was as great as ever. A naturally defensive manager, Bingham was always going to resort to previous tried and trusted methods to satisfy Moores' demands. As Mick Lyons recalled in *Three Sides of the Mersey*: 'I think the London press didn't like us because we were really well organised. We wore these orange/yellow shirts and we got called "Clockwork Orange" or something like that.'

But there was some evidence to the contrary. Latchford returned to the team for the 4-1 demolition of Birmingham on the final Saturday of November, scoring twice in an excellent display of attacking football. They clinically dispatched Leicester City 2-0 at Filbert Street seven days later, the performance impressing the watching Colin Malam of the *Sunday Telegraph*. 'Everton have acquired an unenviable reputation this season for climbing the First Division unworthily by specialising in drawn matches,' he wrote, 'Yet, on the three occasions I have seen them, away from home each time, only once have they displayed any of the defensive, negative thinking also attributed to them. At Filbert Street yesterday, the Merseysiders again suggested that the charges against them are not completely justified.'

The victory took Everton to second in the table before a trip to the mud-filled Baseball Ground in mid-December. Bingham set out his team in typical style and, during a tight, bad-tempered first half, they accumulated three bookings and zero shots on target. But the extra fitness Bingham required paid dividends as the visitors gradually took charge in the sodden conditions. Gary Jones, in particular, was outstanding and unlucky when, having rounded goalkeeper Colin Boulton outside the area and been brought down, he saw his resulting free-kick cannon back off the bar. But the winger played the key role when Everton struck gold on 66 minutes. Jones was able to carry the ball from deep and, spotting an unmarked Bob Latchford lurking menacingly at the edge of the area, measured his cross to perfection and the big striker's angled header from ten yards arced perfectly over Boulton into the far corner for the winner. As table-toppers Stoke lost 3-1 at Leeds United, Bingham's side had now reached the summit – the sixth different team to do so in a title race where leadership had changed hands eight times in three months.

Yet the widespread negative response to tactics overshadowed a moment to savour. Chris Lightbown of the *Sunday Times* had previously been complimentary about Bingham's men but this time he did not hold back: 'If they keep playing like they did yesterday it will be a tragedy if Everton win the League championship this season.' Infamously, Derby County assistant manager Des Anderson provocatively claimed, 'The worst thing that could happen to English football would be for a team like Everton to win the championship. If they do, somebody might be foolish enough to try to copy them. They are nothing more than a team of robots.' Bingham was quick in his riposte. 'Who is Des Anderson? Is he the new Brian Clough? I am sure there are many teams who would like to be in the same position as Everton. It sounds a little like sour grapes.' Meanwhile his skipper fought back. 'What Derby say is rubbish. We are getting a bit sick of being given stick like this,' Roger Kenyon complained, 'How do Derby expect us to play football on a pitch like theirs. It was like running around with divers' boots on.' Horace Yates in the *Liverpool Daily Post* strove to defend Bingham's side and accusations of being over-physical. 'No team of softies ever won the title,' he commented, 'some champions have more flair than others, but in the end it is solidity, consistency and efficiency that prove decisive. These are the qualities Everton are showing in abundance.' Despite Yates' defence, Lightbown and Anderson were not alone in their comments with the perceptive David Lacey using the victory to again target Bingham's side:

> *Everton, who have plodded along, tortoise-like, operating a strict system of percentages both home and away, with the result that they have drawn four more matches than they have won... so negative has been Everton's approach in many of their games that whenever the possibility of their eighth championship is mentioned, the usual response is one of muttered foreboding rather than wholehearted approval.*

Bingham reacted by taking the newspaper clippings and pinning them to the noticeboard at Bellefield. 'Evidence more of sensitivity than a thick skin' as Peter Corrigan of the *Observer* noted. Frank McGhee also remarked upon the manager's defensiveness when the *Daily Mirror* man spent two hours at Bellefield during the following week. 'Anyone who quotes statistics at Bingham will get figures quoted right back,' he declared. But McGhee was also cutting in his conclusion:

> *It is an absolute certainty that they won't win many popularity contests outside their own militant Merseyside home if they do take the title. Their critics, myself included, having been queueing up, taking turns to mock and knock them as dull, defensive spoilers, particularly away from home.*

Bingham rebutted McGhee's claims. 'It is plain daft to suggest that we set out to smother in midfield,' he responded, 'Martin Dobson is naturally graceful. Little Mick Buckley has all the skill in the world and Dave Clements is always looking to attack. It just isn't on to have players like this and play the game defensively.' That was a fair point, as was Bingham's statement that other managers who criticised Everton were merely covering up their own inadequacies. He also gave some clues to McGhee on his own title aspirations: 'I'll only say that the team which wins it will be the team with real strength in depth in the first-team squad which we have; the team with the greatest consistency – which at the moment is us; and the team which is hardest to beat – and we've shown that beating Everton isn't easy.' Next up was a home encounter against second-from-bottom Carlisle United. 'Beating Carlisle at home tomorrow – not hardest job in the world – will consolidate their position at the top,' McGhee confidently predicted.

Summing up the seventies

The typical tale of Everton during the decade combines bad luck and missed opportunities in equal measure. So near and yet so far. Central to that narrative is the game against Carlisle on the final Saturday before Christmas 1974. The promoted Cumbrian side were top early on but the visitors had slipped into the drop-zone although, ominously for Everton, their manager was Alan Ashman, the West Brom boss in the 1968 FA Cup final.

The afternoon was a nightmare for the bulk of the 33,489 crowd. The consensus is the shocking 3-2 defeat to an ultimately relegated side was unlucky and inexplicable. Nothing could be further from the truth as the afternoon showed that those who criticised Bingham's side for lacking championship quality were correct. Two goals ahead through a Bob Latchford double, the visitors then completely outmanoeuvred the league leaders, showing more quality and, just as importantly, the heart and desire. Carlisle scored three times in twelve minutes around the hour mark and the shell-shocked home team showed little promise of netting an equaliser. The victory 'was achieved by playing the sort of football beyond the wit of Everton,' according to Derek Wallis in the *Daily Mirror*. The defeat was a chastening experience for Bingham's side, summed up by Michael Charters in the *Liverpool Echo*: 'It's simply shattering. If Everton had gone out of their way on Saturday to provide more telling ammunition for their critics, they could not have done a better job of it,' he wrote, 'It was the manner of it all. Almost the shame of losing to a side whom they should have crushed.'

Having ceded top spot to Ipswich Town, the brittle Goodison outfit succumbed to Wolves at Molineux on Boxing Day and could only garner a point from a sterile 1-1 draw against Middlesbrough 48 hours later. Bingham's side were now in fourth place, with the farcical scenario of just five points separating the top thirteen clubs. Absurdly, Everton stood just a point behind the leaders having won five games fewer.

Yet Bingham's side recovered form and two victories put them top of the table again in mid-January. After the 1-1 draw at Spurs in November, their manager Terry Neill growled afterwards, 'Call that football? They'll get the game stopped with all those back passes.' Bingham circulated the comments to his players before the return at Goodison on the first day of February and their reward was a tight victory, the only goal arriving ten minutes from time following the sole moment of real quality. George Telfer received Bob Latchford's cross, juggled with the ball before feeding the onrushing Jim Pearson in the inside-right channel, who finished past Pat Jennings to the delight of the 41,000 crowd. Seven days later there was a fourth reverse in 28 league games, 2-1 at Maine Road when new signing Joe Royle played a key role in both goals for Tony Book's outfit. 'They are a very strong team physically who, while capable of putting opponents under a lot of pressure don't create many scoring chances,' the former Everton favourite said after the game, 'The main thing going against them is their predictability.' There was a fortnight's break before the next league fixture – a small matter of the Anfield derby – but in the interim Bingham's side had an FA Cup fifth-round encounter against Fulham.

There had been no smooth passage to that stage. In the third round, Everton needed some good fortune at home to Altrincham, one of the best non-league teams at the time. Typically, the visitors used an over-physical approach to bridge the gap in quality, before shocking the home crowd by forging ahead on 36 minutes, when John Hughes took advantage of a failed offside trap to slot past Dai Davies. The first casualty of the afternoon came four minutes later: frustrated by the hard tackling, Gary Jones was sent off for flooring Ian Morris with a right-hand punch. Worse followed before half-time when John Connolly suffered a double fracture of the left leg following Ian Davison's tackle, although incredibly the referee left the visiting player unpunished. With Everton on the verge of a humiliation, twenty minutes from time David Irving was felled in the area and Dave Clements smoothly equalised from the spot. 'Altrincham matched and often beat their hosts in every department of the game,' was Chris James' opinion in the

Daily Mirror. Rumours of a vendetta against Davison dominated talk before the second game at Old Trafford. 'Some Everton players threatened to get him in the replay,' claimed Altrincham skipper Lennie Dicken, although Clements dampened such gossip: 'Talk of revenge is completely untrue.' The Toffees were more convincing than at Goodison, with Latchford and Lyons scorers in a comfortable 2-0 victory.

The fourth-round draw produced a tricky tie at Bingham's former club, Third Division Plymouth Argyle. Mick Lyons proved a capable replacement for Bob Latchford as the deputy scored twice in a 3-1 victory before an all-ticket 38,000 crowd – including 7,000 who had travelled south from Merseyside. Although Bingham's side put in a professional performance, there was no doubt who was the man of the match. 'The present day transfer market may be in a depressed state,' suggested Alex Goodman in the *Liverpool Echo*, 'but if Everton manager Billy Bingham decided to sell Mick Lyons he would probably be knocked over in the rush of clubs, all with cheque books at the ready.' With Liverpool losing 1-0 at Ipswich, Everton were now the bookmakers' favourites for the cup, odds that shortened to 4-1 when the draw gave a winnable home tie against Fulham.

However, like the Carlisle home game, supporters hold up the 2-1 defeat to the London side as another example of how the fates conspired against Everton. Again, that is wide of the mark. 'Of course it was a surprise,' the *Guardian's* Eric Todd said of the result, 'Not the victory, mark you, but the modest margin of victory. Something in the order of 4-1 rather than 2-1 would have given the emphasis to Fulham's superiority and Everton's inferiority.' The away team denied Everton time and space, playing with real intelligence against the league leaders, who littered their performance with errors. For the first goal, Roger Kenyon and Dai Davies got into a tangle over Les Barrett's cross and Viv Busby scored on the line, for the first of his two goals.[7] Furthermore, although Clive Thomas controversially disallowed Mick Lyons' goal in the second half when Fulham keeper Peter Mellor failed to gather Mick Bernard's high cross, the referee was merely levelling the score. Earlier Thomas wrongly chalked off Jimmy Conway's goal for offside, the player having clearly received the ball from an Everton player. Todd was scathing about the home team.

---

[7] Busby's wife was from Liverpool and the striker was later part of Howard Kendall's coaching staff during the 1997/98 campaign.

'Everton can be dismissed as summarily from this dispatch as they were from the competition,' he concluded, 'They were panic-stricken after Fulham's first goal, pathetically relieved when Kenyon equalised, and shattered when Fulham again went in front.' Manager Bingham told his players not to comment after the game, although Kenyon managed a response on how he felt in the aftermath: 'Sick.'

History lobbed away

Bingham's side had shown the ability to bounce back after a bad result, a welcome characteristic given the next game was at Anfield. A point behind leaders Stoke, the Toffees had two games in hand and although the eventual draw was a good result, significantly their many critics had little ammunition as the visitors contributed enormously to 'a superb match, predictable only in its result, but amazing and exciting in every other way,' according to James Wilson in the *Sunday Times*. The upgrade in quality was primarily due to starting Martin Dobson in the centre of midfield, his best position. Previously the former Burnley player had featured on the right and remained on the periphery. 'Martin gives us class. He also gives us time in midfield because he has such great skill and can keep possession and hold the ball in tight situations,' Bingham declared, 'He's very much a director-general in midfield with his skill and ability to switch the direction of play.'

Dobson did all of this at Anfield, his 'balance, elegant stride and thoughtful use of the ball enabled him to tower over the midfield,' according to Derek Wallis of the *Daily Mirror*. The Everton player also showed a previously hidden combative streak – one 50-50 with Tommy Smith left the 'Anfield Iron' on the floor. Wallis did not hide his admiration for the impressive visitors in the aftermath. 'Some pretty nasty comments have been made about the Goodison team this season and manager Billy Bingham has suffered them largely in silence,' he wrote, 'So it gave him great satisfaction that his team did all the talking for him where it mattered most – out there on the pitch.'

That said, there were no goals to reward Everton's adventure. Gary Jones shot over wastefully and George Telfer should have scored when Latchford pulled the ball back from the byline. But the best chance of the game came in an extraordinary incident in the final moments. Gary Jones' header split the Liverpool defence and left Latchford with a free run on goal. But in a bemusing passage of play, the most expensive player in English football tamely lobbed the ball into Ray Clemence's hands. To be fair the Liverpool keeper showed his experience. 'You have to try and outfox the attackers and that is what I tried to do with Latchford,' he explained, 'I took a step forward but then I held my ground.' Although there were rumours afterwards that Latchford thought the whistle had gone for full time, the Everton striker explained, 'I thought he was going to come all the way and I went to lob the ball over his head. But he did not come and the ball went straight into his arms instead. Ray outfoxed me. But I could not believe I had missed it.'

Three days later Everton easily defeated Luton Town 3-1 to go top before a visit to Highbury on the first day of March. Bingham's side made the struggling Gunners look like a team set for the trap door in a truly masterful display, on the only occasion during the season when they looked true champions. The corner count was 12-1 in their favour and the home team had no shots on target. 'Like a politician who grows into a statesman or a monarch who matures with the years,' mused Brian Glanville in the *Sunday Times*, 'Everton have at last begun to match the status of league leaders.' In the opening period Mick Buckley struck a post and Pat Rice cleared Gary Jones' header off the line, having earlier desperately brought down Latchford for what looked a clear penalty. 'How Arsenal's porous defence yesterday survived a tremendous, six-minute bombardment by Everton early on is a question which defies logical explanation,' Glanville wrote.

Despite their pressure, the visitors had to wait until midway through the second half before striking, when Martin Dobson netted with a diving header from Gary Jones' cross. The winger's free-kick then went to Mick Lyons who headed over goalkeeper Jimmy Rimmer. The visitors' imaginative performance brought rare praise from their former skipper. 'They are like the Arsenal double side of 1971,' Alan Ball said, 'so hard to break down. They'll take some stopping now.' Bingham kept cool. 'Although I won't go as far as to say we'll win the title, our confidence is growing with every game,' he said afterwards. 'It's like a snowball rolling down a mountain, we're gathering momentum all the time.' A week later at Goodison the Toffees ground out a fortunate 2-1 victory over QPR, thanks to a last-minute goal from Bob Latchford. This time Bingham was buoyant: 'The championship is at our feet. We have to do it ourselves and we are not depending on other people. It is all up to us and if we do fall down it will be our own fault.' Two points clear at the top, Everton had ten games left with the first being the most difficult fixture in English football.

'More fun in a public library'

Jimmy Armfield had brought stability to Leeds United after the sacking of Brian Clough and the Yorkshire outfit had moved up to seventh, six points behind Everton. In front of a crowd of more than 50,000, the visitors set out in their usual style in away matches against bigger teams: employ a deep-lying defence that suffocated the life out of the opposition before growing into the game. However, as the contest progressed the importance of acquiring a point became the sole objective and Bingham's side posed no threat. In response the home team had two chances within the six-yard box that Duncan McKenzie and Terry Yorath failed to convert. The end result was a sterile goalless draw, the massed hordes of Everton fans returning over the Pennines with scarves trailing triumphantly out of their cars and coaches because, with challengers Burnley and Derby losing and Liverpool dropping a point, their team was now odds-on favourites for the title.

The aftermath was a tale of how the local and national media – with their different angles of coverage – can hold completely differing views. In the *Liverpool Echo*, Michael Charters was effusive in praising Bingham's strong outfit. Proclaiming that 'I have little doubt that the Elland Road crowd of more than 50,000 saw the defending champions against the champions-elect', Charters went on to say:

> *I have seen many Everton teams in my time, but I can't recall a more efficient, a more effective combination than the current side which manager Billy Bingham has fashioned with a mixture of costly transfers and home-made talent. They are essentially a team in the fullest sense of the word. They play for each other, they have courage, confidence and resilience, they are organised and never stop working. Their team spirit could not be better and of course, they have skill as well, despite what their critics say. No team leads the toughest competitive league in the world without that quality.*

But the national press took the opposite view. In the *Daily Express* David Miller, under the banner headline 'Everton – Ultimate Non-Football', was appalled at 'Everton's defensive mentality which shuffles not eight or nine but eleven men behind the ball when the opposition has it'. The *Daily Mirror's* Frank McGhee admitted to having 'had more fun in a public library'. However, the *Daily Telegraph's* Donald Saunders looked at the wider picture, echoing David Lacey's prediction that draws would be the fashionable result of the campaign. Noting the Leeds game 'may be seen eventually as the moment in which the most open League championship since the war was duly settled' Saunders added:

> *A goalless draw would have been condemned, once, as far too timid a method of clinching success in English soccer's most important competition. Nowadays it seems wholly appropriate to a tournament in which the principal objective has degenerated into the avoidance of defeat. If as seems highly likely, Everton become champions, they will do so because they have lost fewer matches than the other challengers... Everton have merely exploited – more obviously than previous champions – a now outworn system that undervalues victories and encourages caution.*

Saunders went on to justify his thesis by pointing out that Ipswich Town, who trailed the Toffees by five points, had won four games more and their fans would 'probably have enjoyed greater entertainment for their money.' However, he failed to mention that Bingham's side had scored just two fewer goals overall, and six more away from home. Everton were also the only club with more goals on their travels than they had conceded. Yet the fair accusation was that, as prospective champions, the Goodison outfit should have been doing more to entertain.

Brian Clough was another to point the finger at Bingham's team. Writing in the *Sunday Mirror*, he claimed: 'Have you paid to watch Everton this season, and said afterwards: "I would pay a quid to see that again?" I'm not sold on the thought of Everton winning the title... I hope they don't.' He then added, 'Can I ever say to my players: "Let's take a tip or two from the champions?" They would be the worst kind of champions. Unloved and not hated. Neither popular nor unpopular.' However, Bingham could refer critics to the bookmakers' odds: 4-5 Everton, 10-1 Leeds, Liverpool, Stoke. 'The championship is ours... unless we throw it away,' Dave Clements said.

Nevertheless, three days later at Middlesbrough, the league leaders completely undid their effective work in west Yorkshire, going down 2-0 following a poor performance, the visitors failing to recover from a horrendous mistake by Steve Seargeant on nine minutes when David Mills picked up his back pass and scored past Davies. On the following Saturday came a crunch clash: second-placed Ipswich Town at Goodison. In front of a crowd of more than 46,000, the home team were a goal down after 66 seconds through a Trevor Whymark header and they had to thank former player David Johnson for missing two gilt-edged opportunities when put clean through. Everton were forced to go long to Latchford and Lyons at the front – using 'as much subtlety as one of those iron balls used to demolish old buildings' according to the *Guardian's* Paul Fitzpatrick – but Bobby Robson's side paid for their profligacy on the hour. A mix-up in the Ipswich defence resulted in Latchford crossing from the byline and Lyons headed into an empty net. The 1-1 draw was a fair result in an exciting game and Bingham could take heart from some positive press, with Alan Thompson of the *Daily Express* admitting, 'Everton killed all the suggestions that they are negative, defence-minded and dull.'

In the following midweek came a rare war of words across Stanley Park. After Liverpool crushed Newcastle United 4-0 at Anfield to go within a point of the leaders, Kevin Keegan commented, 'Those people across the road will be a bit scared,' leading Roger Kenyon to reply: 'That doesn't worry us. We are not conscious of great pressure. We've still got a game in hand and if we win it we'll be three points ahead again.' On Easter Saturday came a trip to Carlisle United, three points adrift at the bottom. Motor-mouth Emlyn Hughes used the visit to indulge in some proto mind-games. 'True they've got a match in hand – but they've still got to win it,' the Liverpool skipper said, 'I wouldn't like to be in their shoes.' Meanwhile Bob Paisley claimed that 'The situation is suited to a team coming from behind.' However Paisley's predecessor Bill Shankly disagreed. 'There's only one way to look at this First Division title race – if Everton get ten points from their last seven games the rest can forget it because they'll be cutting one another's throats.' Then Kenyon appeared to contradict his earlier claim about the burden of being league leaders. 'The pressure on us is greater now,' the club skipper said, 'some of the teams we've still to play are battling against relegation – and that means they'll be fighting even harder.' Carlisle United were in that category and the Cumbrian side had shocked Everton in December – history could not repeat itself surely?

What news of Carlisle?
'We are coming to the run-in for the Championship and at all costs we want to avoid doing a "Devon Loch", to coin a racing analogy,' Bingham wrote in the Easter Monday match-day programme, 'And so I am looking for 5 points from our

Easter programme against Carlisle, Coventry here today, and Burnley on Friday.'

Before the trip to Cumbria on Easter Saturday, Harry Miller of the *Daily Mirror* added his name to Bingham's long list of critics. Under the headline, 'Draw-bores Everton set to pile on the agony', Miller wrote, 'Everton push depressingly towards their first championship success since 1970 posing an intriguing question.' The now familiar query being whether it was more important not to lose games than gamble and go for the victory. Noting that Everton were on course to win the championship with the fewest ever points, victories and goals, Miller claimed: 'It adds up to championship death by misadventure. The most pleasant sight over Easter would be to see Everton beat Carlisle and Coventry with style and a rush of goals. Unhappily I don't expect that to happen.' Bingham was still downcast about the constant condemnation. 'What I do find annoying, however,' he claimed, 'is the number of people who are prepared to condemn us who haven't even seen us play.'[8]

With challengers Middlesbrough losing and Stoke drawing on Good Friday, Everton had the chance to make Miller eat his words 24 hours later. Sadly, they did not following a pathetic performance against Carlisle that provided proof that Bingham's side lacked the class and character to be true champions. Everton competed for the opening half-hour but then wilted, with Les O'Neill and Ray Train (who cost £5,000 each) gaining a stranglehold in midfield against Dobson and Clements (who collectively cost £365,000), the latter pair's performance being described as 'pitiful' by the *Guardian's* Paul Wilcox.

The home side, who had earned a reputation for playing good if not winning football, eventually overwhelmed the championship favourites. The only surprise was they took an hour to open the scoring, following a hotly-disputed penalty from Joe Laidlaw. Bingham's incompetent and timid outfit had no answer and two late goals gave the bottom-placed side a richly-deserved 3-0 victory. 'The way we played today we couldn't have beaten a Sunday league team,' a scathing Bingham observed afterwards. However the manager's strange comment that 'Clements and Dobson didn't put it together in midfield... The result might have been different if we could have transferred Ray Train and Les O'Neill to our team' was hardly likely to lift morale.

---

8 Bingham's tetchiness also extended to radio. Later in the year, he banned BBC Radio Merseyside's Brian McEvoy from the club for the petty reason of drinking a small brandy on the team coach for health reasons. 'I have no comment to make – but if you print this story you will suffer,' he told the press. They did.

Elsewhere Paul Wilcox stuck the knife in, 'Carlisle stirred up the championship melting pot and exposed the Merseysiders for what they are: a team devoid of imagination who in an ordinary season would have got their comeuppance long before now... How Everton could visit the bottom club intent on only one point was a disgrace.' Even Laidlaw could not resist a dig at Bingham's side. 'I think they are in a false position. They wouldn't be worthy champions if they won it,' he claimed. But a 1-0 victory over Coventry at Goodison on Easter Monday kept Everton top of the table, at the head of five clubs separated by two points:

Everton	46 points	(37 games)
Liverpool	45 points	(38 games)
Stoke City	45 points	(38 games)
Ipswich Town	44 points	(37 games)
Derby County	44 points	(36 games)

Bingham's side were still favourites: 11/10 with Derby at 11/4 and Liverpool 7/1. The stay at the top lasted less than 48 hours, as Ipswich and Derby both won in midweek. The latter were now 6-4 title favourites as the form team in the division, having won three times in six days. Nevertheless, there was an opportunity to return to the summit when Everton played Burnley at Goodison on the Friday night before the Grand National. The visitors were in the title race before two heavy defeats over Easter, which forced the recall of goalkeeper Micky Finn who, at 5ft 8in, was the smallest in the Football League and had conceded seven goals in his only two club appearances. A potentially straightforward home victory was another one of those frustrating games that littered the decade.

Typically, the home team failed to test the agility of the diminutive keeper before the appearance of substitute Dave Clements acted as a catalyst. Before another 46,000 crowd, Bingham's side upped the tempo and just before the hour Latchford headed in Mick Buckley's cross. The home team crucially failed to add a second goal and, thirteen minutes from time, Leighton James fired in a cross and Peter Noble gave keeper Dai Davies no chance from a free header. The point took Everton top, but for only 24 hours as Kevin Keegan's brace gave Liverpool a superb 2-0 win at Leeds and a place at the summit, with five clubs now separated by just a single point.

There were four games left, the first of which was at Luton Town, now bottom of the table. On the second Wednesday in April, Everton travelled to Kenilworth

Road hoping to avoid a repeat of the Brunton Park disaster and for forty minutes the visitors moved the ball fluently around the muddy surface, creating a host of chances but only had one goal to show for their domination when Latchford netted from close range. Yet astonishingly by the break they were behind, thanks to a brace from Peter Anderson. In the second half, the visitors missed several good chances, the closest to an equaliser coming when Gary Jones had a shot cleared off the line, but went down 2-1. The Toffees had been classed as boring and lacking fight on occasion, but that was not the case here – they were just plain unlucky, albeit with some dreadful finishing. 'And when Everton carry out the postmortem on a defeat that could have put paid to their championship hopes,' said Jack Steggles in the *Daily Mirror,* 'they won't need telling they have only themselves to blame'

'We lost because we failed to take advantage of clear chances created by superior football,' commented Bingham afterwards, 'We outplayed Luton but lost.' That was true but just five points from seven games told its own story. However, on the following Saturday, a Martin Dobson goal at Newcastle kept the slim title chances alive, with Everton and Liverpool locked on 49 points, a couple behind Derby with just two games left.

The last home game of the season was against Sheffield United, when Everton once again threw away a game and killed off their title aspirations. In the opening 45 minutes they played their best football of the season, going into the break two goals up, which should have been double. With half-time bringing news that fellow challengers Liverpool and Ipswich were losing and Derby County level, supporters chants of 'We're going to win the league' echoed around the ground. The watching Michael Charters of the *Liverpool Echo* said about the first half that 'the quality of Everton's football was excellent. It was stamped with championship class as Martin Dobson, Mick Buckley and [Gary] Jones powered forward from midfield; it was stamped with championship class in the menace of Bob Latchford and Smallman[9] near goal and there was championship class stamped all over the defence where Roger Kenyon and John Hurst stood rock solid in the middle.'

---

[9] Supporters say Smallman was a lost gem of the 1970s. A promising striker with a silky touch, Harry Catterick had tried to sign him from Wrexham in 1972 but the youngster turned down a move. Bingham had better luck three years later but a long series of injuries wrecked Smallman's career at Goodison, although the consensus was that he was brittle. 'He was, to say the least, inconsistent,' Dai Davies said, 'He was a moody boy, who could score some neat goals on the home ground, but who was almost totally ineffective in away games.'

However, Everton did not possess championship-class resilience and spirit, and those significant failings were apparent in a disastrous second period. A victory may have kept Everton's title chances alive for the final day but in front of a disbelieving 38,000 crowd they fell apart in wretched style. An unmarked Keith Eddy pulled a goal back with a header and on the hour came another calamitous feature of Everton's fortunes in the decade: poor goalkeeping at crucial moments. Dai Davies failed to keep hold of Len Badger's cross and Bill Dearden fired home the equaliser. Six minutes from time, the gifted Tony Currie completed a shock comeback for the largely unimpressive visitors with a crisp finish in front of a dumbstruck Gwladys Street end. In complete contrast to the half-time celebrations, the goal signalled a mass exodus as programmes and cushions rained onto the pitch. Davies recalled the traumatic afternoon in his autobiography, *Never Say Dai*. 'I had a tragically poor game. My terrible mistakes were the main reasons why Everton lost 3-2 and that defeat proved a turning point,' the Welshman said candidly. A 1-1 draw at Chelsea was enough for fourth place and European qualification but, with champions Derby finishing with just three more points, it could have been more.

A new dawn or an opportunity missed?

The failure to land the title in the 1974/75 season is largely seen as a missed opportunity. But that analysis is within the context of the trophyless years that followed. The Everton board had given Bingham three years to develop a team capable of winning the title and fourth place, after a solid seventh spot in the previous campaign, was ahead of schedule. 'In the two interesting seasons that Mr Bingham has been manager of Everton we must still remember that we have come a long way and the whole season will be good experience,' Dave Clements told the *Liverpool Echo*. As one supporter said in the same newspaper, 'Although obviously dismayed at Everton's collapse over the last month, I am sure most Evertonians will appreciate the progress they have made under Billy Bingham's guidance.'

The manager told the *Liverpool Daily Post*'s Horace Yates the reasons for failure. 'I felt we were just not quite good enough, even when we were leading the league,' he surprisingly admitted, 'I could not convey that opinion to the players as they faced the run-in. It was my job to stimulate them, and this I did to the best of my ability... but I always felt we were not just right.' Bingham was correct, a lack of experience and quality meant that team suffered a bad case of stage-fright. Those factors also contributed to the team having a reputation for playing dull, negative football backed by sterile tactics.[10] That said when Bingham took the hand-brake off – as at Highbury and Anfield – his team could be as attractive and expansive as anyone.

Moreover, a total of 25 players were used where, in mitigation, injuries – especially to key players such as Bob Latchford, Mick Lyons (who missed most of the final month) and the stricken John Connolly – robbed the team of an attacking edge, as Everton finished with 56 goals, ten or so fewer than their rivals. 'If a team is going to win the championship you have to spread the goalscoring load. Over sixty goals are needed to win the title,' Bingham said, before pointedly adding that the midfield should have done better. 'They are given freedom to score but they do not put them away,' he admitted about Gary Jones (6 goals), Martin Dobson (5), Mick Buckley (2) and Dave Clements (1). Yet the Everton manager was also satisfied with progress. 'People ask me what went wrong, I don't think much did go wrong. We finished fourth with six points more than last season. Is that failure?'

Yet there was sadness at an opportunity squandered. The 1974/75 title race was probably the poorest quality in post-war league history: Derby were champions because they produced the best run of form when it mattered most – seventeen points out of the final twenty available. Dave Mackay's team were hardly vintage material, virtually winning the title by default after Everton imploded and Ipswich became embroiled in a demanding FA Cup run. Symbolically Derby also won the title without playing, when Bobby Robson's side lost to Manchester City on the Wednesday before the final weekend. During a season where the leadership changed hands on 21 different occasions, the Rams were fortunate that, in the game of championship musical chairs, they grabbed the last seat after 42 games. The fact that the champions did not win the most games, suffer the fewest defeats, score the most goals or concede the fewest speaks volume about the lack of quality.

But more than twenty years later Bingham was still living with regrets over

---

[10] In the final weeks of the campaign top-flight managers were asked, 'Which team, beside your own, would you most like to see win the title?' They nominated five clubs in the seventeen replies, of which Derby and Stoke got the most votes – five apiece. Tellingly, they cast not a single vote for Bingham's side.

the campaign. 'I was sick for Evertonians and for myself. We badly needed that championship to give us the confidence to go on and win things. At the time we were in Shankly and Liverpool's shadows.'

CHAPTER 4
Malfunctioning robots

VIRTUALLY EVERY MANAGER DURING THEIR TENURE HAS THAT moment, the one when they appear to lose control of their own destiny, followed by that slippery slope leading to the sack. For Billy Bingham it was an away game at Maine Road in February 1976.

Yet there had been optimism at the start of the season. 'Everton certainly will be among the front-runners,' wrote the *Guardian's* Eric Todd about their prospects. However, Bingham's side had travelled to Manchester with just two victories in eighteen games. The FA Cup run lasted just one tie, an unlucky 2-1 defeat at Derby County. The Toffees lost 5-0 at Newcastle United a week later, the third time they had conceded five goals that season, much to the chagrin of the *Liverpool Echo's* Michael Charters. 'Everton gave one of their poorest displays for years in crashing 5-0 at Newcastle on Saturday,' he wrote, '... hardly a kind word could be said for this dismal show in which they managed to make what I contend to be an ordinary Newcastle team look very good.'[11] Asked about his manager's prospects, chairman Alan Waterworth gave the dreaded vote of confidence:

---

[11] A decade later the game made headlines because of accusations made by Dai Davies in his autobiography. The Welshman looked to have had a poor game 'but the real truth was that I was paying the price for a piece of pure foolishness by two members of the team the previous night. In their immense wisdom a midfield player and a defender managed to consume a full bottle of whisky and a full bottle of brandy between them. Because of their complete lack of effectiveness I was completely defenceless.'

We are quite satisfied that Bingham is the man who can get things right. Mr Bingham is not under greater pressure from us today than at any other time since he joined us. We believe he can put things right and no time limit has been imposed. What we have to appreciate is that football is a highly competitive business and we fully appreciate that nobody can wave a magic wand. What Mr Bingham has achieved to date has been quite satisfactory and we still hope we can finish in a satisfactory position... Everton have never even thought in terms of a new manager.

'Quite satisfactory' progress was hardly inspiring. 'The acceptance of mediocre cannot be tolerated and the lack of ambition shown right from the top of the club is evident at pitch level,' said one letter to the *Liverpool Echo*. After a 1-1 home draw against Norwich City a week later there were more rumours about the sack, Bingham speaking for the first time about the pressure. 'Of course, I've heard the rumours. They're coming from every direction. But I'm quite happy and intend to get on with my job of running the team, to get them to snap out of their current poor run,' he told Charters. The following Saturday Everton lost 3-2 at Goodison to relegation-threatened Burnley, when the majority of the 21,000 crowd – half of the previous season's average – left before the end and the remainder hurled cushions at the directors' box. The defeat begged the question: why had the campaign gone so badly wrong?

A bad press

Everton were preparing for the 'most exciting season in prospect for the Blues for many years' according to Bingham in the scorching hot summer of 1975. Bingham had no plans to enter the transfer market, contrary to his previous statements of being keen to strengthen the midfield, particularly, in the previous season. But Bingham changed tack after seeing the players on their return. 'Compared with last season, the players are a little stronger, a little more experienced,' he said on the eve of the new campaign. The strategy proved costly,[12] and the manager's pre-season optimism faded when returning winger John Connolly broke his left leg for the second time in eight months, during a pre-season friendly in Holland.

The bookmakers though viewed the Toffees' prospects positively, at 11-1 Everton were fifth favourites for the title, behind Derby (4-1), Ipswich and

Liverpool (6-1) plus Leeds (8-1). Those odds were probably longer after a disastrous opening Saturday at Goodison. Against a Coventry City side that were amongst the favourites for the drop, the home side crashed 4-1. 'Coventry are supposed to be relegation candidates – so what does that make us?' questioned Dave Clements. The 33,000 gate was low for the opening home game but the second highest in the country – a forewarning of how the blight of hooliganism in particular was eating away at football's popularity.[13]

Although four wins in the next six games took Everton fifth, the press were still dissatisfied with Bingham's style of play. In the previous campaign, the manager defended his tactics by claiming they were part of the team's development, like how Don Revie's Leeds gradually moved from their almost brutal, negative methods of the mid-1960s to a more fluid, attractive outfit, without losing competitiveness. Bingham was missing the point. Revie's team would efficiently retain possession in their own half as an art-form, while Everton killed the game as a spectacle by sitting deep in numbers while snuffing out their opponents' threat. That said the Everton manager drew support from the *Guardian's* David Lacey. Commenting on Bingham's rationale, the esteemed writer wrote, 'This may be true. Certainly some of the outstanding Everton teams of the past... have undergone grey formative periods before their true qualities have emerged. Bingham's Everton team have played attractively enough on occasions to suggest that eventually they will match their predecessors for consistent entertainment value.' Matters came to a head following two games in London. At Highbury on the final Saturday in September the visitors came away with a valuable 2-2 draw, after letting a two-goal lead slip.[14] But their negative display of time-wasting brought unanimous criticism. Frank McGhee in the *Daily Mirror* provided some of the sternest commentary:

---

[12] Although when Kenny Dalglish handed in a transfer request to Celtic in August 1975, Everton were favourites to land the striker, with Bingham having scouted the player in secret.

[13] The club's popular *Blue Streak* chartered train for away games had a carriage that doubled as a prison for unruly Everton supporters from the start of the 1975/76 campaign, with 300 fans requiring sixteen security men and policemen.

[14] Irish centre-forward Frank Stapleton equalising two minutes from the end. Eleven days earlier the striker had equalised after 89 minutes in a League Cup tie between the clubs at Goodison. A third, very late strike, by Stapleton against Everton eight years later had devastating consequences.

What Everton did, with the way they played from midway through the second-half of their 2-2 draw against Arsenal, dragged football, unforgivably, right back to the grim days of recent seasons. Suddenly at Highbury all the chilling professionalism that has already sickened and sent away too many paying customers, took over. Suddenly, an Everton team which had been marvellously exciting became totally cynical.

Although Bingham claimed the performance was due to nerves – 'passing the ball back to the goalkeeper from forty yards is certainly not our policy,' he claimed – this was not good enough for McGhee, who counted more than twenty back-passes in the second period. 'A pass back to the goalkeeper when the player is under pressure is understandable,' he went on to say, 'Done deliberately, under no pressure from greater distances, and repeated constantly, it is indefensible. It just eats up time, disturbs the rhythm and, most important of all, cheats the customers.' The following Saturday's *Liverpool Echo* was full of letters of complaint. 'I must write to say how disgusted I was with the team after their tactics at Arsenal last Saturday. I was ashamed to be an Everton supporter,' one letter went, 'For the sake of football and Everton in particular Billy Bingham's attitude to this game must be deplored.' On the following Saturday a 1-0 victory at West Ham brought two points from a similar performance and familiar disapproval over tactics, with home supporters chanting 'What a load of rubbish' at the visitors.

A week later Bingham was intent on producing a more polished display at QPR but suffered the usual consequence when a cautious coach tries to play more expansively, especially when up against Dave Sexton's vibrant outfit. In the opening sixty seconds, seven Everton players charged up the pitch but the home team picked them off, with Don Givens scoring. 'It was a fatal mistake to play the masters at their own game,' said Tony Pawson in the *Observer*, as Rangers eventually romped to a 5-0 victory to go top – the Toffees' biggest league defeat for twelve years. Bingham wisely refused to talk to the press in the aftermath. A first-round exit in the UEFA Cup to AC Milan had hardly lifted the manager's mood either, following a controversial 1-0 defeat in the San Siro after a goalless draw at Goodison. The experienced 1970 World Cup final referee, Rudi Glockner, hardly disproved the long-standing rumours of Italian clubs having an unhealthy influence on match officials with a strange display in Milan. The East German awarded a debatable spot-kick for handling by Mick Lyons and rejected two strong penalty appeals from the visitors. A disgusted Bingham said afterwards, 'It was obvious we would have to get a clear-cut goal for it to count.' In the following home programme he expanded on his emotions, 'I have never felt so futile, helpless or frustrated. That was why I felt on the verge of walking onto the field and telling the lads: "Come on off. We're wasting our time. There's no way we can win here."'

The number one problem

Finding a goalkeeper to replace Gordon West proved difficult. Harry Catterick signed David Lawson for a record fee of £80,000 in the summer of 1972 and although supporters remember the former Huddersfield stopper with little affection, he was a solid presence in his first two seasons. However, when Lawson was hospitalised with a kidney condition in September 1974, Dai Davies was given an opportunity. The genial Welshman was a solid presence but performed poorly at the end of the campaign, so Lawson returned for the start of the 1975/76 season. A thigh injury in late September brought Davies back, only for the Welshman to break a thumb before an infamous League Cup replay at Notts County. Outplayed and outfought by the Second Division outfit, who cruised to a 2-0 victory thanks to two headed goals by Les Bradd, the result left Bingham's side without a win for six games. 'Their second-half performance was without heart; too many heads went down when things went wrong,' was Michael Charters' view for the *Liverpool Echo*. 'They are playing without conviction, with several players off form, giving the overall impression of a team struggling to find its cohesive touch.'

Eleven days later at Aston Villa, the Everton manager took the unusual step of playing a third centre-half in Roger Kenyon at the expense of a midfield player, in a typically defensive move when cornered. The result was a 3-1 defeat. 'Everton, by and large, were pretty dreadful,' was Erlend Clouston's opinion in the *Liverpool Daily Post*. Just when things could not get worse for Bingham, they did. Lawson's thigh problem returned, forcing the Everton manager to play untried eighteen-year-old Drew Brand for the visit to a strong Leeds United team at the end of November. The Scot had signed professional terms only a fortnight before, having played only a handful of reserve games, and that lack of experience was costly on another miserable Saturday afternoon in west Yorkshire. The debutant's vulnerability showed in poor handling as the visitors crashed to a 5-2 defeat – Brand being at fault for two of the goals, although the youngster pulled off some fine saves and the defence offered him no protection. Problems at the back were hampering Everton after Bingham, conscious of the criticism of his side, had told his midfield to push up more. Although the team had greater goalscoring capability the downside was obvious – 31 goals conceded against eighteen at the same stage the year before.

The defeat left Bingham's team dropping like a stone. 'Criticism mounts daily from Everton fans. No one at the club is under any illusions that the slump has to end quickly. Continued failure will not be tolerated,' opined Michael Charters. Bingham came out fighting. 'I think it is a rut rather than a crisis – and it is the first rut of poor results we have had since I was the manager,' he answered. After finishes of seventh and fourth, that was a reasonable stance. However, when asked about a month of seven winless games, the manager remarked that 'Many clubs would not regard that as a slump. But at Everton it is because of the pressures always on us as a club in a city so wrapped up in football.' Those pressures – with Liverpool relentlessly acquiring championships and European trophies – would haunt Bingham and his successor.

Inevitably, the Leeds battering forced a familiar, if unwanted, statement from the chairman. 'We have every confidence in Mr Bingham,' Alan Waterworth said, 'We firmly believe he will get it right. We are leaving it to him to work out... Mr Bingham has our 100 percent support and in any steps he wishes to take we will support him to the hilt.' The New Year would test that statement.

New year, same issues

Although the pre-Christmas period brought two much-needed victories against Birmingham City and Coventry, by the time Bingham's side travelled to Manchester City at the end of February 1976 they were on a run of seven games without a victory. The visitors put in a pathetic display in a 3-0 defeat at Maine Road. 'As poor a performance as I've seen from any Everton team in the past ten years or more,' Michael Charters ruefully claimed in the *Liverpool Echo*.

Former target Dennis Tueart and young winger Peter Barnes pulled the Everton defence apart, but Joe Royle's performance acted as a reminder of the great days of a decade before. The man who later managed both clubs led the line superbly, scoring one and setting up the other two for Asa Hartford and Tueart. Meanwhile City fans jeered the away team's stream of passes back to goalkeeper Lawson and constant foul play. Several players looked as if they were not trying. 'It was torture for the handful of Everton fans there to see this rock bottom performance,' said Charters, 'It must have been both embarrassing and humiliating for the Everton directors, including chairman Alan Waterworth and vice chairman John Moores. Conscious of the traditions and reputation of this great club, I believe that everything possible must be done to restore that fame, now looking very tarnished.' The Everton manager refused to speak to the press after the game and on leaving met a cabal of angry fans, chanting for his sacking. Chairman Waterworth again came out with the dreaded vote of confidence. 'I don't think a manager can be expected to manage if he is not given the backing of the directors,' he said, before adding about the supporters' protests, 'At Everton, if you have a run of bad results you hear this cry. It happened even in Harry Catterick's days.'

The result was a consequence of disharmony between Bingham and his squad that had been simmering for several weeks. 'The atmosphere is terrible. Anyone who wants to see him [Bingham] this week will have to join the queue,' one anonymous player told the press. On Monday the Everton boss closed off Bellefield, with the dropped Mick Buckley and Gary Jones expected to hand in transfer requests. Jim Pearson had earlier held showdown talks with Bingham while the manager rejected David Lawson's request for a move. 'The lads are all cheesed off and would get away if they could,' said one player. Bingham suspected certain individuals were leaking information from Bellefield on team changes and formations.

At the height of the title race twelve months before, Bingham had been complimentary about his team: 'There are very few difficult players on my staff. There is integrity and character in the players which shows itself.' Now Charters was saying, 'The explosive rift between Everton manager Billy Bingham and certain of the players, which burst into the open over the weekend, is unprecedented in my knowledge of Goodison affairs.' Bingham was not the first to suffer from the difficulties arising from the gulf between managing a winning and losing dressing room. 'We know the problems and have worked at them. We have not sat on our backsides,' he said before the Spurs game 48 hours later. 'There is no one more than me that wants Everton to win. I am an absolute true blue and want them to win 150 per cent.' Bingham got his victory, a third in twenty games, by a single goal. But supporters were voting with their feet: the paltry attendance of 18,126 was the lowest on the ground for a league fixture in more than two decades.

Gary Jones – Goodison's missing maverick

The winger's Everton career was a bit of a slow-burner, only becoming a first-team regular in the autumn of 1974, three-and-a-half years after his debut. Jones had been probably Everton's best player during the 1975/76 campaign, however the gifted winger was 'high maintenance' and attracted a disproportionate amount of management attention.

Midway through the season he had scored eight goals in sixteen matches, including two in a memorable display against Aston Villa at Goodison. The press mooted an England call up but there were still issues. Jones was poor in the League Cup defeat at Notts County and asked Bingham to rest him for the visit to Leeds. 'The next day Gary came to me and asked to be left out of today's team,' Bingham said on the Saturday. 'I have been worried about his performance for some weeks and the lad is having a difficult time at the moment with some domestic problems. Psychologically, he was just not right to play and I granted his request to leave him out of the team today.'

The recalled Jones was outstanding in the 2-1 victory at Coventry before Christmas until, like his teammates, form dropped off alarmingly. Relegated to the substitute's bench for the debacle at Maine Road in February, Jones publicly questioned his future. 'Like any player I am ambitious for success and I do fancy a move to another club,' he said 48 hours later, 'I will be seeing Mr Bingham today to talk it all over with him.' Jones told reporters, 'A lot of things have caused this, partly it's financial, because I've not been happy with my terms since the start of the season. There are some players on better terms – which I resent. We haven't won anything this season and I can't see anything being won in the near future.'

Jones' Everton career effectively ended five weeks later. The winger missed a crucial penalty in the defeat at Leicester and then the 24-year-old was poor during a 3-1 home loss to Leeds United. Jones' contribution was negligible and, when substituted, he responded with ironic applause followed by a gesture to the manager's dugout. Jones failed to stay at the ground for the rest of the game and later said he would be making a transfer request. The temperamental star and

Bingham subsequently had a confrontation at Bellefield 48 hours later, one that resulted in the manager fining the player a fortnight's wages with a suspension for the same period. 'I don't accept the fine and the suspension but the fact that I am going to get a transfer pleases me,' Jones said. Yet Jones' argument was with the manager, not the club. 'Due to circumstances I have not been in the right frame of mind to play for him,' he explained. 'I still have a big regard for the club and no quarrel with Everton. This is purely a personal matter.' Bingham's response was caustic. 'I am only interested in players who want to play for Everton. It seems that Jones does not want to play for Everton.'

Jones sadly did not feature for the club again. Sold to Birmingham City in July for £110,000, like many others he soon regretted the decision. Eighteen months later he told the *Liverpool Echo*: 'I made a mistake leaving Everton as soon as I did. Looking back to my transfer, I needed only to have waited a few months and the manager, Billy Bingham, would have left and I could have stayed. I had a feeling before I went that Mr Bingham would be moved out but I was so depressed with the whole situation at Everton. A move seemed the only answer at the time.' That decision was everybody's loss, for Jones lit up many a grey afternoon at Goodison with his own brand of mercurial football.

CHAPTER 5

Dog day afternoons

THERE WAS REAL CASE FOR SACKING BINGHAM IN THE EARLY spring of 1976, because of results and the dressing-room unrest. A 1-0 defeat at Anfield on the first weekend in April took the dreadful run to a paltry four victories in 26 games, with five successive defeats. The loss left Everton a lowly sixteenth in the table, comfortably above the relegation zone but way below expectations. However, a sequence of nine points from the last six fixtures produced a final finish of eleventh. The Ulsterman felt that the failure to land the title in 1974/75 cast a shadow over the following campaign. 'We finished seventh in my first season and then there was the disappointment of being fourth,' he told the *Evertonian* in 1995, 'After that it was a bit of an anti-climax.'

Summer of sorrow

The summer of 1976 was the hottest for more than three centuries and remains the benchmark for all subsequent warm spells. Large areas of the country went seven weeks without any sign of rain as temperatures reached ninety degrees Fahrenheit. It was so hot the tarmac on the M1 melted and the shortage of water led 'minister for drought', Denis Howell, to recommend that people 'take a bath with a friend'.

It was the same story on Merseyside. With daily temperatures above eighty degrees Fahrenheit, for those used to the regular damp, cool summers there was an unusual statement from the Met Office at Liverpool airport. 'There are signs of a definite change,' a spokesman said, 'Temperatures may fall to the mid-seventies.' In Cadbury Schweppes' Liverpool factory, management gave workers afternoons off as chocolate melted in the intense warmth and, following numerous complaints from the water-starved public, Liverpool council turned off the famous Steble Fountain by the Walker Art Gallery, even though it merely recycled water via an electric pump.

While the region sweltered, Bingham took a holiday in France but on returning faced an unhappy bunch of players. Bob Latchford wanted away from Goodison, while Mick Buckley and David Lawson had transfer requests rejected. Bingham had also fallen out with winger John Connolly, who eventually left for Birmingham City in a £70,000 deal.[15] Bingham had brought in Andy King for £35,000 in April and although interested in Preston's Tony Morley and QPR's Stan Bowles, there were no further incomings. 'I have inquired over many players this year, but have not struck lucky,' he told the club's AGM, 'simply because their managers won't let them go.' One player Everton targeted was the great Johan Cruyff. The Dutchman's contract with Barcelona was up in the June and they made an approach two months before, but were scared off when the Spanish club offered him £200,000 to sign a new contract, a figure the Toffees could not compete with.

With further rumours of unrest on the pre-season tour of West Germany, Bingham moved to quash the damaging gossip. 'There is no revolt in the Everton camp. It grieves me to hear the moaners and groaners,' he said. The manager then went on to publicly slam those in the squad he felt responsible:

I am waving the deep blue banner of Everton. The trouble is that our modern society lacks discipline and this is reflected in the actions of some players. They have so much going for them but if you leave them out for one match they immediately want to quit. I want to know where their loyalty is. Or perhaps they are just mercenaries. I have no time for belly-achers at Everton. Perhaps people will say I am old-fashioned asking for loyalty but that's the way it is with me.

Such public condemnation was hardly guaranteed to lift team morale but there was a surprise on the opening day at a sweltering Loftus Road, when the previous season's runners-up were vanquished 4-0. But signs of dressing-room

---

15 Connolly was the fourth Everton player to move to Birmingham City during Bingham's tenure.

tensions were still apparent. Bingham banned Jim Pearson from appearing for the first-team and fined the player a maximum fortnight's wages after accusations of spitting when substituted in the 2-0 home defeat to Aston Villa. 'Serious misconduct following the substitution,' was Bingham's stance,[16] but the player was unimpressed. 'I resent the implications that have been made,' the Scot complained. 'I called Pearson into the office, and gave him a ticking off and his letter of suspension,' said the manager, who placed him on the transfer list. The dispute seemed petty and self-defeating.

Shortly afterwards Bingham spoke about the unrest to Richard Bott of the *Sunday Express*. 'Many of the stories which came out were exaggerated. But some players, when they are out of the side, will always cause problems,' Bingham admitted, before provocatively adding, 'They have no allegiance to anyone except themselves. You know the ones I am talking about. I don't have to name names. But there were never more than four causing unrest.' But four players is four too many and the dressing room would have taken note of their manager's comments.

The off-the-pitch issues were set aside as Everton maintained the early-season momentum until early-October, when a 2-2 home draw against Manchester City deprived Bingham's team of top-spot. Eleven days later that misplaced optimism came to a shuddering end via a hammering at Anfield, one not reflected in the final 3-1 scoreline. With the manager absent whilst recuperating following an operation, the visitors were three behind at half-time, overrun by a Liverpool team who produced a 'bewildering, breathtaking performance' according to Bott. In the second period Everton regrouped and had the consolation of a first derby goal in five years, thanks to Martin Dobson's terrific thirty-yard strike at the Kop end. 'Everton were outclassed. Their defenders were petrified from the start by Liverpool's speed and intuition, and apprehension spread throughout the team,' wrote Patrick Barclay of the *Guardian*, in an ominous portent for future visits across Stanley Park. The champagne that Bingham had kept in his bedside cupboard in the event of a victory remained unopened. Mick Lyons was unconvinced though, his post-match comments scoring top marks for over-optimism and cheerleading. 'If we had played in the first half like we played in the second, we would have

---

[16] Bingham may have had critics, but at least he was consistent, having fined Gary Jones for a similar offence six months before.

won', the skipper said, 'But this is only one match in a long season. We'll still finish on top and we'll beat Liverpool at Goodison.'

Lyons' comments seemed silly as, by the end of November, Bingham's team stood seventh and then crashed 4-1 at a rampant Newcastle when Gordon Lee's side showed championship credentials. The defeat raised further questions about the manager's future as supporters were voting with their feet. A gate of 10,898 for the League Cup tie against Cambridge United earlier in the season was the lowest at Goodison for 23 years and in the late autumn just 23,000 for the attractive visits of West Ham and Derby County were way below the usual figures for those fixtures. The Goodison crowd had also turned on their own, forcing Bingham to leave out their main target for abuse, full-back Terry Darracott, for a Coventry City League Cup tie.

Three days after the rout on Tyneside, fortunes took a further turn for the worse in a farcical visit to The Hawthorns. The visitors were a goal down inside five minutes and on the half-hour came a quite surreal incident when a small Jack Russell dog entered the playing area and referee John Hunting bizarrely allowed play to continue. The white intruder – or brown and white according to the very observant *Daily Mirror* – chased the ball around the pitch for a full two minutes, the 'pressing' tactics forcing Darracott, Ken McNaught and full-back Dave Jones into a series of square passes, until one to the goalkeeper caused chaos. Dai Davies came out for the ball but stopped as the dog went for him and in the confusion, West Brom's David Cross took advantage to dribble past the stranded goalkeeper (and the dog) to fire home. The Jack Russell then followed up and headed the ball into the back of the net. The shell-shocked visitors conceded a third before the break and the game was over.

With Bingham absent, afterwards coach Steve Burtenshaw was seething: 'I think the game should have been stopped because our players were definitely harassed by the dog.' The visitors' complaints drew sympathy from Hunting. 'Cases like this have to be left to the referee's discretion, and I would have stopped the game straight away if I thought the dog was having a direct effect,' the referee admitted before adding, 'I thought by allowing the game to continue I was hoping the dog would go away of its own accord, but I can't argue from the Everton players' point of view.' That said, the controversy over the goal did not disguise a woeful performance from the visitors. But then, unexpectedly and retaining the pet theme, Bingham pulled a rabbit out of a hat.

An early Christmas gift

With George Telfer failing to capitalise on his youthful promise, Bingham was keen to increase forward firepower. The Everton manager rekindled previous interest in Dennis Tueart and tabled a bid in excess of the £275,000 fee Manchester City paid Sunderland two years earlier. City were unwilling to part with the England international and Birmingham City sadly rejected two bids to sign Trevor Francis, whose development into a leading striker from his *wunderkind* early career had made the 22-year-old one of the most sought-after players in the country. After offloading John Connolly to the St Andrews club in September, Bingham made two offers to procure Francis, the second in excess of £300,000, which Birmingham unsurprisingly rejected. The opportunity of pairing Bob Latchford with his former sparring partner [17] was a missed opportunity and Bingham's time at the club may have turned out differently if the talented Francis had journeyed up the M6.

Bingham's frustrating attempts to sign a quality striker continued in vain. The Everton manager, like his predecessor, failed to land Jimmy Greenhoff, who went from Stoke City to Old Trafford, and Blackpool were reluctant to sell Mickey Walsh. Like Catterick, who spent years trying to bring a proven goalscorer to Everton, Bingham found that the market was a minefield for those seeking the most sought-after commodity in football. 'I am still looking for that extra bit of class that can turn a game and I am not afraid to spend,' he said in words right out of the Catterick phrasebook. 'Two or three players come into that category but I cannot get the clubs to part.'

But there was salvation for Bingham across the English Channel. Duncan McKenzie had joined Anderlecht in the summer of 1976 and settled into a comfortable lifestyle off the pitch, living in luxury outside of Brussels with wages of more than £500 a week significantly greater than those at home. However, McKenzie's casual attitude was at odds with the regimented approach of continental football, although unsurprisingly his extravagant gifts made him popular with fans. The 26-year-old was out of the team when Bingham made an initial inquiry in the middle of November. 'It's no secret we need more strength

---

[17] In his excellent autobiography *A Different Road*, the Everton hero described Francis as the greatest player he ever played with. 'He was absolutely phenomenal... on pure natural talent Trevor stands head and shoulders above everybody, absolutely everybody.'

and I'm looking for strikers with class,' Bingham said, 'Duncan would make a good player for us and our crowd because he's exciting.'

The Belgian side gave short shrift to Everton's initial offer of £160,000, saying they wanted £240,000. However, after a prolonged game of cat and mouse, Bingham eventually negotiated Anderlecht down to £200,000 and the complex deal involved club secretary, Jim Greenwood, requiring Treasury permission to move the large amount of currency out of the country. When Greenwood met McKenzie at Manchester Airport, he had forgotten to switch his lights off on his car and the flat battery meant the new signing had to hitch a lift to Goodison from a local radio reporter.

Although Bingham said, 'McKenzie is a player with charisma who would be good for Everton' for some the signing raised questions. 'From within the game, cynical murmurings can still be heard that this is just another alighting point in the butterfly's progress of this enigmatic player,' mused Martin Tyler in *The Times*. 'A career which, the unimpressed say, has never exceeded unfulfilled potential.' James Lawton in the *Daily Express* referred to the way his coach Raymond Goethals had criticised the player for not adapting to Belgian football and failure to apply his skill to the wider needs of the team. Lawton concluded, 'It is a superb talent, McKenzie's, but there are now real fears that it will be unfulfilled.'

With his predilection for throwing golf balls huge distances and jumping over motor cars, critics viewed McKenzie as a bit of a circus act, and a luxury one. They could also point out that Everton were his fourth club in just over two years, although McKenzie may have replied that he was the victim of circumstance on occasions – Brian Clough took him to Leeds during his ill-fated 44-day long spell. However, his former manager, who wanted the striker for Nottingham Forest, summed up the feelings of many: 'I'm surprised there is talk of him moving again. He's 26 and he's hardly had a career at all. He'll have to settle in one place and do his stuff before long or he's going to finish without anything to show for all his talent.' Evertonians ignored that scepticism as the acquisition certainly fired their imagination. McKenzie himself wanted a profitable partnership with the club's British-record signing. 'If I can't do it alongside Bob [Latchford] I can't do it alongside anyone,' McKenzie said at his welcoming press conference. 'It was his presence here that was a reason for my signing. I rate him as the best English centre forward of the present day.'

While the Everton hierarchy were venturing up several Belgian cul-de-sacs in pursuit of McKenzie, they were also negotiating with Derby County over the purchase of 29-year-old midfielder Bruce Rioch.[18] The Rams had sacked Dave Mackay and caretaker boss Colin Murphy wanted the Scottish international as a striker, much to the player's displeasure. Two days before McKenzie signed, Rioch turned down a move because of a new business in which he was involved in the Midlands but, after the club made domestic concessions to the player, the Scot performed an about-turn and agreed terms two days after the striker. That purchase also influenced Rioch. 'Everton's £200,000 signing of Duncan McKenzie from Anderlecht this week certainly helped to change my mind,' he revealed, 'From what I've seen they have players with ability and the McKenzie transfer has added to my view that Everton are a club with ambition and I'm glad to be part of it.' Having sold Dave Clements earlier in the year, Bingham needed a left-sided midfielder but the deal did not feel right: a fee of £180,000 was huge for a player nearing his thirtieth birthday and already preparing for a life outside the game.

Later events indicated the purchases were borne out of panic, the actions of a manager and a club under pressure to do *something*. The expensive duo made their Everton debuts in front of the BBC *Match of the Day* audience at a frozen Highfield Road on the following Saturday. Despite taking an early lead and with the two new acquisitions performing well, Bingham's team slumped to a 4-2 defeat. When Manchester United – without a league victory in three months – inflicted a 4-0 Christmas hammering at Old Trafford, Everton had conceded eighteen goals in five away games, indicating the manager may have better utilised the £400,000 in defence. It was to prove a costly decision.

---

[18] Earlier in the season, Bill Shankly, in a televised interview at Goodison, had described Rioch as one of the finest midfielders in the country.

CHAPTER 6

Torpedoed

THE VINTAGE CLIP REMAINS ONE OF THE MOST RECOGNISABLE and watched online involving Everton. The film features Duncan McKenzie avoiding the clutches of several visiting players as he playfully dummies and tricks his way across the Goodison turf during Everton's 2-0 home victory over Stoke City on 8 January, 1977. 'Stoke can't find a way of taking it from him,' says Gerald Sinstadt on Granada TV's *The Kick Off Match*, before a foul ends the fun for the 33,000 spectators at the FA Cup third-round tie. 'The whistle has eventually brought a marvellous piece of play to an end,' proclaims the admiring commentator as McKenzie smiles at frustrated opponents. However, as Bingham watched the game at his Southport home he was aware of moves behind the scenes to remove him. John Moores summoned Bingham to his Formby home on the Monday afternoon, where he sacked his manager. At 9pm on the same evening, the Everton board issued a typically terse statement:

> *Given the very considerable resources, a club of Everton's standing can put at it's [sic] manager's disposal, the ultimate responsibility for the performances on the field should rest with the manager. The directors have been concerned, for some time, that things have not been going well and despite external criticism have been determined to allow time for a more consistent pattern to emerge. After very careful deliberation, they now feel a change of manager is desirable.*

Bingham appeared shocked at the development, although there had been a leak to the national press earlier in the day. 'Normally we have a board meeting on Tuesday but John Moores told me on Saturday he would like to have a word with me at 8pm on Monday. Going home in the car I said to my wife Eunice: "This looks like it,'" Bingham admitted later. Speaking to the *Daily Express*, the now former manager said: 'I have been fighting in the trenches for quite a while, dodging shells and mortar then I have been torpedoed when I thought we had turned the corner. I've tried to make the team more attractive. I thought the signings of Duncan McKenzie and Bruce Rioch clinched it. But… if you are with a top club you must expect you are there to be shot down.'

The move was surprising as the feeling was Bingham had ridden out the storm. The club were in the League Cup semi-final for the first time, with the opening leg of a very winnable tie against Second Division Bolton Wanderers only days away. Everton had played well against Stoke with John Bean in the *Daily Mirror* proclaiming: 'Everton switched on the Cup smile to leave Goodison basking in the sort of radiance Alex Young used to create in the old, bold days… Strange to think that, less than six weeks ago, Everton's football had forced chairman John Moores to the brink of quitting. Now their slick style seeps right through to new full-back Neil Robinson.' The expensive signings of McKenzie and Rioch were a signal of the board's faith in the manager. Bingham shared that belief: 'I am more optimistic about Everton now than at any period since I came here,' he said shortly before his sacking.

But the Everton board, rightly or wrongly, did not share their manager's confidence. 'We decided this move about a month ago but we deferred it because Mr Bingham was busy signing two new players,' John Moores said, 'We have been doing very well in the Cup but we have been slipping down the League towards the relegation area. We used to get gates of 40,000 but they have been down to 20,000 and we lose money at that figure. The crowds are the bosses and you have to give the public what it wants so we thought it was time for a change.'

Although the majority of supporters welcomed the new arrivals, the circumstances now seemed bizarre. Everton had literally moved heaven and earth to sign Duncan McKenzie – like the Treasury approval to transfer the agreed fee across the English Channel – and Bingham had taken several weeks to capture Bruce Rioch. Yet was Moores really indicating the board were content to sanction these activities, knowing full well they would be sacking the manager in any case? What would happen if Bingham's successor didn't fancy the two new players (or vice versa)? More pertinently, if the board had decided a month before to sack Bingham – why did they not perform the act then? This was typical of the indecisiveness that infected the club's thinking during the decade – they should have sacked Bingham and not signed McKenzie and Rioch, or allowed the transfers and given him time to fully embed the players within the team, one that was still in two cup competitions and on the cusp of a Wembley final. By sanctioning an undesirable combination of the two, Moores allowed for the worst-case scenario: a new manager who did not want one or both of the players, and vice-versa, which is effectively what happened. Bingham had also paid premium fees that the club had little chance of recouping.

Why Bingham failed

Bingham's appointment actually sowed the seeds of his departure. The Ulsterman was, at best, fourth choice for the role. He knew that, the board knew it, as did the players and most significantly, so did the fans, who on occasions showed no compunction in reminding him. Patience with the new manager was always going to be in short supply. 'Controversy was one of the major characteristics of Billy Bingham's reign as manager of Everton,' wrote Charles Lambert in the *Liverpool Echo* after his sacking, 'It was in the air when he was appointed, and has lingered to mark the manner of his departing.'

After a decade of managing relatively small clubs and underdogs at international level, Bingham was naturally pragmatic and more adept at setting up his side to negate the strengths of the opposition. 'His tactics were always geared towards the team, and had more to do with organisation than with individual creativeness,' said Martin Dobson later. Off the pitch, the emphasis on physical fitness and harsh training regimes in the Formby sand dunes may have worked at lower levels, but that philosophy had a limited shelf-life with established stars. Dobson felt that 'For the first year or so I felt the training was too hard. Having to run 3,000 metres a day and meet the weight targets he set us, and then play a game with the reserves in the evening – it just felt like his methods were not geared to the Saturday game. By the time that came along, I felt physically jaded, all the spark had gone.' As one correspondent to the *Liverpool Echo* remarked, 'Bingham's methods produced the most unimaginative, dull, dour, unentertaining Everton team I have seen in thirty years. No matter how successful a team is, it's the way games are won that counts.' Bingham's goalkeeper Dai Davies reflected on those shortcomings in a candid assessment in his autobiography:

I was secretly glad that Billy Bingham did not receive the accolade of winning the First Division Championship [in 1975]. From my knowledge of him he was not a man who deserved that honour. He was a selfish man who had little thought of anything except how to promote himself, and he was not particularly talented either.

Davies was brutal, but there was some truth in that character assassination which goes back to Bingham's appointment. With no elite club experience, the Irishman's natural charm, and not his CV, seduced John Moores in 1973. Thereafter he placed only limited emphasis on attacking play while struggling to make the transition from managing in lower divisions to the top-flight. In truth, he never really got to grips with the different expectations of the boardroom, which were geared for success, to those of lower division clubs who were just happy to survive. His man-management was weak on occasions and counter-productive. 'Bingham was a good organiser,' Mick Lyons said, 'Under Bingham we had a side capable of winning the Championship. He rubbed some people up the wrong way, but this happens in football.' This manifested itself in the way Bingham failed to address the discontent swirling round the training ground that caused the crisis of early 1976 and the disputes over pay that followed.

When four players asked for transfers that summer, Bingham was unmoved. 'If they don't want to play for Everton and are going to cry every time they are out of the team then I am afraid they will have to go,' he said. Such provocative language may have worked lower down the league but was bound to infuriate bigger stars and cause resentment, which was clearly present throughout his last twelve months at the helm. 'He treated Everton players like he treated Southport's players and the difference is that, although they weren't doing well, they were First Division players,' his former Everton teammate Alex Parker (who played for the Ulsterman at Haig Avenue) told Bingham's biographer, Robert Allen. 'Fourth Division players will listen to you and accept what you are saying without thinking of questioning you, but his mistake was that first division players won't.'

Bingham's transfer dealings were another baffling aspect of his reign. The Ulsterman spent £1.3m and recouped close to £1.1m – economically sound but a surprisingly small gap given the restructuring required when he took over and the fact that the board had also made significant funds (of up to £500,000) available. Although Bingham deserved praise for skilfully manoeuvring those stalwarts from the Catterick era out the door – and for good prices – in his first three-and-a-half years there were just two big money signings: Bob Latchford and Martin Dobson. Instead, Bingham had made the same mistake as Catterick in 1970: a belief there was no need for major restructuring as the squad had their best days ahead. 'We have the basis of a good side. It is a young side and with a couple of reinforcements it could be a very good side,' Bingham admitted at the end of the 1974/75 campaign, but the moderate competition effectively acted as a mirage, fooling the Everton manager into believing he had a strong outfit capable of fighting for honours. However, none of that team had the vital combination of ability and temperament to have played in Catterick's and Kendall's championship-winning sides. Apart from Latchford and Dobson, 'there was so little real talent in Billy Bingham's team,' Dai Davies later claimed. But the Everton boss allowed the team to atrophy and when Duncan McKenzie[19] and Bruce Rioch arrived eighteen months later it was too little too late.[20]

Although there was a strong case for retaining his services, given the signings of those two stars, the impression is that the job was simply too big. Leading FA coach Allen Wade said in Bingham's biography, 'I don't think he was ready for Everton. He was intimidated by them,' which was probably true. Afterwards, Bingham rarely spoke, but a November 1977 *Liverpool Echo* interview revealed the sacking left a bad taste in the mouth:

What annoyed me was that I wasn't a failure at Everton. If the club was bottom of the league, you could say all right, you deserve it. But I was rebuilding a team, and was aware of the fact that it still had to be added to. I had lifted them up, taken them out of the rut. I had taken them to the brink of the League Cup final, and felt I had done a reasonable job of stabilising the club. Yes I was a bit bitter over what happened in the end.

---

[19] In a 1995 interview with the *Evertonian,* Bingham said his biggest problem as a manager was finding a partner for Bob Latchford. 'I felt we needed another striker because Jim Pearson and David Smallman were not the right ones for Latchford. You buy players and try them out and hope they gel, but forming a partnership is not easy,' he admitted. 'I went for Duncan McKenzie...he was a player who enjoyed the big games more than the run of the mill league games.'

[20] Before buying McKenzie and Rioch, Bingham had sold twelve players but only purchased five.

Bingham rebuilt his managerial career after returning to Northern Ireland as national team manager in March 1980. Ironically, his biggest weakness at Everton – the accent on fitness and organisation at the expense of individual skill – was ideally suited to getting the best out of a group of players who, with the odd notable exception, were mostly journeymen. Bingham took his country to the World Cup finals on two occasions – as well as defeating holders West Germany twice in qualification for the 1984 European Championships – and their 1982 victory over hosts Spain remains, pound-for-pound, the best achieved by a British country in the tournament. That was all in the future though, the present task for the Everton board was to appoint a successor.

CHAPTER 7

Gordon gives Lee way

'WE WOULD LIKE TO RESOLVE IT ALL IN A WEEK OR TWO AND GET RID of all the uncertainty. The sooner it is settled the better,' John Moores said 24 hours after Bingham's dismissal. Yet Moores had decided to sack his manager a month before and, with no immediate signs of a replacement, the club was in the same position as during the spring of 1973. For a hugely successful businessman, surprisingly he had not learned the lessons of that botched process.

'They are in real trouble'

Everton sacked Bingham on Monday, 10 January and the first reported approach was to England manager Don Revie who, like four years before, turned down the opportunity. Moores and the board subsequently spread their net wide, with former Derby County boss Dave Mackay, Bill Shankly and Brian Clough rumoured to be amongst their targets. But the only men to seriously express an interest were popular first-team coach (and now caretaker boss) Steve Burtenshaw and former player Dave Clements. However, Mackay was the early favourite at 5-2, with Burtenshaw at 3-1 and World Cup winner Jack Charlton and Brian Clough both at 4-1. The caretaker manager was the preferred choice of the Everton players. 'I'd rather have him than anyone from the outside. He is direct and we all respect him and he wants to win,' skipper Lyons admitted.

With Clough[21] and Shankly subsequently ruled out, others voicing an interest

---

21 The club's fears that Clough would take over were well-founded. 'I couldn't work for Sir John Moores,' Clough later told Duncan McKenzie, 'Nothing wrong with the guy but I want to run the club I'm at.'

included former Manchester City coach and manager Malcolm Allison. Ever the opportunist, 'Big Mal' said, 'I can understand Everton's position. There is no doubt their club should be pre-eminent in England as Juventus are in Italy.' For those who regarded Allison's utterances with a certain amount of ennui, this attempted seduction of Moores broke new ground. Allison told the press that he had developed a new coaching philosophy, one he claimed 'would develop footballers stage by stage until it produced all-round players each of whom would also be brilliant specialists, like goalscorers, or great left-sided players, or marvellous headers of the ball.' Allison suggested Everton would be an ideal place to bring these revolutionary plans to fruition. 'They have a marvellous stadium, a dream of a training centre and unlimited resources for buying players,' he claimed, before offering his services as a consultant for three months, 'to see if John Moores and myself could operate on the same wavelength'. That partnership was mind-boggling and one man not convinced was former Spurs player Danny Blanchflower. 'Without doubt Mal it is the best application I have ever heard for a manager's job,' he pithily commented in the *Sunday Express,* 'There is no way John Moores can sleep at night thinking about it.' Sadly perhaps for the press, Allison, whose best days were behind him, was never seriously going to be an option – his extrovert personality and playboy status would never have fitted in with the haughty Everton board.

Another who expressed a desire to take charge at Goodison was, intriguingly, Italian team manager Enzo Bearzot. Out of contract in the June, the future World Cup winner said, 'I am definitely interested. The job with Everton has prestige... I must wait to hear if Everton are interested before making a move.' Although given the red tape involved in employing players and managers from abroad at the time, the board would have found difficulty in bringing in the legendary boss.

Two weeks after sacking Bingham, the side was struggling under Burtenshaw, and a 3-1 home defeat to QPR left Everton close to the relegation zone. 'The situation is now, to say the least, extremely serious for Everton FC,' warned Charles Burgess in the *Liverpool Daily Post,* 'Perhaps that it is putting it mildly. THEY ARE IN REAL TROUBLE.' After the game there were audible chants from the stands of 'We want Clough, we want Clough' and protests outside the ground, leading to more questions for the board about the new manager. Moores tersely replied 'I have nothing to say' when asked about progress whilst new chairman Bill Scott commented: 'We have had plenty of replies to our advertisement, but we cannot do anything until we get the right man.' This was shorthand of course for admitting the standard of applicants had not been great.

Then on the morning of Monday, 24 January, out of nowhere, came an extraordinary development. The *Daily Express* reported Everton had offered Bobby Robson £600 a week to take over at Goodison. 'This stunning move would make him, at over £30,000 a year, the highest paid boss in British Soccer – some £5,000 a year more than Don Revie gets as international supremo.' Like Revie, Robson had turned down Everton in 1973 but four years later not only was the annual salary appealing but the contract offer was up to ten years, with that 1970s phenomenon of a 'golden handshake' thrown in for good measure. Robson, therefore, was more amenable to a move, as he later admitted in his 2005 autobiography *Farewell but not Goodbye*:

> *Technically, I agreed to join Everton in January 1977, after a meeting with Philip Carter and Sir John Moore [sic], the two most powerful men at Goodison Park. We met on a motorway and then proceeded to Sir John's home to clinch the deal. Phil Carter was an extremely nice man and very intelligent. Everton were plainly a bigger club than Ipswich, and had an edge of ambition. To emphasise his desire to have me at the club, Sir John handed me a cheque for £50,000 there and then... It was seven times my Ipswich salary. Was it bribery? No it was a golden hello... I agreed to head north and shook hands on the deal.*

At that juncture, the move was on but then came the devastating – for Everton fans – twist in the tale, as Robson explained. 'I laid down one condition. Nothing was to be announced until I had broken the news to John Cobbold [the Ipswich chairman]. I woke up next morning to a shocking headline: "Robson goes to Everton". I couldn't believe my eyes. I felt nauseous. A thought flashed through my mind – if they could do that to me on the first day, what might happen further down the line?'

Robson, annoyed about the leak before he had informed his chairman, subsequently ripped up the cheque and remained in East Anglia. However, Robson later wrote in his autobiography that '... losing the chance to manage

Everton, at that point in my career, was one of the regrets of my life.'[22]

Given the date of the first press reports of an approach to Robson, this would put the meeting between the three men as the preceding Sunday, or the day after the QPR home defeat. This is the generally accepted view of events, yet in his 1982 book *Time on the Grass* he told a slightly different, but fascinating, story. In late-1976 Robson took a call at home. 'A club in the North-West will be terminating the contract of its manager soon. Are you interested in the job?' Robson recognised 'Deep Throat' from three years before. 'I know you. It's Everton,' he said. 'That's right,' came the reply, 'How do you feel about it?' Robson gave an opening and in early January 1977 the phone went again and it was an Everton director, saying Moores wanted to see him. 'I drove to his home in Formby, Lancashire,' Robson wrote, 'He seemed a nice old man, I liked him a lot.' Over lunch, Moores offered Robson the job. The sticking point was informing the Ipswich board, should he accept. Both sets of directors were close: 'There was an affinity between the clubs and I didn't want that broken,' he wrote. In 1973, Moores had also asked previous targets, Don Revie and Jimmy Armfield, to his home so this is almost certainly the true version of events. It seems highly unlikely that Moores, one of the richest men in the country, would countenance a meeting in a 1970s greasy-spoon cafe.

Moores therefore suggested Everton draft a letter to his employers, an idea which the future England boss rejected, saying he would inform the Cobbold family himself (Patrick was chairman, having just taken over from brother John). Yet Everton did exactly that. 'This letter was handed to me by one of the Everton directors [probably Philip Carter] at a secret meeting at the Newport Pagnell service station,' Robson said, but he shook hands on the deal in any case, repeating his plan to tell the Ipswich board. This must be the meeting (albeit with completely different details) referenced in *Farewell but not Goodbye* as he then wrote that the next day the infamous *Daily Express* headline appeared.

This is an interesting angle given that Everton's renewed courtship of Robson pre-dates Bingham's sacking. The assumption is that the Everton board leaked the story when, given it was run by the southern desk of the *Daily Express*, the evidence points to their Ipswich counterparts. If Everton were responsible, they

---

[22] That may have been true but not for the first or last time, Robson used Everton's interest as a means of improving his own position, immediately signing a new 10-year contract and doubling his salary at Portman Road.

would have given the story to one of the Manchester-based journalists, who were unaware of the developments. Given Everton had been chasing Robson for probably the best part of two months, there had been ample time for the club to leak details, yet they never did and Robson had never been mentioned in the betting. Such an action was also inconsistent with Moores' appreciation of the sensitivities involved. 'If you come, I know it will be hard for you to tell John and Patrick Cobbold,' he had previously told Robson. Understandably, the Goodison hierarchy – who had nothing to gain and everything to lose by the story – were reportedly shocked when it appeared.

Given the two boards were close it is easy to envisage Moores having a conversation with Ipswich about talking to Robson, without his knowledge, so they knew along about the approach and were waiting for their manager to tell them. That explains Robson's surprise when he phoned Patrick Cobbold on the Monday morning and was taken aback on how relaxed his chairman seemed. 'He sounded matter-of-fact, and not agitated as he might have been,' he wrote in *Time on the Grass*. Possibly because Cobbold knew all along.

Either way, there had been a disastrous sequence of events and with no appointment on the immediate horizon, an editorial in the *Liverpool Echo* voiced the frustrations of all Evertonians:

> *It is just over a fortnight since Everton sacked Billy Bingham, and even those Evertonians who regarded this as the dawning of a brave new blue and white world are beginning to get that awful feeling that this is where they came in four years ago. The great debate over who the new manager should be, conducted at first with such great intensity, is beginning to fade away. What follows is the increasing conviction that history is repeating itself – and bewilderment that it can have been allowed to. Everton watchers will need no reminding of the will-he-won't-he weeks of 1973 when it seemed that every big name in British soccer was poised to take the job and, in the end, the directors had to send all the way to Greece for the successor to Harry Catterick. Now those same big names are being juggled with again as the search drags on for Bingham's successor.*

Following Robson's rejection, unbelievably Everton went to another potential target from 1973, Aston Villa boss Ron Saunders – possibly the third choice on the list of targets. Birkenhead-born and a former Goodison player, Saunders always appeared to be a natural for the job but understandably his board turned down the approach. As did Saunders. 'For two and a half years I have worked tremendously hard to build up a team on the field,' he said, 'Now I believe we have an equally good one off the field and are on the verge of great things.'

The failure to act decisively lead to stories of a potential move for former boss Harry Catterick, in a general manager role. Dave Clements had flown back from America to make a pitch for the job and although the Northern Irishman had little chance on his own, there was speculation after the pair held lengthy talks that they could be a master and apprentice at Goodison, in a similar way to how Ron Greenwood and John Lyall operated at West Ham. Catterick, who was now managing Preston, did not exactly dampen speculation. Having admitted to talking to club directors – 'but we spoke in a general way' – the former manager said, 'I can't do anything about it if people keep putting my name up for the job. I know that I may be approached now that I have proved my fitness.' Either way, there was no desire within the boardroom to re-employ their former boss, leading to even more confusion. 'Everton will have to admit – it's been bungled,' read a *Liverpool Daily Post* headline. But just when the board expected to extend the search to the Second Division, up came Everton's knight in shining armour: a tall, angular man based in the north-east.

Meet the new boss

Gordon Lee was a typical footballing product of the 1950s and 1960s, a no-frills full-back who made more than a century of league appearances for Aston Villa. With no obvious alternative career, Lee moved into coaching with Shrewsbury before appointment as Port Vale manager in 1968.[23] Having little money to spend, Lee won promotion from the Fourth Division two years later and, after keeping the Potteries outfit in the third tier, moved to Blackburn Rovers in January 1974. Lee won the Third Division title in the following season, before relocating to Newcastle.

Lee's first season in the north-east was just about respectable, a lowly fifteenth-place position compensated by an appearance in the League Cup final, where they lost to Manchester City. But off the pitch there were issues and Lee

---

[23] Where his first managerial signing was Merseyside and Tranmere legend Johnny King.

came close to resigning several times. The Newcastle chairman, Lord Westwood, on one occasion provided his manager with an uncomplimentary assessment of purchases and the club annoyed Lee by billing him for the hotel he was using. Although they started the new campaign well, supporters were still unhappy with Malcolm Macdonald's transfer to Arsenal for £333,333 during the summer. Lee also had domestic issues, both of his sons remained at boarding school in Lancashire and his absence unsettled them.

When Everton approached Newcastle on the final weekend in January, things moved quickly and, after resigning, Lee moved to Goodison on a reported salary of £20,000 per year.[24] But, like his predecessor, Lee was nowhere near the first choice and chairman Bill Scott faced some awkward questions at the welcoming press conference. Scott stated the board had an original shortlist of three – Bobby Robson, Lee and unnamed other. Once Robson turned down the role, then they approached Lee, having made no contact with the other party (who may have been Revie). Based on Robson's account(s) this would appear conveniently true: he turned the job down on the Monday and Lee was at Goodison within a week.

Yet early on in the process, John Moores said that the club were waiting for replies to their advertisement. 'If we get the right man, then we will close the applications immediately,' the vice-chairman said. Scott had said virtually the same thing after the home defeat to QPR. So why were two conflicting statements given about the recruitment process? Possibly to act as a diversionary tactic while they schmoozed Robson?

All of this uncannily mirrored events from four years before. After waiting more than a month to appoint Bingham, Moores said that he was on the original shortlist, but sceptics claimed the club had never considered him. But Lee was now the man in the dugout and the immediate question was, with a possible trip to Wembley on the horizon, could he end the trophyless seven-year itch?

---

[24] Legendary MP Dennis Skinner tabled a parliamentary question about Don Revie's reported salary offered by Everton in May 1973, and whether it breached Pay Board rules. Lee similarly came under scrutiny within the House of Commons. Labour MP, George Grant, wanted to amend the pay code to restrict salary increases for transferred professional footballers and club managers. About Lee, Grant said: 'This move is increasing his salary from £12,000 per year at Newcastle to £25,000 per year at Everton as I understand it. This plainly should not be allowed. This salary is being paid for by working people, who have to abide by the pay code. I have nothing against Mr Lee personally, but it is a scandal that this kind of thing should be allowed to happen, and it should be stopped.'

'I used to tell myself I was a winner'

During a decade in the dugout, Lee had forged a reputation as a football obsessive whose focus was on the team, not individuals. On hard work and not 'Flash Harry's' as he called them. Shortly after Lee joined, his former player at Port Vale, Roy Sproson, spoke to the *Liverpool Daily Post*. 'He loves honest lads and scrappers dedicated to the game. If you're a cheat he'll kill you,' he said.

Lee therefore wanted honest triers and infamously distrusted skilful players with reputations of giving less than their best. 'You and your coffee house tricks again,' was one of his favourite shouts when a player was overdoing things. 'Talk to me about stars and I say that such things are for astrologers. Mention flair and I think of fires or the width of people's trousers,' Lee famously told James Mossop of the *Sunday Express* after joining. Yet, for all those words, Lee thought that characteristic was overplayed. 'All that stuff about not liking players with skill is so much rubbish,' he once said, 'I admire skill as much as any manager – but I hate to see it wasted by players who think it's enough without dedication to the team.'

Like Bingham, Lee had earned a reputation for negative football and his teams possessed a hardened edge. After his Port Vale outfit lost 1-0 to a fortunate West Ham in the FA Cup third round in January 1973, the usually measured Hammers boss Ron Greenwood was an angry man. 'Port Vale used the most blatant intimidation I have seen. I agree with people who say we were lucky – lucky to come away alive. Even Bobby Moore was intimidated.' Brian Glanville was also unimpressed. 'You would have thought, as Everton fell over themselves to tempt Lee from St James's Park, that he was a cross between Rinus Michels, Herbert Chapman and Helmut Schoen,' he argued in the *Sunday Times*, 'Perhaps he is, though there is nothing in his record to suggest it; a Port Vale team notoriously "physical", a Blackburn team that came up from the Third Division, a Newcastle team that bored everyone to death.'

But Lee had not survived these brickbats without some inner steel and had encouragingly displayed the important attribute of not shying away from difficult decisions. 'They can call me an idiot, they can call me anything they like now that this is happening,' he told the *Newcastle Journal* after controversially selling Malcolm Macdonald, 'but I would not stray from the belief that I am right even if it were to get me the sack eventually. I will always be Gordon Lee. I will always want to be myself. I used to tell myself I was a winner.' The obvious question was – could he be one with Everton? Thanks to his predecessor, there was an early opportunity.

Wember-Lee here we come

Little has changed since, but even by the 1976/77 campaign Everton's record in the League Cup was horrendous, having reached the quarter-final stage only once, when it was first staged in 1960/61. However, during the first half of the season Bingham's team had belied their patchy league form to record several impressive victories, defeating Cambridge United 3-0 at home in the second round before despatching Fourth Division Stockport County luckily at Edgeley Park, thanks to a Bob Latchford header. After an emphatic victory over Coventry City at the next hurdle, 3-0 at Goodison, the side left the pitch to a standing ovation. Skipper Mick Lyons showed his usual optimism about the team's prospects. 'We've got a good chance of winning it now – a better chance than we have ever had, since I have been with the club,' he claimed. But an unkind draw was a threat to those Wembley dreams.

Manchester United (a), League Cup quarter-final

There was a big challenge to come away with anything from the other end of the M62 on the first day of December, Everton having just conceded seven goals in two costly defeats. But Bingham's side did just that. With Tommy Docherty's outfit fielding an inexperienced defence, Everton went on the immediate offensive and, after Alex Stepney had twice saved at Latchford's feet, the visitors shocked the 57,000 crowd by scoring twice at the Stretford End in the space of four minutes. Brian Greenhoff headed Roger Kenyon's free-kick out to Martin Dobson, who from fully 25 yards out struck a sumptuous half-volley past Stepney. With United in turmoil, full-back Dave Jones' run reached the edge of the home area before Andy King's deflected shot speared into the top corner. Just after half-time, Latchford set the impressive Ronny Goodlass free and King converted the winger's centre, directly in front of the 5,000 jubilant Everton fans. 'Their team, often derided by those who remember Ball, Kendall and Harvey, even turned on a little bit of swagger once the third, unanswerable goal had gone in,' said a surprised Patrick Barclay in the *Guardian*. The visiting hordes chanted 'Wembley here we come' after the final whistle, but Alex Goodman in the *Liverpool Echo* probably summed up their frustrations too. 'Why oh why can't they play like this more often?' he enquired.

Bolton Wanderers (h), League Cup semi-final (first leg)

The semi-final took place at Goodison six weeks later, but it seemed light years given the turmoil during the interim. Steve Burtenshaw had temporarily taken over the reins but in his first game in charge, at Ipswich, Everton suffered a mauling with only David Lawson's heroics keeping the result to a manageable 2-0 defeat.

The visitors were a Second Division outfit capable of competing with top-flight clubs and, like many teams, Bolton were the opposite of their manager. Ian Greaves was a former 'Busby Babe' who was tough, uncompromising but capable.[25] However, the Burnden Park outfit played a tactically aware and measured type of game, in the style of continental teams rather than using traditional, physical English methods. In their ranks were former Manchester United winger Willie Morgan plus a trio of Merseyside-born players: a young Peter Reid, Paul Jones and danger man, striker Neil Whatmore, who had scored in every round. Centre-half Sam Allardyce ironically was suspended, his place taken by blond-haired defender Mick Walsh, one of Howard Kendall's infamous 'Magnificent Seven'. 'There is nothing for us to be afraid about,' Greaves said beforehand.

In front of more than 54,000 fans paying record receipts of £64,000, the game panned out as expected: the visitors competitive under a snow-threatening sky and in an icy, biting wind. Having said that, the nervous home team were superior early on and went ahead on the half-hour. A corner from Ronny Goodlass drifted into an empty space filled by the onrushing Duncan McKenzie, who planted a header past future Blues stopper Jim McDonagh. After the break, Burtenshaw's side retreated further into defence as Bolton dominated the midfield, but the home side looked like taking a one-goal lead to Burnden Park until, with just two minutes left, goalkeeper David Lawson clumsily took too many steps, an unusual offence punished with an indirect free-kick. Willie Morgan tapped the ball to Whatmore who smashed it into the net, sending

---

[25] Ironically, Greaves turned down the opportunity to replace Gordon Lee at Newcastle and was also on the shortlist to take over from Tommy Docherty at Manchester United in the summer of 1977.

15,000 travelling supporters into raptures. The goal was the first conceded by Everton in nearly nine hours of cup football during the campaign. A 1-1 draw perhaps pushed the tie in the direction of Bolton as an exasperated Burtenshaw let rip afterwards. 'I told them the second half was disappointing and too many people did not accept the responsibility of wanting the ball. Certain people we rely on to put their foot on the ball just did not do it in the second half,' he complained. The *Daily Mail* was ruthless: 'Managerless and, for the most part, clueless, Everton were embarrassingly outplayed in last night's first leg of their semi-final on their own Goodison Park.' However, by the time of the second leg four weeks later, Everton had a new boss.

Bolton Wanderers (a), League Cup semi-final (second leg)

Lee's first two league games in charge did not go well: a 2-0 defeat at Aston Villa followed by a troubling 2-1 home setback at home to Leicester three days before the second leg. At that juncture, the Toffees had not won a league game for three months, a run that left the club two points above the relegation zone. 'The overriding impression after seeing unhappy Everton slide to another defeat was the size of the task confronting Gordon Lee as he tries to create a team worthy of Everton's name and tradition,' were Michael Charters' words in the *Liverpool Echo*. But thankfully Everton had displayed their best form in cup matches, something Lee alluded to before the second leg. 'I suppose everyone is expecting Bolton to win, but football in general and cup football in particular can be very strange. But I want us to win and I want to go to Wembley,' the Everton manager said. His opposite number was circumspect. 'Our biggest enemy would be to feel that we were already in the final,' Greaves admitted, 'Everton have many talented players and they are the First Division side.'

For the huge Toffees' away support the Bolton manager's concerns were justified on an evening where a bank of floodlights failed completely and a loose pass knocked out the referee. Cannily Lee had publicly told the squad after the Leicester defeat that there would be big changes for the next league game – in other words perform at Bolton or you will be dropped. The threat certainly worked as, composed and organised from the off, the visitors were a different beast from a team facing a relegation battle, showing their top-flight class as Bolton failed to perform.

With Martin Dobson imperious, Everton's midfield completely disrupted the rhythm of Peter Reid and his colleagues and Lee's side deservedly went ahead after 24 minutes with a quite superb goal. Goodlass picked the ball up from a Dobson throw-in, skilfully skipped to the byline and Bob Latchford met his pinpoint cross with a regal header. The burly striker displayed the new spirit by running towards his new boss with a clenched fist. 'Yes it was good to see Bob do that,' said Lee, 'the game is all about heart, all about feeling.' With David Lawson barely tested, Everton gave Bolton an undeserved lifeline when Allardyce tripped Duncan McKenzie and the striker picked himself up to take the penalty. But after stopping his run-up after a few strides to protest against goalkeeper McDonagh being too far off his line, the striker fired wide. Suitably encouraged, Greaves' team upped the tempo but the visitors held on comfortably. 'Getting to Wembley is great, but I want to forget about the League Cup now,' the manager said afterwards, 'Cup football is very nice, but it doesn't last very long. People forget it.' But he did add a positive message: 'But it will be nice to see the blue and white of Everton going to Wembley on March 12.'

Aston Villa, League Cup final, Wembley

Everton finally showed their cup form in the league before the trip to Wembley, winning three successive games to move to fifteenth. Meanwhile Aston Villa had endured no such hardships, standing fourth in the league whilst, like their rivals, still progressing in the FA Cup – in December they had achieved the result of the season, thrashing champions Liverpool 5-1 at Villa Park, with all their goals coming in the opening period. Villa had one of the era's best managers: Ron Saunders,[26] who was in the final for the fourth time in five seasons. The son of a Birkenhead coal-heaver exuded total self-belief, was a notorious disciplinarian, but liked his teams to play with attacking gusto. In a twist of fate, both managers were facing one of their former clubs.

The Villa defence included the fine attacking full-back, John Gidman, a well-balanced midfield featuring Frank Carrodus, the cultured and wiry Scottish playmaker Alex Cropley plus Kirkby-born Dennis Mortimer, a box-to-box midfielder who successive England managers criminally overlooked. The real quality though was up top. Andy Gray needs no introduction, the Scot was in his

---

[26] Exemplified by the fact that the week before the final Saunders picked up a record tenth manager of the month award.

second season in English football when he became the first to win both the PFA Young Player and Player of the Year awards. But the future Everton legend's striking partner ultimately had the greater influence on the final. Brian Little was a hugely intelligent and mobile forward with outstanding skill and understanding of the game – and crucially a clinical finisher. His hat-trick in the second leg of the semi-final against QPR had clinched the final berth. 'I played upfront with other fine players, but few, if any were better than Brian,' Gray said in his autobiography, *Gray Matters*.

Villa's development on the pitch under Saunders left them clear favourites (8/13 on against 11/8 for the Toffees) but Lee was optimistic. 'Everton have not won anything for a few years,' he said, 'but I like to believe it could be our turn now. We have to work hard for success.' The Everton manager could also take confidence in that, apart from the cup-tied duo of Bruce Rioch and recent addition, Stoke full-back Mike Pejic, he could pick from a fully-fit squad. Unusually Lee announced the team three days beforehand: *Lawson, Jones, Darracott, Lyons, McNaught, King, Hamilton, Dobson, Latchford, McKenzie, Goodlass. Sub: Telfer.* Villa had comfortably completed the league double over the Toffees earlier in the campaign but failed to justify their favourites' tag as both teams conjured up probably the worst ninety minutes witnessed under the twin towers, best summed up by Steve Curry of the *Daily Express*:

> *Fear, the most destructive single element in football, turned the League Cup final into the most embarrassing Wembley finale to any post-war competition. Whatever the outcome of Wednesday's replay between Aston Villa and Everton, however well the teams play – and they can hardly be worse – nothing can obliterate the ineptitude of Saturday's match.*

The 96,000 crowd, paying receipts of more than £300,000, fell victim to a yawn-inducing game featuring no less than 82 back-passes – an average of approximately one every seventy seconds. Although the two teams ultimately cancelled each other out, Everton were clearly the better in the opening period, with Martin Dobson outstanding in a first-half display that overshadowed the strong Villa midfield. Chances were at a premium and Duncan McKenzie's cheeky early chip, which landed on the top of John Burridge's goal, was the closest either side came to scoring. Meanwhile a dogged Blues rear-guard kept a clearly unfit Gray in check.

In the second half Dobson felt the effects of a hip injury and, as his influence waned, the Villa central trio saw more of the ball with Lawson saving at Gray's feet in one goalmouth scramble. With fifteen minutes left, the two teams retreated towards the safety of a replay four days later and, at full time, the players appeared unsure of what to do before climbing the Wembley steps to shake hands with the many (bored) dignitaries and engaging in a barely deserved lap of honour. The only entertaining part of a woeful afternoon occurred when referee Gordon Kew stopped the game after the break and spoke to the players, who searched the pitch for spurs that had fallen off the boots of the marching band who played at half-time.[27]

After the game, both managers agreed that the reason for the mediocre fare was largely psychological. 'It was too big a strain for the young players,' explained Lee, 'I think the occasion drained them.' To worsen matters, the Football League had decided to forgo extra time several years before, to avoid the sight of tired teams flogging themselves through another half-hour. Having just seen the players do that for ninety minutes the crowd were entitled to see the chance of a result. As Duncan McKenzie said after the game: 'Who is going to be interested in the League Cup winners by Wednesday? It will be a non-event.'

Aston Villa, League Cup final, replay

In answer to McKenzie's question, 55,000 fans at Hillsborough, paying £115,000 in gate receipts, were certainly interested in the outcome. Injuries forced two changes, Dobson's hip kept him out while Dave Jones had a knee problem, with Roger Kenyon and Mick Bernard stepping in.

The second match[28] was a more intense and exciting affair than the Wembley bore draw, although that was not particularly hard. With Lyons moving into midfield to counter the dangerous Mortimer, Everton again started the better

---

[27] Spectators did not know what was happening and Bryon Butler, commentating on BBC radio, initially hypothesised that the referee was actually calling the players together to plead for greater commitment and positive play.

[28] The first replay between Everton and Aston Villa remains the only domestic final since 1966 not broadcast in either highlights or live form. The major attraction for television cameras on the night was Liverpool's European Cup match against St. Etienne.

team as Villa struggled on a difficult pitch. Latchford had two opportunities – a looping header that goalkeeper Burridge tipped over and when put clean through, from what seemed like an offside position, the stopper smothered at his feet. With the stalemate poised to last an eternity, ten minutes from time came the goal to clinch the cup – or so it seemed. When John Deehan clipped the ball past David Lawson at the near post there appeared to be ample opportunity for Kenyon to clear but – perhaps rusty in his first appearance for three months – the centre-half forgot any sense of co-ordination, lost his footing and only succeeded in dragging the ball over his own goal-line.

Everton threw everybody forward but when all hope appeared lost, ninety seconds from time Lee's outfit got the salvation they – and their magnificent support – deserved. With the Villa defence camped in their own penalty area, McKenzie's chip was headed on by substitute Jim Pearson and there was Latchford to prod the ball into the net in front of the delirious Everton fans at the Leppings Lane end. Understandably, after more than three hours of tense combat, extra time brought no further goals and the prospect of unchartered territory for English football – a second replay for a major domestic final. 'In the first half we overpowered Everton in every department without creating anything really definite,' said Saunders after the game, 'But give them credit, they battled well.' Leading Toffee supporter Mick Lyons was typically optimistic: 'We played our hearts out and never gave up. We'll win it you'll see.'

Aston Villa, League Cup final, second replay

It was four weeks before the teams could lock horns again with penalties on the menu if there was another stalemate. The venue for the second replay was Old Trafford, with the vast travelling army hoping for a repeat of December's triumph over Manchester United. With Bernard injured, Neil Robinson filled the right-back berth – the third different player in that position in the three games – and Dobson was back in the side for Kenyon, Lyons reverting back to central defence with Ken McNaught. Villa were without the injured Andy Gray.

The opening thirty minutes was horribly familiar. 'The first half was so boring that it was of interest only to diehards on both sides,' wrote Horace Yates in the *Liverpool Daily Post*. That said, Everton surprisingly went ahead for the first time in the tie on 38 minutes. Villa centre-half Chris Nicholl clattered Latchford in the inside-left channel and after Goodlass' free-kick was headed back into the danger zone by McNaught, the Everton centre-forward showed his predatory instincts, stealing a yard to sweep the ball over the line for his 22nd goal of the campaign.

Villa understandably turned the screw in the second half, twice coming close to an equaliser when Cropley shot wide, following a brilliant Little pass, and when Mortimer's superb strike from 25 yards went outside the post. Although Little buzzed around the box effectively, Villa could not find an equaliser but ten minutes from the end, just as Everton fans thought a first trophy for seven years was within touching distance, Saunders' side drew level from an unlikely source. Northern Ireland centre-half Chris Nicholl had only scored three goals during the campaign, so there was little danger when the defender picked up the ball in the right-back position and drifted past Jim Pearson and headed towards the centre of the pitch. What happened next is etched in the memory of the 54,749 spectators present, who took total receipts for the final to more than £500,000. From 35 yards out Nicholl's venomous left-footed shot swerved and dipped to the right of a clearly unprepared David Lawson, who appeared to run a few steps before vainly throwing himself forward.

Punch-drunk, Everton conceded again within sixty seconds. The ball was played into Little at the edge of the area, Robinson reached it first only for the clever Villa striker to dispossess the young full-back. There appeared to be little danger but, as the ball ran towards the byline, Lawson suffered a rush of blood, sprinted from goal, and allowed Little to slip it under him. Once again, the former Huddersfield goalkeeper was at fault in a big game for Everton.

Yet, a final that had veered spectacularly out of control was not finished. With Villa supporters prematurely celebrating what seemed like the match-winner, Everton forced a corner straightaway. Burridge failed to clear Goodlass' near-post cross and, after Dobson and Latchford had headed towards goal, skipper Lyons nodded home at the second attempt. 'There was pandemonium in the Everton section of the crowd occupying the Stretford End,' according to Horace Yates. A final that had produced only three goals in almost five hours of play had now witnessed the same number in 150 seconds.

The remainder of normal time produced no further excitement, nor did the extra period – until two minutes from the end. In one of those nonsensical moments that characterised Everton's decade, Lee's team committed football suicide after 328 minutes of the final. Villa substitute Gordon Smith crossed from the right, Goodlass' partial deflection sent the ball towards the six-yard box and, after Terry Darracott unaccountably let it run on, Little reacted first to fire home from three yards out in front of the massed ranks of blue support. The full-back later told the authors of *Three Sides of the Mersey* his version of events: 'As I've gone to clear, Ronny Goodlass, who's playing left-side in front of me, has got back,' Darracott explained, 'It's clipped his toe so it's taken out of my range and it looked, to all intents and purposes, like a mistake by me. That's the way people read it.'

A cruel way to lose a final, but as Alan Thompson said in the *Daily Express*: "History will say that Villa deserved to win the Cup but the hearts of the romantics will still go out to Everton.' Consoling words were not enough though for those Everton fans in the immediate aftermath, and keeper Lawson summed up the prevailing mood: 'It was a real sickener.'

CHAPTER 8

Moores: part of the problem

JOHN MOORES' ASCENSION TO POWER AT GOODISON IS WELL-documented. After becoming one of Britain's wealthiest men on the back of his Littlewoods empire, the Eccles-born businessman became chairman of the club in 1960. Working in collaboration with Harry Catterick, during the first half of the decade their drive, discipline and, just as importantly, his company's money created the first modern football club. Moores was also a visionary but his attempts to turn Everton into a worldwide superpower were thwarted by the footballing authorities, whose insularity blocked his wish to open the borders to the best footballing talent from abroad. 'Imagine a first team line up with such personalities as the Pele's, the Garrincha's and Puskas' and Di Stefano's of the world,' he said in 1964.[29]

Moores retired as chairman twelve months later but remained on the board and the Littlewoods chief was still the de facto leader as Everton won a seventh league title in 1970. But after that triumph, Moores – with nearly half a century of the stresses and strains of being a business leader behind him – was understandably beginning to lose that ruthless edge and Midas touch. By his later admission, when Harry Catterick fell ill in early 1972 and showed no signs of a prompt return, then the best outcome should have been a parting of the ways.

With fortunes sliding to a worrying degree, Moores took over again as

---

[29] As first revealed in *Money Can't Buy Us Love*, Moores made two attempts to bring Puskas to Goodison. In the first, he planned to circumvent the maximum wage laws of £20 a week by making the Hungarian a Littlewoods director. As ever, Moores was ahead of the game, with accusations in recent years that various clubs have used third parties to make 'off payroll' payments to employees to circumvent FFP rules.

chairman that summer but, uncharacteristically, allowed Catterick to soldier on. Even when he sacked his manager in April 1973, there was no immediate successor and Catterick effectively remained in charge for the rest of the campaign. Moores then made a mess of appointing a replacement and ended up with Bingham. The Littlewoods chief was therefore learning one of the game's truisms: hard-nosed, ruthless and successful business people are almost certainly going to lose common sense and objectivity when running a football club. Moores was sadly proving to be no exception.

As supporters lost patience with Bingham in the early winter of 1976/77, so did Moores. Not present at The Hawthorns for the infamous dog-assisted 3-0 defeat, having travelled to Bloomfield Road to scout Blackpool's promising striker Mickey Walsh, Moores was furious when hearing the result and he told a waiting journalist, the *People's* Norman Wynne, that he 'was thinking about resigning from the board. I'm upset for our fans and at the way our gates have dwindled'. Within 24 hours, the story made backpage headlines and in response Moores made an official statement on the Monday:

I am very disappointed with the current performances of Everton and know that many of our devoted supporters feel the same way. I have worked unstintingly for Everton for many years and it saddens me to feel as I do that we are not getting things right at the moment. It is this disappointment at our collective failure to give the fans the kind of football we all want to see that has prompted me to think seriously about making way for someone else. Naturally, I am discussing my feelings with my fellow directors because we want only one thing – a successful Everton F.C.

Moores' threat pointed towards problems at boardroom level. There had been two chairmen since his resignation in 1973, Alan Waterworth and Bill Scott, but they were effectively his nominees, and were always wary of such an overbearing personality. Consequently, muddled leadership followed, with accusations that those in charge were fearful of making big decisions in case they incurred Moores' wrath.

As Bingham struggled, Moores drew little sympathy from a large section of the support, who saw him as part of the problem. One wrote to the *Liverpool Echo*: 'He has complete control of the club and anything that has happened since his joining the board has been at his behest or with his approval... so any shortcomings here must rest with Mr Moores,' before adding, 'We have the unfortunate selection of Mr Bingham as manager. His track record as a manager never justified his appointment... He [Moores] had the power to see the things he complains of never happened and he still has the power to put things right.' Moores' attempt to redress the balance was to sack Bingham and reset the club. Former Spurs captain Danny Blanchflower was never a big fan of Moores and his *Sunday Express* column pointed the finger of blame at the Littlewoods chief:

> *He wants everything. He wants to win the championship and the FA Cup, as well as the Pools. So he took sides with Everton, and their deadly rivals Liverpool keep winning trophies. It must taste like the grapes of wrath to John Moores. Now he gets older and more desperate to win those things he has not been able to buy – the cherished trophies that the great game denies him. He showed his impatience recently when he threatened to resign. He showed it again last week by sacking manager Billy Bingham not long before the club's League Cup semi-final with Bolton. How restless and jumpy he must be.*

Ironically, Blanchflower accused Moores of impatience after the vice-chairman could have sacked Bingham and avoided a good deal of mud-slinging twelve months before, when results were poor and there were rumours of a dressing room revolt. The fallout from the Ulsterman's dismissal continued in the press during the following week, many continuing to blame Moores, and the fact that poor performances were emblematic of wider failings within the club. Writing in the *Daily Mirror*, Derek Wallis referred to Moores' statement in the previous November that he was reviewing his position because of 'collective failure', and then added:

> *If it was a collective failure, why has Bingham been made a scapegoat? Why have there not been other resignations? And why was Bingham allowed to carry on until he had signed McKenzie and Rioch, and then denied the time to enjoy the fruits of his labours – particularly as Everton are in the League Cup semi-final and had an apparently impressive win in the FA Cup last Saturday? What makes the Everton directors and Moores think that*

Malcolm Allison or Brian Clough or whoever they choose might be more successful than Bingham would have been, given a little more time to complete the job he started three and a half years ago.

Wallis went on to ask whether Bingham should have been 'kicked out, when the team he had so painstakingly and patiently reconstructed might, just might, be on the threshold of something big'. That was a fair point, but Wallis then added, 'Try as I might, I cannot rid my mind of the thought that Everton used Bingham. The directors allowed him to persuade McKenzie and Rioch – players they wanted – to join the club after lengthy negotiations and then discarded him.' The left-field theory explains many things – for a start, Moores' statement that the board decided to sack Bingham in early December and the call from 'Deep Throat' to Bobby Robson around that time. Secondly, Bingham could be charming and persuasive and the Goodison hierarchy realised this was an asset in buying players. Also, with Bingham needing to stabilise the side, he did not need a player with McKenzie's attributes at the time. 'His ability is so individual that he is almost impossible to slot into a team plan,' Peter Taylor wrote in *With Clough by Taylor.* That explains why the player was, at best, fifth or sixth choice on his list of strikers. However, the fact that the manager was willing to go to inordinate lengths to capture McKenzie indicates somebody else was pulling the strings – Moores. If Bingham had used the same determined approach with Birmingham City, then ultimately Trevor Francis could have ended up at Goodison, albeit for a fee of more than £300,000.

Finally, the wheels were set in motion around the time Moores threatened to resign. The chairman had voiced concern over falling gates and that the club was 'not giving fans the kind of football we all want to see'. Within a week Everton were bidding for one of the great footballing crowd-pleasers of the time. This all points to Moores driving the purchase of McKenzie in particular, with Bingham being used as a facilitator. As Wallis asked, 'Who was running Everton Football Club at the time – the manager, directors or John Moores?' The answer was obvious really.

The roots of this situation lay in Harry Catterick's six-month lay-off in the first half of 1972. Although coach Tommy Casey was nominally in charge, the club bought players – such as Bernie Wright and John Connolly – with no clarity on who was taking decisions. Whether a recovering Catterick was able to fill that vacuum on his return is debatable, especially when Moores returned as chairman. Intriguingly, Billy Bingham subsequently maintained there was boardroom interference in the signing of Bob Latchford. 'I was reluctant to let Howard Kendall go because I thought he could have done a job for us,' he later said, before adding obliquely, 'but I was being pressurised by various people to get somebody big.' Given Moores – and Catterick who was still at the club – were long-standing fans of Latchford, the purchase hints at assuaging the desire of the board rather than meeting the team requirements.

At a time when managers were becoming increasingly empowered, the board's dysfunctional reputation undoubtedly put off those strong-willed, self-sufficient candidates that the club were looking to attract, like Bobby Robson or Ron Saunders. One supporter's letter to the *Liverpool Echo* lay the failure to quickly land a top-class replacement for Bingham in the hands of one man. 'Mr John Moores reminds me of the jockey who retires but still wants to ride the horse. There is little doubt that he IS Everton. The chairman and directors just make the number up. He is still the boss, manager and the captain... is it any wonder that top soccer managers have refused to come to Everton?' he asked, before adding, 'To return Everton to former greatness needs a manager of the Shankly and Revie type, who always insisted on doing the job they were engaged for, not to stand for interference.'

Bingham spoke about the pressures from the boardroom some years after his removal. 'I thought people were a little bit impatient, especially Sir John Moores,' he said, 'He wanted success immediately and no manager can guarantee that.' Setting aside that Moores gave Bingham nearly four years, the Ulsterman's successor should have noted his departing words. 'It needs a certain sort of personality to be able to take the pressure and I was quite willing to see it through. Any man who has the job will have to accept that. It is part of being in charge of a team with Everton's traditions.' The last word on the sacking goes to Bingham's ally, the Belfast-based journalist Malcolm Brodie:

> One wonders, however, if it is only managerial changes that Everton require. Wealth and 'the other considerable resources a club of Everton's standing can put at the manager's disposal' (to quote the official sacking statement) are not everything. A club needs a soul and sensitivity and one doubts if these have existed for some years now at Goodison Park.

CHAPTER 9

Clive's Madame Rose-tinted spectacles

AT THE START OF 1977, LOCAL PSYCHIC 'CONSULTANT' MADAME ROSE peered into her crystal ball and predicted the year ahead. Apart from the usual tip for the Grand National, there were warnings about postal services but she did forecast a new lease of life for the docks. Fans in the city were only interested in predictions for the two clubs, and her words carried a fascinating message. 'At first very high hopes and expectations – a trophy almost within reach – bitter disappointment,' she claimed, before adding, 'here I am talking about the colour red.' Across Stanley Park there were encouraging signs. 'But the colour blue radiates confidence and triumph,' the mystic claimed. Lee's team failed to lift the League Cup but had moved through the rounds in the FA Cup, albeit with a few close shaves, and come April they still had the opportunity to fulfil her prophecy.

On the Ball, on the beach

After overcoming Stoke City, Everton travelled to Swindon at the end of January on the same weekend that stories emerged about Gordon Lee. Bizarrely there was more soothsaying, when a clairvoyant appearing on ITV's preview show, *On the Ball*, forecast a Swindon victory after a replay. The County Ground pitch was notorious for resembling a beach and the prevailing weather conditions evened-up the contest to produce a classic cup tie in front of an all-ticket crowd of more than 24,000. Some typical ingenuity from Duncan McKenzie put the visitors ahead, the striker skilfully controlled Terry Darracott's long cross and in one movement lifted the ball over the advancing keeper before volleying into the empty net. The home team replied when Lawson was out of position from a deflected free-kick and Dave Syrett equalised. Latchford put the Toffees back in front after the break from inside the six-yard box, but the Third Division outfit equalised in extraordinary fashion. There appeared to be little danger when Kenny Stroud picked up a clearance, but the midfielder fashioned a tremendous shot from fully thirty yards that arrowed into the top corner. The game stayed at 2-2 but Swindon had been unlucky. 'Everton were out-run, out-fought and outclassed by a Third Division side,' remarked Stuart Pyke in the *Sunday Express*.

With Lee now in the hot-seat, there was even more panic at Goodison three days later, with Trevor Anderson putting Swindon ahead just twelve minutes from time. On the previous Saturday, Lee took charge of Newcastle's home defeat to Manchester City and was now on the verge of making FA Cup history in suffering two defeats within a week, but five minutes later the home team equalised via the outstanding Martin Dobson. The equaliser whipped the 38,000 crowd into a frenzy and, with less than sixty seconds remaining, full-back Dave Jones strode forward and, as the Swindon defence parted, the youngster curled home a glorious winner.

The subsequent crowd invasion showed how Everton supporters craved even a sniff of success, but they were watching a team short on ideas and confidence. Speaking about the task facing Gordon Lee, Paul Fitzpatrick in the *Guardian* noted that 'his pleasure will be tempered by the knowledge that he has an immense task ahead if he is to restore Everton to former grandeur.' The tough fifth-round game at Cardiff City made that task harder until McKenzie provided a moment of genius. With the game locked at 1-1 the striker had a clear run on goal with only keeper Felix Healey to beat. The Everton man told the *Liverpool Echo's* Alex Goodman what happened next:

> *My first thought was to chip the ball over Healey but he realised what I was going to do and went back towards his goal. And he wouldn't dive at my feet when I tried to show him the ball and take it round him. This time other defenders were back but I knew none were going to tackle me because in a case like this their first reaction is always to get back and guard the goal.*

Finally there was a gap on the line and I just kept my head. But as I was
going to shoot the first time, Brian Attley came across so I changed my mind
at the last minute and put it the other side of him. In the end the ball went
through his legs.

McKenzie's 53rd minute strike ultimately proved to be the difference
between the two teams, keeping Madame Rose in the game as well. The sixth
round gave Lee's team a home draw against Derby County and, at odds at 7-1
to lift the cup, they had stealthily climbed up the betting stakes. But by the time
of the quarter-final, Lee had fired the opening salvo in one of Goodison's most
newsworthy relationships.

Doctoring Duncan

Duncan McKenzie used to relate a tale of a conversation with Gordon Lee: 'He'd
say, "Eleven Mick Lyons, eleven Duncan McKenzies – who'd win." I'd say the
McKenzies. And then he'd say "How can you say that – he's a better goalkeeper
for a start."'

The story sums up the philosophies of the two. Lee was the football man, a
professional for whom the game was about hard graft and teamwork, with little
time for romance. McKenzie was the polar opposite, an individual, a moody,
talented and incorrigible entertainer who thrived on the big stage. 'If you asked
him to describe the sort of footballer he hated most,' McKenzie later said, 'I was
that man.' The dichotomy lay in the circumstances that brought them together.
'It's great to be at Everton. It's great to know the boss believes in me, has put his
faith in me,' McKenzie admitted on joining the club. The issue, of course, was that
manager was Billy Bingham.

Inevitably, at Lee's welcoming press conference a journalist brought up the
name of Everton's enigmatic star. 'I want players with skill and I think it is
beautiful to watch those players express themselves,' Lee commented, before a
proviso, 'But I will not accept that if it is done to the detriment of the other players
in the team.' The words were hardly reassuring to the player, but McKenzie
remained in the side until an incident after the Cardiff victory, which the striker
recalled in his autobiography, *The Last Fancy Dan*. Lee was annoyed in the way
McKenzie had toyed with the Cardiff defence before scoring. 'There was no pat
on the back from Lee, who moaned to me "Why didn't you f------ hit it?" I couldn't

believe the remark and said that I bet he'd rather me hit the ball over the bar,' the player said. 'We were so far apart in our opinions it was frightening. I wondered what more I could do.'[30] Predictably, something was going to give and Lee dropped McKenzie for the sixth-round tie against Derby, after just one goal in ten games. As the striker admitted, his head would drop if not scoring. Although the decision was justified, Lee probably wanted to impose his authority within the dressing room but to complicate matters, replacement Jim Pearson scored a fine diving header as Everton reached the semi-finals following a 2-0 victory at Goodison.

Recalled for a league victory over Spurs, McKenzie found himself out of the following weekend's visit to West Ham. Lee's pre-match comment that 'the players who are consistent stay in – those who are inconsistent go out' was probably referencing one man. Even after the game – an entertaining 2-2 draw that witnessed a memorable Ronny Goodlass goal from just inside the opposition half – the story did not go away. When the press mentioned the dropped star's name afterwards, Lee was apoplectic. 'McKenzie has played twelve games without scoring a goal,' the Everton manager angrily remarked (although it was actually one in eleven). 'All I see of him is on TV and in the newspapers. He hasn't done anything on the pitch.'[31] The former Leeds player was out of tune with the times. 'McKenzie is an anachronism, an enigma. He is a direct throwback to the less sterile soccer days,' Peter Thomas said in the *Daily Express*, 'Today, football is full of managers who are so powerfully moved by the success of Leeds and Liverpool that the shadows are growing longer every day for players like McKenzie.' Given Lee scarcely hid his immense admiration for the Anfield club then there was no surprise in his stance over the talented maverick. Eleven days later McKenzie was not even on the bench for the second replay of the League Cup final, and spent the game summarising for local radio. Two decades later the striker opened up about his relationship with his manager to the *Evertonian*:

---

[30] Yet the two were not as far apart as generally thought, with McKenzie using Lee as a 'stooge' as part of his post-playing career on the after-dinner circuit. 'I think over the years Duncan has made more of this rift than there was back then,' Bob Latchford wrote in his autobiography, 'Duncan is a raconteur. He'll exaggerate stories and he's very good at doing it to humorous effect in order to sell himself…I think over time this has damaged Gordon's reputation and legacy.'

[31] Lee was not alone in this opinion. 'For a start he can stop talking his head off with journalists and keep himself off the television screen' was the advice given to McKenzie by Brian Clough, of all people.

It couldn't have been a worse scenario than for Gordon Lee to be my manager. Before he had even met me he said that I wasn't his type of player and that I should be in the circus... During the entire two-year period I was there, Gordon Lee tried to get rid of me so I had no option but to go...You were looking over your shoulder all the time. Every time there was a stop in play you expected your number to be held up and substituted.

However, Lee reaffirmed his trenchant views to Richard Bott of the *Sunday Express*. 'I want players who can do it for me on soft grounds, hard grounds, in slime and snow, at Lincoln as well as Liverpool... that is what this game is all about. Without it the clever stuff, what people call flair, is stupid, amateurish.' That was a valid point but Lee failed to acknowledge that the best teams had a balanced combination of both and his disciplined, hardworking approach would only get Everton so far. Consequently, critics later accused Lee of sending out dull, one-dimensional teams. 'Mr Lee must be told that we at Everton do not want or will not accept a team of robots. We have been brought up to expect so much more,' one letter to the *Liverpool Echo* went, 'Lack of cups we will tolerate, but the negation of true football for mere honest endeavour we will not.' To be fair, that was a common viewpoint but, to Lee's credit, he kept supporters largely content for two years.

Although McKenzie's days at Goodison appeared numbered, that was not the case. Although Lee was keen on offloading – using the striker as a makeweight in a proposed deal with Southampton for Mick Channon – the forward regained his place and finished the 1976/77 campaign with ten goals in thirty games. At the start of the following season the striker said, 'People say I'm a lazy player, but I don't think I am. My job is scoring goals, but I want to be everything this season. Perhaps I should become a greedy player, so that when I score a goal I should go out looking for more.' All appeared well when McKenzie started the 1977/78 campaign with a creditable seven goals in eleven games. 'A lot of water has flowed under the bridge between me and the boss,' McKenzie claimed, 'but I can say the relationships between us are as good as they possibly can be.' Having said that, even Lee's comments after a 3-0 win at Sheffield United could be included in the barbed category: 'I am pleased for the lad. He has done well for three games in a row.'

However, a broken foot at QPR in early October 1977 left McKenzie on the sidelines and, after returning over Christmas, there were just four goals in 21 games in the rest of the campaign. The arrival of the hardworking Mickey Walsh from Blackpool in the summer of 1978 effectively ended McKenzie's Everton career, which was a cause for regret as a lost opportunity. As Derek Wallis said in the *Daily Mirror*, McKenzie 'was a player who seemed to be going everywhere without getting anywhere,' and Lee could have provided the direction and discipline the player needed. Whereas, for Lee, McKenzie provided an ideal opportunity to develop his natural management style by incorporating a mercurial talent within a disciplined and hard-working set-up. However, McKenzie did leave supporters with several treasured memories in his two-year stay, none more so than in one of the most infamous games in the club's history.

The Maine chance

The city of Liverpool enjoyed a memorable sporting month in April 1977. While Red Rum was famously winning a record third Grand National at Aintree, there was consternation when local radio reported that Anfield was on fire, with fifteen machines fighting a massive blaze. The legendary Billy Butler, on BBC Radio Merseyside, had put out the story as an April Fools' Day joke – only for it to backfire as the prank ended up with apologies to both Merseyside Fire Brigade and the club itself.

On the pitch, there was mood for optimism on either side of Stanley Park. While Liverpool had an unprecedented treble of a domestic double and the European Cup in their sights, Lee's side had moved up to thirteenth by the middle of the month. But the FA Cup captured the attention and, whereas Everton rode their luck to reach the last four, Liverpool had taken advantage of a series of home draws to progress.

The city held its breath on the Monday after the quarter-finals, with the possibility of a first Merseyside derby at Wembley. However, there was a familiar sense of anti-climax as the draw paired the two together for the fourth time out of five in the semi-final.[32] The reaction of both camps said plenty about their relative mind-sets, whereas Lee claimed that 'Liverpool are the best

---

[32] Curiously, this was the third FA Cup semi-final derby game in the post-war era and, appropriately, Everton had also beaten Derby County earlier in the competition in all three years.

team in the world', Tommy Smith was confident. 'It is a pity that we shall have to beat Everton at Maine Road and not Wembley,' the Anfield Iron arrogantly predicted. To add spice to the encounter, the two teams locked horns at Goodison on the following evening, when Lee provided an indication of his future thinking when under pressure. With McKenzie still out, the Everton boss controversially dropped winger Ronny Goodlass, selecting Mick Lyons in midfield. After an even first half, the home side were under the cosh throughout the second period as they luckily ground out a goalless draw. 'If football is about skill, then Liverpool know all about football,' Michael Charters said in the *Liverpool Echo*, 'Their skill was so far in front of Everton, particularly in a one-sided second half when Everton were hardly given a kick, that they are still way in front in the local battle for supremacy. Everton have a long way to go to match the men from Anfield.' Nevertheless, nine games unbeaten provided an indication of some steps in the right direction.

As the big game approached, scheduled for Maine Road, the key issue for both teams was selection. With Roger Kenyon and Dave Jones out, Andy King was struggling with a toe problem whilst Martin Dobson had an injured groin. However, the biggest headache for Lee was Bob Latchford, who badly damaged an ankle in the 3-2 victory at Derby County seven days before. 'I can't think of being without Latchford on Saturday. While I have been here he has hardly missed a chance,' he said after the game. Lee's other problem was whether to select the enigmatic McKenzie, who scored the winner at the Baseball Ground. 'He worked hard but was always just part of a good team performance. You won't get me talking about individuals,' the Everton manager said in typically stubborn style.

Before the semi-final the Everton manager made the reasonable point about Liverpool's success being based on home form, before adding, 'Liverpool are fifty per cent less effective away from Anfield. At home an invincible record but away we have won as many games as they have –and scored more goals.' Mick Lyons felt the game was a chance for redemption. 'We are fed up with being losers,' the club skipper admitted, 'Of course we want to reach Wembley again. But this time we want to come back with the Cup. We want success and we want to give our fans success because they have given us such marvellous support this season.'

As the Blue and Red hordes travelled down the M62, their scarves hanging out of cars and coaches made for memorable and colourful scenes, with seventeen special trains departing from Lime Street for Manchester Victoria. Meanwhile, ticketless supporters had camped overnight outside the ground hoping their early bird tactics would pay off, as ground tickets priced at £1.50 were changing hands for more than £10. Team news hardly enhanced the mood of Everton fans unable to gain admission: although Dobson passed a fitness test, Latchford was out. Manager Lee also sprung a major surprise by gifting Mick Buckley a first appearance of the season.

The Everton manager's horoscope in that morning's *Liverpool Daily Post* made for interesting reading. 'You may be entertaining false apprehensions today – you seem to be in an over-anxious mood, especially about what you are handling in the way of work.' His state of mind may have contributed to making another, baffling, change. After the League Cup final defeat, the manager dropped Lawson with Dai Davies stepping in before the semi-final, where he had performed well in two victories. The Welshman was naturally expecting to retain his place, but there was a shock less than an hour before battle commenced. 'As I played cards with some of the other players,' he recalled in his autobiography, 'I was called out by Lee and told that Dave Lawson would after all play in the game. It was quite a shock, but when I went back to the rest of the team and told Dave, his shock was just as great as mine. "Shit! Shit! I haven't prepared" was his reaction.' A match-ready Lawson was a weakness, an unprepared Lawson a liability, as it sadly proved.

The weather had been wet and windy beforehand and there was a tremendous downpour twenty minutes before kick-off, leaving pools of water in the penalty boxes and centre-circle. The prediction beforehand was the conditions would produce a typically stodgy, combative semi-final. The game was anything but – the epic clash remains one of the most memorable derby matches, in front of 52,500 spectators paying £140,000, twice the previous record for the ground. 'On a waterlogged pitch, the Liverpudlian Derby gave us a superb semi-final; one of the best for years,' wrote Brian Glanville in the *Sunday Times*. Praise indeed from the great man.

Bob Paisley had one selection dilemma: the former Everton player, David Johnson, or young David Fairclough. The Liverpool manager chose the latter and, in the opening minute, the flame-haired striker set the tone with a thrilling diagonal run from the touchline to the edge of the Everton box, only to miskick as the ball stuck in the sodden turf. Everton were quickly on the front-foot and responded with three clear chances. 'We saw in the first ten minutes that the game would be exceptional; full as they were of incident and near escapes,' Glanville wrote. After gaining a stranglehold on the game, Lee's side promptly went behind. Kevin Keegan's ball from the left found Terry McDermott on the edge of the box and, after evading the challenge of Buckley, the midfielder chipped the ball over the stranded Lawson, ridiculously eight yards off his line. Rightly voted BBC's Goal of the Season, the keeper's faulty positioning surely influenced the scorer. Rather than fold, the underdogs knocked their opponents out of their cultured stride, midfield pressing forcing Paisley's side into a series of errors before the Toffees deservedly levelled prior to the break – their first equalizer in a derby game for nearly thirty years. Terry Darracott's long ball went towards the corner flag on the Liverpool left but an over-confident Emlyn Hughes slipped and Jim Pearson, who creditably sensed a mistake in the hazardous conditions, nipped in. The forward's cross evaded a phalanx of defenders before landing at the feet of McKenzie, who dug the ball out of the mud and saw his left-footed strike slip out of Ray Clemence's reach via Tommy Smith's thigh.

The second half was a different story. Paisley's side gained a foothold in the middle as the drying pitch and slackening pace of the game worked in their favour. After 73 minutes, Lawson's weak punch from Steve Heighway's free-kick skied the ball upwards and Jimmy Case's header arced over the goalkeeper and a despairing Mick Lyons. Lawson foolishly claimed that Kevin Keegan had impeded him, but the hapless goalkeeper actually succeeded in flooring the striker whilst punching the ball. Everton had conceded five goals in two epic games in Manchester during the month and Lawson was at fault in four.

With the match following the expected script there was not just one, but two, stings in the tail. The first came as the red half was prematurely celebrating a trip to Wembley. Duncan McKenzie, 'who managed to illuminate even this superb battle with individual artistry' according to the *Observer's* Peter Corrigan, flicked on Lawson's long clearance and, after receiving Pearson's return pass, moved into the inside-right channel and his cross perfectly bisected three defenders and Clemence to reach the onrushing Bruce Rioch, who had a simple tap-in. Having equalised twice, Everton fans in the ground had hopes of a winner. However, a second twist involving referee Clive Thomas remains one of the most infamous moments in the club's history.

Doubting Thomas

Towards the end of extra time in the 1981 League Cup final, Liverpool controversially opened the scoring against West Ham. However, when full-back Alan Kennedy fired home over the prone and offside figure of teammate Sammy Lee, the referee should have disallowed the goal. He failed to do so and although the Hammers equalised, their manager John Lyall was still angry afterwards, calling the referee a cheat on the pitch. The man in black was Clive Thomas, who not for the first time in a high-profile game made a controversial and blatantly-wrong ruling.

Twenty-four hours later on BBC's *Match of the Day*, Jimmy Hill passed comment on the official's behaviour, in a perceptive critique rarely seen today. After noting Thomas remained a top-class referee having toned down previous flamboyance, the presenter pointed out that 'His supreme confidence in his own ability may be his Achilles heel, if the mood takes him he will stretch a law or the application of a law beyond its natural limits as we have seen on more than one previous occasion. Yesterday I believe that attitude resulted in an illogical decision.' Viewers may have remembered that the referee had controversially disallowed a Brazilian goal against Sweden from a corner in the World Cup three years before, Thomas bizarrely whistling for full time as the ball was in flight. But for Evertonians, Hill could only have been referring to one incident in the dying embers of the semi-final at Maine Road.

The constantly quoted facts are worth revisiting. Mick Buckley found Ronny Goodlass in space on the left and McKenzie headed on the winger's cross to substitute Bryan Hamilton, who helped the ball into the net. Cue pandemonium on and off the pitch as the long-suffering Everton players and fans celebrated a probable winner. Everybody thought it was a goal – apart from Mr Thomas. With the Liverpool players desperately apportioning blame, the man from Treorchy blew for what he later called an 'infringement'. In his autobiography, *By the Book*, published seven years later, Thomas recalled the controversial moment:

> *The score was 2-2 with only a couple of minutes left when a cross from the right [was actually the left] resulted in what Bryan Hamilton and at least 30,000 Everton supporters thought was a winner: beating Liverpool and reaching Wembley, a double triumph. I was satisfied, though, looking at Hamilton when the ball was passed to him, that he was offside. I blew*

accordingly but the Everton players had drowned Hamilton in their celebration and, even more unfortunately, linesman Colin Seel was on his way back to the halfway line, also satisfied with the goal. Although McKenzie was the best footballer on the field, I had to blame him for his last touch of the ball on to Hamilton because, by then, Hamilton was indeed offside. I could not blame the linesman for not seeing this final touch, nor indeed the Everton players, nor Gordon Lee, the manager, who was raging on the touchline.

The immediate reaction of those on the day was one of disbelief. Duncan McKenzie later recalled seeing the injured John Toshack in the dressing room area asking Thomas about the disallowed goal. 'An infringement occurred, John, and you should know better than to ask,' the referee replied. The Liverpool player later told McKenzie 'Well, I'll be the first to admit – you were robbed'. Lyons recalled Thomas coming into the dressing room: 'We said "What did you disallow the goal for?" and he said "There was an infringement of the rules of the Football Association." So we said, "What do you mean"? He said, "There was an infringement of the rules of the Football Association. Watch it on telly and I'll be proved right."' For his part, Hamilton informed the waiting press, 'The ball hit me on the hip and went in. There was nothing wrong with it as far as I was concerned.'

Surprisingly, given his later comments, Jimmy Hill made an impassioned defence of Thomas on that evening's *Match of the Day*, stating the Everton player was offside. 'There was never any doubt in my mind that Bryan Hamilton was offside and I'm delighted the cameras proved me right', Thomas claimed. Yet many were not convinced. In 1977 the offside rule stated that any player level with an opponent should be penalised when the ball is played, but analysis of the video shows that Hamilton is clearly onside when McKenzie makes contact, standing outside the six-yard box whilst Liverpool defender Joey Jones is on its line. The subsequent movement during the flight of the ball fooled Thomas. The Everton player took a step towards goal while Jones moved out and the positions reversed: when the Irishman touches the ball he is now standing closer to goal than his opponent is, but that was irrelevant because the referee applies the law when McKenzie played the ball, a point that strangely *Match of the Day* missed. Irrespective of that fact, Emlyn Hughes in the right-back position, who went over to cover Goodlass, is also playing Hamilton onside.

Thomas' subsequent comments in his autobiography – that he was the only one who could have seen McKenzie's touch – displayed the arrogant side that Jimmy Hill later criticised. The Everton striker's header was visible to everybody, including linesman Colin Seel, on the other side of the pitch in line with Hamilton and Jones, so perfectly placed to judge whether the Everton player was offside. In a pressurised and fast-moving environment, Thomas was not the first to make a wrong offside call, but the big mistake was a failure to engage with Seel, an experienced official who was so confident that he ran to the halfway line.[33] Thomas did not entertain such a notion because it would have cast doubt over a conceited belief that his judgement was unimpeachable. Presenter (and Evertonian) Will Hanrahan interviewed Seel on BBC Radio Cumbria in 1981 and the linesman let slip that, after the game, Thomas told him 'there was an offence, let's get our stories straight,' to which he replied, 'you mean your story. I saw nothing wrong with it.'

Thomas provided further elaboration in his autobiography. After explaining the offside aspect, the match official offered up another get-out-of-jail card. 'Mind you, I am also convinced that Bryan Hamilton handled the ball too. The angle of the pass meant to me that there was only one way in which he could have "scored", and that was with his arm. If I had not blown for the convenient offside, you Everton fans, I would still have disallowed the goal for hand ball.' The sheer arrogance of Thomas here beggars belief, in the space of a micro-second the official had the spatial awareness and 20-20 vision to decide there were two offences, even though Thomas could not have possibly seen where the ball hit Hamilton. Thomas' decision was an assumption and had no factual basis – the linesman was better-placed and clearly did not see any offence. Significantly, three Liverpool players within five yards of Hamilton could see the midfielder's right hand in relation to the ball and none complained.

Hamilton later explained what happened. 'I can remember Duncan McKenzie getting to the byline and crossing the ball over,' the Irishman told the *Liverpool Echo*, 'It came to me in mid-body position. I couldn't get a head or foot to it, so

---

33 Thomas took the completely opposite view in 1981, when interviewed on *Match of the Day* after controversially allowing Liverpool's goal to stand in the League Cup final. Then Thomas consulted with his assistant only after the West Ham players told him too. 'That was bad refereeing,' said the Welshman about his initial failure to talk to his assistant. Yet, four years earlier he was perfectly happy not to speak to Seel. Again, this is one of the several inconsistencies surrounding the incident.

I turned my hip and it hit the hip bone and flew into the corner. I was at the near post at the time about six yards out. I looked at the linesman but it seemed okay. The next thing I knew, it was disallowed.' A television freeze-frame undoubtedly confirms this. At the point of contact with his midriff Hamilton's arms are trailing slightly behind him – something Thomas should have noticed given his self-proclaimed visual gifts.

Then in 1996, there were further revelations, of a sort. Speaking on BBC's entertaining retrospective, *Match of the Seventies,* the Liverpool skipper Emlyn Hughes confessed: 'I was on holiday with Clive recently and he told me "Emlyn, you know I might just have made a mistake that day."' Everton fans' feelings that Thomas may have shown some uncharacteristic humility, after two decades of pain, were sadly misplaced. Before the final show of the series the continuity announcer, in a portentous voice usually reserved for, say, announcing the death of a head of state, said, 'An interview in an earlier programme about an incident in the 1977 FA Cup semi-final between Everton and Liverpool concerning a disallowed goal, suggested the referee, Clive Thomas, later admitted his decision to have been a mistake. Clive Thomas has assured us this is not the case, and we accept that and are happy to apologise for the suggestion.' The theatrical statement was rightly in keeping with the farcical chain of events since the semi-final, which also included Thomas' definitive view of the incident, as delivered in 1988 to the BBC's Gerald Sinstadt and Brian Barwick for their book, *Everton v Liverpool: A Celebration of the Merseyside Derby.* By then, the offside angle had now disappeared completely:

> *How I saw it was relatively simple – although it proved not to be a simple incident in the way it reverberated around football not only in this country but all over the world. From the angle of the cross, there was no way that Bryan Hamilton could have controlled the ball without the use of his arm. In no way could I say that from behind I could have seen the ball make contact with his hand or his arm. But I was hundred percent certain that he couldn't have controlled it any other way. So I disallowed it. For handball.*

Note how Thomas ridiculously puts the incident in a worldwide context, massaging his ego in a manner that Jimmy Hill felt hindered his decision-making. But the unanswered question was why the Welshman – so certain previously that the offence was offside – was now claiming it was for only handball, an aspect not mentioned at the time. The only conclusion I can conceive of is that the man from Treorchy had been making it up as he went along since the moment Duncan McKenzie's header travelled in the direction of Bryan Hamilton.

Returning to the scene of the crime

The Thomas controversy overshadowed Everton's superb performance at Maine Road and Lee's men were unlucky to most neutrals. 'Everton deserved to win it,' was Brian Glanville's opinion. However, Lee was also angry that the press focused on how the draining effects of chasing glory on three fronts hampered the Anfield side. 'Rather than find excuses for Liverpool after Saturday's match I would prefer if people gave credit to Everton. I am annoyed and the lads are annoyed that they have not been given the praise they deserve,' he declared, 'I do not see it that Saturday was our only chance to beat Liverpool. They led twice and yet we are still in the tie. I wonder if they can recover after falling behind.' Of course Liverpool could, because they had the quality and resilience of champions. Lee should have been asking if his team was good enough to raise their game again at Maine Road on the Wednesday, against a side that undoubtedly was going to play closer to their potential.

Lee was still sweating on Latchford's fitness: 'If Bob's anywhere near fit I will play him,' the manager said beforehand. However, when asked what this would mean for McKenzie, the conversation went down a familiar path. 'Why can't you talk about other players in the side?' Lee complained, 'If that's all you want to discuss I am not answering any more questions.'

In the end, Latchford was still unfit, but whether the record signing would have made any difference is debatable, as Liverpool displayed their undoubted superiority and made a mockery of Lee's questioning of their ability. Solid at the back, dominant in midfield and with the inclusion of David Johnson adding extra penetration, early on it was clear that Everton missed the boat four days before. That said, Everton were architects of their own downfall, conceding a penalty when full-back Mike Pejic needlessly pushed Johnson in the back under the eyes of the prowling Thomas, who awarded a spot-kick converted by Phil Neal. Again, this shows one of the reasons why Everton endured a trophyless decade: players with nous do not pointlessly push opponents in the penalty box at the start of a semi-final. Although the underdogs briefly rallied, they barely tested Clemence and two goals in the final five minutes sealed their fate. Although Lee reasonably claimed the late strikes distorted the picture, Everton were second best, the defeat emphasising that hard-work and team spirit will only get you so far. As Duncan McKenzie said 24 hours later, 'With their luck they will win the lot this season, but to be fair, I thought that while they had a few players on Saturday who did not want to know, we had our share last night.' Martin Dobson reflected the views of players and fans after the replay. 'We put on enough pressure to have achieved a far more realistic result than that,' the midfielder said, 'And after promising to win two cups we are left with nothing.'

Supporters have long forgotten the replay, but the first game understandably remains in the memory of Evertonians. Referee Thomas made a mistake originally disallowing the goal, which happens. It was his behaviour in the immediate aftermath that irks. Thomas should have consulted linesman Seel, who was far better placed to spot any offence, and was satisfied that neither happened. (Seel was certainly better placed to note that Hughes was clearly playing Hamilton onside). If the referee had done so then the goal should have stood. But Thomas' well-known overconfidence in his own ability precluded him from doing so and buttressed his opinion that he alone was correct and everybody else – the linesman, the Everton players and officials – were in the wrong.

Everton fans understandably have complained over the years that the fickle nature of fate has not been in their favour. Sometimes this has been misplaced – all clubs have bad luck on occasions – but Thomas' decision possibly prevented them from enjoying a rare moment in the sun at the expense of their rivals. A trip to Wembley could have temporarily lifted the psychological burden that had engulfed Everton over the previous seven years. There would not have been a mid-1980s type revival – Lee was nowhere near a top-class manager and the squad had many weaknesses – but a final appearance and potential trophy could have bought time and lessened the pain for supporters. 'Most of us have never won a medal of any sort. Look at me,' Mick Lyons said earlier in the campaign, 'I have been at Goodison eight years and won nothing. Like the rest of the lads I get sick of having Liverpool's success stuck in my face week after week.' For all that, it is important to remember that Thomas' decision did not cost Everton the game, for they still had a second opportunity in the replay. A good team would have regrouped and dug in again, like in the 1984 League Cup final, but Lee's side failed to do so and to blame the defeat on the psychological impact of the disallowed goal only masks their shortcomings.

However nearly forty years later Lee still bore the wounds inflicted by Thomas, which were re-opened for Brian Viner's brilliant account of the era, *Looking for the Toffees*. 'That game,' he told Viner, 'was the most disappointing thing that ever happened to me in football, or probably in life. I will never, ever forget that. I'll take it with me to my grave.'

CHAPTER 10

Unlocking the Latch

WHEN THE GREAT JOURNALIST HUGH MCILVANNEY SPOKE ABOUT George Best after the Irishman died, he made the valid point that it was wrong to use edited highlights to judge a player's career. Any honest appraisal should include the good and the bad. However, supporters understandably judge their own favourites by the best days, ignoring the poorer spells and/or problems off the pitch.

Alex Young is an Everton player who falls firmly into that category. By his own later admission, the Scot's Goodison career consists of two distinct periods. From 1961-64 the forward was a key part of Harry Catterick's first great team, his deadly striking partnership with Roy Vernon the bedrock of the 1963 title-winning campaign. But the latter half of his Everton career was a disappointment: a tale of injuries, off-the-field issues and conflict with Catterick, as changes in the wider game marginalised his role. Young may have complained that the Everton manager harboured a grudge but, as *Money Can't Buy Us Love* explains, this was incorrect.

Finding his touch

Another player, surprisingly, who falls clearly into that category is 1970s hero Bob Latchford. Like Young, he was a Goodison idol, but also somebody whose Everton career was one of extended peaks and troughs. There were three distinct periods in the celebrated striker's time at the club. The first covers joining in February 1974 to Billy Bingham's departure. Although there were goals, the forward struggled to adapt and ended up agitating for a move largely, but not solely, for financial motives. The second is the glory of the first two years under Gordon Lee, when he rightly cemented his status as a Goodison legend. Finally, there are the dog days of 1979-81, with injuries and further disputes behind the scenes as Lee's reign imploded.

Supporters largely forget the weight on Latchford's shoulders when joining the club. Everton were in the shadow of their illustrious rivals and the board saw the acquisition of a British-record signing as symbolising a brave new world, with Latchford the key player in the Goodison revolution. However, the price tag of £350,000 added another layer of pressure for the essentially introverted striker, one that weighed heavily for a significant period. 'Basically, I'm shy and you can't put something into your character that isn't there,' Latchford said three years later, 'I admit that being Britain's costliest player has been a burden... I wished I had cost only £250,000. The sooner someone breaks my transfer record the better.' Yet seven goals in the first thirteen league games indicated a smooth transition and his second campaign was one of further progression, with an acceptable strike-rate in an era of obsessive defence and cautious tactics. 'In his first full season for Everton, Latchford has marked up 19 goals,' Michael Charters remarked in the *Liverpool Echo,* 'It does not make him the best in the country... but it does show that Everton have a striker to be feared.'

Failing to land the title cast a shadow over the start of the following campaign – Latchford claiming in his autobiography that Bingham's response was to tighten up discipline even more in pre-season, with a damaging impact on morale – but the striker began by netting in four successive league games. Yet the former Birmingham player was still not making the most of his wide range of qualities, particularly physical. 'People think you are a hard man but inside you are like a kitten,' Bingham once told him. 'You have everything, pace, strength, skill, accuracy. Use it.' But the striker rarely did. For all his attributes, Latchford seemed to lack confidence in his own ability. First-team coach Stuart Imlach later said in *Three Sides of the Mersey*: 'He would go about training as if it just didn't matter. We were in the gym one day and I had a right go at him, gave him a right mouthful, and he got me by the collar and could have murdered me. I just said to him, "Thank God, I got a bit of reaction out of you." This was the type of fellow he was.'

On the pitch, if not finding himself on the score-sheet, the record-signing was accused of not offering enough and regarded as a luxury. 'Latchford, remains, for me, an irritating player who often contributes little to a match and then steals its thunder with a moment's magic,' opined Derek Wallis in the *Daily Mirror* after the 3-0 home win over champions Derby County in August 1975. 'If I'd paid all that money for him I would expect much more effort and ambition than Latchford put into this match and most others I have seen him play.'

Following a goal drought, manager Bingham made headlines by dropping the expensive purchase for the visit to Stoke City in early November. 'I have been unhappy with Latchford's form,' the Everton manager explained, 'He has only scored one goal in the last eleven games. I have been very patient with him and that patience has been overstressed now. It wasn't a sudden decision. It's been on my mind for the last two or three weeks because he's had opportunities and chances to score goals but has not been putting them away.' Latchford himself was sanguine about the whole affair. 'Whether the boss thinks I've been playing well or playing badly, the simple thing is I'm a goal-scorer and I haven't been putting the ball into the net,' he said. Elsewhere there was support for the manager's action. 'Most Everton fans will applaud his bold and sensational decision,' Michael Charters wrote, 'They have watched Latchford struggle in embarrassing fashion to re-discover his scoring touch.' Rumours from the Midlands inevitably spoke of a return to home territory as, with gates falling amid an economic downturn, even Everton were not above the cash crisis.

But typically, Latchford was back a fortnight later and regained his scoring touch immediately, netting in seven successive games. But as Bingham's team struggled in the new year, with stories of player unrest, so did Latchford, who then missed two months following a cartilage operation. That said, even in a mixed season characterised by poor form and injury, a goal return of twelve goals in 31 league appearances was solid, however the campaign left some scars. 'Last season [1975/76] was a disaster – for the club and me. We had a bad pre-season tour and it carried on from there,' he told Richard Bott of the *Sunday Express* later in the year.

Wanting away

Those wounds did not heal immediately and in early June 1976, the striker wanted a move. 'Latchford, a £350,000 signing from Birmingham City, sent in a written transfer request before Mr Bingham went on holiday and it is understood that he is unhappy at Goodison because he has not been offered a rise for the new season,' Alex Goodman revealed in the *Liverpool Echo*. But when Bingham returned his stance was clear: 'Latchford stays. There is no way he can have a transfer.' Bingham's rationale was that Government pay curbs – aimed at reining in rampant inflation – restricted the club's offer. 'I would like to give people rises but there is a £6 limit on some wage earners and other people earning over £8,000 cannot have a rise at all,' Bingham explained. Given Latchford sat in the latter category, there was little room for manoeuvre, especially as the club exercised their right to a two-year extension on the same terms. Latchford's problem therefore was the restrictions within his original contract. 'I was so naive, so green it was ridiculous, with hindsight there is no way I should have agreed to the terms,' the striker later claimed.

Although Latchford's request appeared to show a lack of loyalty, in many ways it was completely understandable. During 1975 pay rose nationally by more than 25 percent due to rampant inflation, while players on long contracts had to sit back and watch on as their salaries were worth less and less. With income tax rates (set at anything up to 83 percent) swallowing up the wages of high earners, the life of a top-flight footballer in the middle of the decade was not as affluent as it seemed. Asking for a move, with an improved contract, was one way of bridging the gap. There was also a suggestion that the Everton hierarchy, whose relationship with players was traditionally one of master and serf, used the prevailing economic conditions to reinforce their authority. The government policy was not binding, so there was still room for flexibility and Everton's refusal to budge was an unsubtle method of putting players in their place. As others pointed out later, it was a club sadly lacking in soul[34] at this juncture and no wonder that some, notably their star man, were deeply unhappy.

For all that, the Everton board formally rejected Latchford's demand before a second request prior to a pre-season tour of Germany, which suffered the same fate. In Saarbrucken Latchford was dismissed, uncharacteristically, for retaliation, indicating perhaps that all was not well – a state of mind that did not improve when a third request for a move was also rejected a week later. 'He keeps writing them and we keep turning them down,' Bingham replied

---

[34] Those accusations were still there at the end of the decade. The *Liverpool Daily Post's* Charles Lambert asked new chairman Philip Carter on the club's 'impersonal relationship' with the public in 1979. 'I would disagree violently,' was Carter's reply, 'I don't think you can isolate the club's image from the fans, and the fans we have both at home and away are a credit to us, and a part of our total image.' As ever Carter was showing his intelligence, carefully avoiding discussing the board's shortcomings.

when pressed about Latchford's flood of transfer requests.

Elsewhere, others shared the striker's thinking. Kevin Keegan[35] was someone who had expressed an interest in playing abroad for better rewards and Latchford was keen on following suit. 'Germany, France, Belgium or Spain – it doesn't really matter,' the striker admitted. 'Abroad there is more thought given to the player and I have to think of myself and my family. If the tax system here were changed it would help, but I don't think it will be.' The irony is that even if put up for sale, there were few, in economically challenged times, who could afford the striker. Indeed the only club willing to take advantage was Barcelona, who made a reported inquiry in August 1976, courtesy of a John Keith exclusive in the *Daily Express*, but nothing came of it.

The stand-off was unedifying, but as Latchford told Richard Bott in September 1976, the dispute was primarily, but not exclusively, about money, and experiences abroad influenced his attitude. 'I was talking to a West German journalist on our pre-season tour,' Latchford said, 'and he told me ordinary players earn £2,000 a month in their first division. It's the same in Spain. No wonder Kevin Keegan can't wait to get out there. And I have to ask myself "What am I doing here?"' The travails of the 1975/76 season lay behind his decision. 'I feel as though my career has stood still for two years. I haven't had a sniff of an England cap,' he told Bott. 'Yet my record is as good as any striker England have used. If it's not going to happen here I will have to accept it. If it means going abroad for success I'll go. I might even finish up in America.' Such indecisiveness indicated a lack of self-belief, a characteristic of Latchford's that affected his own performances on and off the pitch, curious for someone who possessed a multitude of striking gifts. As he confessed to Bott:

> *My trouble is I don't believe in myself enough. I've never had enough self-confidence. And when I lose the bit I have, everything starts to go wrong. It's a mental battle. I know I have the ability and can score goals. But sometimes I come off the pitch and say to myself "What's the matter with you? Why didn't you make things happen? What was the end product?"*

---

[35] Keegan went to Hamburg in 1977 for an annual salary of £120,000 per year, more than five times his earnings at Anfield. Not only that, but the tax system in Germany was significantly less punitive than the UK.

I thought that last Tuesday night after the Ipswich game [in August 1976].
I know they only came for a result and played it tight, I ran about, put the
effort in, but what did I achieve? I tell you, I was rubbish.

Regardless of his own words, Latchford started the 1976/77 season with the intention of eradicating those demons. 'I am going to win this mental battle with myself. I'm going to be harder, too. If defenders want to mix it with me this season, they'll get it back,' Latchford proclaimed and he started the campaign in fine form. Unfortunately, for Everton supporters, the determination to look for a future elsewhere was still there. 'Goal-happy...but still everyone knows that I want to leave Everton and that I have had transfer requests turned down,' the striker admitted in the *Liverpool Echo* in September. 'The situation hasn't changed at all but five goals in the first six matches have made me very happy.'

A key part of the improvement was the embryonic relationship with fellow striker George Telfer. 'The more they play together the better they will become. Last season, injuries split up the partnership and it takes time and experience to get a good understanding. George is getting that experience now and improving all the time,' Bingham said after the two players had shared the goals in a 3-0 victory over Stoke in September. Regular gametime to skilful left-winger Ronny Goodlass had also added an extra dimension to the team. Having signed as an apprentice almost a decade before, the local-born player had waited until Christmas 1975 to make his long overdue debut. A tricky, old-fashioned winger, Goodlass gave Latchford something previously missing: quality from out wide. Latchford's strike against Stoke signified this change, the ball was quickly moved to the left and Goodlass' pinpoint delivery was met with a diving header at the near-post, a trademark goal in the following two fruitful years. 'The introduction of Ron Goodlass into the team has given us the chance of a new pattern of play,' Bingham said afterwards.

Nevertheless, the dispute with the club was still unresolved. After more discussions in November, Bingham announced, 'We cannot give Bob a new contract because of the Government's pay restrictions but if he were to win an England cap it could change his status under those regulations and I would then be prepared to sit down with him and discuss a new contract. That's his incentive, that's his carrot and it applies to any player.' Although welcome news, there were still persistent rumours over a move back home. 'If Birmingham came up with the right sort of offer I would certainly have to give it serious consideration,' Latchford had said previously. On the pitch, the goals continued to flow: a strike against Derby in mid-November took him into double-figures for the campaign in just seventeen games, but there was just one more in eight matches before Bingham was on his way.

For club and not country

The arrival of Gordon Lee galvanised Latchford as the striker returned to the prolific form of earlier in the season. But there were initial issues as Lee later claimed. 'He had a problem when I arrived,' the new boss admitted, 'He wanted to leave.' Those wishes were set aside as Latchford, although sadly unfit for the FA Cup semi-final, scored in fourteen of the final 22 games, taking his season's tally to 25 from fifty matches: a ratio of a goal in every other game, which it virtually was, as he never scored more than once in a match after the season's opener at QPR.

But the long overdue international recognition proved sadly elusive. Tipped for a call-up in the World Cup qualifier against Luxembourg in March 1977, manager Don Revie picked Stuart Pearson, Joe Royle and Paul Mariner ahead of him – all good players, but in a game where goals were everything surely there was a place for the most prolific English striker at the time. 'There wasn't a thought in my head about playing for England against Luxembourg so I wasn't in the least disappointed when I wasn't included,' Latchford admitted. But performances in the following season ensured the England management could not ignore his claims for international recognition.

Season in the sun

Latchford's 1977/78 campaign is the stuff of legend, the most memorable for an Everton player since the days of Dixie Dean. But there were few signs that glory days beckoned in the preceding summer. Although there was a productive pre-season of four goals, the burly frontman was still looking to depart and held talks with Lee before a summer tournament in Morocco. Although Lee promised to get back to the directors, Latchford did not seem convinced. 'If the situation is still the same as before in as much as if nothing happens I will have to put in another transfer request,' the player said, 'I would be happy to stay at Everton but it is simply a matter of money. If I cannot get what I want at Everton then I must look elsewhere.' Interestingly Latchford said previously that there were other issues involved, not just money. With Lee now in charge, they were just financial, indicating that Bingham was also a problem.

With Latchford now in the final year of the contract, there was little incentive for the board to renegotiate and the impasse continued. By September, the Everton boss denied speculation that the club were selling their star striker. With arrangements in the offing allowing players to freely move at the end of their contract, subject to the clubs agreeing a fee, Latchford still wanted to go. 'If freedom of contract is agreed then I'll be on my way as soon as my contract with Everton expires,' the forward told the *Liverpool Echo's* Alex Goodman.

The forward was off to a slow start on the pitch. Suspended for the opening day defeat by Nottingham Forest, because of a sending-off at Birmingham in May, Latchford had to wait until mid-September for his first league goal of the campaign, during a 5-1 victory at Leicester City. However, another 5-1 away win, at QPR in early October, made the football world take notice. The purchase of the gifted Dave Thomas on the left added another dimension to the attack and, on eighteen minutes, the winger and Latchford combined in trademark fashion. The striker had already scored and when Thomas found space, Latchford met his pinpoint cross with a beautiful diving header at the near post. 'It was one of those goals you dream about but rarely see,' Gordon Lee said, 'I don't think anything could have been done to stop it.'

The Everton manager appreciated the added variety provided by the new signing. 'It is important for Latchford that he [Thomas] gets the ball in the penalty area at the right time and with the right pace behind it.' Latchford added two more in the second half to take his tally in the league to seven in ten games. 'I've set myself a target of thirty goals for this season,' he said presciently afterwards. 'There is no question he is the best centre-forward in England – and on his day the best in the world,' an admiring Lee proclaimed. Overshadowing his personal triumph was the fact Latchford was still in conflict over his contract, although Lee now refused to discuss the issue in public.

But November's game at Goodison against Coventry City fired the imagination of Everton supporters. The striker had scored twice in both previous home matches, but went one better against the Midlands club in a memorable 6-0 victory. Already a goal up from Martin Dobson, Latchford scored his first with a header, from a suspiciously offside position, and just before the break added another. But at 5-0, Latchford's final goal two minutes from time remains in the memory of a generation of Toffees. Full-back Mick Pejic took possession near the corner flag and moved the ball to Martin Dobson, who found Dave Thomas on the left wing just inside his own half. Let Gerald Sinstadt, commentating on *The Kick Off Match*, pick up the story: 'Thomas... acres of space for him... two men to cross to... Latchford [who volleys in with his left foot]... what a glorious goal!... that's the goal of a championship side... the mark of tremendous finishing and accuracy from Latchford.' The hat-trick hero ran into the arms of a jubilant Gordon Lee, who later called it 'a day you dream about but seldom have.' After the game Latchford paid tribute to his teammate: 'All thanks and credit to Dave Thomas who is playing superbly on the wing. His crosses are lethal and he was involved in four of our six goals.' Joe Mercer was at the game and on local radio afterwards the great Evertonian understandably got lost in the moment, comparing Latchford to Dixie Dean and Tommy Lawton whilst reminding listeners that Thomas' wing-play brought back memories of Tom Finney and Stanley Matthews.

At the start of the season, the *Daily Express* offered a £10,000 prize to a player from the top two divisions who reached thirty league goals. The hat-trick against Coventry had taken Latchford's tally to fourteen before the halfway point. Consequently, bookmakers installed the striker as 5-1 favourite to grab the money. Two seasons before Latchford had been 100/1 at the start of the campaign and in 1976/77 had not even been mentioned in the betting. 'I'm not saying it's impossible but it will need someone to have a really exceptional season,' he said when pressed about his chances.

By this time, Latchford had finally won international honours, when caretaker manager Ron Greenwood selected him for the crucial World Cup qualifier against Italy at Wembley earlier that month. The former West Ham boss watched Latchford score twice at Goodison against Newcastle in October and before the home match against Birmingham City two weeks later, the striker said, 'I know this is my last chance to convince Ron Greenwood that I should play against Italy, and I shall be aiming to score as many goals as possible. I want that England place, and this could be the game to tip the scales in my favour.' Latchford scored twice in a 2-1 victory.

Although some labelled the Everton hit-man as just another broad-shouldered striker, there was more to his game than that. Latchford could play with a range of partners, at Birmingham he could lay off the ball for a runner like Trevor Francis, whilst at Everton the forward accompanied deeper lying players like Duncan McKenzie and Jim Pearson. Alternatively, Latchford could play centrally with two wingers and bring attacking midfielders into play. The Everton man had a quiet game against Italy and was substituted, despite Greenwood playing two wingers as a supply line. At 27 years of age, the Everton forward was never going to be a long-term solution for the national team, especially as failure to qualify for the 1978 World Cup finals brought rebuilding. Latchford, by his own admission, never felt part of the national squad – although five goals in twelve games was not a bad return – and lacked the all-round game to flourish at the highest level. That said, the feeling is the call-up came three years too late. Selection then may have given the striker more confidence and provided leverage in the pay disputes that blighted his middle years at the club.

However, even during a successful campaign, there was still tension over a new contract, with Latchford rejecting an opportunity to become one of the best-paid players in the country 'over what the trade unions called fringe benefits' in his own words. Although Lee said, 'at the bottom of him I think he still does [want to leave] when his contract is up next summer,' the striker claimed the Everton manager was forcing the board to make a move. 'Ideally I want to stay at Everton… but I would happily sign for five, even six, years if it suited Everton and we could agree terms,' the striker said. His manager was still impressed: 'He has got on with his job, trained marvellously, played even better, knocked in goals.'

New Year drought

By early January, Latchford was still on course for the elusive prize, having found the net on five occasions in December. 'I'm not going to think about getting thirty goals until I've got twenty-nine but having said that I will be very disappointed if I don't get to the thirty mark when I am on nineteen now,' the striker admitted. But having then said, 'I just hope that I don't dry up too much over the next three to four months,' ironically the goals did just that. As Lee's team struggled, Latchford's strike rate plummeted compared to the previous rich harvest, scoring in just two of the next nine league games.

During that period Latchford missed two games with a groin injury, including the visit to bogey ground Maine Road – the fifth successive time the forward had missed out on a trip there through injury. With ten games left Latchford was nine goals short of the target before, with odds lengthening, the trip to Newcastle on Good Friday. According to the *Daily Mirror*, his performance 'confirmed the England forward is back in the scoring business.' The striker netted the first goal of the afternoon in breath-taking fashion. Duncan McKenzie flicked on George Wood's goal-kick, via a brilliant back-heel, and Latchford's first-time half-volley from outside the box arrowed into the net. Twenty-four hours later there was another goal against Leeds, a 35th minute header when the England man got in front of centre-half Paul Hart to nod past David Harvey. There should have been another on the hour. Latchford took the ball from Hart but, just as he was about to strike, in nipped Duncan McKenzie to lob over the Leeds keeper. 'I took the ball off Bob's toes – well you know bad his shooting is,' the scorer joked. 'How do I rate my chances,' Latchford said about the prize, 'Well the odds started to turn against me a few weeks ago... I'll start thinking about thirty if I get to twenty-nine.'

McKenzie may have stolen a potential goal on Easter Saturday but the Goodison magician played a key role in the resurrection of Latchford's chances. 'What Duncan did was distract defenders,' Latchford told author Martin O'Boyle, 'He pulled them out of position which helped me find more space and consequently score goals.'[36] At Old Trafford two days later McKenzie's first-half cross evaded the entire United defence and goalkeeper, hit the far post and rebounded kindly for Latchford to score. When the number nine converted Thomas' cross it was the seventh league game where he had scored two or more goals. This was untypical as, strangely, for such a prolific scorer Latchford had difficulty in making the most of favourable conditions. In the two-and-a-half years prior to the start of the 1977/78 season the forward scored in 33 league games but on only one occasion did he net twice. In *Three Sides of the Mersey*, Stuart Imlach said about Latchford, 'I mean, he scored lots of goals, but once he got a goal he seemed to go into his shell. I said, "When you get one, you want two, when you get two, you want three, and if you get three that'll do for me."' With confidence building, the striker was now heeding the former Everton coach's instructions: he had accumulated 25 goals from fifteen scoring league games in the campaign, against sixteen in fifteen during 1976/77.

The target was now five goals from seven matches. That became four from six

---

36 30 – The Story of Bob Latchford's 1977/78 season

on the following Saturday morning. In the early kick-off against Derby County, due to the Grand National, Latchford scored the winner with a header from another Thomas cross. The inevitable question came afterwards. 'Well I'm a little bit closer now,' he smiled, 'It's nice to push the total along, but it's still going to be a hard task.'

The stand-off over Latchford's contract finally ended shortly after, with the striker signing a new three-year deal. 'I never really thought I would leave Everton,' said Latchford, 'It was just a question of playing as well as I could, scoring goals, and hoping things would work out well.' He then made a salient point: 'I always felt they would come up with something, because it would cost them more to replace me than to keep me.' On the following Saturday the target was reduced to three following the opening goal in a controversial encounter at Highfield Road, one not enough to save the Toffees from a 3-2 defeat. Against Ipswich Town a week later the striker hit the target from a most unusual source: the penalty spot. Latchford later told Martin O'Boyle about his aversion to spot-kicks:

> *I didn't take penalties for three reasons. Number one: I wanted the goals to be shared around the team. As a striker I got my fair share of goals and it was only right that other people were given a chance. Number two: I didn't really consider them to be a true goal. Yes, they counted on your goalscoring record, but they were a bit too easy to come by. Number three: I wasn't very good at them.*

Just after the hour mark of a moribund home game, Latchford tested his thesis after Russell Osman[37] felled Martin Dobson. The striker had never taken a penalty as a professional but those present would never have guessed as he smashed the ball over a despairing Paul Cooper into the roof of the net. 'I just tried to keep my shot down and whacked it, so the prize is still there to go for, although it's not going to be easy,' the match-winner told the *Daily Express* afterwards. The equation was down to two goals in three games but, with favourable odds, the striker drew a blank in visits to West Brom and Middlesbrough during the following week. This left one game – Chelsea at Goodison on the final

---

37 England great Terry Butcher made his debut in this game.

day of the season. Latchford was not optimistic. 'It looks like your firm might be keeping their money after all,' he told Alan Thompson of the *Daily Express* at Ayresome Park.

For added symbolism, Dixie Dean had journeyed to the ground to make league history exactly fifty years earlier to the same week. As Latchford later admitted, for the first time since that memorable occasion Everton supporters came to Goodison more interested in witnessing individual glory than a victory. Yet the similarities with his esteemed forerunner's greatest day ended there. Whereas Dean scored twice in the opening six minutes to lessen the pressure, Latchford had no such comfort and was goalless as the famous Littlewoods clock at the Gwladys Street end was close to showing half-past four. With Everton leading 3-0 Mick Buckley crossed, Mick Lyons flicked the ball on and Latchford headed home. A couple of minutes later there was an unusual reaction of audible groans when Lyons scored. Rather than flick the ball onto Latchford, the defender incurred the wrath of the 40,000 crowd by heading past Peter Bonetti. 'I could have killed Mike (Lyons) when he scored instead of heading the ball on to me, except he was really apologetic for it,' the striker told the *Daily Express* afterwards.[38]

However, with thirteen minutes left came the moment that truly lifted Latchford into the pantheon of Everton greats. Perhaps in an attempt to right a wrong, Lyons backed into the man-mountain defender, Mickey Droy, and went down with a theatrical fall. To the surprise of many, the referee pointed to the spot. Latchford described what happened next in his autobiography:

Dobbo [Martin Dobson] took me aside as the Chelsea players continued to protest. "Just keep your head down and blast it," he whispered, I knew exactly where I wanted to put it – to Bonetti's right side. There were no nerves. At the referee's whistle, I blasted the ball with my right foot. The roar of the Gwladys Street signalled that I'd fulfilled my task. I ran to the fans and sank to my knees. Fans and players raced towards me. I'd done it.

---

[38] One of the features of Latchford's campaign was the relative lack of coverage in the national press, obviously to deny the oxygen of publicity to a rival publication. This omission was exacerbated when two days later was the first ever Mayday bank holiday - meaning no Monday print coverage of the achievement either. [This surely isn't true? There were papers on bank holidays in the 90s when I was a paperboy – albeit that they'd be quite thin] It is yes, I was a paperboy then – no Echos either.

Pandemonium followed as large numbers of supporters invaded the pitch accompanied by a joyful soundtrack from the terraces. There were more celebrations akin to a title victory at full time. As Lee told the *Liverpool Daily Post* in 2002, 'I was sitting on the bench when an old fellow, who seemed to me at the time to be eighty years old, climbed over the railing from the terraces, ran on to the field and hugged Bob. When he came back past me he was crying like a baby with tears of happiness.' 'The money side of the award is secondary to me,' Latchford admitted afterwards, 'The prestige and sense of achievement in reaching the target is the part that has thrilled and pleased me.'

The hero also provided a clue to the ecstatic celebrations to the *Observer Sport Monthly* three decades later. 'We qualified for Europe, we got to FA Cup semi-finals, we were competing for championships,' he said of that time, 'But it was dark days because we ended up coming short. And Liverpool were so dominant.' But on that afternoon, the striker provided a huge ray of sunshine amongst those clouds and provided many of those present with their most cherished Toffees moment.

CHAPTER 11

Rebuilding

LATCHFORD'S *ANNUS MIRABILIS* TOOK PLACE DURING A SEASON where Lee was rebuilding the team. However, there was problem. 'There is also the question of money to consider. We lost over £100,000 last year,' Lee told the *Liverpool Echo,* 'And it is wrong for people to assume that we have plenty of money to spend.' Lee had learned enough in the final months of the previous campaign to understand that there was a need for new faces:

> *You know what I am looking for... consistency. Okay the lads worked hard for me last season and took us to Wembley in the League Cup final. But you don't have to be a great side to do that. The FA Cup semi-final with Liverpool proves my point. The first game... great, we were the better side. The replay... we didn't shape. Players who did it for me on the Saturday couldn't produce on the following Wednesday. Now I'm on the way to finding the balance I want.*

Looking after number one

The goalkeeping position needed an overhaul as Lee learned immediately that David Lawson and Dai Davies were not good enough. The manager's primary target was a familiar name: Stoke City's Peter Shilton. Within 48 hours of the replay defeat to Liverpool, the Everton boss offered Stoke £300,000 for the England international but there were snags: the Potteries club reportedly wanted a player-exchange deal and they were still under the threat of relegation. Manchester United were also in the picture, having pulled the plug on their

£275,000 deal twelve months before over Shilton's wages. Stoke chairman Albert Henshaw naturally denied the speculation. 'These reports are completely unfounded,' he said, 'there is no truth in them at all.'

But the position changed when Stoke were relegated in mid-May. 'We want Shilton to stay and we hope that he will,' admitted his boss George Eastham, 'But we want to have happy people at this club and it really is a matter for Shilton himself to decide.' Although Lee rejected the rumours there was no denying who was in pole position. 'England international goalkeeper Peter Shilton will almost certainly move to Everton during the summer,' Nick Hilton revealed in the *Liverpool Echo*.

For unknown reasons the trail went stone cold. Salary concerns may have come into it – by signing an index-linked contract three years before, Shilton was by some distance the highest-paid player in the country but he surprisingly remained at Stoke until Brian Clough took him to the City Ground for £270,000 in September 1977. Having cooled interest in Shilton, Lee turned his attention across the Pennines to Leeds' keeper David Harvey, who was out of favour at Elland Road. The Yorkshire club rejected Lee's initial bid of £65,000 but the two clubs settled on a fee of £85,000 only for the deal to collapse when the player could not agree terms.

The transfer inaction frustrated the Everton boss. 'It has all been very frustrating. I have spoken to lots of people and got precisely nowhere,' he complained, 'the trouble was that most people wanted to do swap deals.' However, Lee subsequently travelled to Blackpool to buy Scottish goalkeeper George Wood for £150,000. The 24-year-old had arrived at Bloomfield Road in 1971 and after a period vying for the goalkeeper's jersey with John Burridge, Wood played at centre-forward for the reserves and worked as a bricklayer. However, the Scot progressed quickly to become one of the most sought-after stoppers in the country. Wood's arrival led to a surfeit of goalkeepers – seven at all levels – and the first casualty was Dai Davies. The Welsh international had rejected the chance to move in a swap deal with Wood but found Wrexham far more amenable after an interesting interlude. Travelling to Kuwait with the Welsh national team, officials refused him entry because of an Israeli visa in his passport – the legacy of an appearance for Everton on an end-of-season tour six years before. The goalkeeper was ignominiously marched to a plane and flown home.

Lee was in the market for a forward and, after a failed bid for Wood's teammate

Mickey Walsh, the manager bought winger Dave Thomas from QPR for £200,000 as an exciting alternative. The 27-year-old had almost come to Goodison five years before and was openly delighted about the new challenge: 'It is a fantastic move for me. It looks as though the tide has turned for Everton and I have come at just the right time.' For Lee the signings were a statement of intent: 'With two new faces, I've something to offer the fans. It will even ginger them up at Anfield. They'll be saying "Those so and so's. They're having a go, they're going to compete." And that's good.' Whether the dual purchase sent tremors through the Anfield boardroom was debatable.

The Everton manager also had to balance the books and reduce the bloated playing squad. After selling Bryan Hamilton and Mick Bernard, Lee made a controversial move. Centre-half Ken McNaught impressed Ron Saunders in nullifying Andy Gray in the League Cup final and during early summer the Aston Villa manager bid £200,000 but, with a deal looking certain, the defender pulled out over the length of his contract. But four weeks later the Birmingham club renewed their interest, expressing a desire for McNaught and Mick Lyons, dropped by Lee at the end of the previous season. With too many central defenders on the books, the Everton boss was happy to see both go. McNaught eventually left for £200,000 while Lyons remained. 'I've been here since leaving school and when it came down to making a decision I found I just didn't want to leave,' the skipper said. McNaught's sale was perplexing as the Scot had shown no inclination to go, having recently married and moved into a new house. McNaught was the best defender on the books with his peak years ahead and success at Villa magnified the mistake, lifting the title in 1981 and European Cup twelve months later. However, Lee was also showing great faith in the nineteen-year-old Mark Higgins.[39]

In the opening months of the 1977/78 campaign Lee continued with the wheeling and dealing. The arrival of Dave Thomas had jeopardised the future of Ronny Goodlass and the popular winger took the unusual step of moving abroad to Holland, where he flourished for three years at NAC Breda and ADO Den Haag. Bruce Rioch's brief spell at the club ended when the midfielder returned to

---

[39] Higgins initially made his mark as a hugely promising schoolboy international. 'There is a whisper that one of the boys playing for England on Saturday, Mark Higgins, is a footballing natural in the Duncan Edwards mould.' wrote Brian Clough in his *TVTimes* column in June 1974

Derby County after a ten-month stay. The Scot had recently generated controversy with a bad challenge on Czechoslovakia's Marian Masny when on international duty, with Leicester City's Alan Birchenall and Stoke City's Geoff Salmons also criticising his robust methods. After the FA Cup game against Cardiff City, the Bluebirds' manager Jimmy Andrews claimed Rioch had gone over the top with three of his players. Although Rioch protested his innocence, the midfielder admitted to Richard Bott of the *Sunday Express*: 'There are some players in the game you have to wary of. Perhaps I am one of them.' It was probably no coincidence that Everton sold Rioch immediately following a League Cup tie against Middlesbrough at Goodison, when a notorious late and high tackle on Ian Bailey resulted in the youngster being carried off. Remarkably, the midfielder escaped justice. 'Frankly had I been the referee and had seen on the pitch what I saw from the press box Rioch would have been down the tunnel,' wrote Derek Wallis in the *Daily Mirror*. Rioch travelled back to the Baseball Ground a week later for £150,000, explaining that his wife had not settled in the region. Lee used the money to buy Trevor Ross from Arsenal for £170,000, the player returning to Goodison following rejection as a teenager after two years at the club.

'The team of 1978 will be Everton'

Lee's transfer deals were a compelling backdrop to his first full season in charge. Before the campaign started, the manager was in a positive mood with Chris James of the *Daily Mirror*. 'I'll be reasonably satisfied at the end of the season if we've made progress and show consistency,' he said. 'Then we will have something to build on. I would like to think we could get back into Europe because a club like Everton ought to be there and could do well.'

Lee's pre-season optimism proved misplaced after the side lost their opening two league games, the first infamously to Brian Clough on the great man's return to the First Division with Nottingham Forest. But two McKenzie goals brought a deserved win at Villa Park as Lee's men started a long unbeaten run. A week later a startling result made people take notice, as Everton went to Filbert Street and returned with a comprehensive 5-1 victory. 'There was much more discipline in our play,' a delighted Lee remarked, 'We created chances and scored goals and we defended with composure and control.' That said, the Everton boss was still not satisfied with the midfield balance. 'I am looking for something between Middlesbrough's defensive qualities and Manchester United's attacking style,'

Lee revealed, 'People raved about our game with Wolves last week [a goalless draw at Goodison]. But I didn't see it that way. Neither team would win the championship on that showing.' A key part of Middlesbrough's solidity was the protection provided by the 24-year-old Graeme Souness in midfield. Lee was a big fan of the Scot's ability to control a game and clever distribution and there were reports that the Everton boss had put in a bid, with reserve striker David Smallman offered in part-exchange. Nothing came of the approach and Souness, of course, went to Anfield four months later.

Lee's concerns about the midfield looked unnecessary as his side took five points from three games in early October, with Alan Thompson of the *Daily Express* purring after Everton had much the better of the 1-1 draw against Manchester City. 'Manchester City might be top of the heap this morning, but the team of 1978 will be Everton. Whether that forecast becomes fact at the end of this season or midway through next is entirely up to them.' The Toffees ran riot at QPR a week later, recording a further 5-1 victory that left them fifth. 'Whisper it not to Bill Shankly, but there are now two teams in the city of Liverpool,' suggested Russell Thomas in the *Guardian*, 'Everton's long awaited revival continued on Saturday with a performance of genuine class worthy of their current position.' So how had Lee engineered such a revolutionary change? Aside from the goals of Latchford and wing-play of Thomas, the defensive backline of centre-halves Lyons and Higgins, plus full-backs Pejic and Dave Jones, was disciplined, hard-working and took no prisoners. Regardless of Lee's thoughts, in midfield there was a nice equilibrium – the defensive solidity of the experienced Rioch, the class of Martin Dobson and goalscoring prowess of Andy King. Lee had dragged the best out of the unpredictable McKenzie. 'I spelled it out to him that we stood or fell as a team, that no amount of clever tricks would compensate for a lack of help for his mates,' the Everton manager told Tony Hardisty of the *Sunday Express*, 'I don't kid players and they have no chance of conning me. I can spot a phoney a mile off – and they go through the door. McKenzie's no phoney. He has worked as hard as the rest and still pleased the spectators with his skill.'

Two weeks later Lee's team went to Anfield in third place and returned with a goalless draw after a dreadful, physical game that, at least, showcased the prowess of George Wood – 'their finest goalkeeper since Gordon West' wrote Michael Charters in the *Liverpool Echo*. That said, not for the last time in the campaign, critics accused Lee's team being overly-physical when pressurised and this led to 'an eminently forgettable match – not a good advertisement for Merseyside football' according to Charters. In the home game against Newcastle a week later, the capricious nature of the game caught up with the Scottish goalkeeper. Alerted to the good form of the stopper, national team manager Ally McLeod was at Goodison but Wood spotted him in the car park beforehand. Whether the encounter affected the Everton goalkeeper is unknown, but a jittery display followed as the bottom-placed team earned a 4-4 draw. 'I think I've blown my chances now,' said the goalkeeper about his international prospects, 'I would rather not have known that Ally McLeod was watching. He's not going to come back to watch me again is he?'[40] Lee did not point the finger at Wood but reserved a rocket for the team. 'We were pathetic and that goes for the whole side,' he admitted in the aftermath, 'You can preach attacking football all your life but you must never lose sight of your defensive principles.'

After maximum points from their next two games, away at Derby and at home to Birmingham City, Lee's team escaped with a point from Portman Road after a crazy afternoon. With the game goalless on the hour mark, the match veered out of control spectacularly and the visitors required three equalisers in a six-goal thriller, with a 92nd minute Mick Buckley goal resulting in the manager's Mourinho-esque sprint down the touchline as the unbeaten run stretched to seventeen games. Now in second place, Lee may have been delighted but Brian Glanville in the press-box did not share his joy. 'The present First Division must be the poorest for years,' he claimed in the *Sunday Times*, 'A team as moderate as Nottingham Forest would scarcely lead were it not so. A team as ordinary as Everton would not lie second.' Lee's team responded to Glanville's claims in the best possible way seven days later. The 6-0 win over Coventry featured not only the famous Bob Latchford hat-trick but a superb display of attacking football in a remarkable game where the visitors won the corner count 13-2.[41] The watching Alan Thompson was certainly impressed again:

---

[40] Events proved Wood correct, McLeod did not. The keeper had to wait until the 1979 for his debut, when Jock Stein was in charge. In Wood's third game, the Everton custodian wrote himself into the history books, in a manner of speaking, by conceding the first international goal scored by Diego Maradona.

[41] There was a curious coincidence about the win. The victory was the biggest on the ground since the 8-0 hammering of Southampton in November 1971, when Joe Royle scored four times. On the day of the win over Coventry, the striker again scored four in a game, on debut for Bristol City.

When goals are scored by players wearing 7, 8, 9 (hat-trick), 10 and the best player on the field by many light years is wearing No 11 then you have something special in the realm of football. In a word: Everton. What have they got? Answer: The lot. A modern version of the football that used to be seen everywhere in England.

Having said earlier that Everton were his team of 1978, Thompson admitted 'I now have a correction to make. They are the team of autumn 1977.' Typically, for the Lee era there was a sense of anti-climax on one of the landmark days. Informed Everton were top as Nottingham Forest had lost, his glee turned to stunned silence in the dressing room when the true goalless scoreline emerged from the City Ground. That said, given their momentum there seemed only a question of time before the Toffees reached the summit.

Their title aspirations also received unexpected support from an unlikely source: former Anfield foe Kevin Keegan. Now plying his trade at Hamburg the England star said, 'I don't expect Liverpool to win the League this season – they're too tired both mentally and physically. I think Everton can win it.' For the first time Lee also started to talk in terms of winning the championship, telling the *Sunday Express*:

We have a lot of skill and strength. Nobody can give me a valid reason why we shouldn't win the title. We have what you need to win something – first-class team spirit. I have the happiest dressing room in the country – and I'm responsible for it. We have players with guts and finesse. We have people who score goals and others who will die to stop us conceding them. We have a good balance. I'm pleased with how it's gone since I took over from Billy Bingham.

Any team with title pretensions also had to convince the London press of their class and the challengers had an opportunity on the first weekend in December, during a visit to struggling Chelsea. The Toffees returned up the M6 with a 1-0 victory derived from a familiar source: Thomas directed a corner towards the near post and Latchford's head did the rest. But on the day Lee was named Manager of the Month, their performance still received mixed reviews from Fleet Street's finest. When asked about press criticism, Lee understandably went on the offensive. 'They are good professionals and I take it as a compliment if southern reporters are knocking Everton and the North in general – because it shows they are playing better than southern teams,' he pointed out, 'I don't mind criticism – you have to accept it along with the praise. But this was from people who see us once in a blue moon. It's like deciding you dislike someone after only meeting them for a couple of seconds.'

Lee's points were valid but the manager's insistence that hard graft and teamwork came before flair and individual glory was hardly appealing to the press. 'Frank Sinatra's "My Way" expresses a sentiment I don't encourage in my teams,' Lee told the *Sunday Telegraph's* Colin Malam, 'A star player, in my opinion, is someone with good individual ability who uses it for the good of the team, and not simply for self-glorification.' That was reasonable but the downside was his side lacked star quality and an identity with the footballing public, which could only change if Lee's team possessed a real depth of ability that could ultimately bring success, in the same way as Kendall's 'team of no stars' did a decade later. Having said that, although the *Daily Mirror's* Frank McGhee admitted he was 'haunted' by an Everton challenge for the title, Lee may have pointed out some salient facts: the Toffees were the leading scorers in the country with 39 league goals and had recorded the only two 5-1 away victories in the top-flight.

Middlesbrough were next up in the league and beforehand Graeme Souness joined in the baiting of the Goodison outfit. 'Of the teams we have played so far I would put Liverpool, Leeds and Manchester United in front of them to name but three,' the Scot said, 'Gordon Lee obviously has something. His powers of motivation must be special. But I cannot honestly see them winning the title. The bubble will burst and maybe we are the team to do it.' Souness may have been talking a good game but Lee served up the coldest dish in response: a 3-0 thrashing at Goodison.

Now 21 games without defeat, Everton were favourites for the title: 2-1 with William Hill and 7-4 at Coral. A difficult goalless draw at Birmingham City followed, leaving Everton in second place, two points behind leaders Forest but four ahead of Liverpool. As ever the Christmas period was key to the title-race and the team had four tough games: Manchester United, Leeds United, Arsenal and, crucially, Forest. Lee issued a rallying call. 'We couldn't have had a harder programme in terms of opposition... at the end of the season when we look back,

I hope we will be able to pick out the Christmas period as one of the reasons why we have done well,' he said, 'If we can come through this period successfully, the prize will be within our grasp.'

Blue bubble bursts

Long unbeaten runs usually crash and burn in spectacular fashion. That happened with Lee's outfit in the Boxing Day fixture against Manchester United, when the visitors – who had just lost 4-0 at home to Nottingham Forest – surgically took apart the Toffees in freakish fashion before a 48,000 crowd at Goodison. Dave Sexton's side had seven shots on target – and scored with six of them. Lou Macari, a persistent thorn in the side of the Goodison club, scored two, his second one of the best goals seen on the ground. Running at full speed into the area, the Scot met Gordon Hill's cross on the full from twenty yards to crash the ball past a startled George Wood. Ridiculously the score was 5-0 for the visitors after 69 minutes but late goals by Latchford and Dobson, either side of a Sammy McIlroy strike, at least got the home team on the scoresheet in an astonishing 6-2 loss.

Twenty-four hours later further cracks appeared, Everton performing even more poorly at Elland Road in a 3-1 defeat. The returning Duncan McKenzie took to the field to a great ovation from both sets of supporters, but the striker endured a miserable afternoon. Three goals down after 49 minutes, the visitors exhibited one of the more prominent characteristics of Lee's teams – ill-discipline when things were going against them. Displaying unacceptable levels of provocation, 'Everton took defeat with poor grace and sportsmanship' wrote Patrick Barclay of the *Guardian*. Referee Ken Burns booked three visiting players with 'Everton stretching the patience of their opponents, the onlookers, and eventually Mr Burns,' according to Barclay. Alan Thompson in the *Daily Express*, so complimentary before Christmas, described the Toffees as 'ill tempered, disorganised and belligerent' before adding that 'If this is to be Everton's method of chasing the title, then they will not be mourned by many if they miss it.' The concession of nine goals came as a shock to the system. 'We've forgotten some of the simple defensive things,' Lee warned. 'We scored six against Coventry and then conceded six against Manchester United. It might be good entertainment for the public but it will not win us the title.'

A brilliant goal by Andy King helped restore some sort of equilibrium following a 2-0 win over Arsenal four days later, before the top-flight's most important match of the season. Nottingham Forest had taken five points from three games over Christmas, establishing a five-point gap before Lee's team travelled to the City Ground at New Year. Defeat was not an option but that looked the case when, despite an encouraging start, Everton were a goal down after 25 minutes. A long pass from Forest's Kenny Burns left Peter Withe and Roger Kenyon duelling for the ball and the big striker hit the deck after a poorly-timed challenge from the Everton defender. The referee, Ray Toseland, pointed to the spot, John Robertson converted from twelve yards and the visitors lost their composure for the remainder of the half.

Everton grew into the game and suspicions within the 44,000 crowd that Forest's wastefulness could prove costly were realised five minutes from time, the referee awarding a second penalty when Burns handled in the area. With regular taker Andy King appearing to abrogate responsibility, new signing Trevor Ross confidently stepped forward to score past Peter Shilton. The hard-earned draw kept Lee's team within touching distance of Forest but he was in combative mood afterwards. 'I thought the decision over their penalty was disgraceful,' he remarked, 'Had we lost because of that I would have been really upset. But I always thought we were going to get something.' After two heavy defeats, fans could take encouragement from the manager's argument that his team had shown great resilience in taking three points from teams first and third in the table.

After a tough Christmas programme, January was just as challenging. Lee's claims about restored confidence appeared justified with some revenge for the League Cup final defeat following a 4-1 victory over Aston Villa in the FA Cup at Goodison. Everton again defeated Villa seven days later in the league and with Forest drawing the gap was four points. 'Professor Gordon Lee, after a little experimentation here and there, appears to be getting the chemistry right again,' wrote Paul Fitzpatrick in the *Guardian*. The Toffees' return to Elland Road for a League Cup quarter-final tie tested that theory. After three minutes, hopes of redemption for their Christmas performance appeared vindicated when Dave Thomas opened the scoring. But the visitors gradually lost their poise and, on the half-hour, goalkeeper Wood came out for a cross and collided with Mike Pejic, leaving Tony Currie with an easy finish. Five minutes later a shaken Wood allowed Peter Lorimer's shot to squirm over the line before Lyons inexplicably let a corner to pass at the near post and Eddie Gray tapped home. Three goals in eight minutes knocked the stuffing out of the away side, and Lee's mood at half-time worsened when Mark Higgins was dismissed before the break for a second bookable offence. A late penalty made it 4-1 for Leeds.

Sensing the home team had set out to protect themselves after their physical battering in the previous meeting, Lee was not happy afterwards. 'There were things that went on out there that displeased me,' he complained, 'It is very sad when a player is sent off for a professional foul and other players get away with it when they go over the ball. The fouls began in the first few minutes. Had something been done it would have been different.' Lee's comments drew little sympathy after Everton's aggression on the ground in December. Caught on the rebound, three days later a 3-1 defeat at Wolves left Everton's title aspirations as bleak as the ice-covered pitch. Now six points behind Forest, the team was clearly not as good as the long unbeaten run indicated. If the duo of Thomas and Latchford failed to fire, there was a lack of other attacking options. At the back the committed but limited Mick Lyons and inexperienced Mark Higgins were always going to struggle at some point, while midfield protection had largely disappeared with the sale of the experienced Rioch. Goalkeeper Wood was not the truly solid presence his early-season form indicated.

The FA Cup fourth round had also delivered a tough assignment, away at Middlesbrough. Strangely, both clubs found themselves in Jersey beforehand, visits that did not go according to plan for either. Terry Darracott slipped over and dislocated two fingers while Dave Thomas sustained a training injury that kept him out of the tie. But for one young Middlesbrough player the trip almost had disastrous consequences. The incoming tide left the seventeen-year-old Craig Johnston stranded at Elizabeth's Castle, half a mile from St Helier. As there was a team meeting scheduled, the Australian *swam* back to the mainland in the wintry waters, a journey which took ninety minutes.[42]

A now dry Johnston made his debut at a wintry Ayresome Park in the last opportunity for Everton to salvage something from the campaign. Lee dropped McKenzie and recalled George Telfer in a 4-4-2 formation, but for the second time in ten days, Wood let down his manager. After six minutes, the goalkeeper scarcely connected with a punch and when the defence failed to clear, John

---

42 Ironically Johnston's absence was not noticed. 'Where have you come from?' asked the receptionist at the hotel. 'Australia' was his reply, which had an element of truth. Given the midfielder's future history with the Toffees, he should have stayed there.

Mahoney hammered the ball home from 25 yards. Four minutes later Wood failed to gather another cross and David Mills fired home from fifteen yards. Two goals down after ten minutes in a season-defining game was a dreadful start and, overrun in the middle, the visitors went 3-0 behind on 52 minutes when Mills netted his second of the afternoon. Lee brought on McKenzie which immediately made an impact. Telfer pulled one back and with the home team panicking, Latchford struck the post. Unfortunately, there was no reward for a spirited fightback other than a Lyons goal at the death. After conceding ten goals in three successive defeats, Lee blamed not just the rear-guard for ending trophy hopes. 'It was all about bad defence, and I don't mean the back four,' he ranted, 'Defence goes throughout the team, and while our midfield players are skilful players who can score goals they must also accept defensive responsibilities.' Unsurprisingly when asked whether axing McKenzie had contributed to the defeat, Lee was typically evasive: 'That is a hypothetical question. We lost the game because we gave away three goals.'

Although there was a call to arms from Lee after the game to stop Forest, like their rivals Everton were unable to rein in Clough's side. Despite winning seven of their next ten league games, Lee's team never closed the six-point gap and a late-season dip meant Liverpool pipped them for second spot. There was consolation though in Bob Latchford's thirty-goal league campaign and a tally of 55 points was the highest since the championship season of 1969/70. However, with their territorial rivals retaining the European Cup at Wembley in May, overtaking the Anfield side was clearly going to be a Herculean task.

CHAPTER 12

King for a day

OF ALL THOSE WHO HAVE SAT IN THE GOODISON HOT-SEAT IN THE post-war years, none was affected by the success of their close rivals more than Billy Bingham's successor. 'I'll be proud if we escape from that Anfield shadow this season, because I knew it was going to be my biggest problem since the day I took the job,' Lee said at the start of his first full campaign. Liverpool were the footballing equivalent of Banquo's ghost for the manager, a spectral presence across Stanley Park, yet paradoxically nobody was more vociferous in their admiration for the Anfield club than the Everton boss.

Reverence across Stanley Park

So why, towards the end of the decade, was he feeling the pressure? It was all down to a matter of timing. When Shankly's team won the league and UEFA Cup in 1973, the two Merseyside giants stood at ten major trophies apiece after almost eighty years of combat. Even when Liverpool lifted the FA Cup twelve months later, there was no sense of a shifting of the tectonic plates, more a reflection of the natural ebb and flow of footballing fortunes. However, the appointment of Bob Paisley in the summer of 1974 changed all that history. A 1975/76 double that matched Shankly's achievement three seasons before was one thing, but the lifting of the European Cup twelve months later (plus the now obligatory league title) put clear water between the two clubs both in terms of success and broader recognition, especially abroad – one that sadly widened into a gulf thereafter. 'The entire existence of Gordon Lee must surely be a nightmare,' Brian Clough once said, 'What possible pleasure can there be in life for the manager of Everton when rivals Liverpool keep on winning everything in sight?'

That said, there was a respect between the clubs that seems light years away from the tribal nature of the modern game. After the Anfield side lifted the title in 1973, John Moores was ready to pay tribute. 'I am sure all Evertonians will join me in congratulating Liverpool on their success,' he said, 'They have maintained a fantastic standard over a lengthy period and well deserve the title of champions.' Whether Moores would have uttered those words if Harry Catterick had been manager is a moot point. The former Toffees boss took the professional view, caring little for outsiders. Such introspection was out-of-date by the early-1970s and the appointment of Billy Bingham was an attempt to break down barriers both inside and outside the club. The 41-year-old was immediately willing to extend the hand of friendship towards Anfield. 'Bill Shankly is a wonderful man and I have the greatest possible respect for him,' the new boss said, 'yet I don't intend to copy him. He does his public relations job wonderfully well; I hope to do the same for Everton but in the way I see it should be done.' When the *Daily Mail's* Colin Wood hosted both men for a meal prior to the start of the 1973/74 season, Shankly said that it was the first time he had fraternised with any Everton boss.

The respect continued in Bingham's first campaign. 'I can sense a change of feeling at Everton,' Shankly said later in the year, 'I have met Billy Bingham and he is a man who can do a lot for that team.' The Scot's belief that 'I would like to see Everton doing well next season because it will benefit the whole city of Liverpool' reflected John Moores' long-held view that local competition drove ambition. When the Liverpool manager resigned the following summer, Bingham returned Shankly's earlier compliment. 'He has had tremendous success for Liverpool,' the Everton boss admitted, 'He's done a marvellous job. I've nothing but admiration for Bill Shankly. He's getting out on top.' Such was the *entente cordiale*, Michael Charters in the *Liverpool Echo* later wrote that 'The feelings of mutual respect and regard between our two senior clubs have never been higher in my memory. And that is so good for the game and for the sporting reputation of our city.'

This positive change was largely due to movements at boardroom level. Alan Waterworth replaced Moores as Everton chairman in the summer of 1973 while John Smith took over the reins at Anfield. The two had plenty in common: both families had political links and they were magistrates who had known each other for many years. When Smith took over, one of his stated aims was to build bridges. 'I would like to see Liverpool and Everton become even more friendly than they are,' he said, 'They are representatives of a great footballing city and I am sincere when I say I would like to see Everton doing well.' Smith was as good as his word and after the goalless draw at Anfield in February 1975, the two chairmen took the unprecedented step of putting out a joint statement about the supporters who, in a time of rampant hooliganism, behaved impeccably:

> *Saturday was an unforgettable occasion not only for the quality of the game – one of the best derby matches for years – but also for the sense of atmosphere and sporting commitment generated by the crowd. Not one incident involving the fans has been reported. Their sporting behaviour, despite their fierce partisanship, was a model for all. When you remember that both clubs are deeply involved in the championship battle, the fact that so many supporters behaved in such exemplary fashion reflects the greatest credit on them all.*

Smith said afterwards that 'If Liverpool don't win the title we hope Everton do' while his Everton counterpart said the opposite. The two chairmen also started a tradition of meeting in the *Liverpool Echo* offices before the season began to issue an address to supporters, one that continued when Bill Scott succeeded Waterworth in the summer of 1976. Scott was keen to continue the relationship and both sets of directors travelled together to the FA Cup semi-final at Maine Road. After their August 1977 meeting, Smith told readers:

> *There has never been a greater degree of unity between the two clubs as there is at present... This togetherness is not only good for football in the city, but for the city itself in a broader sense. We set an example to the others. There is no more mature soccer city in the land than Liverpool, thanks to the behaviour of the fans of both clubs. I sincerely hope that Everton achieve the success we have enjoyed at Liverpool because this would be for the good of Merseyside as a whole.*

Although cynics could argue it was easy for the red side to encourage a rapport whilst being the best club in Europe, they were genuine moves to bring the clubs together. Bob Paisley was cut from a completely different cloth to Shankly, but even he visited Bingham's bedside when the Everton manager was hospitalised in October 1976. Having said that, there are always exceptions. After Liverpool toured the city in May 1977, Emlyn Hughes made his crass remark about 'Liverpool are magic, Everton are tragic' in front of the thousands gathered in front of the Town Hall.[43] The 'punishment' quite rightly was a grovelling apology in the opening programme of the following season.

Regardless of those developments, on the pitch Everton could not escape the remorseless presence of their rivals despite attempts to break free – 'I think you will see the shadow of Liverpool receding a lot' were Bingham's words after signing Duncan McKenzie and Bruce Rioch. Gordon Lee inherited the burden of annexing power from across Stanley Park and his response was an attempt to disarm his rivals through typical honesty that bordered on naïveté. 'Their greatest strength is that they keep the game simple and they do it better than anyone else,' he said before the 1977 semi-final, 'You can't argue with the facts. Look at their record. It's frightening.' Lee used to say people did not like his candid nature, but no wonder critics questioned whether Everton players had a psychological barrier when facing their rivals.

Closing the red gap

Although the economic downturn similarly affected both clubs, on the pitch Liverpool continued to operate at a different level. As well as winning trophies, the red half retained local bragging rights in the Merseyside derby throughout the decade. After David Johnson scored the winner at Goodison in November 1971, Everton had gone fifteen matches without a single victory against their rivals at the end of the 1977/78 campaign. In the thirteen league matches played during that period, Everton had scored just one goal – Martin Dobson's firecracker at Anfield in October 1976.

Fate often seemed to conspire against the Toffees and supporters could point to several unfavourable referring decisions. Previously unheralded Liverpool players saved their finest hour for the big game – notably, Alan

---

[43] For balance, a chastened Hughes did say six months later that 'I have tremendous respect for Gordon Lee and the job he is doing at Goodison. Everton are capable of winning the championship this season.'

Waddle's only career goal in December 1973. But the closing minutes at Anfield in April 1976[44] was a further example of Liverpool's monopoly in producing unlikely heroes. There had not been a single derby goal in nearly eight hours since Waddle's strike, and a fifth successive goalless draw was on the cards when Martin Dobson took a throw-in on the halfway line at the Kemlyn Road side. But Liverpool substitute David Fairclough nicked the ball from Roger Kenyon's weak return, turned on his heels and slalomed through three players before his right-footed shot beat Dai Davies at the near post. It was a great solo goal by the youngster, but one assisted by two individual errors. That was sadly a common occurrence at key moments during the decade, an indicator that collectively the players were simply not good enough.

Everton enjoyed their best league season for eight years in 1977/78, but the old failings were still there. They were eight points ahead of their rivals, having played three games more, before the Goodison derby in April and Mick Lyons was in typically optimistic mood: 'There have been times when we thought we were ready for Liverpool and then found we weren't,' he said, 'Now I believe we are because this is the best Everton side I've ever played in.' Once again his team were found wanting when a victory would have clinched second place and, in league terms at least, made them top dogs on Merseyside. 'Everton were totally outclassed, unable to penetrate a stern, resolute defence, lost for an answer to masterly control in midfield and unable to tame an attack which left them floundering repeatedly,' wrote Derek Wallis in the *Daily Mirror*, 'In truth, to quote [Emlyn] Hughes, Everton really were tragic last night.' The visitors should have won by a landslide but had only one goal to show for their dominance, ironically scored by former blue, David Johnson.[45]

In order to close the gap, Gordon Lee spent the summer of 1978 targeting a striker, as he felt the forward blend was not working. Earlier in the year, Lee had tried to bring Trevor Francis to Goodison but efforts to renew interest ended when the forward signed a new deal and he turned to Blackpool's Mickey Walsh.

---

44 Famously the match kicked off at the unlikely time of 11 am on the Saturday morning, because of the Grand National later that day.

45 Excluding own goals, Johnson was the first player to score for both teams in the fixture. At the time, the striker held the unusual distinction of netting the winner for both clubs' most recent derby victories, having scored in Everton's 1-0 win at Goodison in November 1971.

The Irishman may have a poor reputation with Evertonians but he was much coveted and Blackpool had previously rejected bids from Leeds, Liverpool and Birmingham City. When the Fylde club subsequently refused Lee's £300,000 offer, he was left bemused. 'Blackpool don't seem to know what they want,' he admitted, 'That's why I have forgotten about Walsh for the time being.' Yet a month later, using the double-speak trademarked by Harry Catterick, the Everton manager said, 'I am interested in quite a few players, and Walsh is one of them. Everything depends on circumstances.' Lee was referring to the fee, and when Everton upped the offer to £325,000 Blackpool accepted. 'If you think a player is good enough for the First Division, an extra £25,000 is neither here nor there,' the Everton boss said.

Although Lee was confident the player could flourish in the top-flight, the huge outlay was a gamble and the opening game at Chelsea defined Walsh's time at Everton. Struck in the mouth by Mickey Droy, the striker lost a tooth and required surgery. Walsh scored just once in the opening thirteen league games by early November, missing chances in big matches that frustrated fans conscious of his fee. Lee subsequently defended the forward: 'Mickey has got to adjust. He had come from the Second Division and will take time to get used to the pace.' That was a reasonable point but supporters were entitled to ask whether, given the price tag, three months was more than sufficient time to acclimatise. 'Why doesn't Gordon Lee be honest with the supporters and himself,' one fan wrote to the *Liverpool Echo*, 'He must know by now that Mickey Walsh is not First Division class.'

The move had clearly come too late in the 24-year-old's development, something even Walsh confirmed to Richard Bott in the *Sunday Express*: 'My only regret is that I didn't get the chance two years ago. I would have been a much better player by now.' Out through a broken toe for six weeks, the striker returned in January but the striker had lost his goal touch and confidence. After five further ineffective performances, he moved to QPR in March in exchange for Peter Eastoe.[46]

---

[46] When Keith Chegwin went on the road on BBC's Saturday morning show *Swap Shop*, the production team used the outside broadcast equipment from one of the Match of the Day games later in the evening. In December 1978 when Liverpool played at Anfield, Walsh was a guest of 'Cheggers'. With no goals available, the piece showed only a number of near-misses in an Everton shirt.

Lee also added his former Newcastle skipper Geoff Nulty to the squad, the Prescot-born player joining for a fee of £50,000. But Lee's other signing raised a few eyebrows. Colin Todd was one of the premier English defenders of the decade, winning two titles with Derby County. The north-east born player was also the best man-marker in the business and, with Roy McFarland, was one half of a formidable central defensive pairing. Lee eventually paid £300,000 – a huge outlay for a player only three months shy of his thirtieth birthday. 'I'm delighted because I've admired Colin for a long time,' said his new boss. Lee may have been content but Todd immediately had reservations. 'He had big plans for the future,' the new signing later wrote in *Toddy*, 'But we never hit it off. Our relationship started fairly badly and then got worse; we just weren't each other's cup of tea, it was as simple as that.'

Elsewhere, the Everton manager was not tempted to join the trade in overseas players that opened after the lifting of restrictions. Like Harry Catterick, the Everton manager believed the English top-flight was the hardest in world football, and only the very best could succeed. Consequently, Lee had earned some bad press after the World Cup during the summer by proclaiming, 'We have nothing to learn from the Continentals'. After Spurs signed Argentine World Cup stars Osvaldo Ardiles and Ricardo Villa, *Shoot!* magazine asked Lee whether he would be following suit. 'When I sign a player I want to find out all there is to know about him, down to what toothpaste he uses,' he answered, 'I couldn't possibly hope to know that by snapping up somebody who had impressed me in the World Cup finals.' Furthermore, the Everton manager's distrust was a result of stereotyping overseas players as 'fancy-dans' unable to withstand a punishing season. 'Lee has definite views as to what constitutes value to a team,' John Roberts of the *Guardian* commented, '"Pisspot players," is his phrase for those who, he considers, flatter to deceive, and more than a few continentals have been categorised thus.'

Everton started the 1978/79 season at Chelsea, winning 1-0 thanks to a typically spectacular Andy King goal in front of the *Match of the Day* cameras. With Ardiles and Villa making their Spurs debut on the same day, Jimmy Hill's view was that overseas players should be welcomed as English football was too insular. That was correct but, given Lee's previous views, the presenter asked him whether English football leaned too much towards aggression to be successful, and Lee responded in his rich black-country burr:

Possibly so. Possibly we may a little bit. I think perhaps particularly when we play abroad we might have slight problems. Maybe we have too many powerful players when we do go abroad but I still believe it's all about balance. My memory always goes back to when England won the World Cup. People like Nobby Stiles as an example. I think he was the perfect balance when England won the World Cup in 1966. Alf Ramsey had the right type of team. He had the right balance. I think to win any major competition you need power and desire and courage and strength as much as you need the skill. And obviously what you want is the right balance and have a little bit of both and I hope I've got them!

Lee's memorable thirty-second cameo featured in the BBC's review of the programme during the decade, mainly because of a typically clever editorial piece by Jimmy Hill: preach the benefits of overseas players and follow up with somebody who plays the little Englander to perfection. That said, the interview revealed a lot about Lee. Most importantly, he came across as an extremely nice chap, finishing the chat with a warm smile – there was an endearing, innocent charm to the Everton manager on occasions. Also, through his willingness to talk football and his beliefs about the game, Lee engaged with the press and supporters in a far better way than his predecessors did. Yet, like his counterparts, the Everton boss could burn a short fuse and often gave the impression of being permanently distracted.[47] As was noted at the time, with his manner, build and height it was easy to see a hint of Basil Fawlty about him.

But the interview also re-affirmed the Everton manager's wonderfully unreconstructed view of the game: when he spoke about 'balance' it was the players' characteristics rather than the tactical set-up of the side. However, the power and strength that Lee desired was largely the province of experienced professionals and consequently the squad was ageing, populated with players whose best years were behind them. New signings Todd and Nulty were close to

---

[47] In his 1988 book *The Blues and I*, Kevin Ratcliffe spoke about Lee's selection dilemma ahead of the 1980 FA Cup semi-final replay against West Ham. The choice was the future club skipper or winger Joe McBride. 'As we headed for the lift, Gordon stepped out,' Ratcliffe wrote, 'Then while we were getting in and the doors were closing, he suddenly said to me, "You're playing." And to Joey, "You're not." It was just another example of how he always seemed to be thinking about something else.'

thirty years of age, elsewhere there were Martin Dobson (30), Mick Pejic (29), Dave Thomas (28), Bob Latchford (27) and Mick Lyons (27). With players such as Andy King, Trevor Ross, Mark Higgins and Billy Wright still in their early twenties, there were few close to, or at, their peak, which is always a danger with any squad – ageing players are too busy concentrating on their own form and fitness to help younger counterparts.

'Suddenly I am not so dead chuffed'

Lee's strategy of building a squad for the now appeared to be paying dividends in the opening months of 1978/79. After the victory over Chelsea, Everton won two home league games in the following week before thrashing Wimbledon 8-0 at Goodison in the League Cup. The perfect league record ended when a Martin Buchan injury-time equaliser robbed them of a deserved victory at Manchester United. Lee's comments following the 1-1 draw typified the way Liverpool affected him. Bob Paisley's side had also won their first three league games and on the same afternoon hammered Spurs 7-0 at Anfield. 'Hell's bells, what a week this has been. I thought we had done well last Saturday until I heard that Liverpool had thrashed Manchester City [4-1]. Then when they crashed out of the League Cup and we scored eight I thought we were on our way,' a frustrated Lee told waiting journalists in the bowels of Old Trafford. 'We looked to have this game sewn up and I was dead chuffed. Then Martin Buchan hit a bolt from the blue and I came in and found that Liverpool had hit seven and suddenly I am not so dead chuffed.'

Everton's centenary season also added extra pressure to Lee, whose approach was more cautious than before. The manager had repeatedly warned his players about switching quickly to attack, leaving them vulnerable and he was keen to avoid a repeat of the turn of the year, when the defence leaked goals. Also, the feeling was teams had worked out Everton: crowd out Dave Thomas and cut off the supply to Bob Latchford, something Liverpool had done perfectly at Goodison in April. Consequently, wanting more options, the manager instructed the team to build slowly from the back, and it was no coincidence that Todd was one of the best ball-playing defenders in the top-flight. Twelve months before supporters were used to watching Dave Thomas speeding down the wing, now the team treated them to possession *ad nauseum* at the back before cautiously breaking forward. Like it or loathe it,

Lee subsequently outlined this change in rationale to the *Liverpool Echo's* Charles Lambert:

> *What I want to develop is a constructive team, making the best use of the players we have. If you attack too quickly, you risk delivering the final pass too fast and it therefore becomes inaccurate. If you get your strikers and midfield players all in the final third of the pitch, you lose the space you need. There are times when you might be forced to throw the ball up and fight for it, and you've got to change your ideas and mix the tempo of the game. But sometimes you have to take time to build up your attacks. Everton's defenders now have an important role in the side's attacking policy. They have to decide whether they should play it around at the back before moving forward. And when they do make a pass, they are expected to make it accurately – or to go forward themselves. I want defenders to be constructive and accurate.*

The Toffees faithful did not exactly welcome the change, which coincided with the sale of crowd favourite Duncan McKenzie to Chelsea. 'Their present dull and ultra defensive style, not to mention the intensely irritating time wasting possession, is making a lot of Everton supporters wish they had not bought season tickets,' wrote one angry fan. Yet Lee could point to results as justification. Everton were still unbeaten going into October without playing with the panache of twelve months before and, unsurprisingly, the southern press had their knives out. After a 1-1 draw at injury-ravaged Aston Villa in mid-September, the *Sunday Times'* Rob Hughes claimed Lee's team 'makes you almost vomit at the way they outspend almost any club in the land and then, knowing the state of the opposition, subject such talents as Martin Dobson and David Thomas, half a million pounds of forward creativity, to utterly defensive duties.' As much as Hughes, for some reason, was not necessarily a fan of the club during his distinguished career, on this occasion he was correct – the Toffees did not record a single attempt on goal in the second half. After a hard-earned 1-0 win at Ipswich a month later, Charles Burgess in the *Guardian* was equally critical: 'It is alarming to think that the team lying second in the First Division are there not because they impress and win with forward-looking attacking ideas but because they are extremely, boringly difficult to beat.'

There was a further reason for Lee's change in style. Everton were hanging onto the coat-tails of Liverpool, as probably the best team in Anfield history was making a brilliant start to the campaign. Results were now everything and Lee wanted to win games more efficiently. 'I have heard the jibes that we are effective rather than exciting,' he told Tony Hardisty of the *Sunday Express*, 'That kind of talk makes me sick. My job is to produce a team that wins matches.' After the 1-0 victory at Ipswich left Everton three points behind following an unbeaten ten games, Andy King spoke about the rivalry. 'We are criticised only because we haven't won anything yet,' he said, 'nobody will be complaining if we have four trophies on the sideboard at the end of the season. Although we have more on our plate, the championship looks like a two horse race between Liverpool and ourselves.' Asked about the change in style, the midfielder again referenced Paisley's free-scoring team, who had accumulated 33 goals in their opening ten league games, against a moderate thirteen by Everton. 'People accuse us of being boring. Well, Liverpool were boring for ten years and kept winning things,' King remarked, 'I've played in two derby games and on both occasions I was bored to tears by Liverpool.' King however agreed with the suggestion that the visitors could have won by more with greater ambition: 'We should have won 3-0... and how many teams win 3-0 at Ipswich.' 'Only one this season,' a journalist replied, 'Liverpool.'

Forever autumn

The final Saturday of October 1978 is enshrined in the memories of all Evertonians of a certain generation. A golden autumnal afternoon of ethereal light that ended seven years of hurt. A time for believing, for one day at least, that the possibilities were endless.

When Merseyside's big two clashed at Goodison, both were unbeaten after eleven league games with Liverpool leading the way having dropped just a single point. Paisley's side had rampaged through the top-flight, amongst their 35 goals were 7-0 and 5-0 victories at Anfield against Spurs and Derby County respectively, four at Manchester City and seven goals in East Anglia at Ipswich and Norwich. The addition of Kenny Dalglish and Graeme Souness since the 1977 European Cup victory added an extra creative dimension to the formidable line-up. Paradoxically, the Anfield side were already out of two cup competitions – Second Division Sheffield United had shocked them in the League Cup, while Brian Clough's Nottingham Forest famously removed the holders from the European

Cup at the first time of asking.

Meanwhile Lee's team were in second place, four points behind, unbeaten in their sixteen matches in all competitions. At Goodison Everton had scored 23 goals and conceded just two. But having accumulated enough points to have topped the table at the same stage of most other campaigns, frustratingly the Toffees were still in the red shadow. 'It is hard not to feel a twinge of sympathy for Everton who so far have achieved all that could be reasonably expected of a club, desperate, in their centenary year, to bring one of the major trophies to the Goodison side of Stanley Park,' mused David Lacey in the *Guardian*.

With Lee's team fighting on all fronts, the derby came during a number of season-defining matches. Four days later Everton were due in Czechoslovakia to defend a narrow 2-1 lead over Dukla Prague[48] in their UEFA Cup second-round tie, having previously overcome Irish minnows Finn Harps 10-0 on aggregate. Then two intriguing match-ups against champions Nottingham Forest, at the City Ground in the league and then in the League Cup at Goodison.

Lee was cognisant that a derby defeat would seriously damage title hopes before a third of the season was completed but a victory could have an unlimited impact on morale and confidence. He had already earmarked the importance of the encounter following the draw at Old Trafford eight weeks before. 'I don't know when the derby game is – I can't look that far ahead,' the Everton manager claimed, but then let slip he knew exactly when it was. 'But if things keep going this way, the fans will need their passports to get into Goodison the last Saturday in October. Only Merseyside-born folk will be admitted.'

Before the biggest league derby for years, Lee's main problem was an injury to skipper Mick Lyons, who received seven stitches in a gashed knee at QPR the week before. But assisting the Everton cause was six Liverpool players on international duty in midweek, while only Bob Latchford had been away from Bellefield. The big striker was finding his feet after a slow start to the league campaign, scoring five times in the preceding five games.

---

[48] Lee's geography was never a strong point. When Everton's opponents for the second round were announced, the Everton boss proclaimed all-knowingly to the press: 'We've been drawn against a Czech team called Dukla Prague, but the second leg is not in Prague, it's in a place called Praha.' Lee once asked a group of local journalists who the best team in Holland was. They replied it was PSV Eindhoven. Lee was having none of it: 'Bruges for me.' When they politely pointed out Bruges was in Belgium, Lee retorted 'Well I mean that part of Europe.'

The other threat came from midfielder Andy King, who had netted eight goals already. King was a rare beast – a southerner who settled seamlessly into life at Goodison. Credit for his signing goes to Billy Bingham, who later explained to the *Evertonian* how he bought the chirpy midfielder. 'I got Andy for £35,000 after pretending I didn't want him,' Bingham recalled, 'The Futcher brothers at centre half were the ones everyone was talking about, and Luton wanted £120,000 for them. I offered £100,000 for them and then prayed the bid wouldn't be accepted. They did reject it and so I went back to them and said I would take Andy King because he would be a useful squad player. They accepted that.' Available for the final three matches of the 1975/76 campaign, King scored twice in his second game at Derby County and there were 23 goals in the following two seasons – a decent return for someone who was inexperienced and not a striker. However, there were periods of inconsistency and King, for all his *joie de vivre,* suffered from pre-match nerves that affected his performance on big occasions. (Mick Lyons was King's room-mate before the League Cup final at Wembley and said that on the morning of the game his teammate's back was 'more or less paralysed' because of nerves. Tommy Smith had watched the Goodison derby in April and said that King's performance was one of the most nervous he had seen in the fixture.) But the midfielder was maturing on the pitch and had been Everton's best player during the season.

Everton great Joe Mercer outlined the enormous task. 'I would love to see Everton beat them, and make no apologies about that,' he told the *Liverpool Echo*, before ominously adding, 'If they do beat Liverpool, they will have beaten the best team in Europe and probably the hardest team to beat in the world.' Paisley's team were unbeaten in 23 league matches and prospects became more daunting when Lyons was unfit, with the experienced Roger Kenyon stepping up. The twenty-year-old Billy Wright partnered Kenyon, having broken through at the end of the previous season and the maturity of the nephew of Tommy Wright had impressed one of his uncle's teammates. 'He is very composed, knocks the ball round well and is not afraid to take up attacking positions,' said Brian Labone. As Evertonians dreamt of a first derby victory in seven years, Joe Mercer was asked how to beat Liverpool before the game. 'You have got to out-run them, out-tackle them. And you can't play defensively, so you have to push up and play in their half,' he said. Thankfully on the day of the game Lee's side did all of that – and then some.

Beneath the most glistening autumnal sun imaginable, for the first time in five years both teams entered the field of play together, with two unfamiliar skippers: Emlyn Hughes was injured so Kenny Dalglish captained the visitors while Martin Dobson led out Everton, whose supporters filled the packed arena with a cacophony of noise and countless streams of paper – in tribute to the ticker-tape reception given to hosts Argentina in that summer's World Cup. A vibrant and determined home side took hold of the contest in a manner not seen in the derby for the best part of a decade, jettisoning the shackles that had impacted their previous limp performances. They were *competing*. After Bob Latchford had put a typical near-post header wide and then fired straight at Ray Clemence, the newly perm-haired striker wasted a golden opportunity to put the Toffees ahead. Alan Hansen left Mike Pejic's clearance for his keeper, but the forward took advantage of the indecision, nipped between the two and watched helplessly as his header bounced wide while the hyperactive Gwladys Street fans held their breath. Destined never to net in a derby game, Latchford probably should have scored.[49]

Everton largely gained a stranglehold because Paisley thought full-back Phil Neal could not cope with Dave Thomas and earmarked midfielder Jimmy Case to stay wide and remain close to the winger. Having set-up in a 4-3-3, Liverpool found themselves a man down in the centre against Dobson, Nulty and King, who made their numerical dominance count and allowed their opponents little time or space. The home team had a further great chance in the opening period – Clemence only partially clawed away Dobson's header before Case cleared off the line. As the teams trooped off at half-time, home supporters probably thought that their side had wasted a great opportunity.

Everton kept up their tempo thankfully in the second period, coming close when a diving Nulty was only inches away from a tantalising Walsh cross. At that point, their derby goal drought at Goodison had lasted ten hours and seemed destined to never end but then, on 59 minutes, it happened. Everton's strength was on the left-hand side of the pitch and after some patient interplay between Pejic, Walsh and Thomas, the ball reached the full-back about fifteen yards

---

[49] Conversely, Latchford scored in all four appearances for Birmingham City against Liverpool before moving to Goodison, and netted for Swansea in his first game against Liverpool after leaving in 1981.

inside the Liverpool half and Dobson knocked down his long pass. Andy King told Brian Barwick and Gerald Sinstadt in their *Everton v Liverpool: A Celebration of the Merseyside Derby* what happened next:

> *I remember as it fell to me I saw Graeme Souness showing his foot, so I hit the shot first time with the outside of my foot. Graeme said afterwards that I mishit it. It was one of those that commentators call great goals but I call lucky goals. It could have gone anywhere. When this one ended up in the net, I made a beeline for the bench and Micky Lyons because he was the all-time Evertonian. I knew how much he wanted to play, and I knew what the goal would mean to him.*

While King sprinted across towards a jubilant dugout, elsewhere there were memorable scenes of unrestrained joy. 'Goodison Park goes absolutely mad!' proclaimed the watching John Motson in a memorable BBC *Match of the Day* commentary. After the game King admitted intending to keep the shot low but, by striking with the outside of the boot, the ball swerved and dipped. This helped carry it away from Clemence's left and out of the goalkeeper's reach.

Not surprisingly, with Liverpool keen to retain their seven-year unbeaten derby record, the visitors attempted to turn the screw but found a rejuvenated Kenyon and the impressive Wright in determined mood. The closest the visitors came to an equaliser arrived when a deflected Alan Kennedy shot fell into the path of a clearly offside David Johnson. Although the former Everton man squeezed the ball past Wood at the near post, the linesman correctly flagged to the delight of the Everton keeper who turned and celebrated in front of the relieved crowd. The home team should really have wrapped up the game on 73 minutes, Thomas fired past Clemence only to see a back-pedalling Hansen hook the ball off the line.

Although an outgunned Liverpool tried in vain for an equaliser, in mounting tension the home team held on for a well-earned victory. 'Everton deserved to win more comfortably than the result showed,' Alan Thompson claimed in the *Daily Express,* 'Indeed a three-goal margin would not have unduly flattered them.' Spectators climbed the recently installed fences and invaded the pitch, the fans proving a problem for the police, as did the BBC's Richard Duckenfield, as he later related:

My brief was to get a live interview for 'Grandstand' as soon as possible after the final whistle. Andy King was the obvious person to talk to, so I approached him as the players were coming off. I'd barely lined him up in front of the camera and congratulated him when I felt rather than saw this looming presence, and a voice said, "Get off the pitch." The next thing I knew, Andy, the microphone and I had been bundled on to the track. Subsequently, I discovered that we had been removed personally by the inspector in charge of the pitch area. He told me, "My instructions are that at the end of the game there will be nobody on the pitch – and that means nobody."

Thankfully, the camera was rolling and captured the pure comedy gold of the whole incident – which lasted only seconds – for posterity, as a startled Duckenfield tries to interview the match-winner while the burly copper aggressively pushed the pair onto the sidelines. When the police eventually allowed King to speak, he summed up the feeling of all Evertonians: 'I couldn't have dreamed about it, it's beyond a dream.'[50] Gordon Lee was equally delighted after the game. 'My players did all the talking for me and they did it where it mattered – on the pitch,' the manager said. Naturally, Lee then had to reference his close rivals. 'Liverpool are a great side, they have won League championships and European Cups. But we have beaten them today and it's as simple as that.'

Lee also said that 'if we were not frightened of Liverpool we are frightened of nobody' and others hoped the victory could lift the psychological burden. 'By beating the Liverpool jinx, Everton have taken another step up the ladder that leads to the top,' wrote Charles Lambert in the *Liverpool Echo*, 'Over the previous eighteen months they had proved to the rest of the country that they could play. Now they have proved it to the other half of Merseyside as well.' Gordon Lee later described it as 'A magical day, I could sniff our victory in the air before a ball was

---

[50] Liverpool man-of-the-match Phil Thompson was interviewed after the game where he conformed to the stereotype of all late-1970s footballers. Resplendent in an open-necked shirt with big, pointed collars plus a medallion, the bubble-permed defender uttered the immortal line: 'I'm as sick as a parrot.' Bob Paisley was typically ungracious afterwards. 'We played to Everton's type of game,' he said.

kicked. I had a feeling that it was to be our day and I could see defeat in the faces of the Liverpool squad long before the final whistle.'

But the final word on a momentous victory goes to the missing skipper. 'People were smiling as they walked along on Sunday morning,' Mick Lyons remembered, 'Some came up to me with congratulations, even though I hadn't played. They would say: "You were happy yesterday." But I think they really meant it as much for themselves.'

CHAPTER 13

Lee's winter of discontent

THE PHOTOGRAPH REMAINS A DEFINING IMAGE OF GORDON LEE'S reign. The date is 3 February, 1979 and a wide-angle shot shows the Everton manager standing alone, ball in hand, on the snow-covered pitch in the frozen wasteland of Molineux. The referee had just announced the game was going ahead, against the manager's wishes, and a further photograph shows Lee angrily storming away. One journalist joked Lee's burning rage could have assisted clearing the snow. Everton subsequently failed to compete, falling to a 1-0 defeat and afterwards a fuming Lee called for a change in the FA laws. 'Referees are amateurs and are not qualified to judge,' he complained, 'I am not upset just because we lost, I argued against the game being played beforehand. It was just a joke. There were six inches of snow on it in parts. You might just as well have let 22 labourers loose on it.'

On the slide

The result typified the way the season had unravelled since the derby victory. With Liverpool already out of Europe, the Toffees travelled to Czechoslovakia three days later to defend their first-leg lead against Dukla Prague, knowing progression presented an opportunity to make their own mark. The game should have been an easier assignment but, typically, having moved smoothly into a two-goal lead at Goodison, Everton allowed the visitors a crucial away goal near the end. In Prague, the visitors were disciplined and, as the game entered the final minutes, Dukla appeared to have run out of ideas. But, like at Goodison a fortnight before, there was drama. Standing in his own box, Dave Thomas foolishly tried to lift the ball over Miroslav Gajdusek, but the Dukla player regained possession and his curling shot evaded George Wood before nestling in the far corner. There was no way back for the visitors, who went out of Europe after trailing in the tie for all of ten minutes. A soft individual error had hampered Everton once again. 'It was a bad goal to give away,' said Lee, 'Just as their goal in the first leg was a bad one.'

But, perversely, three days later Lee's side produced one of their best performances at the City Ground. Facing a Nottingham Forest team unbeaten in 38 league games, they dominated the home side to such an extent that a goalless draw was widely seen as a miscarriage of justice. Solid at the back, where Lee had picked Billy Wright and Colin Todd to successfully counter the ball skills of Tony Woodcock and Garry Birtles, the visitors were denied by the human shield, Peter Shilton. Even when Dobson's header bypassed the goalkeeper, full-back Viv Anderson cleared off the line. Brian Clough admitted: 'Everton were firing machine guns at us most of the time and for long stretches we couldn't even get into their half of the field.'

Three days later Everton wasted the good work on the Trent. Facing a weakened Forest at Goodison in the fourth round of the League Cup, for the second time in a week Lee's side wasted a big opportunity to progress into the latter stages of a cup competition. Before a huge 48,000 crowd, the home team had a lucky break early on when Kenny Burns misjudged the flight of a corner and headed past Shilton. Clough's side survived a first-half barrage and Everton paid for their largesse after Mickey Walsh hesitated with only Shilton to beat and the goalkeeper saved at his feet.

With Lee having picked the same two smaller central defenders, Clough had told Burns and Larry Lloyd to make their presence felt in the opposition box and within minutes of the Walsh chance, Lloyd equalised after Wood fumbled a corner. Then, on 72 minutes, full-back Viv Anderson put the visitors ahead with a superb strike from distance. A Tony Woodcock header put clear water between the teams before a Bob Latchford consolation merely added to the frustrations of the home supporters. After the 3-2 defeat, it did not go unnoticed on Merseyside that a fortnight before Andy King had bragged about Everton still being in four competitions while Liverpool were in two. The defeat had now sadly restored the status quo.

Skating on thin ice

Everton continued their unbeaten league start, taking ten points from a maximum twelve and in doing so still looked like potential champions. After an entertaining 2-2 draw at Arsenal, Alan Hoby in the *Sunday Express* wrote that 'the clockwork blues of Goodison are without weakness. They have a powerful, fluent, well-drilled outfit. And in Martin Dobson, Andy King and the former Gunner, Trevor Ross, they have a formidable midfield trio.' A 3-1 victory at Birmingham featured a superb display by Colin Todd, who scored one of the great Everton goals. Striding forward from the back, he received a perfect pass from Andy King and crashed home a superb first-time shot from distance. 'You can say what you like about Gordon Lee,' said Peter Thomas in the *Daily Express*. 'But this fellow is certainly turning into something of a Soccer superman. If there is a manager around at the moment who can unseat his magnificent neighbours Liverpool, then the insular and earthy Lee is the man.'

But unseating Liverpool became Lee's Achilles heel. On the Saturday before Christmas Everton travelled to Coventry City protecting the only undefeated league record in England. Highfield Road had proved a graveyard for Everton in the previous two campaigns. The 4-2 defeat in December 1976 in icy conditions spoiled the debuts of Duncan McKenzie and Bruce Rioch while a 3-2 loss in April 1978 was a battle. Injuries left Everton with only nine men and Coventry scored their winner while George Wood was on the floor with blood pouring out of a gash over his eye. The police ended up restraining the visibly angry Everton manager.

Everton went to the Midlands as the country was on the cusp of the notorious 'winter of discontent', when widespread strike action against the Labour government's restrictive pay policies brought chaos.[51] The mass disruption also took place during one of the worst winters on record and, with the cold snap beginning to bite, Highfield Road was a refrigerated landscape. Three goals down with fifteen minutes left, the visitors scored twice in a heroic fightback but the

---

[51] The industrial unrest was the worst since the 1926 General Strike. Some images burned in the memory, such as the rubbish piling up at Leicester Square in London. Typically, amongst the multitude of stoppages, one in Liverpool drew the most headlines. The city's gravediggers went on unofficial strike and, with nobody to bury or cremate the dead, bodies piled up. Liverpool City Council hired a factory in Speke to store corpses and made plans to bury the dead at sea. Thankfully, the union called off the strike action before that eventuality became real.

home team had already inflicted the real damage. Lee was furious, feeling the referee should have postponed the game. 'It was a farce having to play with a third of the pitch covered in snow,' the Everton manager complained, 'how can skilful players play in the snow? The ball wouldn't roll.' The grievance would become a recurring theme in the coming weeks. With Liverpool's game postponed, a victory would have taken Everton top. After both teams won on Boxing Day, the Anfield side were a point ahead and did not play in the league for six weeks. Yet incredibly, at the end of that period Lee's team had not filled the top spot once.

Before Christmas Lee reflected on the lessons of the previous season. 'In the first month of 1978 we were knocked out of both FA and League Cups – and lost another League game at Wolves,' he said. 'Now we are coming up to the same period again and we can't afford another bad patch.' But the warning signs were there. As well as the Coventry defeat, there was a disappointing 1-1 home draw with Spurs before the postponement at half-time of the New Year's Day match at Bolton Wanderers.[52]

Although Lee could argue his team was carrying injuries, having dropped three points in two league games Everton faced a tricky FA Cup tie at Second Division Sunderland. After the postponement of the initial game, a Wednesday night clash at a freezing and snow-filled Roker Park had all the hallmarks of a giant-killing and so it proved. In front of a 28,000 crowd, the home side overran the dreadful visitors for an hour, racing into a two-goal lead and a late header by Dobson was purely a consolation. Once again the defeat raised questions about the character of the team (and manager) when under pressure. 'It was a night for big hearts – and their hearts were bigger than ours,' said Lee wistfully afterwards. The *Liverpool Echo* pulled no punches: 'His team has become widely known as an efficient, hard-working and grimly determined outfit that bores the pants off people and provides few moments of real inspiration.'

With West Brom now usurping Everton as Liverpool's main rivals, three days before the trip to Molineux Lee's team wasted an opportunity to go top after a

---

52 New Year's Day 1979 weather-wise is statistically the worst day for league football in history, with only three games completed. Everton's match at Bolton was abandoned at half-time with the game level at 1-1. There were allegations that referee Trelford Mills told one Everton player early on that he would be abandoning the game at the break and in the intervening period Bolton's Peter Reid suffered a serious knee injury after colliding with George Wood. Elsewhere, a day notable for Gary Lineker making his professional debut, for Leicester City.

disappointing 1-1 draw with Aston Villa at Goodison, when Dave Thomas equalised in the final seconds. The crowd of 29,079 – decent considering the weather but the lowest at home for two years – booed the players off at the end, much to the chagrin of the goalscorer. 'The crowd pay their money and they're entitled to criticise, but if you're going to get success there's nothing better than a lift from your supporters,' Thomas said.

The draw left Everton second in the table, level on points with West Brom having played a game more, with Liverpool a point behind with two games in hand on the Toffees. The mood of the away supporters at a snowbound Molineux three days later did not improve when news came through that Liverpool's 2-1 win over West Brom took them top. An Everton victory would have left the Toffees at the summit.

Frozen hell at The Dell

Thanks to the only hat-trick of Andy King's career, Everton finally reached top-spot after a 4-1 victory over Bristol City seven days after the Wolves defeat. The sojourn was brief. Although Liverpool regained the lead three days later when Everton travelled to Southampton on the following Saturday they were still in contention, although pre-Christmas momentum required restoration. For Lee, the trip to The Dell sadly proved to be a watershed like the 3-0 defeat at Manchester City was for Billy Bingham three years previously. Beforehand, the majority of supporters viewed the Everton manager as the saviour – even after the recent hiccup the man to restore former glories to Goodison. Afterwards Lee was just another jobbing manager, battling against the tide.

The problems were initially weather-related. Everton had travelled to Majorca in the week before the game, but bad weather delayed their flight home until the Friday morning and there was a further six-hour coach trip from London. With the match in doubt because of the frozen conditions, the squad had to remain on Merseyside until referee Colin Downey inspected the Southampton pitch – a system that prevented unnecessary long-distance travel in the event of a postponement. The party hung around on Merseyside for longer than necessary as Downey was late for the inspection and when the referee wanted a further look on the Saturday morning, the team had to travel anyway. With the possibility of a wasted journey, Everton then protested that the 10am inspection time was too late as there was a special train carrying supporters leaving at 8.45am.

Lee accompanied Downey on the Saturday morning and was furious that the referee gave the green light. 'The pitch inspection was a joke,' he complained. 'And I shan't be attending any more of them. It was an utter waste of time because the referee didn't want to talk to me. I asked him to wear football boots but he wouldn't. The fact that the referee did not wear football boots suggests to me strongly that he thought it was dangerous.' Although Lee pleaded with Downey not to play the game, he was wasting his time. That said, although the pitch was icy and snow-covered, it was perfectly playable and all the Southampton players wore studs. Before kick-off, Lee warned there could be 'four or five broken legs before the end of the afternoon'.

Southampton romped to an easy 3-0 victory, as only Colin Todd – the sole thoroughbred in the Everton line-up – showed the necessary ability to adapt to the difficult conditions. After a half-hearted performance from the visitors, Lee went on the attack. 'The middle of the pitch was solid ice. It was unplayable and it was a death trap,' he stormed, 'Andy King has knee ligament trouble and may need an operation. Pat Heard, Mark Higgins, Neil Robinson and possibly Dave Thomas and George Wood are all injured as a result of the pitch.' Yet Lee's hysterics were difficult to fathom – King needed a knee operation in any case, and an opposition tackle injured the midfielder. Lee's further statement that 'My players could have been killed and King's career could be finished,' had no factual basis. Asked why, with all these wounded players, Lee did not use a substitute, the manager responded that he did not know which of his injured players to take off. When a journalist pointed out the referee had not called on a trainer or played injury time, Lee replied 'that's your opinion.' Earlier in the season Lee had said, 'I always believe that if you go out on the field with negative thoughts in your head you are already halfway to being beaten.' Yet the risk was his continual complaints about wintry surfaces could impact performances, and this is what happened.

But Lee was not finished. There were rumours that the presence of BBC cameras had influenced the decision to go ahead and unsurprisingly the Everton boss took the bait. Noting that all three league defeats had been televised, Lee said, 'I wouldn't like to think that TV was putting pressure on,' before warning that 'If I find it is true and have the evidence I'll report it to the League and would like an investigation. I went to the Southampton ground at 7.45 on Saturday morning and the TV vans were in the yard. When the referee made a second inspection at 10 o'clock, the cameras were already in position.' But Alec Weeks, producer of *Match of the Day*, pointed out the BBC had been due to show Everton's postponed home games with West Brom and Aston Villa, before claiming it was 'ridiculous to suggest that we have any bearing on whether games are on or off'. The press ridiculed Lee's claims in the days that followed. The consensus being that his negative attitude affected the players. 'Has Gordon Lee cost his Everton team the league title?' Steve Curry asked in the *Daily Express*, 'Before a ball was kicked he had brainwashed his players to the idea that they were going out to risk their career. They played like a team treading through a minefield while Southampton got on with the job.' But the Everton manager remained unrepentant, informing the *Liverpool Echo*:

> *I think the public have got the wrong idea about me these last few days. I am not too worried about that, but what does worry me is that the points I am making about having to play on dangerous pitches... It is not exaggerating to say that someone could be killed. If a player falls badly and hits his head on a frozen rut it could kill him.*

Lee's comments on frozen pitches were not without merit, but their timing and emotive language left him open to criticism and accusations of sour grapes. The enormous amount of postponed games showed that referees were cognisant of the risks and the pitches at Wolves and Southampton were playable. The biggest danger on icy pitches was not death, but muscle tears because of the inability to stop or change direction quickly. Lee should have delayed any comments until the dust (or ice) had settled, concentrating instead on coaching his team to adapt to Arctic conditions. As one correspondent to the *Liverpool Echo* remarked: 'How on earth can you put a professional footballer in the right frame of mind for an important match within minutes of telling the media that the playing surface involved is liable to be responsible for the premature ending of a player's career?'

After Lee's post-match bluster at Southampton, all the injured players, bar Neil Robinson, mentioned in despatches at The Dell were available for the home game against Ipswich at Goodison seven days later. Beaten 1-0 after Billy Wright missed a penalty, there was a familiar response from the Goodison faithful: massed throwing of cushions after Lee's team had shown little appetite for the fight. 'Everton are still third in the table, but that cannot disguise a gloomy Goodison picture,' said Charles Lambert in the *Liverpool Echo*, 'Bad results, loss of form, falling gates and a series of injuries have given them much food for thought.'

With genuine title aspirations at Christmas, Everton had won just twice in ten games and were out of the FA Cup, whilst slipping away from league contention in their centenary season. Although Lee could argue there were injuries, all his key players largely stayed fit. The one area where Lee had a genuine grievance was full-back Mike Pejic's injury against Leeds before Christmas. The left-hand axis of Pejic-Dobson-Thomas was the source of the team's attacking threat and Lee felt that his absence was crucial. 'Was it coincidence we lost at Coventry in the next month to surrender our unbeaten League record,' he admitted later, 'Was it coincidence that Bob Latchford scored only four more league goals – less than one every five games – when he has a career average of a goal every other match? Was it coincidence that the form of Martin Dobson, who had been playing some of the best football of his time at Goodison suddenly suffered?' In isolation, they were reasonable points but Lee should have built a more balanced team and both Dobson and Thomas lost form at the same point twelve months before, so his argument was not necessarily true. However, the injury to Pejic unbalanced the defence – in the away game at Wolves there were four centre-halves – and disrupted the side. There was a distinct lack of leadership on the pitch and the team was showing little resilience, which was not surprising given Lee's outspoken remarks over icy pitches had provided a ready-made excuse.

The manager's recruitment policy in the preceding summer had clearly not worked as well. The gamble with Mickey Walsh failed and the purchases of Colin Todd and Geoff Nulty looked like a short-term means of stability rather than a concerted effort to reach the next level. Therefore, Lee had not addressed squad weaknesses – such as on the right, which required a full-back and natural width going forward. As one letter to the *Liverpool Echo* went: 'Our season is now over and to my mind the future of the club looks bleak. Gordon Lee has fashioned a hardworking, cheerless, unimaginative and predictable team. These qualities will keep us near the top, but we will never reach the summit until we find flair, poise and rhythm.'

Lee's poor management of the controversy concerning icy pitches only succeeded in ripping away the veneer of invincibility established over the previous two years. His repetitive outbursts revealed a manager with a pretty thin-skin who had difficulty controlling his emotions and, on occasions, his players. Such was the paranoia over poor surfaces Mick Lyons was still complaining on *Match of the Day* after a televised defeat at West Brom in April, having previously told Richard Bott of the *Sunday Express*, 'Our midfield players like the short stuff, you can't expect an elegant player like Martin Dobson to suddenly start landing long balls upfield. Is it our fault that we have not been able to adapt or the fault of a system that makes us play on bad grounds?' The answer was obvious. For a century, organised football had always suffered from poor pitches over the winter months and the best teams adapted their game accordingly. As Horace Yates said in the *Liverpool Daily Post* after the defeat at Wolves, 'It was the same for both sides and there was absolutely no comparison in the way the sides adapted to it. Tactically, Wolves were simply light years ahead of Everton in that respect.' Consequently, the message from the club skipper was absurd and sounded like an excuse: it was difficult to imagine a player from Liverpool or Nottingham Forest, teams that won trophies, making the same statement.

Everton eventually finished fourth at the end of the 1978/79 campaign, having won only two of the last thirteen matches. A decent outcome but an anti-climax after a superb start. Although there was a sour feeling to the second half of the campaign, critics could not underestimate Lee's feat of taking Everton from eighteenth in the league to a third- and fourth-place finish in his two full seasons. Such rapid progress would be a cause for celebration elsewhere but on Merseyside any feat was always calibrated by achievements across Stanley Park. With Liverpool champions for an eleventh time, this comparison irritated players and supporters. 'I can understand their frustrations,' Mick Lyons said of the fans, 'Everything we do is measured against what Liverpool have achieved and I know our supporters get Liverpool rammed down their throats at work.' By the start of the following season there were even more reasons for Everton supporters to dread entering the factory or office floor.

CHAPTER 14

Rebels with a cause

ONE OF THE PROBLEMS WITH FINISHING THE SEASON POORLY IS wounds fester over the summer and become infected by the time August arrives. That occurred with Everton during 1979. Even before the start of the 1979/80 campaign the club was in crisis, with Lee admitting 'I have problems and I am under pressure. I realise this. But I will do things my way and sink or swim on that basis'.

There was clearly tension at the end of the previous season after a relatively harmonious two years. With players out of form, Lee dropped both Latchford and Dobson. Striker Peter Eastoe arrived from QPR and on the same day Lee purchased the experienced Brian Kidd from Manchester City for £150,000 – like a number of his signings a relatively large amount for a player nearing thirty. With Dave Thomas injured in April, Lee switched to a 4-4-2 formation for the first time, using a flat midfield with no natural width. The result was a series of dour performances that did little to placate the fans and press alike. 'There is a dogged joyless quality about much of their play,' Robert Armstrong wrote in the *Guardian* after a 2-0 defeat at West Brom in April. Lee had also built an unbalanced squad with a surfeit of centre-halves but no right-sided defender and so he played Todd at full-back, a position the former Derby player disliked immensely. There were reports Pejic, Dobson and Latchford all wanted a move away at the end of the season, the latter in exchange for Aston Villa's Andy Gray.

There were issues off the pitch too. Popular coach Steve Burtenshaw had left during the summer of 1978 to manage QPR, having enjoyed a close relationship with the squad. Burtenshaw was the antithesis of Lee, a worldly-wise cockney who saw a life outside football and encouraged the players to express themselves. If the Everton manager lost his temper, the more tranquil Burtenshaw would smooth things over. In his place came Eric Harrison, who was more in Lee's image – hardworking but someone with a slightly austere view of the game. Harrison's strength was youth coaching[53] and he took some of the associated disciplinary mind-set into the dressing-room when dealing with senior professionals, which was always going to cause tension.

Matters came to a head on a disastrous pre-season tour in early August. Lee was keen to persevere with 4-4-2 and not only did the arrival of Kidd and Eastoe threaten the place of Bob Latchford, but also the purchases of Imre Varadi and Eamonn O'Keefe allowed the possibility of two mobile front-men. Furthermore, there was no place in the system for Dave Thomas. John Bailey arrived from Blackburn for £300,000 and provided a youthful and mobile presence at left-back, earning the vote over Mike Pejic. During the mini-tournament in West Berlin, the Everton boss consequently left out Thomas and Latchford for the second game against local team Hertha, much to their displeasure, while an unhappy Todd filled the right-back position. With tempers fraying in the heat, the former Derby player took his shirt off in protest and there were frantic scenes in the dressing room at half-time, as Bob Latchford recalled in his autobiography:

> *People were shouting and arguing and suddenly Eric [Harrison] started on Dave Thomas. Tizer [Thomas] was one of the most unassuming and placid members of the Everton squad. I don't know why Eric chose to have a go at him, but he started ranting about his rubber souled boots... Tizer for the first and only time I'd ever known, blew it... 'F--- this and f--- you; I'm not playing.' This was pre-season.*

Any chance of some sort of détente between management and senior players disappeared by the final pre-season game, at home to Dutch side Roda Kerkrade, when three – Pejic, Thomas and Latchford – submitted transfer requests. Like others, Everton were concerned that the new freedom of contract regulations made players act as if their obligations had concluded and,

---

[53] After leaving Everton Harrison went to Old Trafford where, of course, he developed the fabled 'Class of 92'.

noting that all three wanted completely new terms when under contract, the club provided a robust response:

Written transfer requests have been received from three players who are unhappy at the terms offered to them – even though they all have at least one year to serve on their existing agreements. The requests from Bob Latchford, Mike Pejic and Dave Thomas will be granted in due course. But the players concerned will only be transferred when it is in the best interest of the club.

In some ways the trio's frustration was a consequence of Lee's strategy of retaining a large corps of senior professionals looking to maximise earning potential in their final years at the top. But as PFA chairman Gordon Taylor said about the dispute, 'We warn players about the dangers in negotiating long-term contracts... But once such a contract has been signed we expect a player to honour it just as we expect any club to honour their side of the bargain.' There is sympathy for Lee in that context and whatever their differences, senior players should not have acted collectively in such an unprofessional manner on the eve of a new campaign, especially over contractually-agreed wages. Their actions could only have had a negative effect on the already fragile morale of the squad. That said, Taylor claimed that 'I understand the trouble at Everton is not about cash as a clash of personalities.' Central to that was Lee's inability to understand the better players needed special treatment. 'Mr Lee has had problems dealing with talented individuals in the past,' Ian Hargraves wrote in the *Liverpool Daily Post*. 'And it does seem he has difficulty in understanding the rather special requirements of such players, who generally thrive on encouragement.'

Twenty-four hours later all three, plus the 'injured' Colin Todd, were absent as Everton lost 3-1 at Goodison to Roda. The sparse crowd booed off the team whilst chanting the names of the missing players, who subsequently denied that their actions were financially motivated. 'In my own mind there are a few other reasons why I want to leave,' admitted Dave Thomas, 'My heart is not with them at the moment. Mentally I'm just not right to play for the club.' For his part, Latchford said, 'I think I have given Everton good service, but it is time to part. I am 28 going on 29 and it is a good stage of my career to move.' 'It is far from money,' said Pejic, 'It is something that has been brewing up for more than twelve months and I feel annoyed that the club has said it is to do with money.' The unhappy Colin Todd was also demanding a transfer.

However questionable the motives, issues had been bubbling under the surface and the dispute placed Lee in a difficult position: either make peace or move the malcontents on. The manager was keen to call their bluff. 'I will never have players who are unhappy at Everton,' he said, 'if someone is unhappy all they have to do is to speak to me: I will discuss it with the board and if it is in the best interests of the club he can leave. I believe that if a player doesn't want to play for Everton, then he has to be transferred. If I have to play youngsters, I will do so.'

With Lee not for turning, a tangled web of transfer activity followed at a time when fees were spiralling out of control, after Trevor Francis became the first £1 million British player earlier in the year. When it ended, Everton had lost three senior stars. Initially, with Andy Gray unsettled at Aston Villa the planned exchange deal with Latchford failed. Then Dave Sexton was keen on signing Dave Thomas for Manchester United, but Lee was only keen on a swap involving Micky Thomas, which ended any chance of business.

Having sold Martin Dobson to Burnley, Lee turned his attention to Wolves' Steve Daley, who was also attracting the attention of Manchester City. Lee offered Latchford and Thomas as part of a complicated exchange deal dependent on Wolves getting Gray from Aston Villa. Having travelled to Molineux, both Everton players surprisingly declined the move, putting the saga effectively back to square one. Lee wanted West Brom's David Mills, using Latchford as bait, only for Ron Atkinson to refuse a player exchange. Latchford then twice turned down a switch to The Hawthorns when Atkinson wanted a cash-only deal. With Villa eventually selling Andy Gray to Wolves, Latchford also rejected a move there, understandably given his Birmingham City roots. The player's reluctance to move was a source of frustration to his manager. 'He has turned down three English clubs: Wolves, West Brom and Aston Villa, and I honestly don't know what he wants. But he is not doing himself any good.' Belgian side Anderlecht also expressed an interest but the price tag scared them off.

By September the Gang of Four were surprisingly still at Goodison. But then Pejic moved to Aston Villa for £150,000 and Todd went to Birmingham City. 'My relationship with the manager deteriorated as the [1978/79] season progressed, and I was as surprised as anyone to be back for pre-season training. It was mercifully short-lived,' Todd confessed in his autobiography. Thomas eventually went to Wolves in early October for £420,000,[54] only after turning down a switch to Old Trafford, for financial reasons, after Dave Sexton made a late bid. 'The money aspect of the move was important as it is short career, and you have to get out of it what you can,' the winger said afterwards, but he made a mistake. Thomas failed to settle at Wolves, fell out with manager John Barnwell and within a year was off to Vancouver.

And then there was one. The stand-off between Latchford and Lee continued, and forced Jimmy Armfield, now at the *Daily Express*, into drafting an open letter to the striker:

Take some advice from an old pro, and get your boots back on. I know you'll be sitting at Goodison today watching your mates and it will be killing you. The confrontation between you and Everton is doing neither any good. They aren't getting anything out of you, and you aren't doing your career any favours ... You're a long time finished in this game, make the most of it while you can.

Whether Latchford heeded Armfield's words is unknown, but the forward showed signs of wanting to make peace. 'Although I'm looking to get away at the earliest opportunity I would be more use to Everton than sitting in the stand,' he said, 'If the manager wants me to play I would bury my differences and forget all my problems once the game began.' Lee was in no mood to build bridges however: 'Either he wants to play for Everton or he doesn't. But he's on the transfer list, which indicates he wants to leave the club.' With Lee effectively putting a gun to his striker's head, Latchford's desire to move was entrenched: 'I still want to leave Everton, and I'm still prepared to talk to anybody.' Then, after exhausting all his options, Latchford suddenly withdrew his transfer request and announced that he would fight for his place. The move was a welcome one for Lee: if things were going badly off the pitch, on the park was no better.

---

[54] The fee is good example of how transfer values can spiral out of control quickly. Everton had initially been happy to accept £300,000 for the winger but the record deals involving Steve Daley (£1,450,000) and Andy Gray (£1,469,000) in September 1979 had a trickle-down effect. 'I don't think my transfer fee will ever be beaten,' Gray told *Shoot!* magazine.

CHAPTER 15

Sniffing the hot dog

'TO SPEND AN ENTIRE SEASON NEVER OUT OF THE TOP FOUR PLACES in what is universally regarded as the toughest national league in the world is encouraging, but not success in the terms in which we understand the word at Everton,' said chairman Philip Carter at the club's AGM in July 1979. 'Our aim in the 1979/80 season will be nothing less than to win the League Championship, and the manager and playing and coaching staffs will be given every possible backing and encouragement by the directors to achieve this target.'

Ambitious words indeed. Although Everton supporters welcomed the desire, for a beleaguered manager under pressure they were words that he could have done without hearing. When Colin Todd left the club, he admitted that 'they've got good players, but they are also under pressure because of the neighbours next door. I was at Derby eight years, and I never felt the pressure. When I came to Everton I felt it straight away.' The more Liverpool won, the more they ramped it up on Gordon Lee.

'Everton are in genuine danger of being relegated'
Perhaps that burden was one of the reasons behind the players' rebellion. Lee was a football-obsessive and this impacted on his management style on occasions, particularly when under pressure. 'He was a smashing bloke, who was wrapped up in his football,' Mick Lyons said, 'He could never seem to relax, and if you don't switch off in this game, it can eat you up.' An inability in maintaining close relationships can be a product of that personality, as is the tunnel-vison required to pursue perfection. Both came into play here. Although he correctly criticised the players for their role in the pre-season dispute, the fall-out had exposed the manager's weaknesses. Lee was too busy pursuing his obsessions to pick up the

signals from an unhappy dressing room and once that disquiet became apparent, he did not possess the necessary man-management skills to smooth over the differences – there was no room for negotiation. As Bryan Hamilton said: 'I think he was more comfortable dealing with ordinary players than superstars. He seemed to be able to understand people better when they worked hard.' The seven weeks' delay in resolving the dispute was hugely damaging. 'The time that it happened, and the transfer activity that followed, had a big unsettling effect on the selection of the side and also the performances of the players,' Lee later revealed, 'We have had to replace players in a side that is still getting to know each other.'

Notwithstanding problems with the Gang of Four, the Everton manager was also rebuilding the squad during the summer. However, Lee was not the first Everton manager to endure a frustrating time in the transfer market and he failed to land Manchester City's Asa Hartford and Nottingham Forest's Martin O'Neill. 'I just can't get the player I want. I had a go for Hartford and O'Neill, and there is a shortage of the class of player I want,' he complained. Eventually Lee bought Garry Stanley from Chelsea for £300,000 and eventually acquired Hartford for £500,000 at the end of August, after the midfielder's bizarre stay at Nottingham Forest had lasted less than a month.[55] In theory Lee made a good signing to assist his aim of adding a more scientific approach. 'They [the supporters] appreciate players in midfield in the category of Harvey, Ball and Kendall,' he said, 'Asa is one of only a few in recent years to enter that mould.'

However, the opening day 4-2 defeat at home to Norwich City was an early indicator that Carter's aim of title-winning glory had no chance of fruition. With Billy Wright and Todd in the centre of defence, their weakness in the air – the visitors' four goals were all headers – undermined the incompetent home team in front of a crowd of 26,000, the lowest at Goodison for the opening game in forty years. The watching Patrick Barclay of the *Guardian* commented that Lee 'strung up on the gallows by the ineptitude of his team's performance against Norwich must now wait to see whether or not Everton's directors will pull back the trap door on his stewardship.' The Everton boss received one of the earliest votes of confidence in league history in response. 'You have the full support of both

---

55 Hartford's first journey to Goodison did not go as planned. The Scot drove to Anfield by mistake and had to be redirected by two young Everton fans.

myself and the board and I'm confident you will produce a better squad,' said chairman Carter.

There was no sign of the skilful, passing style from the back that Lee had promised, instead his side played dull, attritional football. Form was patchy and it took until mid-October to record a first home league victory. European dreams were over by that time. Drawn against Feyenoord in the UEFA Cup, Everton lost the away leg 1-0 when George Wood dived over Rene Notten's shot. Lee was unhappy about his keeper: 'We can't continue to give opponents silly goals,' the manager said, before Wood repeated the clanger at Goodison, allowing a swerving Richard Budding shot to pass him with fifteen minutes left for the only goal. 'You can't legislate for giving away goals like that. It was worse than the one in Rotterdam,' Lee caustically remarked as his side crashed out. The Everton manager dropped Wood in November, replacing him with the hugely promising Martin Hodge. A big dressing room presence, Wood failed to fulfil his early promise and like the rest of the team suffered from inconsistency and was prone to expensive mistakes.

With Everton hovering above the drop zone, domestic cups were the only chance of bringing some respite to a characterless campaign. Three years before, a good run in the League Cup acted as a diversion to poor league form so, when the Toffees travelled to Grimsby Town at the end of October, hopes were high of history repeating itself. The game against a mid-table Third Division side instead became one of the most embarrassing episodes of Lee's tenure. The visitors showed an aristocratic touch in the opening period and got their rewards when Brian Kidd converted a Garry Stanley cross. Yet as the rain swept in from the North Sea, within nine minutes they trailed 2-1. Mike Brolly was a 25-year-old journeyman who arrived from Bristol City for a mere £5,000, but he joined the list of those unheralded players who have haunted the club over the years. The midfielder scored both goals, each created beautifully by Bob Cumming, a deep-lying midfielder who tormented Everton throughout. Backed by a rabid full-house of more than 22,000, the home team played with such intensity and intelligence that the visitors were restricted to few chances in a classic cup tie played at breakneck speed.

Although Lee's team staged a late rally, the home side held on for a famous victory, one that again raised questions about the manager's future. Asked about Lee later in the week, Philip Carter said, 'What happened at Grimsby in no way reflected on the position of the manager. Obviously, we were disappointed, but as far as I'm concerned it was one of those things that happen. The manager is being given considerable time and money to rebuild the team and we're happy with the way things are going.' Whether supporters were was questionable.

The one common theme of Lee's reign is that the manager would start picking fights when feeling the stress of the job, invariably with the wrong target. On the following weekend, in a bizarre development it was Martin Peters. After a dour goalless draw at Norwich City, afterwards Lee accused the World Cup winner of killing the game by playing as a third centre-half, even though Peters was employed as a deep-lying midfielder who came close to scoring three times. The outburst sparked a war of words between Lee and Norwich counterpart, John Bond. There had been bad feeling following the game at Goodison, when Bond accused Brian Kidd of breaking his son Kevin's nose. 'I don't know how Everton can spend so much money and play that way. I think they are a joke,' said the Carrow Road boss. But Lee hit back. 'He always criticises established clubs,' the Everton manager said, 'Until he wins something or takes Norwich into Europe I am sure he is a good joke himself.'

Everton supporters found little humour thereafter. Lee's insistence with 4-4-2 and no width meant a midfield of Garry Stanley, Andy King, Trevor Ross and Asa Hartford. Although the latter acted a creative presence, the other three offered little in the way of leadership, guile and pace. Only Andy King was a goalscorer capable of running beyond the forwards. The ageing, immobile strikeforce of Bob Latchford and Brian Kidd relied largely on service from the wings, yet Lee had not replaced Dave Thomas nor looked for forward options on the right. With the money received for Thomas, Lee bought right-back John Gidman from Aston Villa for £650,000. The Liverpool-born player was an excellent addition but the two deals diminished attacking options. Ten players who had appeared for the club in the previous campaign had now left, and eight players had made their debut in the current season but, with more than £2 million spent, Lee possessed a hopelessly unbalanced, miscast outfit playing dull, one-dimensional football. Former manager Harry Catterick was not impressed. 'His pattern of buying has left me mystified,' Catterick told the *Sunday Mirror*, 'When I study his player recruitment I cannot see what he is seeking. It's like watching a house being built in red brick, then black ones appear from nowhere.'

However, Lee was stubborn about criticism of his team's style. 'I think we can be as successful as we were over the last two years,' he told the *Liverpool Echo's* Charles Lambert, 'Whether it looks as good without a natural winger is open to doubt. But providing you can develop the right sort of rhythm with players in a 4-4-2 formation you can produce an attractive side which scores goals, and that's what the public wants.' However, after a decade without a trophy, supporters wanted more than just aspirational statements. In the natural team-building cycle, after three years in the job Lee should have shipped out those players surplus to requirements and fans would have been watching a fully-formed starting XI playing in their manager's chosen style. Yet effectively Lee was talking in terms of a rebuilding job. Yes, there was some mitigation with the departures at the start of the campaign, but Mike Pejic was surplus to requirements and Colin Todd was always going to be short-term solution.

Also, fans – and the board – wanted good football and a title-winning side, not a club that regarded finishing third and fourth as a 'success'. Realising those dreams were hardly helped as Everton won only two of their eleven league games before the end of the year and in mid-November Lee was criticised after praising the players on *The Kick Off Match* for their commitment following a 2-0 home defeat to Middlesbrough – a team that had scored in just two of their previous nine league games. Nevertheless, Lee's team reached the nadir on the final Saturday before Christmas when a Goodison crowd of just 26,000 witnessed a wholly incompetent display in a 2-1 defeat to Manchester City. The home team seemed unable to make the simplest of passes and the display even left the voluble Malcolm Allison lost for words. 'I always find it difficult to assess a game we are involved in but on top of that I don't know how bad or good Everton were,' the Manchester City manager said. John Keith of the *Daily Express* was certainly not short of an opinion though. 'Everton's performance before the interval was one of the most abject I have ever seen from players in the famous royal blue,' he wrote. Unsurprisingly, a salvo of cushions thrown from the stands greeted the players at the end. 'The buck stops at me and it's up to me to put things right,' Lee told the *Liverpool Echo*, 'I've not been sleeping too well but it's no good kidding. Giving goals away and missing chances has been the story of our life, and it's these two things which football is all about.'

Having hovered just above the bottom three all season, alarm bells were ringing as 1979 ended. Everton had started the decade top of the table on the way to a seventh league title. At the end of it, the unthinkable had now become more than just a possibility. 'Everton are in genuine danger of being relegated,' warned Charles Lambert, 'It couldn't happen to a club of the stature and resources of Everton? That's what Manchester United and Tottenham thought, and they found out the hard way that they were wrong.'

A chance for redemption

As the decade closed, Lee reflected on his time at Goodison. 'We've been near to winning a trophy four times since I came to Everton three years ago. I'm sick of going so close. I want to win something. That must be my immediate ambition,' he told John Keith. 'At twenty other clubs I might be regarded as a success, but not at Everton and certainly not by me. When I joined Everton from Newcastle I said that competing with Liverpool in the same city is like attempting to climb Everest. It's something you have to live with but now I'd dearly like to get one foot on top of the mountain at least.'

But in early 1980, the manager was merely stumbling around the foothills, desperately trying to find the right blend. As ever though, the FA Cup provided an opportunity to drag something from a campaign that had few redeeming features. The draw was kind to Everton, giving them a relatively easy ride against Aldershot and they overcame the Fourth Division side 4-1. It was equally generous in the next round, ultimately pitting Lee's team against another Fourth Division outfit.

FA Cup fourth round, Wigan Athletic (h)

'I am glad 1979 has gone,' said Gordon Lee before the Toffees played Wigan Athletic in the fourth round. But a New Year's Day victory over Nottingham Forest and the win over Aldershot had generated some optimism. 'There is a good spirit among the players... I am very pleased the way the younger players are coming through,' Lee said before the tie.

Wigan were newcomers to league football, having been elected two years before. But there seemed little chance of progression in the FA Cup when the draw sent the Latics to Second Division Chelsea in the third round. With the game postponed until after the fourth-round draw, Everton club secretary Jim Greenwood made it clear Wigan were the preferred option, purely for financial reasons. The non-league side wanted 10,000 tickets for the game, against the 3,000 Chelsea needed and the bean-counters were happy when a Tommy Gore goal for the visitors produced a major upset at Stamford Bridge.

The Fourth Division outfit had no less than six Liverpool-born players in their squad, two of whom, Joe Hinnigan and Tony Quinn, had been on Everton's books. On the last Saturday of January, Greenwood's hunch proved correct, a crowd of more than 51,000 (paying ground record receipts of £88,890) crammed into Goodison and the visitors, backed by a huge army of supporters, gave a good account of themselves.

Lee had spiced up his side by selecting youth-product Joe McBride[56] as a winger, to try and provide a greater attacking presence and the young Scot put the Toffees ahead on the half-hour. Thereafter the tie degenerated into a match of petty squabbles. Wigan centre-half Neil Davids played the role of pantomime villain during a running battle with Bob Latchford, but with twenty minutes left the striker headed home from a corner before Kidd wrapped up the game with a beautiful left-footed finish. However, the real drama occurred in the final minutes. Tempers frayed after Davids appeared to deliberately run into Latchford in full view of the referee, leaving the Everton man on the ground clutching his head. With the Everton number nine uncharacteristically burning a short fuse, moments later teammate Kidd was booked for dissent before a corner. As the ball came across the Mancunian then elbowed Davids in the head and was immediately red-carded by Willis, who eventually restored peace after a mass brawl seemed likely. Shortly after, home supporters roundly booed the away team as they left the pitch. Interviewed by Granada TV's Gerald Sinstadt after the game, Davids spoke about an incident missed by the cameras, as he lay on the ground after Kidd's red card, 'There was a bit of a fracas and somebody ran up and kicked me in the head, right in the face, but luckily I had my hands over my face.' Pressed by Sinstadt about the identity of the mystery player, Davids replied, 'I'm not sure,' before adding with a smile, 'But I have an idea.' But as Patrick Barclay of the *Guardian* wrote, 'If Davids was referring to Bob Latchford whom the Wigan defender had gratuitously ill-treated earlier, he was hardly the one with reason to complain.'

However, the incidents again raised questions about the discipline of Lee's

---

[56] McBride's father, Joe McBride senior, was one of the most prolific post-war strikers in Scottish football. A visit to watch his son at Goodison led to a memorable blooper from a local radio commentator: 'Joe McBride, watched today by his father, Joe Bride McSenior.'

team, who had accrued three red and 36 yellow cards thus far, dreadful numbers in lenient times and the worst in the top-flight. Ian Hargraves in the *Liverpool Daily Post* claimed that it was 'clear evidence that the club appear to have abandoned all attempts at self-discipline.' Meanwhile Barclay said, 'Undoubtedly there was provocation, but discipline is not the prime virtue of this Everton team, and it is time for Gordon Lee to instil some.' The Everton manager was having none of it. 'I speak to the players regularly about it but it is no good sending frightened men onto the pitch – they might as well not be there,' was Lee's attitude. Barclay was not convinced: 'With some exceptions, their performances have displayed a mixture of gratuitous violence and the aimlessness of a scratch team.'

FA Cup fifth round, Wrexham (h)

At 9-1 to the lift the cup, the draw was again kind, providing another home tie against a lower division team. That was the good news, the bad was the Everton boss received another vote of confidence. The week before the Welsh club arrived at Goodison, Bobby Robson's Ipswich Town defenestrated Everton on the ground, running out comfortable 4-0 winners on a humiliating afternoon for the Toffees.

At the end, the home players trooped off as cushions replaced after the Manchester City game rained down like confetti, while afterwards a crowd of 300 fans gathered around the main entrance, chanting 'Lee out' before being dispersed by mounted police. 'We were pathetic, disgraceful, a shambles,' an angry home manager rapped after the game. 'I felt sorry for my colleague,' the future England boss said, 'When the crowd starts this kind of thing all they do is damage the club.' However, in a now familiar interjection, Lee's chairman once again came out in support. 'We're backing our manager,' Philip Carter declared, 'He's going through a bad patch but Gordon is the same man he was in the last two seasons when we finished third and fourth in the table.' Yet fans were not necessarily of the same voice, as one complained in the *Liverpool Echo*: 'Our patience is wearing thin. The directors have a responsibility to the supporters... How long do we have to suffer this rubbish?'

Always sensitive to the mood off the pitch, the Everton boss cut a characteristically morose figure before the game against Wrexham. 'What a situation – we could win the FA Cup and we could also be relegated,' the manager quipped. Revisiting one of his pet subjects – the transfer requests at the start of the season – Lee asked the question 'When did a player last want to leave Liverpool?' The statement revealed how the Anfield side continually loomed large in his thoughts. That was understandable. David Miller once wrote in the *Daily Express* that being the manager of Everton was a thankless task, likening the relationship between the two clubs to that of Britain's greatest entertainers. 'It is almost as doomed as Ernie trying to upstage Eric,' he wrote. Lee hardly enhanced the Goodison mood by pessimistically claiming the Second Division side would be 'formidable opposition'.

Having said that, if Lee's intention was to warn against complacency, it worked as home supporters amongst the 44,000 crowd forgot previous indiscretions to provide passionate backing. Gary Megson had recently arrived from Plymouth and the ginger-haired midfielder put Everton ahead after six minutes. Peter Eastoe added a second just after the break before Mick Vinter pulled a goal back. Trevor Ross then kicked off the line before the visitors' prolific Dixie McNeil fouled the midfielder in the area and the former Arsenal player scored from the spot. In a tight, combative game of little quality, the home team clinically punished the mistakes of their opponents and further goals by Eastoe and Latchford, plus a consolation from Vinter, produced a final 5-2 scoreline that was harsh on the visitors.

Lee was understandably jubilant. 'What an answer from the players to the people who have been having a go. All they have to do tonight is hold up five fingers,' he proclaimed before adding a memorable soundbite: 'We are only two games from Wembley. It's the sniff of the hot dog.' Lee also felt the win banished the ghosts from seven days before, with a sense that revenge was on his mind. 'Today there was no danger. If it had been Ipswich this afternoon I would have fancied us,' he said before admitting that another crack at the East Anglian side would be welcome. The footballing gods immediately went to work. When listening to the draw made from the bowels of Lancaster Gate 48 hours later, the manager would have noted that, with two balls remaining in the velvet bag, both clubs were still in there. Lee had got his wish. And another home draw too.

FA Cup sixth round, Ipswich Town (h)

'Ipswich might be playing the same club and some of the same team,' the Everton boss said. 'But they won't recognise them. Ipswich will find it very different this time because even though we won't have such a strong team – our preparations have been better.' That said, the crucial encounter came at the end of another difficult week. On the previous Saturday, the death of Dixie Dean at Goodison overshadowed a bitter derby defeat and the club's greatest-ever player was laid to rest in emotional scenes 24 hours before the tie. Also, the odds were stacked. Whereas Everton had taken one point from three games since the fifth round, Ipswich were purring: sixteen games unbeaten since early December having just inflicted one of the great hammerings, a 6-0 rout of title-chasing Manchester United at Portman Road, when visiting goalkeeper Gary Bailey saved three penalties.

Team selection was easy: several players were missing through injury and both Asa Hartford and Trevor Ross were suspended. Bob Latchford had not featured since the Wrexham game but, having scored in every round, Lee recalled the striker as a 'cup specialist'. The other change was an unusual tactical manoeuvre that was a gamble. Lee spoke about it after the game: 'We knew Ipswich wouldn't change their style, so we had to do something that would give them problems.' Eric Gates had caused havoc in the league game, filling the creative role just behind strikers Paul Mariner and Alan Brazil. Although a commonly used ploy now, then it was very unusual. 'Playing between the lines' was not a familiar phrase in the footballing lexicon but, to counter, full-back John Gidman eventually moved into the centre of the park to pick up the diminutive, but clever, striker.[57] Unusually, this meant playing three at the back but the change worked a treat. Not only did Gidman perform the job brilliantly but also Gates never tracked back and the talented defender was therefore a threat up front. On 29 minutes, Terry Butcher misjudged his perfect cross from the left and Latchford's clinical header finished the job. Whether being dropped motivated the striker is unknown, but Latchford had one of his best games, foraging tirelessly and chasing back whilst still looking a continual goal threat.

Elsewhere, the minute's silence before the game for Dean may have focused minds and stimulated the home team, for their performance was full of passion, with barely a 50-50 ball lost. The visitors enjoyed as much possession as in the

---

57 The original plan was for Gary Megson to mark Gates with Gidman picking up Arnold Muhren. With the scheme not working, after ten minutes the defender took over his teammate's role.

league game, but Wright and Lyons man-marked Brazil and Mariner superbly. A goal to the good, the home team kept Ipswich at arm's length until, on 75 minutes, Russell Osman fouled Brian Kidd twenty yards from goal, Andy King knocked the ball to the forward who fired home through the wall. In a breathless finish beneath the early spring sunshine, substitute Kevin Beattie's goal with a towering header was too little, too late and the crowd erupted more with relief at full time. Lee's gamble had paid off. 'Tactically we were superb. We out-thought and out-manoeuvred them... We beat the best side in the country by skilful football,' Lee said afterwards. 'There is life, plenty of it, in Everton yet,' wrote Derek Brown in the *Sunday Times*.

The victory was hugely symbolic, two Everton number nines scoring in the week their most illustrious predecessor had gone. 'The lads wanted to do it so much for the fans and the boss,' admitted Mick Lyons, a pall-bearer at the funeral, after the game, 'And in a way we wanted to do it for Dixie Dean too.' Everton were reigning cup holders when Dean was born, to bookend his life they were now aiming to lift the trophy immediately after his passing.

FA Cup semi-final, West Ham United

The three other remaining teams were Arsenal, Liverpool and West Ham United. Everton thankfully faced the Second Division outfit at Villa Park. However, in the days of a much narrower gap in quality in English football, John Lyall's side were a top-flight outfit in all but name. Their ranks contained players of outstanding quality in Trevor Brooking, Alan Devonshire and goalkeeper Phil Parkes. The central defenders were Billy Bonds, one of the best uncapped England players, and Alvin Martin, Bootle-born and released by Everton as a youngster.

Lee had few options with just thirteen available players. The hardworking and clever Peter Eastoe had partnered Brian Kidd in the previous two matches that brought three points, as relegation worries eased. Consequently, Bob Latchford warned 'The odds are against me playing' and the team-sheet confirmed the striker's worst fears – he was substitute. Lyall expected the semi-final to be tough and that was the case as the two teams fought to a standstill in an epic encounter at a sweltering Villa Park, where an unusually warm spring had produced a barren, rock-hard pitch. Intriguingly the referee was Colin Seel, Clive Thomas' wing man at Maine Road three years before. Like Thomas, Seel would end up being the villain of the piece.

With Asa Hartford controlling the midfield and John Bailey attacking purposefully, Everton – in all blue – started the better against a nervous West Ham, showing the difference in experience. Parkes saved superbly from Eastoe before Lee's team got the goal they deserved. Just before the break, Alan Devonshire shoved Andy King in the back and referee Seel harshly pointed to the spot. Some Everton players could not believe their luck. 'I have to say honestly that I don't think it should have been awarded,' Asa Hartford admitted later. However, Seel responded: 'I was six yards away with a clear view. Both players (King and Stewart) moved to head the ball and there was a definite push by the West Ham player.' Kidd's spot-kick went straight down the middle. But the remaining seconds in the half were action-packed: Devonshire and Ray Stewart had already been booked for arguing over the penalty decision and Ross suffered the same fate for fouling the former. Seel had already warned Ross twice before the booking and the Everton player was taking his role of midfield destroyer literally when, right on half-time, he scythed down Brooking. Seel, who was several feet away, reached for a yellow, realised the midfielder had already been booked and controversially changed his mind. The failure to dismiss Ross was a crucial moment in the context of what happened later.

Although West Ham re-emerged with a more positive approach, the most important moment of the tie occurred just after the hour. Stewart's shot poleaxed Ross and, as the midfielder lay on the floor, Martin Hodge attempted to clear the ball into touch so his teammate could get treatment. But Stewart tried to keep the ball in play and came to blows with Brian Kidd before the linesman pulled the Everton striker away as Seel, too far away to see the incident, came over. After consulting his assistant, Seel gave Kidd a red card while, amazingly, sparing Stewart punishment, even though he had already been booked. Kidd was a gentleman off the pitch but burned a short fuse on it and Eric Harrison had to physically restrain the striker. After pointing aggressively at the linesman a boiling Kidd was eventually persuaded to leave the field of play.[58] Although admitting he had not seen the incident after checking on Ross, Seel defended himself later: 'I could only go to the linesman, Ken Redfearn... he said that blue number nine had thrown a punch at an opponent and that in his opinion number

---

58 It was Kidd's third career sending-off in the competition, the first player to achieve the unwanted feat in the 108-year history of the FA Cup.

nine should be sent off.' However Lee claimed, 'If one had gone the other should…
it looked only a skirmish.'

To dismiss only one of the combatants was nonsensical and Seel's irrational
action seemed an attempt to balance out those perceived first-half errors that
favoured Everton. Down to ten men, Lee's side wilted in the heat and seven
minutes later caved in. The excellent Devonshire went down the left, his
beautifully weighted pass found Brooking in space towards the byline and with
Hodge (who otherwise had an excellent game) unwisely getting caught in no
man's land between his goal and Brooking, the midfielder pulled the ball back for
Stuart Pearson to finish into an unguarded net. Although the underdogs deserved
the equaliser, Everton could feel hard done by. With Latchford on as a substitute,
West Ham pegged back the First Division side for the final twenty minutes.
Thanks to Pat Holland and Bonds missing chances and no extra time, Everton
lived to fight again and a replay at Elland Road – although that was thanks to
another controversial decision, when the referee disallowed Geoff Pike's strike
three minutes from the end because Trevor Brooking was offside 35 yards away.
'So often Cup semi-finals are eighteen-carat bores… this match was a rousing
exception,' according to Ronald Atkin in the *Observer* of a stirring ninety minutes
in Mediterranean-like sunshine.

Despite tabloid calls to be omitted, Seel was still on refereeing duties when
the two teams reconvened on a humid Wednesday evening, although he was
hardly looking forward to the appointment. 'I feel like a pilot who has been in an
air crash and has had to climb back into the cockpit,' the Carlisle printer admitted.
Injuries and suspensions forced Lee to reshuffle his resources. Latchford came in
for Kidd, Gidman moved to midfield with a nineteen-year-old youth product,
Kevin Ratcliffe, called in to bolster the defence having performed creditably at
Old Trafford on his only previous appearance a month before. The Everton
manager's rationale was similar to the quarter-final, using Gidman to stop the
threat of the wiry, skilful Devonshire on the West Ham left. But he used the full-
back against Ipswich within a fluid 3-4-3 attacking system with Joe McBride
providing natural width. At Elland Road, he left out the Scottish winger and
retained the 4-4-2 system, making a tactical blunder by giving the midfield an
unnecessarily defensive look against Second Division opponents.

With West Ham hit by injuries, Everton were favourites on a ground where
they had not tasted victory for nearly thirty years. After Seel and his linesmen

managed to achieve the near impossible feat of both sets of supporters booing them, as at Villa Park Everton enjoyed the better of the exchanges, although their only real chance arrived when Billy Bonds kicked Wright's shot off the line. In the second half, the London side began to find their passing range, with the vibrant Devonshire at the centre of virtually everything, while Everton relied on long balls to their forward duo. That said, apart from a couple of Pearson near-misses and a Bonds goal disallowed for pushing, the Hammers failed to break the deadlock before Seel blew for extra time.

The stalemate lasted four further minutes. Three Everton players made a mess of picking up a loose ball, Brooking took up possession and fed Devonshire on the left touchline. The midfielder played the ball to Pearson at the edge of the box, took the return and after Wright's crude attempt to floor him, kept his balance to fire low past Hodge. Despite Lee bringing Imre Varadi on as a third striker, Everton rarely threatened until six minutes from the end. For once, Everton got to the byline and Billy Wright's low, fast centre was met by a classic Latchford near-post header, the striker jumping on the hoardings to celebrate in front of the massed Evertonians. The magical moment seemed likely to take the tie to a third game at Highfield Road on the following Monday.

But dramatic endings characterised Lee's reign at Everton. With less than 180 seconds of the replay remaining, yet again there was heartbreak. Brooking's cross from the flank eventually fell to right-back Frank Lampard, standing in the centre-forward position, and his soft header agonisingly creeped inside Hodge's right-hand post. The scorer's celebration – a 360 degree rotation around the corner flag – only added to the surreal nature of the goal. West Ham manager Lyall said a moment of brilliance would decide the tie, however the winner was anything but. Everton had little time to mount a counter-offensive, Varadi carelessly running the ball out when well-placed to cross seemed horribly in tune with the Lee era. When the full-time whistle came, Everton could have few complaints. A visibly upset Lee said, 'We just have to forget tonight if we can, but it's going to be hard. I can't think of a more cruel way to lose.'

The 1980 semi-final defeat to West Ham sits comfortably within the mythological tales of luckless Everton. They are legion – occasions when the fates conspired against the club. The usual characteristics include refereeing (the 1977 semi-final), injuries (Brian Labone at Old Trafford against Liverpool in 1971) or an unheralded player producing something out of the ordinary (Aston Villa's Chris

Nicholl). Yet these events hide an uncomfortable truth – ultimately Everton were not good enough. That 'unlucky' narrative applies to Elland Road. Lampard's goal was indeed out of character – he scored only 22 in more than 600 West Ham appearances – but the winner emphasised the two clubs' attitude. Whereas Lee used his right-back in midfield as a defensive measure to stop West Ham playing, Gidman's opposite number popped up as an auxiliary centre-forward to score the winner. Everton deserved nothing with that sort of mindset. West Ham's bravery won a tight cup tie but that was not Lee's *modus operandi*. Ultimately, Everton, a division higher than the victors, did not deserve to go to the final. Equally sadly, one of the characteristics of the cup run was that senior players Bob Latchford and Mick Lyons, who were desperate to win something, were their star performers. It was Lyons, led off at Elland Road in tears, who gloomily spoke for most Evertonians after the game:

> *We had tremendous support and if ever we were going to Wembley it was this year. Everything was right. So we've got no excuse. People can criticise us as much as they like and we've got no comeback... When we equalised I thought we could pinch it or at least get a replay. Then they got that second goal which was unbelievable. The ball bounced loose and went to their player.[59] But the number of times it bounced loose and never went to us. You feel as if you're going to be an eternal loser. You feel you're never going to win anything in your life. But with saying that, I thought on the night that West Ham deserved to win. Every year you grow older and this year was my best ever chance to get my name on a cup.*

---

[59] This was not correct. After David Cross headed Brooking's cross into the heart of the box, Frank Lampard was standing in an unmarked position between Kevin Ratcliffe and Lyons, one of whom should have been picking up the full-back. The West Ham winner was not a result of bad luck, but poor marking. The main contributor to the goal is therefore Lee's decision to break up his established centre-back pairing to enable John Gidman to play in midfield.

CHAPTER 16

'Eversell'

ALTHOUGH THE INTERTWINING OF FOOTBALL AND FINANCES IS viewed as very much a modern phenomenon – when balance sheets are more important than clean sheets – that is not necessarily the case. The importance of generating cash almost certainly goes back to lifting the maximum weekly wage of £20 in 1961, when players were free to negotiate their own deals and, by the end of the decade, the biggest stars became assets in their own right, expecting salaries to match their importance on and off the pitch. This acceleration in rewards was such that, by the end of the 1960s, the likes of Alan Ball could expect a basic pay packet more than ten times greater than at the start of the decade. In the final year before the lifting of restrictions Everton paid less than £30,000 in wages – just over a decade later the bill was close to £250,000. Consequently, the biggest clubs had to generate additional funds to retain their best players and remain active in the transfer market.

Eversell or Everhell?

Everton were one of the first clubs to try and maximise their potential off the pitch. The £1m reportedly spent on the Main Stand in Goodison Road in 1969 acted as a catalyst for the concept of 'Eversell' in the following years. The marketing and commercial strategy was the brainchild of promotions manager David Exall and initiatives included expanding the restaurant facilities plus increasing the numbers of pitch-side advertising hoardings. Although such enterprise is standard in the modern era, they were intrusive for many. As one correspondent to the *Liverpool Echo* explained:

> *'Eversell' means that at Goodison, the supporter is now a witness (or victim?) of the first ninety-minute advertising package deal in the history*

of the game in this country. Not only is the ground covered with even more hoardings, but now, half an hour before kick-off, at half-time, and throughout the whole game (via the electric scoreboard), one is assailed by advertisements. The reason for this is, increasingly, the only legitimate reason for anything at Goodison these days – making more money... Everton has become a corporation catering for businessmen; Liverpool supporters feel an important part of the club; we Evertonians feel mere cash units.

That said, even before Bingham's arrival, steadily falling attendances meant that in 1972/73 the club had failed to make a profit for the first time in six years. Gate receipts of £430,000 were half those across Stanley Park and Exall admitted: 'It must be appreciated that when results are unsatisfactory and attendances drop, as they have done at Goodison in the last two seasons, then that is the time when the need for extra cash becomes greater.'

Everton's consequent commercial activities[60] resulted in accusations from supporters that they were more interested in being a 'money-grabbing club' than providing a successful football team. Early in the following campaign, Exall spoke in the matchday programme: 'We can only refute these charges, Everton will, as always, attempt to present attractive and winning football in a first-class setting. We are a well-organised club, business like, but with our priorities in exactly the right place.' Either way, significantly a leading official had to defend the club against supporters' accusations.

Exall also made the valid point that improving catering facilities was not just a financial initiative. At a time of upward social mobility, the game was gradually moving from the cloth-cap image towards providing fans with more choice. 'These are the kind of amenities which supporters have been crying out for years,' said Exall, 'Far from reducing supporters to mere "cash units" they give them a place and identity within the club structure.' Furthermore, as John Moores later explained there was another reason for the negative comments. 'I think people's criticism of "Eversell" is well wide of the mark,' he said, 'They have seized on this aspect of the club's affairs to complain about. I think it is temporary. If we could start winning, the criticism of the advertisements and the rest would stop.'

---

60 Everton were selling 40,000 bingo tickets a week at one stage during the decade, in places as far away as Jersey.

But the primary role of generating additional income was to replace the falling money at the gate on match-days. During the turbulent 1970s, English football shed 5 million spectators. With cash-strapped Merseyside feeling the effects of a declining economy more than most, then for Everton and Liverpool that was a priority.

Before the brink

Buoyed by government investment and the boom years of the 1960s, during that decade the Merseyside conurbation achieved close to full-employment for the first time since the 1800s. However, this proved only temporary respite for a region that had been plagued by unemployment all century.[61] In the latter half of the 1960s the long-term economic decay started, most notably within the port, where jobs halved due to modernisation, contraction of shipbuilding and repairing. The decline also affected job numbers in port-related transport and distribution.

In the year Billy Bingham took over at Goodison, three further events had a dramatic impact. Firstly, the economic fallout of the international oil crisis following turmoil in the Middle East. More significantly, the entry into the Common Market placed further pressure on the port as international trade moved towards the south of the country. Finally, the Liberal Party – thanks to a redrawing of the electoral boundaries – gained control of the city council but crucially not with a majority. With no strong leadership and energies wasted on squabbles with the Conservative and Labour parties, local politicians were ill-equipped to respond to the crisis. 'The city lacked the capacity to confront the fiscal, administrative and social consequences of its rapid economic decline,' wrote leading academic Michael Parkinson in *Liverpool: Beyond the Brink*, 'It failed to take a series of difficult decisions to rationalise the management and financing of the city.'

During the summer of 1973, unemployment in Liverpool stood at 7 per cent. Central government, in particular, had not addressed large closures in the

---

[61] Contrary to popular belief, the region's problems are not limited to the last forty or so years. During the depression of the 1930s Liverpool had an unemployment rate fifty percent higher than the national average, by the late 1940s this had risen to 250 percent. Historically, Merseyside has had an unemployment rate twice that of Manchester.

engineering industry during the previous four years. Consequently, twelve months after Bingham arrived, unemployment rose to more than 50,000, with an unskilled out-of-work labour force of 27,000 chasing just 855 vacancies. With companies such as Triumph, Plessey, Lucas, English Electric, Courtaulds and Birds Eye shedding jobs by the thousands, the unemployment figures for the area ran way above the national average.

The region's other problem was little industrial expansion or new investment. Whereas nationally the number of white-collars workers had grown by twenty percent, on Merseyside the figure was a fifth of that. Attracting new business was proving difficult, not helped by the area's poor reputation for industrial relations – although data showed this was a myth, with lower strike days on average than similar areas and a figure artificially inflated by the disproportionate presence of more strike-prone industries. When unemployment stood at 10 percent by the late summer of 1975, the worst since the 1940s, the Merseyside Industrial Development Office came up with the novel idea of providing the city's clubs with leaflets printed in foreign languages for distribution on pre-season tours, spelling out what the area had to offer.

They may have shown willingness to make the region look attractive, but Everton and Liverpool were also suffering the impact of the economic decline, and they were not alone. 'Football is in a serious state,' Football League president Lord Westwood told the House of Lords in the middle of the decade, 'There are few professional clubs making a profit.' The matter in hand was an amendment to the Safety of Sports Grounds Bill to allow clubs access to Government grants or loans as they were not commercial enterprises. The fact that football was pushing for a relatively small amount of funding spoke volumes about the parlous state of its finances, although the sport could feel hard done by. 'No matter what we do in football we don't seem to be able to win,' Westwood told the Lords, pointing out that the Pools paid more than £70m in dividends each season, while the game got nothing. Everton's reward for putting more seats in the new Main Stand had been a significant increase in its rates bill. The nationwide police bill for the season was £750,000 – a huge sum for the time.

The growing shortage of money impacted gates still further. At Goodison, less than 60,000 fans witnessed the first two home games of the 1975/76 season, a figure that would have been close to the opening match a decade before. With Football League rules dictating a minimum admission price of 65p, attendances were falling around the country – although Bingham's controversial opinion that increasing unemployment was the main factor was widely pilloried until he received support from the Liverpool chairman. After a crowd of just 27,000 watched the table-toppers at Anfield against Arsenal in early December 1975, John Smith claimed 'Because of the very high unemployment in this area, we can expect attendances to fall... people are pruning their personal budgets because of high living costs and the decline in attendances must be seen against the employment position.' Bingham responded by saying, 'I was very pleased to read Mr Smith's comments. He has confirmed what I have been saying all season.'

Bingham's theory gained credence in April 1976 when 16,974 attended the midweek home match against Stoke, a post-war low for a top-flight game at Goodison. 'It was very disappointing but it is a sign of the times,' said club secretary Jim Greenwood, 'People are finding that money is short but it is success they want.' Even with other sources of income, football finances were still largely dependent on gate money. A break-even figure of 30,000 meant Everton were vulnerable as crowds plummeted – from 40,000 to 27,000 per game in the 1975/76 season and there was a damaging loss of £43,000 reported at that year's AGM. Indeed, there was speculation during the stand-off with Bob Latchford that the club needed to sell the striker to balance the books. 'Soccer interest is declining on Merseyside,' said the *Liverpool Echo* portentously.

However, there was still a place for those believing there was a link between attendances and quality of football. As one disgruntled supporter stated about the drastic fall in Goodison attendances at the AGM, 'They [the supporters] are not prepared to come to watch this sort of rubbish. You get better matches in a box of Swan Vestas.'

Answers overseas

The mid-1970s also saw the genesis of that other modern phenomenon: lucrative overseas friendlies. Clubs previously journeyed abroad to northern Europe or, occasionally, places like the United States. But with increasing globalisation other, less established, countries realised the developmental and financial benefits from inviting English teams over. For Everton the first journey into the unknown was a two-week tour of Malaysia and Singapore in May 1974 that involved a friendly against a Malaysian XI plus a triangular tournament with Coventry City and Derby County. In front of big crowds, Bingham's team finished bottom of the mini-league but, with the tournament sponsored by a major brewery, the financial rewards compensated.

Three years later, Everton appeared in the King of Kings tournament in Rabat, Morocco, a tour that got off to an inauspicious start as Duncan McKenzie later recalled. 'I spoke French and was acting as interpreter on a trip to Morocco when Gordon [Lee] was asked how he liked Africa. He replied: "What do you mean Africa? Don't you know we're in Morocco?"' In their semi-final Everton lost on penalties to a full-strength Czechoslovakian national team before going down 1-0 to Moroccan champions WAK Casablanca in eighty degrees heat.

Two years later there was a surreal development when Everton left a freezing Britain and journeyed to Colonel Gaddafi's Libya in March 1979, where they inflicted the national side's first defeat at their new stadium in Tripoli. 'It was good experience and a useful work-out – especially with most of the games being snowed off in England,' said Lee afterwards. The *Daily Mirror* also reported in 2011 that the visit had an immediate impact with the Libyan leader joining the ranks of the club's celebrity fans. 'Gaddafi's love of the Toffees is said to have begun when Everton visited Libya on tour in 1979,' the paper claimed, 'The dictator was so impressed he immediately changed the Libyan national side's kit to all-blue, and rewarded each of Gordon Lee's side with a luxury Arabic carpet.' Puzzled customs officers at Heathrow confiscated the gifts. Two months later Lee's team returned for two friendlies against the Egyptian national team in front of a national television audience. After a 1-0 defeat in the first game, the visitors reversed the scoreline in the second, with a mass brawl after Trevor Ross' dismissal. But the perils of trips abroad remained: Lee partially blamed the dreadful performance in the 4-0 defeat by Ipswich at Goodison in February 1980 on a visit to Israel during the week.

Put it on your shirt

Football was slow to grasp commercial opportunities during the 1970s but in the latter half of the decade, with rising costs and liability for ground improvements following the 1977 Safety of Sports Grounds Act, clubs were keen to explore matchday sponsorship. Manchester City were the first to act in early 1977 and Everton followed suit later in the year – their first sponsored game was against the Maine Road club when a local firm, Brook Hire Ltd, paid the princely sum of £2,650 for the privilege. Initially the club expected to take £50,000 each season but there was clearly an untapped market: every home match had a specific sponsor during the following campaign as annual income from the venture increased to £75,000.

Nevertheless, the greatest prize of all was the controversial issue of shirt sponsorship. Embraced in places like West Germany – which had allowed company names on shirts since 1973 – in England the Football League and FA had stubbornly rejected overtures from clubs. Infamously non-league Kettering Town, under the direction of maverick Derek Dougan, wore shirts sponsored by Kettering Tyres in 1976 and found themselves threatened with a £1,000 fine. Twelve months later both the English governing bodies were still against it but such obstinacy merely delayed the inevitable and within twelve months the FA caved in. However, not all clubs were enthusiastic, for some putting a sponsor on the team kit was akin to desecrating holy ground and, more pertinently, the television ban on advertising limited their value.

But in the summer of 1979 Liverpool were the first English club to agree a shirt-sponsorship deal, worth £50,000 for twelve months, with Japanese electronics giant Hitachi. Although the agreement made financial sense, Hugh McIlvanney in the *Observer* voiced his concerns. 'A case can be made for such commercialism but it does not convince all of us,' he wrote, 'The impression given is that, for the moment, Liverpool may have lost track of their identity as a great football club and begun to see themselves primarily as a business concern.' But in a sport facing increasing costs and falling gates during an economic recession, clubs had to put themselves on a sound financial footing or risk extinction. As David Lacey noted in the *Guardian*, 'The fact that Liverpool, one of the wealthiest clubs in the League, feel the need for outside support may be taken as a symptom of soccer's growing liquidity problems.'

There were certainly financial constraints at Goodison by the end of the decade. Even with lengthy cup runs in 1976/77 there was a record loss of more than £100,000, with wages alone coming to more than £500,000. In the two years that followed, Gordon Lee's policy of paying large fees and wages for experienced players added a further strain and then the new freedom of contract regulations loosened clubs' hold over their stars, whilst the North American Soccer League was offering more attractive salaries and lifestyles to players in frozen Britain. Both developments hiked up wages.

The first sign of the tightening of the purse strings at Goodison came in early

1979. Lee was one of the many fans of Birmingham City's Trevor Francis and was keen to reunite the striker with Bob Latchford. 'They go together like fish and chips' Lee once said about the pair. The Everton boss had carefully put together a deal for £750,000 plus an unnamed player[62] with both Francis and Birmingham satisfied with the offer. At the eleventh hour, chairman Philip Carter surprisingly pulled the plug on the agreement, with Francis heading to the City Ground as Britain's first million-pound player. 'I don't think anyone can argue that Francis might have made a difference to us,' Carter said, 'But weighing that against the price asked I have got to say that Everton considered this carefully and decided in the overall interests of the club that we would not participate in this particular auction.' Carter went on to reasonably explain that the directors were only guardians of the club and therefore compelled to act in a sensible manner. 'If you look at the accounts over the years it is only too obvious that the club does not make a lot of money,' he explained, 'in the last few years we have been losing money.' However, the chairman's explanation cut no ice with the long-suffering fanbase, who had seen Liverpool buy players with real star quality like Kenny Dalglish and Graeme Souness over the previous eighteen months. Signing the coveted striker would have signalled Everton were still competing at the high end of the transfer market and given a struggling team a shot in the arm. 'We hear that there's not the money at Everton. Rubbish! It seems Forest, a so-called small-time club, could offer the money for Francis while the Everton directors couldn't,' wrote one supporter in an angry missive to the *Liverpool Echo*.

The club's annual report in the summer of 1979 reflected Everton's decline, their income of £1.6m being only two-thirds that of Liverpool, who were increasingly reaping the rewards of continual presence in Europe. Whereas Liverpool now had a multi-national company sponsoring them, Everton had a shirt deal with New Brighton firm Jaka Foods, who put Hafnia, one of their brand names, on the blue jersey.[63] However, this applied only to non-televised games and Carter attacked broadcasters for their inconsistent application of the rules. 'Sponsors of nearly every sport receive coverage on television which is

---

[62] Almost certainly Colin Todd, Everton having pipped Birmingham to his signature earlier in the campaign and he was unsettled at Goodison. Todd went to St Andrews later in the year.

[63] Whereas Liverpool players received various electronics goods following the Hitachi sponsorship, their rivals had to make do with a visit to Jaka Foods on the Wirral.

denied to football,' the Everton chairman complained, 'To me this doesn't make sense.' Carter was correct – television was the only winner, reaping increasing advertising revenues and audiences whilst attendances diminished. Meanwhile sponsors in golf, athletics and motor racing enjoyed exposure on the small screen denied to football, restricting potential deals to a third or a half of their true value.[64] Despite continual protests from Everton and Liverpool in particular, having just signed a four-year TV deal there was little the clubs could legally do and unsponsored shirts continued in televised matches until 1983.

Like the rest of football, in 1979/80 the club's financial position worsened. Gates had fallen to just under 29,000 against 40,000 two seasons before. Lee's transfer strategy had seen a net loss on deals of £820,000. The financial realpolitik priced Lee out of acquiring Chelsea's Ray Wilkins and Coventry's coveted striker Ian Wallace. Chester City's Ian Rush was another player Lee could not afford, the striker going to Liverpool for £300,000.[65] The manager therefore found himself in the invidious position that many of his successors faced: needing to offload to buy. 'If I could sell some players, then I could do some business,' he said, 'I haven't got £750,000 to spend. Not many clubs have that kind of money available.' Yet supporters could point out that chairman Carter had said in the summer that the board would always back their manager if he wanted an outstanding player.

The failure to get another deal over the line proved hugely significant. At the end of the 1979/80 campaign Lee's two main targets were Newcastle United's centre-forward Peter Withe and Bolton Wanderers midfielder Peter Reid. Withe eventually went to Aston Villa but Reid was positive about moving. A free agent after his contract expired, the Liverpool-born player admitted, 'I've got to be interested in joining a big club like Everton – and I think I could do a good job for them.' However, by early July, Reid seemed to be heading to Wolves before Lee

---

64 There were some inconsistencies in coverage. Film was broadcast of Everton's infamous defeat at Grimsby in October 1979 with the sponsors' names on their shirts. Conversely, TV companies could go to ludicrous lengths to avoid showing logos. In the away game at Crystal Palace in February 1981, Everton goalkeeper Jim McDonagh had to change into a spare jersey at half-time, one that had the sponsor's logo. The *Match of the Day* cameras then showed no close-up action in the visitors' penalty area in the second period to ensure they met broadcast rules.

65 Although Rush later incorrectly claimed that Lee did not fancy him. To complete a triumvirate of stories involving Anfield strikers past and present, Lee went on a scouting mission to watch John Aldridge play for Newport in the Welsh Cup final and tried to buy the unsettled David Fairclough from Liverpool.

stepped in with a bid of £600,000, which Bolton accepted. That was the easy bit. The hard part was getting Reid to agree terms, which proved a step too far. Then Arsenal subsequently withdrew from a £500,000 deal, after also rejecting Reid's pay demands.

Before the start of the season, Lee spoke about over the failure to land transfer targets and it did not take a genius to guess about whom he was talking. 'I worry about the future of the game,' the Everton boss commented, 'some of the demands being made by players are frightening, and if they continue they will put fellow members out of work.' But later Reid denied the accusations. 'There was all this stuff in the press about my "outrageous demand"', he claimed, 'All I did was compare the Everton and Arsenal offers with what Wolves have agreed to pay me. I'm not a greedy person. Ask anyone who knows me well.' Although nobody realised at the time, the failure to land the midfielder was a blessing in disguise for everyone at Everton bar Gordon Lee.

CHAPTER 17

Another false dawn

LEE WAS CERTAINLY A MANAGER UNDER PRESSURE IN THE SUMMER of 1980, not helped by some curious transfer dealings. At the AGM Philip Carter had stated that 'The board will find Gordon Lee extra resources in order to build a first class squad capable of winning the highest awards.' Although Carter would not provide the funds for Trevor Francis, the chairman had quietly told his manager that money was available to buy Paul Mariner from Ipswich, rumours indicating Bobby Robson was willing to sell. But Mariner stayed put. Elsewhere, Lee was finding it difficult. 'Gates are down and we have had a bad season financially,' he said, 'And it is harder for me to get players than it was twelve months ago because of our position in the league.' Consequently Lee made only one meaningful purchase, goalkeeper Jim McDonagh from Bolton for £250,000, after selling Brian Kidd to the Burnden Park club. Now effectively third choice, George Wood moved to Arsenal for £150,000. Lee unsuccessfully tried to lure Nottingham Forest's sought-after striker Garry Birtles to Goodison in a triple exchange for Bob Latchford, Andy King and Trevor Ross.

History repeated

After constantly claiming that a frictional pre-season in 1979 had a damaging long-term effect, Lee promptly fell out with two senior players. The Everton boss had wanted to offload Andy King but attracted little interest and, after an eighteen-year-old Steve McMahon had impressed in two pre-season friendlies, the former Luton player was dropped for the pre-season trip to Spain. Also left at home, Trevor Ross asked for a transfer before Lee ludicrously banned both players from talking to the press while the squad was abroad. 'This attitude of not letting players speak to the press dates back to Victorian times,' said PFA chairman Gordon Taylor, 'It doesn't make for good man management.'

Although Ross stayed, King left for QPR in a £400,000 deal in September. The midfielder later admitted off-the-field issues may have hastened the departure, with his bubbly nature undoubtedly at odds with Lee's regimented approach. Acting as the 'cheeky chappie' may have been acceptable in his teenage years but King's immaturity irked his manager. 'I was young and stupid, did some crazy things,' he told the *Sunday Express* two years later, 'I got a reputation for being a bit of a nutcase.' King also elaborated on his well-known gambling problems in the same interview:

> *I was down the betting shop every day. Don't ask me why I got hooked. Perhaps it was frustration, it used to bug me that some players came to the club for big money and rolled up in a nice new car because of their big percentage. I had broken my nose for Everton, busted my ankle, walked off the pitch dripping blood... yet I couldn't get the contract I thought I was worth. But someone else could have a stack of money and a new car before he had kicked a ball for the club.*

The midfielder gave further background to his leaving to *The Evertonian* in 1996. 'The football side was changing totally and ideas were different under Gordon Lee,' King explained, 'He changed the team constantly and we were always facing an uphill struggle to emulate those across the park. They were the greatest side in Europe at that time. Then I encountered injuries. And considering all that, I made the terrible mistake of going down to QPR for more money. That was a terrible decision.' Few players have had an affinity with the club like the bubbly midfielder and he was quickly longing for a return. 'I had gone from the First Division to the Second Division and then spent two years praying and begging to get a chance to come back to Goodison,' King admitted.

However, yet again, the Everton boss was showing no sign of learning any lessons. The negative headlines plus the involvement of the players' union was a carbon copy of twelve months before. 'Mr Lee said he didn't want a repeat of that this year,' wrote Charles Lambert in the *Liverpool Echo*, 'Yet here we are, one week from the big kick-off, and there is every sign of a rift between the manager and two of his players.' At an acrimonious shareholders' meeting, one attendee asked, 'Are we content with mediocrity... All I can see are overweight, undertrained, overpaid mercenaries playing for Everton.' However, in a stormy question-and-answer session at Everton Supporters Club, Lee provided a rallying call that brought the audience to its feet:

> *I know the standards at Everton are high. But don't misread me. There is no way I am going to hide and run into a corner. I like players who stand up to be counted and are not frightened to make mistakes. I am no different as a manager. I will stand up and be counted and be criticised – but no way am I going to run away. I might get the sack, but I don't lack courage to try and do a good job.*

'The ambition here is boundless'

The brief film clip regularly pops up on social media. Before the home game against Wolves on the first Saturday of September 1980, *Match of the Day* reporter Tony Gubba wanders around the Goodison trophy room. 'Ambition here is boundless,' Gubba claims before pointing to a large cabinet and explaining: 'When they built this Fort Knox showcase a few seasons ago in which to hang the club's sporting scalps, they sent a man round to Liverpool with a tape to measure the European Cup just to ensure they built a compartment big enough to take that great trophy when they win it.' The BBC man – who had lived in Liverpool – then walked in front of the new cabinet and almost apologetically informs viewers that it contains only a large clock and a presentation box holding five medals originally belonging to 1930s stalwart Jimmy Stein.

Reflecting on the start of the 1980/81 season, Charles Lambert tells Gubba that Everton 'haven't set off in a style that convinces fans that better times are ahead.' That was a fair assessment. With little money to spend and feeling ordinary players were overpriced, the manager would consequently place faith in his youngsters. Lee had signed one of those prospects early in the year. Graeme Sharp was a nineteen-year-old striker making a name with Dumbarton – having scored sixteen goals in 34 games during that season. The young Glaswegian was first rumoured to be heading south in February when Wolves were said to be making a £150,000 bid,[66] with Manchester United, Southampton and Notts County also interested. After watching Sharp at the end of March, Lee agreed a deal with the Scottish side for £127,500 but Dumbarton had promised to sell the

---

66 The plan, ironically, being for Sharp to be the understudy to Andy Gray at Molineux

youngster to Aston Villa, and the change of mind famously angered their boss Ron Saunders. 'This is just the sort of action that brings the game of football into disrepute, it is disgraceful' the Villa manager remarked, 'I am complaining about Dumbarton, whose word is clearly not their bond.'

The young Scot started at Sunderland on the opening day of the season when Lee fielded six players aged 22 years and under whilst nineteen-year-old Paul Lodge sat on the bench. Although laudable, the visitors struggled at a sweltering Roker Park, a 3-1 loss featuring a comical own goal by Billy Wright who coolly lobbed the ball over the advancing Jim McDonagh. Former Blues midfielder Mick Buckley was in the Sunderland team and he piped out a warning: 'Gordon Lee is a genuine manager but all the chopping and changing can't be doing his team any good. I think he is asking too much of the kids he has put into the side.'

Peter Eastoe was significantly a goalscoring substitute and the striker went on to enjoy his best season at Goodison. The Tamworth-born forward was a precocious youngster, winning a string of England Youth caps but failed to break into the Wolves and QPR first-teams, either side of a profitable spell at Swindon that brought 43 goals in 91 league matches. Eastoe took some time to settle at Goodison before netting eight goals in sixteen games in early 1980. Much under-rated, he was a clever striker, especially when with back to goal and had a smooth appreciation of those around him. 'He treats the ball in the manner of the continental forward,' wrote Erlend Clouston in the *Guardian*, 'Not turning with it, but laying it off and using his pace to round his marker.' The 27-year-old was a cool finisher and perhaps only a lack of dribbling speed stopped him from reaching top class. Eastoe netted the winner in the opening home league game of the season against Leicester City and was outstanding against Wolves, scoring in a 2-0 victory. Lee told Gubba after the game: 'I think his first-half performance today was near international form, he played out of his skin, took his goal well – he's a very, very good player.'

The victory left Everton thirteenth but from nowhere Lee's outfit won their next five league games. Having not recorded an away victory for a year, Everton went to Villa Park and defeated the eventual champions 2-0, with Eastoe scoring a classic diving header. Seven days later, Crystal Palace, the 'Team of the Eighties', were vanquished 5-0 at Goodison. Clouston commented that Everton 'produced passages of sustained high quality play that must rank as the best seen at Goodison since 1970.' Just two weeks before there had been calls from supporters interviewed on *Match of the Day* for Lee to go, now they were giving the manager and his team a standing ovation at the end – BBC Radio Merseyside transmitted thirty seconds live without commentary. The game was a personal triumph for Bob Latchford, who plundered a ten-minute hat-trick and overtook Joe Royle as the club's leading post-war league goalscorer, with 103 in 224 games. On the following Saturday, Lee's team were even better in repeating the scoreline at bogey ground Highfield Road. 'Everton were brilliant and I don't believe anyone could have beaten them today,' said Sky Blues boss Gordon Milne, 'For us it was ninety minutes of torture. Everton were ruthless, clinical and heavily punished our mistakes.' The 5-0 thrashing could have been more, as the visitors twice struck the woodwork in the closing moments. A jubilant Lee proclaimed afterwards that 'quite simply, we were brilliant.'[67] A week later, his team overcame Southampton 2-1 in a tight game at Goodison.

A key factor in the revival was the influence of Steve McMahon. The Halewood-born youngster was famously a ball-boy at Goodison and took to first-team football with the abrasiveness and self-confidence that characterised his peak years later in the decade. 'He is a player with all-round qualities,' Lee said, 'He has the ability to pass, he has determination. He has awareness of defensive responsibilities, he can win the ball, get into scoring positions and finish by scoring goals.' The midfield dynamo got the first of his Everton career during a 3-1 midweek victory at Brighton when the visitors became the first club to reach 3,000 top-flight league games. 'Two months ago Gordon Lee must have been worrying about his job,' said Brighton boss Alan Mullery, 'Now he has got an admirable team playing excellent football.' A sixth successive league victory, their best run since the 1970 title run-in, left Everton third, after starting the season 50-1 outsiders for the title.[68]

Lee, admirably and uncharacteristically, had sacrificed his footballing principles by asking younger, more inexperienced players to play in an expansive style. 'I have had more satisfaction this season from matches we have drawn 2-2

---

67 The victories over Palace and Coventry remains the only time since 1931 that the Toffees have scored five goals or more in successive top-flight games.

68 Odds that incurred the wrath of one Everton fan, who was so annoyed that he smashed the screen on the counter of a Wirral bookmakers. The miscreant's defence in court was 'It was a disgrace that Everton should be quoted at such a price'. His reward was a £20 fine.

than I did last season from games we drew 0-0,' Lee later told the *Liverpool Echo*. 'Yet professionally, I can't really believe that's right. If you get away with a 0-0 draw, you have kept a clean sheet and that gives you something to build on and you might win the League.' However, the splendid sequence of results acted merely as a mirage. The defence was not good enough and the Toffees kept just one clean sheet in the next twelve league games, with only three victories. Mick Lyons had many qualities but he was unable to command the defence like Brian Labone, or, say, Roger Kenyon.

With football in crisis amid falling gates, Lee was also conscious that managers had an obligation to entertain and after an unlucky 2-1 defeat at Norwich City in November, Joe Royle – now a Canary – admitted, 'They are the best footballing Everton side I have seen.' Then after a thrilling 2-2 draw in the Potteries in early December, Lee said that 'I have had a lot of excitement from the majority of games we have played, and after the game at Stoke last week I went home thinking that the Everton supporters must have enjoyed the game too.' A 4-3 victory over Brighton at Goodison seven days later took Everton fifth. 'We are only five points behind the leaders... we are not doing badly,' Lee admitted. But two defeats over Christmas condemned Everton to mid-table mediocrity and, like twelve months before, Lee was now relying on the FA Cup.

CHAPTER 17

'They've got a big trophy cabinet and nothing to put in it'

LEE NEEDED A TROPHY BUT THE FATES WERE GOING TO PROVIDE little assistance in his efforts to remain at Goodison. With league form deteriorating to an alarming degree, in a familiar tale the only chance of success remained in the FA Cup. But the draw was unkind: knock-out specialists Arsenal, who were aiming for a fourth successive final appearance. A home game was the only consolation.

FA Cup third round, Arsenal (h)

The Gunners had not lost an FA Cup match outside of Wembley since February 1977, with just ten defeats in 68 games in the competition in a decade. 'They are well organised, with a lot of experience – more than we have – and they are difficult to score against,' Lee admitted, 'They are rarely involved in high-scoring games, but we have home advantage and we have got to make it pay.' The Everton manager's main decision was whether to retain the youthful central defensive partnership of Billy Wright and Kevin Ratcliffe or recall skipper Mick Lyons. Lee chose the former option which, in the context of the way the game panned out, proved crucial.

In front of a 34,000 crowd, the howling wind made playing conditions difficult and contributed to a dour encounter. With Asa Hartford and the outstanding Steve McMahon running the midfield, Everton enjoyed the bulk of possession but Terry Neill's outfit had not earned a miserly away reputation for nothing and the Everton attack of Imre Varadi and Peter Eastoe got little change out of the composed Gunners backline, with David O'Leary superb. After eighty minutes of neat Everton approach play that failed to breach Arsenal's yellow brick wall, Lee took off Varadi and brought on Lyons in attack – a time-honoured ploy. 'Making that change was like throwing a dice,' Lee admitted after the game. The intervention altered the flow of the contest and a direct approach reaped rewards five minutes from time. With a replay at Highbury on the cards, Joe McBride broke free on the left and crossed. After the game, the visitors' outstanding full-back Kenny Sansom described what happened next. 'I should have cleared the ball with my right foot but I tried to run it out to the corner flag with my left, nine times out of ten it would have been alright; instead it swung in late and bounced off my ankle into the net.'

With the visitors committed to attack, Everton broke away in the last minute and Lyons squeezed the ball in at the near post, although Willie Young's desperate clearance looked to have stopped it crossing the line. But linesman Peter Hindle flagged immediately and John Bailey rewarded him with a kiss. The 2-0 result was just about right, with James Mossop of the *Sunday Express* saying, 'The connoisseurs of the game – and I like to be included – will argue that Arsenal deserved all they got.' The Everton manager had enjoyed a bit of luck at the right time. 'I like to think we have beaten the favourites,' a jubilant Lee said, 'We needn't fear anybody now.' But the Monday lunchtime draw produced a contest against the club he feared and admired more than anyone else did.

FA Cup fourth round, Liverpool (h)

Four years after the defeat at Maine Road, Lee had the opportunity for some revenge at last.[69] But it was going to be tough. By the end of the 1970s, Merseyside derby matches had become niggling, soulless affairs. Lee's team always tended to become over-physical against better opponents and, with Paisley's players hardly shrinking violets, the games became frenzied and brutal. One, at Anfield in

---

[69] Liverpool had beaten non-league Altrincham in the third round at Anfield whilst Everton were overcoming Arsenal – 3 January, 1981 remains the last occasion both teams played at home simultaneously.

October 1979, remains the most diversely action-packed derby game of all-time.[70] Everton went into the fixture with an appalling disciplinary record, accumulating seventeen bookings, plus an Andy King red card against Wolves, in the opening months of the campaign.

After some shadow boxing in the opening ten minutes, Liverpool went ahead in comical circumstances. Mark Higgins headed down Alan Kennedy's speculative pass to Lyons, who promptly lobbed the ball over George Wood.[71] Everton equalised via a Brian Kidd header before Ray Kennedy put Liverpool ahead. Midway through the second period Andy King levelled matters via a third successive derby goal with the visitors' second and final attempt on target. There was mayhem three minutes later. There had been an undercurrent of bad feeling – Graeme Souness had been booked in the opening period essentially to calm him down – and Garry Stanley's robust tackle on David Johnson was a cue for an extraordinary twenty-man brawl in front of the Kop. Amid much pushing and shoving, Terry McDermott and Stanley exchanged haymakers and referee David Richardson sent both off.[72] After a comedy own goal, three further goals, two red cards and a boxing match between both teams, there was further drama moments later, albeit from an unexpected source. The Everton boss later described what happened. 'Jimmy McGregor [the Everton physio] keeps nudging me. "Look at this," he says, and I can't see anything,' Lee said in *Everton v Liverpool: A Celebration of the Merseyside Derby,* 'He digs me again, and says, "Hey – look at this." And then I see two policemen bringing this girl streaker round the ground.' With the naked intruder removed from the pitch, the game eventually finished 2-2.

---

[70] The game taking place on 20 October – a date synonymous with the fixture. Graeme Sharp scored a memorable winner at Anfield on that day in 1984. There was a rare postponement, through a waterlogged pitch, twelve years later. Finally, 20 October, 2007 witnessed a 2-1 defeat for Everton in possibly the only football match in history named after the referee.

[71] The own goal producing a priceless anecdote. That evening Lyons was enjoying a drink in the pub with Andy King, where an over-enthusiastic Everton supporter pestered the club captain. When King asked the fan to leave as an embarrassed Lyons wanted to be alone, things took an unexpected turn. Rather than abuse Lyons, the fan admitted, 'I'm made up with him. He's won me forty quid. I had him in the sweep to score the first goal.'

[72] Reported at the time to be the first dismissals in derby history, however research by the author in 2004 established that Everton's Alf Milward was sent off at Anfield in 1896.

The return game was possibly the most disgraceful Merseyside derby in its long history, on the day when Dixie Dean sadly passed away at Goodison. Referee George Courtney allowed the settling of scores from October and for several new feuds to continue unabated. Lee set the tone by placing Lyons up front, wearing the number five jersey, hoping that his captain's muscular presence would unsettle the Liverpool defence. However, with Hartford and Ross due to attend a disciplinary panel, there were early bookings in the space of thirty seconds for Kidd and Lyons, who both crossed the twenty-point mark to face suspensions themselves. 'William Ralph Dean, known to the world as Dixie, served football honourably and memorably during his lifetime,' wrote Colin Wood in the *Daily Mail*, 'But the men of the blue and red shamed it in his final hours.'

After nineteen minutes of over-physical play from the home team, including eight fouls in the opening ten minutes, the visitors went ahead. David Johnson fired home after George Wood had weakly blocked Kenny Dalglish at the edge of the box, rather than clearing out both the ball and Liverpool player. The Scot was also at fault for the second goal, losing the ball after being too feeble under pressure from Dalglish before Billy Wright handled Ray Kennedy's shot on the line. Lee claimed it was a foul afterwards, but Courtney quite rightly waved away Everton protests and Phil Neal converted from the spot.

The game continued its wicked way, full of ugly skirmishes and macho posturing before, on the hour mark, came the moment synonymous with this brutal encounter. A serious flashpoint was inevitable and when Jimmy Case clattered into Geoff Nulty, the challenge left the Everton player with shattered knee ligaments. Case farcically received a booking for an obvious red-card offence. Nulty left the field on a stretcher and never played again.[73] One incident, ten minutes from time, summed up proceedings. The Liverpool bench decided to remove Johnson from the fray, for getting too involved in petty squabbles. During that time, the Liverpool striker was booked for dissent. The 2-1 defeat left a desperate Everton in the relegation mire. 'Neither side can take credit from this shambles,' said Norman Wynne in *The People*. No manager showed any contrition in the aftermath, with Lee making little effort to shake off responsibility for his team's contribution to an ugly, abrasive contest. 'After what I saw today nothing

---

[73] Four years later Nulty's legal team issued writs to both Liverpool FC and Case, who received his when sitting on the substitute's bench for Brighton. There were no further reports of any action taken though.

surprises me,' he claimed, 'If I said what I thought of the referee I would probably be thrown into jail.' As ever the Everton manager also blamed the defeat on the fickle nature of the footballing fates, even though his side had been completely outplayed. 'There were three things that sickened me,' he complained, 'one was the Hansen foul on Ross which was in the penalty area. Then there was the foul on George Wood before they got a penalty. And the injury to Nulty was like a knife in the stomach.'

Paisley, meanwhile, hit back, 'It was a bit like playing against the Welsh rugby team at times. I thought we were at Cardiff Arms Park.' Although there was some truth in that, his players were far from innocent and Case was responsible for the worst moment of the game, which his manager naturally denied. 'I'm not condoning anything. It was a foul. But Jimmy never went in high. He had over-run the ball but his foot was on the ground when he challenged.'

The opening derby of the following campaign, in October 1980, provided a chance of restoring some credibility to the fixture. With English football in crisis, there was an acknowledged need to provide more entertainment and there was a call to arms from both managers for better fare. 'It is up to everyone to set a standard and keep filth out of the game,' said Paisley. Their players responded in brilliant style during a 2-2 draw, which featured chances galore in a game where Liverpool fought back from two goals down after 21 minutes. 'Pace, passion and little pause for thought delivered one of the great old style derby contests, a goalmouth thriller in which in the first half particularly the memories came too fast to absorb,' was Rob Hughes' reaction in the *Sunday Times*, 'That was Goodison yesterday when a ninety-minute adrenaline charge splendidly wiped away the smear of last March when a tackle by Case terminated the career of Geoff Nulty.'

By the time the two teams reconvened in the FA Cup three months later, Everton were sliding down the table. Meanwhile Liverpool were suffering a mid-season blip that would eventually lead to an uncharacteristic fifth place. Unsurprisingly, the demand for tickets was the main issue. When the rivals had last faced each other in the cup on Merseyside, at Goodison in March 1967, the provision of screens at Anfield allowed more than 100,000 fans across both grounds to watch Everton's victory. Like then, Liverpool's secretary Peter Robinson was the prime mover behind the screening of the game on the Saturday evening across Stanley Park but the FA, who wanted all ties played at 3pm, rebuffed the request. At a time of flagging interest in the game, such archaic thinking was anachronistic.[74]

Lee had several selection issues. Ever-present Jim McDonagh had picked up an ankle injury and Martin Hodge replaced him while Kevin Ratcliffe had impressed and retained his place at John Gidman's expense. Up front for the Toffees was Imre Varadi, who had brought some much-needed pace to the team after replacing the injured Bob Latchford before Christmas. 'His pace may frighten opponents,' Lee once said, 'But his finishing frightens the life out of me.' The cup tie would see both characteristics. Paisley's team were missing the injured Alan Hansen and Alan Kennedy. On a beautifully crisp and sunny winter afternoon, Liverpool were the marginal favourites at 6/4, against 15/8 for the home team.

The other notable aspect of the game was the referee: Clive Thomas. To his undoubted pleasure, on the night before the game BBC Radio Merseyside interviewed the Welshman while he relaxed in the swimming pool of the city centre's Holiday Inn hotel. Booed onto the pitch, the theatrical Thomas virtually danced his way to the halfway line in a show of publicity-conscious defiance. In truth, he had a quite superb game, ensuring matters never got out of control, although there were 46 fouls and six players booked – literally, as the previous week had seen the termination of the first attempted use of yellow and red cards.

Everton maintained a breakneck speed throughout, channelling their aggression in a more controlled manner than the infamous game ten months earlier. Although as Hugh McIlvanney noted in the *Observer* after twelve fouls in the first fifteen minutes, 'From the start the players were inclined to give the ball the kind of attention that a pork chop might have expected from a pack of ravenous dogs.' To the delight of home supporters in the sell-out crowd of 53,804, paying a record £112,524 in gate receipts, on seventeen minutes Everton went ahead. The ball was lobbed towards Asa Hartford in the inside-left channel and

---

[74] The clubs eventually struck a deal with the London-based Viewsport to show the game at four venues: the Liverpool Stadium in the city centre, the Liverpool Odeon and ABC cinemas in Liverpool and Southport, with unplanned technical problems at the latter. Workers could only start installation in the early hours of the Saturday morning, due to a late-night showing of another type of blue movie. The £5.50 price of entry – twice as much as the dearest stand ticket at Goodison – proved prohibitive and interest was poor, with barely 300 people present at the 3,500 capacity Liverpool Stadium. Kenneth Wolstenholme was the commentator for the game.

after Terry McDermott missed the interception, the Scot played in Peter Eastoe. Ray Clemence partially blocked the Everton striker's shot and the fans in the Gwladys Street agonisingly held their breath as a desperate Phil Neal pursued the ball as it trickled towards the goal. Although the England full-back reached the ball before it crossed the line, his hooked clearance struck the onrushing Avi Cohen and rebounded into the net.[75]

The home side retained an element of control, with Varadi a threat, constantly moving to wide positions to test the Liverpool full-backs. That said, Liverpool had their best chance to equalise just before the break. Kenny Dalglish was at his best when receiving the ball with his back to goal and the Scot wriggled away from Ratcliffe brilliantly, only to see his left-footed shot strike the inside of the diving Martin Hodge's thigh and go out for a corner. Perhaps, for once, the fates were smiling on Everton. Further indications they were came when the teams appeared after the break, Dalglish remaining in the dressing room to get stitches in a gashed foot. (Although the forward's absence went unnoticed to Kenneth Wolstenholme, who only realised the Scot was not on the pitch with fifteen minutes left.)

The game's only real flashpoint came early in the second half. John Bailey's back-pass was half-a-yard short and substitute Jimmy Case – public enemy number one at Goodison – slid in and caught Hodge in the chest. Lyons stamped on Case as he lay on the ground and Graeme Souness waded into the Everton skipper. Referee Thomas managed to put a lid on proceedings before they got out of hand. 'I was acting like a boxing referee breaking up clinches,' he said in his autobiography, 'And I gave Case a public warning. Souness was a lucky man not to be sent off.'

After Clemence had saved brilliantly from Varadi, the Everton man added a second on the hour mark. Phil Thompson got caught underneath Asa Hartford's high, hanging ball from deep on the Everton right and, after the defender slipped, Eamonn O'Keefe nipped in. The midfielder appeared to take the ball too wide in rounding Clemence, however Varadi scored at the far post from his measured

---

75 Eastoe claimed the goal at the time – the ball was over the line 'by at least two feet' he said – and Everton credited him as the scorer in their records. Liverpool said it was an own goal by Cohen. Nevertheless, that evening's *Match Night* on Granada showed conclusively that Phil Neal had cleared the ball before it crossed the line. The confusion provided a headache for the bookmakers, who in a rare show of kindness paid out on Eastoe (at 9-1 to be first scorer) on the basis the club had attributed the goal to the striker.

pass. Or it looked like a pass. In his excellent autobiography, *I Only Wanted to Play Football*, O'Keefe made a confession:

> *I was in – with only Ray Clemence, the Liverpool goalkeeper to beat. I took it past Clemence, to the left but – horror! – had I taken it too far? I stopped the ball to the left of the penalty area – it was an acute angle but 'scoreable'. Clemence was trying to get back into his goal area and I bent it with my right... Nightmare! I'd overcooked it and it was going to miss the far post when, from nowhere, came Imre Varadi and volleyed the ball into the roof of the net!*

Famously, the man born in Hammersmith to Hungarian parents[76] then mistakenly ran towards the Liverpool supporters massed in the Enclosure, only to receive a pie in the face for his celebrations. However, a frantic ending rekindled memories of October after Case converted Ray Kennedy's cross at the near post with fourteen minutes left. Varadi then missing two gilt-edged chances, the second of which occurred when the forward rounded Clemence, only to scoop the ball over the bar before Everton hung on for a memorable victory. 'It hasn't been a game of classic open football,' said Granada TV commentator Gerald Sinstadt at the finish, 'It's been a game we will not forget.' Hundreds of young supporters climbed the eight-foot high steel railings, most drawn to skipper Lyons, a winner at last after twenty derby matches. They were indeed symbolic scenes: the uniform tight jeans, Adidas trainers, Kicker boots and mushroom 'wedge' haircuts indicators of a new terrace culture.

A major factor in the victory was the outstanding performance of Steve McMahon, who tackled with aggression but used the ball intelligently. 'Liverpool's midfield has seldom looked so anonymous,' said Chris James in the *Daily Mirror*. Jubilant fans carried Lee into the Winslow pub.[77] The surprise victory also brought unusually kind words from Bob Paisley. 'In my 42 years with Liverpool

---

[76] After Varadi signed, Lee was asked about his nationality. 'He's Uranian,' was the reply.

[77] Lee's pre-match preparations did not go to plan. Eric Harrison handed two footballs to the Everton boss in the dressing room as the team-talk was taking place. When that finished Lee handed the balls back to Harrison who shouted, 'What the f--- have you done Gordon?' Both had 'Best Wishes, Gordon Lee' on them. They were the match-balls.

I can never recall an Everton team that has been stronger than us,' he admitted, 'We were playing into their hands and Everton were like vultures, I want them to go on and win the cup now.'

But the person who could take the greatest pride in the victory was skipper Mick Lyons. A match programme earlier in the season had asked the defender for his career highlight. 'Still hoping for one,' was the wistful reply. Following the derby victory, one of the bravest and most die-hard of all Evertonians could rest easy at last.

FA Cup fifth round, Southampton (a)

'We have been the unluckiest side of all in this season's competition,' said Gordon Lee of the fifth round tie, an away game after six successive home draws. 'The Cup is about fate, after we beat Liverpool, the last tie I would have picked was away to Southampton.' The draw had indeed produced one of the toughest challenges left. Kevin Keegan had joined the Saints during the previous summer and under his influence, Southampton had hovered around the periphery of the title race. Entering the encounter in prime form, Lawrie McMenemy's side were thirteen games unbeaten with ten victories, having accumulated 27 goals in that time. They were always formidable opponents at The Dell, having scored in every match during the campaign, while Everton had lost their previous four visits there without scoring. For Lee there was a chance of some redemption, for exactly two years before he had incurred widespread criticism after the infamous 3-0 defeat in icy conditions. The Saints boss was also feeling the pressure. 'This is the game of our lives – it's that difficult,' claimed McMenemy.

Thankfully for Lee, the late winter sunshine produced perfect playing conditions on the south coast in a tie not only played on Valentine's Day, but Keegan's thirtieth birthday. The Everton manager showed little love, assigning John Gidman to a man-to-man role, one which the defender performed to perfection. In a tight game largely played in a narrow channel either side of the halfway line, the visitors showed a defensive discipline sadly missing since autumn. Lee set up the backline with Billy Wright at right-back and Ratcliffe effectively playing as a sweeper behind Lyons. The future skipper was outstanding, showing the impeccable reading of the game and pace that characterised his later years. Lyons, on his 400th appearance for the club, missed the best opportunity of the game, heading just wide before the break when well-placed. In the second period, Varadi should have scored but allowed Southampton keeper Peter Wells to smother his shot. Although Jim McDonagh made three smart saves, the visitors were good value for their draw as Lyons triumphantly raised his fists to the 6,000 Everton fans. 'Bruising stuff, on a difficult pitch,' wrote Brian Glanville in the *Sunday Times*. 'You could, were you to be polite, call it typical Cup-tie football.' The Everton manager indirectly agreed with Glanville's view. 'That match was about courage and big hearts,' he said after the game, 'about commitment and physical strength.'

The two teams reunited at Goodison three days later, in front of 49,000 supporters – although there was probably more with many Gwladys Street season ticket holders housed in the Enclosure due to overcrowding. In another ragged encounter, chances were even scarcer than on the Saturday. The grim, soulless encounter drifted into extra time with no real likelihood of either breaking the deadlock, with the visitors replicating Everton's tactics on the south coast of containment and disciplined defence. The tie was heading for a third match when out of nowhere after 104 minutes came the only goal. John Gidman's measured delivery from the right was more potent than before, Lyons' flick appeared to catch the Saints defence off guard and Eamonn O'Keefe bustled his way through the challenge of two players before firing into the roof of the net. It was fairy-tale stuff for the Manchester-born midfielder, who two years earlier had been driving vans on the night shift for the *Guardian*, in order to focus on football during the day.

Although a poor game, the victory remains one of those famous evening matches under lights that act as the cornerstone of the Goodison legend. Kevin Keegan – with one eye probably on Anfield after his acrimonious departure four years before – paid tribute to the home support. 'The crowd won it for them… The fans are a credit to the club and I wish we had them down at The Dell,' the England skipper remarked, 'I wish Everton luck. It's about time they won something. They've got a big trophy cabinet and nothing to put in it.' At 7-2 joint-favourites with Spurs, the bookmakers thought they had a decent chance of doing so.

FA Cup sixth round, Manchester City (h)

'The way it's going we'll probably get Ipswich in the quarter-finals,' Lee said after the draw at The Dell, in typically optimistic fashion. They did not, but the last-eight tie was still tough. After rebuilding their league campaign with two successive wins, Everton were 11/10 favourites to beat City, who were a generous 5/2 to record their second Goodison victory of the campaign. In the opposition dugout was John Bond, who had not hidden from criticising the club (and Liverpool) in the past – possibly because of rejection for the assistant manager's role at Goodison in 1972. The former Norwich boss had rejuvenated City since taking over from the sacked Malcolm Allison the previous October, moving them into a mid-table position, just behind Everton. The Maine Road outfit had recently taken Liverpool to the limit in their League Cup semi-final and were unlucky to lose 2-1 on aggregate.

Apart from the suspended John Bailey, Everton were at full-strength while City welcomed back Tommy Hutchison from a pelvic strain. The winger was to become the pantomime villain in a bitterly-fought game that, even by old-school FA Cup standards, was a real blood and thunder affair in front of a sell-out crowd of 52,791 spectators. Everton were also battling history, having won only one of their previous twelve games against City.

Having seen how Everton's midfield had snuffed out Liverpool, Bond's side clearly attempted to fight fire with fire during a testing encounter that reflected the desire to succeed of two clubs living in the shadows of more glamorous neighbours. Consequently, they played with the fear and desperation associated with a semi-final, in a game of fifty fouls. 'Like two crazed tanker drivers fighting for the same mile of motorway,' Richard Bott wrote in the *Sunday Express*, 'They charged into a sixth-round tie that was reckless, tingling and often terrifying.' For some, those characteristics merely added to the occasion. 'Most of the afternoon was deeply entertaining with a marvellously exciting ebb and flow,' opined Leslie Duxbury in the *Observer*. That players would give no quarter was apparent even before battle commenced. Referee Peter Willis was about to let the visitors start proceedings when Mick Lyons reminded the official that City had won the toss to choose ends and the home team should be kicking-off. After a slow start on a soft, sticky surface, City took control and were unlucky not to go ahead when McDonagh saved a Kevin Reeves header and then Steve Mackenzie's fierce drive struck the bar. With City dominant and against the run of play, two minutes before the break Varadi broke free on the right and O'Keefe helped on his cross to Eastoe, who finished with clinical efficiency.

Having gone ahead at a psychologically important point, the home team then threw away their advantage immediately. In added time, Reeves headed down

Bobby McDonald's driven cross from the left and Gerry Gow neatly clipped the ball over McDonagh. 'They've equalised just when it mattered most, just when it mattered most,' proclaimed the great David Coleman on *Match of the Day*, in his final commentary on the ground. But referee Willis handed the home side another opportunity to seal a semi-final berth just five minutes into the second period. Imre Varadi's performances during the FA Cup had drawn tributes from outsiders, notably one footballing legend. 'He looks like a good Continental player,' Bill Shankly said, 'He can control the awkward ball, and that is enough to make him unique in today's football. Yes he's a very promising boy.' Varadi was superb against City, running young centre-half Tommy Caton ragged, and when the striker turned in the box and the defender hauled him to the ground, the referee awarded a penalty. A week before Trevor Ross and Steve McMahon both failed from the spot in the televised 3-2 victory at Crystal Palace, but the former bravely stepped forward and gave Joe Corrigan no chance.

Varadi took centre-stage shortly after. 'Ray as he is known at Everton lacks a bit of composure when he has got into a scoring position,' Lee confessed to Colin Malam in the *Sunday Telegraph* after the derby victory, 'I'm praying his finishing will improve with experience.' Those prayers sadly remained unanswered five minutes after the penalty. Varadi intercepted Bobby McDonald's careless back-pass, rounded Corrigan and watched in horror as his hurried shot went into the side-netting, albeit from a tight angle. The miss was to prove a (or maybe *the*) pivotal moment of Lee's reign. Everton continued to press after the let-off but failed to land the killer-blow and paid the penalty with five minutes remaining. The visitors broke out of defence and with the disorganised home backline in a blind panic, Mackenzie and Reeves cleverly set up Paul Power, who lobbed the ball over McDonagh before celebrating in front of the Manchester City fans at the Park End, who had outshouted a strangely muted home support during the game.

There was further drama within seconds when referee Willis dismissed Kevin Ratcliffe after he appeared to butt City's Tommy Hutchison by the corner flag, with the winger going to ground somewhat theatrically. The decision seemed a soft one but afterwards Hutchison, sporting a bruise over his left eye, told the waiting press: 'I didn't even hear a whistle. The next thing the lad butted me. I don't know whether it was intentional or not but he certainly hit me with his head.' Despite the best efforts of both sides, the game eventually ended all-square. Neither deserved to lose, but then again they had not done enough to secure a semi-final spot. Having said that, Lee was understandably the more frustrated figure at the end of the game. Twice Everton had City on the canvas but failed to finish their opponents off, primarily due to Varadi's crucial miss. Having won all ten home FA Cup ties as Everton manager, there was a real danger that game eleven would put Lee in mortal danger, with a difficult replay at Maine Road. 'Everything we did wrong today we'll do right on Wednesday,' proclaimed Lyons.

FA Cup sixth round replay, Manchester City (a)

Naturally, the closing moments of Saturday's game dominated the lead-up to the replay, with Lee slapping a ban on Ratcliffe from talking to the press but the future club skipper broke his silence. 'Hutchison got me sent off,' said the young defender, 'I'm disappointed that a player I admired got me sent off. If he hadn't made a meal of it, I wouldn't have had to go. A man butted hard enough to go down like a ton of bricks doesn't get up and take a free-kick. It was no more than a brush of heads.' However, the *Match of the Day* cameras appeared to support Hutchison's version of events. 'Everton must be trying to stir things up,' the winger said in response, 'Perhaps they want me to pull out of the replay, but there's no chance of that. Ratcliffe can say what he wants. Millions saw what happened on TV. What can I add to that?' Lee slapped a fine on Ratcliffe 'for intent and because he made contact' but tempered the punishment after analysing the video.

When the war of words had concluded there was still the replay. After the final whistle at Goodison, there had been an ugly altercation in the tunnel, when Everton players angrily confronted Hutchison but, thankfully, the encounter in rain-sodden Manchester was not the vendetta-driven affair some feared. In fact Willis described it as one of the best games he had refereed. The first half was evenly-contested with chances for both teams but, as the game progressed, the home side's taller and more experienced players appeared more suited to the mud. After a spell of City pressure, midway through the second period came the crucial moment of the game. McDonagh and Lyons both went for the same cross and the ball reached full-back Bobby McDonald at the edge of the box. The Scot's low left-footed drive skidded across the damp turf and reached the net via two deflections. For the first time in the tie, City were ahead and the shell-shocked visitors conceded a second goal minutes later when an unmarked McDonald headed home Hutchison's cross. With Everton heads dropping, it was almost cruel when Power ran from deep and took a return pass from Dennis Tueart before wrapping up the contest. Eastoe's late strike was merely a consolation for the 13,000 travelling fans and Lee's team, who sadly came up short once again.

Afterwards the Everton manager felt the second goal was crucial. 'We left McDonald unmarked and gave him a free header,' Lee complained. 'You can't expect to get away with that and we deserved to get punished. We probably deserved to lose the game because of that.' But when the dust had settled the Everton manager reflected positively on a thrilling cup run witnessed by more than 250,000 supporters. 'We have shown tremendous spirit and commitment and I think the fans have appreciated that,' Lee remarked. Yet there will still no Wembley day-out for his club and Derek Potter of the *Daily Express* brutally described Lee's outfit as 'A side that had already done enough to deserve a place in the final and now rather sadly ends up on the soccer refuse tip.' It was a harsh, but true, verdict with an unspoken question. Where did the defeat leave Gordon Lee?

CHAPTER 19

The day the trumpet blew

ALTHOUGH THE MANCHESTER CITY DEFEAT ENDED ANY CHANCE of a trophy, there was still much to play for. Twelve league games remained and although in tenth position, Everton had matches in hand and were a couple of victories off the European places. With entertaining football before Christmas and promising youngsters coming through, chairman Carter and the board were happy with progress, with the Everton boss claiming he had cash to improve the squad. For Lee, therefore, it was business as usual, the Everton boss talking about signing Peter Shilton for £750,000 and flying over to Germany to check on the unsettled Tony Woodcock at Cologne. Lee said that he had narrowed down his problem area 'to defence and attack' which left few others untouched, to be fair.

'Cartered' out

But the home game against Leeds United three days after the replay defeat cruelly defined the rest of the 1980/81 season. Ahead 1-0 and cruising Everton carelessly gave away two late goals in a damaging loss. The first of six successive defeats that took the Toffees to the periphery of the relegation zone before a further 2-0 home loss to Norwich City in mid-April proved disastrous. The home supporters within the paltry crowd of 16,254 slow-handclapped and booed the Everton players, with widespread chants of 'Lee out'. To add further pathos, Joe Royle scored his final career goal, a reminder for both parties of a glorious era that Lee had tried, and failed, to emulate. The chairman and directors met at the ground afterwards and Carter issued a terse statement:

The marked decline in our playing performances since March 11, when we were knocked out of the FA Cup after a very good run, is a matter of grave concern to the board. The board has backed Mr Lee whole-heartedly throughout his four and a quarter years at Everton but the positions of the manager and the coaching staff are now under review and a further announcement will be made before the end of the season.

There was a distinct lack of sensitivity in Carter's actions. The chairman had previously told Lee that he would be making a statement but did not disclose the content and the first time the Everton boss heard the words was when a radio reporter played them back. Although the board's frustration was understandable – under Lee the club was going backwards – in many ways the timing was nonsensical and reflected badly on the Goodison hierarchy. Lee was never going to convince the board that he was the right man for the job in a handful of games, on the contrary the Everton boss could only do himself further damage. Also, the statement only added pressure to a manager and squad facing a relegation fight. Therefore, Carter should have sacked him there and then. 'It is wrong and unfair that Mr Lee should be given this added burden,' wrote Charles Lambert in the *Liverpool Echo*, 'In any case, nothing Mr Lee does in the remaining five games will prove much that the board doesn't know already.' Notwithstanding the sympathy vote, Lambert went on to paint some painful home truths about the Everton boss:

Whatever happens in this period of 'review' Gordon Lee's record still stands as that of a man who has often looked like winning something but has never actually done so. In his four seasons at Goodison he has consistently been among football's also-rans. Often among the best of the rest. But never a winner. That is clearly not good enough for Everton, Saturday's statement didn't answer that problem either.

Lee later told Richard Bott in the *Sunday Express* that the black Saturday was 'the day the trumpet blew' but typically he came out fighting. 'I accept that I have made mistakes,' he responded, 'It's my job to get the best out of the players. It's my responsibility and I'm not going to run away. It's more important for me to

Billy Bingham returned to Goodison in 1973 a decade after leaving as a player. His four-year reign ended trophyless however. [ALAMY]

Mick Lyons at Anfield in February 1975. Few players wore the Everton shirt with greater pride and commitment but his career symbolised the club's frustrations during the decade. [COLORSPORT]

Duncan McKenzie at his welcoming press conference with Billy Bingham in December 1976. Remarkably, by this time John Moores had already decided to part company with the Everton boss. [ALAMY]

Peter Shilton and Bob Latchford share a joke at the Victoria Ground in February 1977. The striker was at the start of a golden two-year period at the club while supporters felt the missed opportunities to buy Shilton were hugely damaging. [COLORSPORT]

Martin Dobson celebrating Duncan McKenzie's equaliser at Maine Road in April 1977. The midfielder was a cultured presence for both Billy Bingham and Gordon Lee. [COLORSPORT]

An infamous moment in Everton history. Bryan Hamilton believes he has scored a probable late winner at Maine Road in April 1977, but referee Clive Thomas thought differently. [ALAMY]

Bob Latchford celebrates reaching thirty league goals for the campaign in April 1978 in one of Goodison's most memorable moments. [ALAMY]

Brian Kidd puts Everton ahead from the spot in the FA Cup semi-final against West Ham at Villa Park in April 1980. The striker's second-half dismissal ultimately contributed to more heartache for Lee's team. [COLORSPORT]

Nobody worked harder to bring success to Goodison than manager Gordon Lee, but sadly there were no trophies to show for his four years in the dugout, although fans remember the first half of his reign fondly. [COLORSPORT]

Imre Varadi in action during the crucial FA Cup quarter-final against Manchester City in March 1981. His second-half miss with the goal at his mercy was a key moment in Gordon Lee's reign. [ALAMY]

Philip Carter welcomes new manager Howard Kendall in May 1981, the chairman's support two-and-a-half years later was rewarded with unparalleled success. [ALAMY]

Adrian Heath joins Everton for a club record fee of £700,000 in January 1982. Two years later his goals played a major part in the Goodison revival. [ALAMY]

Jim Arnold punches clear under pressure from United's Frank Stapleton in the FA Cup quarter-final at Old Trafford in March 1983. Despite the Irishman's last-gasp winner, the epic game showcased the enormous promise of Kendall's youthful side. [COLORSPORT]

A momentous day in Merseyside football history – the first derby match at Wembley in March 1984. The confidence from going head-to-head with their rivals in the League Cup final proved vital. [COLORSPORT]

Peter Reid drives past Liverpool's Mark Lawrenson in the 1984 League Cup final. The inspirational midfielder's contribution to Everton's success was priceless. [COLORSPORT]

Neville Southall in the FA Cup semi-final against Southampton in April 1984. 'The most consistent goalkeeper in the First Division this season,' the great Gordon Banks said at the time. [ALAMY]

The first sign that the balance of power on Merseyside was shifting, as Everton parade the Charity Shield at Wembley in August 1984 after a 1-0 victory over their closest rivals. [ALAMY]

A rare view of Trevor Steven's match-clinching goal against Bayern Munich sets the seal on Goodison's greatest game.
[JIM MALONE]

Graeme Sharp celebrates his title-clinching goal over QPR. After Howard Kendall rejected his transfer request earlier in the season, the Scot responded with thirty goals in all competitions.
[COLORSPORT]

Derek Mountfield opens the scoring against QPR on the day the title was clinched in May 1985, one of a remarkable fourteen goals that season for the centre-half. [COLORSPORT]

The two Kevins – Sheedy and club skipper Ratcliffe – after the title was clinched against QPR in May 1985, both men were crucial to the team's success. [ALAMY]

Kendall's team receive the acclaim of 50,000 Evertonians on the day the title was clinched, amidst emotional scenes, against QPR on Mayday Bank Holiday Monday. [JIM MALONE]

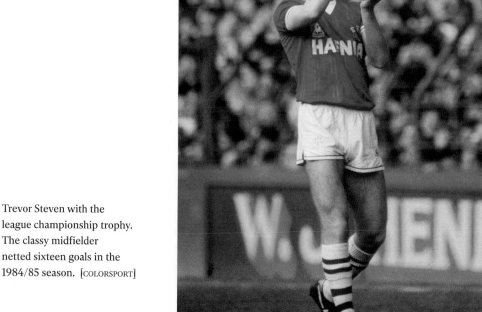

Trevor Steven with the league championship trophy. The classy midfielder netted sixteen goals in the 1984/85 season. [COLORSPORT]

Everton with the new First Division trophy before the West Ham game in May 1985. [COLORSPORT]

Howard Kendall at the De Kuip Stadium, Rotterdam, May 1985. The victory over Rapid Vienna established Everton as the best team in Europe. [ALAMY]

The Everton team line-up for the European Cup Winners' Cup final on the greatest night in the club's history. [COLORSPORT]

Always the man for the big occasion, Andy Gray celebrates opening the scoring in the European Cup Winners' Cup final. [ALAMY]

After joining the club for £250,000 in November 1983, Andy Gray became an Everton legend, capable of changing games through the force of his own personality. [COLORSPORT]

stand up now than ever before.' Brave words but the failings of the ill-balanced defence, one which habitually conceded costly late goals, put Lee on the brink. 'Successful sides don't lose goals, we have attacked we have entertained we have scored,' he said in the aftermath of Carter's statement, 'But I have to accept the balance has not been right.'

Everton unsurprisingly struggled and before the home match against Middlesbrough a week later – a 4-1 victory in front of just 15,706 fans – Lee spoke about the demands in what seemed a valedictory message. 'More than anything else in my career, I have wanted success for Everton,' he wrote in the matchday programme, 'And despite the pressure that has built up because of our recent results, nothing has changed... But at the end of the day, I am really a fatalist. I believe that teams are fated to win the League or Cup, and probably it's the same being a manager. I am either fated to do well at Everton or fated to lose my job.'

Lee lost his final home game on 25 April, 1981 against Stoke City. The 1-0 defeat featured the lowest post-war home gate in the top-flight of 15,532 spectators, but there was also a pointer to the future. Paul Bracewell was in the Stoke side, as was Adrian Heath, who had the privilege of netting the final Goodison goal of the Lee era. Two days after a 1-1 draw at Wolves on May Day Bank Holiday, Lee was sacked. 'There have been cup runs in each of Mr Lee's four seasons, but at Everton we have always seen the League Championship as the true measure,' Carter said. 'Our decision was reached after long and careful consideration, and with much regret.' The chairman's additional comment that 'He has worked extremely hard and impressed with his integrity. Unfortunately he has not been able to achieve the standard set,' was hardly a glowing testimony to Lee's four-year odyssey.

Goodbye Gordon

'I have always been a fatalist, I have always said and argued that you make your own luck in football. But now I begin to wonder,' Gordon Lee told Richard Bott in his final days as boss, repeating the message of the Middlesbrough programme, 'If I have made mistakes, at least I know what they are. And I will stick to my principles because I believe in them.'

There in a nutshell was Lee's management shortcomings set out in tablets of stone. Fatalism in the sense that as his Goodison tenure progressed, Lee increasingly referred to the 'bad luck' that he had suffered or expected to suffer, which did not exactly engender a sense of confidence. 'I've come to be a bit philosophical about cup ties,' the manager explained before the encounter against Manchester City, 'I've been involved in so many last-minute equalisers, near misses, and replays that I've stopped caring... perhaps, at long last someone up there will decide it's our turn.' Like several players of that era today, Lee continued to reference the times when the cards seemed unfairly stacked, taking aim at the usual targets. 'I will never forget when we played Liverpool in the FA Cup semi-final at Maine Road,' he wrote in the final home programme of the 1970s, 'I still believe we won that FA Cup-tie. I have seen the TV recording time and again, and I'm still convinced that we scored a winning goal and beat Liverpool. That was a horrible experience for all of us.' It was not necessarily 'horrible' as the disallowed goal did not remove Everton from the competition – Lee perhaps should have explained why his team failed to compete in the replay?

The suspicion therefore is that Lee's increasing belief that the fates had already plotted his managerial course engendered a certain type of paranoia, for example in his irrational and misguided outbursts against frozen pitches in early 1979. Referencing the three infamous league losses at Coventry, Wolves and Southampton, Lee said later in the year that 'playing on such surfaces gives a clear advantage to the less skilful team because the side which is capable of the better football has to sacrifice that extra ability in order to adapt... The fact that we lost those three games to sides not as good as ourselves proves my point because we were reluctant to abandon our footballing principles and were unable to adapt.' Lee should have abandoned his principles and adapted so, with that sort of mindset, in his final two years results were probably a series of self-fulfilling prophecies. Such negativity also informed his side's dreadful disciplinary record at the time – which he did little to suppress – that was also a reflection of Lee's frustrations in the dugout. 'If they had recorded as many points as cautions, the fear of relegation would surely have been banished long ago,' wrote Patrick Barclay in the *Guardian* in April 1980.

Even as he was about to lose his job, Lee was still referencing how the odds were stacked. 'It was a sickener to lose in the last minute of the replay of a [West Ham] semi-final last season, and this time we should have beaten Manchester City at Goodison,' he said, 'In most years, any side that beat Arsenal, Liverpool and Southampton would have virtually won the cup but we didn't have any easy games. I think a lot of people here thought it was going to be our year for the cup.'

Lee later remarked about Mick Lyons' own goal in the derby that 'you couldn't help asking yourself that couldn't have happened to Bob Paisley,' conveniently forgetting that Liverpool's Avi Cohen had put through his own net in the FA Cup fourth round tie at Goodison. Whether Paisley was still cursing his luck eighteen months later was debatable.

One of Billy Bingham's favourite sayings was that 'Excuses are easily found. Wise men look for reasons,' and that applies to Lee, who in the final years of his tenure focused far too much on the former and not enough at the latter. Managers who make their own luck are adaptable, have a strategy and a way of executing that plan. If things go wrong, they work out a solution. All that was sadly largely beyond the Everton boss. 'Mr Lee's failure at Everton was ultimately down to the fact that the club, with its demands and its traditions, was just a bit too big for him,' was Charles Lambert's conclusion in the *Liverpool Echo*.

There are two stages to a manager's timeline at a club. The first is motivating those players they have inherited, whilst filling the obvious gaps. A capable manager, which Lee undoubtedly was, can draw on their experience and reputation and lift the dressing room to get results. Through focusing on his principle of hard graft, Lee was able to achieve that in his first two years in charge. 'When I arrived I felt the club was on course for the Second Division, but I got a good response from the players,' he said after his sacking, 'The two things a manager hasn't got is [sic] time and money. I weighed the financial situation up with the directors and the time factor. The only way to get immediate success was to get players with proven quality and experience in the right price bracket like Mike Pejic and Dave Thomas. This type of player needs a fresh challenge to start him off.'

Having bought some breathing space, the second stage is much more difficult – moving to the next level by building your own team, using your own players and in your own style. Most managers fail to achieve this, even if they have negotiated the opening challenge. (Joe Royle and Roberto Martinez are later examples at Goodison.) Lee's reign at Newcastle was too short to be tested on this[78] and at Everton the unyielding belief in his philosophy made the transition difficult. The Everton manager's main – and some would say, only – footballing creed was,

---

[78] Remarkably it took nearly four years for the two clubs to agree the compensation package due to Newcastle for Lee.

of course, that hard-work was everything, or as one correspondent to the *Liverpool Echo* remarked: 'His belief that workhorses can match truly talented players over a forty-two game season.' 'People are knocking me, but all I am doing is to stick by the principles I believe in,' Lee said in early 1979, 'If the championship slips away and I get the sack I will still stick to the principles and thoughts I have about football.' However, after the 1-0 victory at Chelsea on the opening day of the 1978/79 campaign, Richard Yallop summed up the Lee philosophy in the *Guardian*:

> *Close seasons come and go, but nothing changes Everton, or their manager. The same efficiency, organisation and physical application provides the foundation for occasional glimpses of skill outside the ordinary, and there is the same professionalism in Gordon Lee, who observed that his side stopped running towards the end on Saturday because of the heat.*

The final quote is the important one, hinting of Lee's flawed obsession with being a footballing perfectionist to the detriment of the bigger picture. Lee said the best derby he took part in was a goalless draw in 1977. 'Every player denied everybody else,' he explained, 'There was so much closing down, nobody could pass the ball. I remember thinking when I got home that, of its kind, it was almost the perfect game by both sides. It was an exhibition of how to be a good player when not in possession of the ball.' With beliefs like this, Lee therefore largely ignored the wider creativity needed by his team to derive real progress.

The short-term nature of his initial transfer activity also hindered the Everton manager's chances of building something long-term at Goodison. 'Having been third and fourth in the League and missing out in the semi-final of the cup, frustration sets in,' he said about his ageing players, 'They see their hopes of success going further away because they are a year older.' Those frustrations resulted in the great revolt of the summer of 1979 – essentially a vote of no confidence from senior players in the future direction of the club under his stewardship.

Lee's recruitment was neither inspiring nor well-planned. Although the Everton boss could argue he had bought Dave Thomas, thereafter few acquisitions – if any – appreciably enhanced the quality of the squad. He should have brought in younger blood in the summer of 1978 and subsequent new arrivals were largely at the same age and level (or even worse) than those they replaced. Lee swapped a 31-year-old Martin Dobson for Asa Hartford, who was nearing thirty and cost a club-record fee, which was not good business. Jim McDonagh for George Wood. Lee spent more than half-a-million pounds on Garry Stanley and Gary Megson in midfield and recouped the money by selling Andy King. Not only that, but there was little logic in his dealings. During the summer of 1979, having told Geoff Nulty to fill a familiar role at the back like at Newcastle, Lee then spent £300,000 on Colin Todd three weeks later, forcing the 29-year-old into the middle of the park when, by his own admission, his legs had gone. Lee then sold Thomas which left no senior winger at the club, but six midfielders.

The other feeling is that, by blocking the move for Trevor Francis in early 1979, Philip Carter did not have 100 percent confidence in his manager. Even at that stage, with the team struggling on the pitch and Lee increasingly agitated off it, the suspicion is the chairman realised his manager was not good enough to justify handing over a British record fee. However, his track record over the previous two years earned some security. That stasis continued until a shortage of cash forced the manager down the route of fielding a younger team. Consequently, there was a huge turnover of playing staff. Lee used 49 players at Goodison and only four of the eleven brought in during his first two years were still there at the end. Lee also knew his transfer policy restricted youth, saying, 'It's true that the club has bought a large number of its first team players, and, consequently, the apprentices and young professionals possibly felt they would have to wait a long time for a chance.'

There was an over-reliance on out-of-form players throughout the second half of his reign and little evidence that Lee knew his best team. A relatively minor selection issue in the 1-0 home defeat to Manchester United in March 1981 crystallised the manager's relative absence of footballing nous and imagination. Lee picked Kevin Ratcliffe as substitute and, in the second half, took off John Bailey and replaced him with the future Everton skipper. When there was only one substitute, Lee was swapping left-backs at home when trailing.

These shortcomings ultimately produced poor results against the big clubs of the time. Although his derby record was not the worst – four defeats in twelve games – results against the better teams were generally rotten. Even in Lee's first two seasons in charge, Everton were effectively flat-track bullies, rarely troubling the leading sides in the division. Lee managed Everton in 35 away games over four years against Liverpool, Nottingham Forest, both Manchester teams, both north London clubs plus Leeds United and West Brom. There was just one victory, at Old Trafford in March 1978. Those who queried whether the Everton manager's belief that hard-work was enough to get results against quality opponents were correct. Moreover, as many have said since, the departure of Steve Burtenshaw and appointment of Eric Harrison was also a major contributor to Lee's ultimate downfall. 'Eric Harrison was in your face and a bit OTT,' Kevin Ratcliffe told author Simon Hart for his series of hugely enjoyable interviews with Everton players of the time, *Here We Go: Everton in the 1980s*, 'He would make you a bag of nerves shouting at you and his promotion from reserve-team football didn't go down well with the first-teamers losing Steve and getting Eric, a non-league player.'

For all his obvious faults, there was a certain amount of romantic tragedy about Lee's time in charge. Although it went awry later, the manager really could not have done more in his first two years. For many Evertonians of a certain generation, the 1977/78 season remains their favourite campaign, even ahead of the successful times a decade later. Lee gave debuts to Kevin Ratcliffe and Graeme Sharp while Gary Stevens and Kevin Richardson both came to the club on his watch and were first-team regulars shortly after his departure. Lee also signed John Bailey from Blackburn Rovers and tried to acquire Peter Reid. Younger players such as Steve McMahon, Martin Hodge, Gary Megson and Brian Burrows went on to have long and productive careers elsewhere.

But ultimately, like virtually all managerial jobs, his tenure ended in failure. Asked by the *Liverpool Echo* in 1997 to reflect on his departure, the fatalist in him came to the surface again, when recalling the pivotal moment of his reign:

We're 2-1 up against Manchester City in the FA Cup quarter-finals. We've beaten Arsenal, Liverpool and Southampton and our name's on the trophy. Eight minutes or so to go, Imre Varadi is clean through. It's so simple he's got to score. He CANNOT miss! Joe Corrigan knows he's beaten. He's saying 'put it where you like, son'. So 'Ray' puts it past a post. Right at the death, Paul Power tries a lob. Jim McDonagh is off his line and he's never going to get to it. It's 2-2 and, instead of relishing a semi-final, we're facing a replay. We lose that 3-1 and we're out of the Cup. And that's the end of me, too.

Yet also beyond doubt is that Lee was a decent man. Those who dealt with him appreciated his courtesy. After Nottingham Forest defeated Everton 3-1 on the opening day of the 1977/78 season, Brian Clough said, 'I feel sorry for beating an honest man like Gordon Lee when there's a lot of crooks I'd like to stuff.' Before joining, Lee told the Everton directors he put job satisfaction and a settled home-life above anything else. 'My ultimate loyalty is to my family,' the new appointee said.

As someone who thought only about football, his absent-mindedness produced a wealth of glorious anecdotes. The famous tale of Steve Burtenshaw discovering that the Everton manager was still in his slippers when Lee was driving them both to Newcastle on a scouting mission. The boss was still wearing them with his suit inside St James Park. Mick Lyons later described working with his manager to the *Liverpool Echo*:

> *Gordon was determined to bring success to Everton. Every conversation you had with him eventually turned back to football. We would be playing cards and he would throw down an eight and call it a 'Martin Dobbo'. On one occasion we had a long coach journey home from an away game. It was very hot and we stopped at a pub for a meal and a few pints. I ended up sitting next to Gordon and as soon as I put the drinks on the table, he was on about our performance. He used the glasses to explain himself and my pint was the centre forward. Every time I tried to pick it up, he would say 'Leave Latchy alone for a minute'.*

One of the mysteries of Gordon Lee is his post-Everton career. Here was a manager who had, at most, two seasons of failure in more than a decade in the dugout. At Newcastle and Everton he had challenged at the top of the table and possessed an excellent record in cup competitions. 'I can think of only five or six managers who have a better track record than me – Brian Clough, Bob Paisley, Bobby Robson, Terry Neill, Ron Saunders and, possibly, Dave Sexton,' he correctly claimed. Fourteen clubs offered Lee jobs, but surprisingly none were First Division. Of those, only Chelsea had experienced any sort of success. Lee wanted the Stoke City role, but the board went for Richie Barker. West Brom also rejected the former Everton boss, who then turned down the Wolves job in January 1982 – a wise move as they were struggling financially and then relegated from the First Division.

Lee, with more experience and ability than most managers in the top-flight during the first half of the 1980s, eventually found himself in the Third Division with Preston[79] for two years. In December 1985, the Irish FA interviewed him for the Republic of Ireland manager's role (a couple of hours after Jack Charlton) in the glamorous surroundings of Knutsford services. After a two-year sojourn at KR Reykjavik ended in 1987, his final job was caretaker boss at Leicester City four years later. But Goodison defined Lee. Once asked about how he regarded his time at the club, he replied, 'It depends what you call success, but I will never accept it as failure.'

---

[79] At least the former Everton manager was consistent in his message. Interviewed by Jimmy Armfield in the *Daily Express* on taking the job, Lee told the great man, 'We were 2-1 up against Manchester City in the quarter-final. Imre Varadi could have made it 3-1. He missed the chance and five minutes from time City equalised. In the end they won. If Varadi had scored I could still be at Everton and John Bond might be out of work. Football's like that.'

CHAPTER 20

The impossible job

'Everton simply cannot afford to get it wrong this time.' The words of Peter Parry, chairman of the Shareholders' Association, about the search for a new manager. Parry was correct too. After two failed attempts to replicate the success of the Catterick years and more than a decade without a trophy, Everton had fallen behind their traditional rivals, particularly those across Stanley Park. With the scourge of hooliganism and the economic recession continuing to erode attendances, ongoing failure on the pitch could have drastic financial consequences. 'Their [the board's] task will not be easy,' wrote Charles Lambert in the *Liverpool Echo*, 'Burdened as they are by the suspicion that if the next man fails to rehabilitate the club Liverpool will probably be even more firmly entrenched as the top dogs in the city by the time the next managerial change comes around.'

Although the consensus is that Howard Kendall was first choice, that was not the case – there were some reservations over his lack of top-flight managerial experience, after just two seasons at Blackburn Rovers. Bobby Robson had turned down a move to Goodison on two previous occasions but the hierarchy were intent initially on making it third time lucky, particularly as rumours hinted the future England manager wanted a change of scene. This development provided a glimmer of hope in the Goodison boardroom, yet the circumstances were different to before. Ipswich were in the UEFA Cup final and, under an earlier agreement made by league chairmen, clubs were not allowed to make an official approach during the season. Robson also did not come cheap and Ipswich's compensation demands had previously scared off mighty Barcelona. If Robson wanted to leave, other clubs would have been interested – Manchester United had just sacked Dave Sexton and Sunderland were preparing a £1 million offer over ten years. Everton also had a tour of Japan planned for the end of May and Philip Carter was sensibly keen to appoint a manager before then.

With the cards stacked against Robson, the bookmakers installed Kendall as favourite. However, because the fanbase wanted a big name, he was also a risk. 'It has been galling for Evertonians this week to realise that the club is no longer apparently in the market for a proven leader already with a top club,' wrote Lambert. With Robson unavailable, a lucrative contract tied Ron Saunders to Villa Park and the board saw Brian Clough, not for the first time, as a loose cannon. To Carter's credit the chairman did not make the same mistake as John Moores and turn the appointment into a public saga and, within a week of Lee's sacking, the board appointed their 34-year-old former player. The step was a brave one.

Home is the hero

For all the reasonable doubts about a lack of top-flight experience, Everton were still recruiting one of the most talented young managers in English football. After three years at Birmingham City, Kendall enjoyed two rewarding seasons at Stoke City, with eighteen months as a player-coach under the tutelage of Alan Durban. After helping the Potteries club back into the top-flight in 1979, Kendall took the reins at Blackburn Rovers, who had just suffered relegation to the Third Division. The new manager immediately took the Lancashire side to second-place and promotion. Durban's impact on Kendall was obvious – the Welshman had earned the reputation for being a somewhat dour but effective manager and, with just 58 goals in 46 league games, the Ewood Park outfit were the second-lowest scorers in the top half but possessed the meanest defence. 'The influence of Alan Durban has been obvious in his Blackburn team with its excellent defensive record, its rigid 4-4-2 and its lack of friends,' Patrick Barclay wrote of Kendall in the *Guardian*.

There was further progress in the 1980/81 campaign,[80] Blackburn narrowly missing out on promotion to the top-flight on the final day, having averaged just a goal per game but conceding only 29, which nobody else bettered. After two

---

[80] There was an unusual incident in Blackburn's game against Shrewsbury Town at the end of August 1980, when Kendall, who was not a renowned penalty taker, broke the goal-frame with a powerful spot-kick.

years at Ewood Park, Kendall's team had scored only 100 goals in 88 league games but conceded just 65. They were the statistics of a manager who knew how to win efficiently and recognised the importance of a clean sheet. That is a key point in assessing Kendall's Everton reign: in the dark days the side was not struggling due to a leaking defence, more a lack of goals. At Ewood Park, there were plenty of suitors elsewhere. Terry Venables left Crystal Palace for QPR in October 1980 and the Selhurst Park club offered Kendall the job.[81] Although initially saying that 'I am flattered and excited to be linked with a club like Palace' the Blackburn manager wisely, as it happened, remained in the north-west.

Given his record as Ewood Park, at the new manager's welcoming press conference Kendall was asked about his reputation as a defensive coach. 'That's most unfair,' he replied, 'There is no way I haven't encouraged everyone to play positively, including the defenders. The fact is that Blackburn happen to have better quality defenders... But I promise you this. There's no way I will ever string five players across the back or field three defenders in midfield.' Another statement hinted at future recruitment. 'If you haven't got players with a genuine will-to-win you've had it.' One man who was an advocate of the new appointee, notwithstanding querying his lack of experience, was the manager who brought Kendall to Goodison fourteen years before. 'I have been a great admirer of Howard ever since I had him as a player,' said Harry Catterick, 'I always thought he had it in him to be an outstanding manager.' The Everton great's other statement about Kendall was strangely prescient given events of late-1983. 'I can only plead with the fans: For God's sake be patient, and give the lad time. He's still learning and he can do a great job.'

There was also a sense of destiny about Kendall returning to Goodison as a boss. 'Coming back as manager was a fulfilment of a personal ambition,' he told James Mossop of the *Sunday Express*, 'When I left Stoke for Blackburn I was struck with one awful thought... in leaving the First Division I was forfeiting the chance of running out at Goodison again.'

The Magnificent Seven

When Kendall departed Everton in 1974 he was the best player at the club. The problem seven years later was that he was still one of the best. Consequently,

---

81 Not the last time the managerial trajectories of Venables and Kendall would cross of course.

Kendall needed to perform a complete overhaul of the squad, given the way Lee had failed to manage transfer dealings in his final years. The Everton manager was left with some positions overloaded with players of the same type. 'I will try and put it right as I can, but to finish fifteenth and nineteenth in the league suggests there is a lot of work to be done,' he admitted. The Everton manager's initial meeting with the players was brief, according to Eamonn O'Keefe. 'I'm sure that you're aware of my appointment and I intend to have a successful time here, with or without your support,' Kendall said, 'If anyone wants to leave, they can – but it will be in my time and it will be at a time that suits Everton Football Club. That's all gentlemen. I will no doubt talk to you at some stage in the future.' With the board making considerable funds available in the summer of 1981, the new boss was certainly active, bringing in the fabled 'Magnificent Seven'.

Number 1 – Alan Biley, £300,000, Derby County

With those infamous Rod Stewart blond locks, Leighton Buzzard always seemed an apt name for the birthplace of Alan Biley, a player defined by his haircut rather than a fruitful goalscoring career either side of a traumatic spell at Goodison. The streaky mullet was named the best footballers' 'barnet' of all-time in one 2003 poll. 'I'm so pleased, I can't tell you,' Biley later told the *Evertonian*, 'I made the *Observer* top ten of all time while I've gone from eighth to sixth and fourth in some papers.'

Yet such misplaced pride disguised the fact that, for a decade, the bubbly blond-bombshell was one of the most prolific and popular strikers outside the top-flight, with 93 league goals from 212 appearances before joining. When Kendall signed Biley in early July, he proclaimed: 'He has a proven goal-scoring record over several years… He has a lot of pace, an eye for goal, and is surprisingly good in the air for a lad of about five foot eight inches.' Biley wanted to bring some much-needed flamboyance to Goodison. 'I suppose my ideal is to be on stage, singing into the mike and juggling a football,' he declared after joining, 'You could say I'm a bit of a poser. But I enjoy life, love my football. And this move to Everton has been terrific.'

Although Kendall claimed Biley was a proven goalscorer, all but nine had been outside the top-flight and it was abundantly clear that, like Mickey Walsh, the striker had been over-promoted. That did not seem the case after a debut goal against Birmingham City, when Biley 'set Goodison alight with his pace, skill and enthusiasm and he thoroughly deserved his 88th minute goal,' according to the *Daily Mirror's* Chris James. 'I like to have a rapport with the fans,' the striker admitted afterwards, 'I like them to see me enjoying myself and in turn I like to see them enjoying themselves.' Sadly, after another goal at Leeds in his next outing, that rapport disappeared as Biley lost confidence and form.

Biley's time at Goodison appeared up as early as November, following a laboured 1-0 defeat at Arsenal. 'You don't make excuses when certain parts of your side haven't done it on the day... I would have taken off Alan Biley if I could,' Kendall said, after laying into the striker in the dressing room. 'He blamed me for the goal. He blamed me for the result, everything. And I make no bones about it, I came home on the coach and I cried my heart out,' the striker later told *The Evertonian*. With only one goal in nineteen matches, inevitably Biley was on the transfer list. 'Alan Biley has not been doing enough for me, and the situation has come to a head,' said Kendall. Biley eventually went to Portsmouth where he kept up his one-in-two goal ratio, becoming a Pompey hero as they romped to the Third Division title.

After finishing Biley continued his colourful career and Andy King was a regular visitor to his health club in Biggleswade. The charismatic striker also did the management rounds of local non-league sides where there was a familiar question of priorities. 'I always get in with really good hairdressers that will come to my club and do it if I want something special,' he declared, 'But at the moment I'm just back to the old highlights.'

Number 2 – Neville Southall, £150,000, Bury

£200 per game. The transfer fee of Everton's greatest post-war player. In his autobiography *Love Affairs and Marriage*, Kendall described being alerted to the ability of the great man by a good friend who was the landlord of The Neville pub in Llandudno – 'I knew then that we were fated,' Kendall wrote – and after watching the Welshman play for Winsford Town, he tried to sign Southall for Blackburn. But with two senior goalkeepers at Ewood Park the board rejected the request and he moved to Bury where he was player of the year. Unsurprisingly, the new Everton manager moved quickly and signed Southall.

Southall's first two seasons were stop-start affairs, with his own inexperience and the good form of Jim Arnold keeping him out for long periods. After the 5-0 home shellacking by Liverpool in November 1982, Southall went on loan to Port

Vale for a month. He was one of the best goalkeepers in the country within a year. 'When I first arrived I thought I would give it until Christmas and if I wasn't in the first team I'd go somewhere else,' he told the *Liverpool Echo* before his 1995 testimonial, 'I certainly never thought of a long term stay here.' Thankfully for Evertonians everywhere, it was.

Number 3 – Micky Thomas, exchange for John Gidman, Manchester United

Thomas was – and still is – one of the game's great characters. Gordon Lee had previously expressed an interest in signing the midfielder but when Ron Atkinson wanted full-back John Gidman, the two clubs agreed a swap deal, with Everton also receiving a cash adjustment. Thomas was a boyhood Toffee, who had watched the team from the Gwladys Street terraces and Kendall beat six other clubs to his signature.

A wiry, mobile presence, Thomas gave some much-needed craft and flair to the midfield until his Goodison career was strangled at birth in November. Having returned from injury, Thomas told Kendall that he did not want to go to Newcastle with the reserves. The manager warned him about the consequences but Thomas failed to turn up for the coach on Saturday morning and, forced to train with the juniors 48 hours later, Kendall sold him to Brighton during the week for £400,000. 'He refused to play, and that was that,' Kendall explained, 'There is no way any player on our staff tells the manager who he puts in this team. I sold him for the good of the club, myself and the fans.'

Although Kendall was quite correct in putting a marker down, this was not in the script when Thomas joined. 'I am an Evertonian through and through, and looking back I do regret what happened,' he later recalled, 'I regret that incident more than anything else that has ever happened to me in football.'

Number 4 – Mike Walsh, Jim McDonagh plus £90,000, Bolton Wanderers

The often detrimental comment that the 'Magnificent Seven' were six poor signings and a genius is incorrect with regards to Mike Walsh. The blond defender was a proven top-flight operator, who had performed excellently in the middle or at left-back for Bolton. Out of contract during the summer of 1981, the defender wrote to all 22 First Division managers to say he was available and Kendall pounced. 'He is a good player who would be a tremendous addition to the squad,' a delighted Everton boss said. The Irish international was in the Everton team from the start of the campaign, forming a solid central defensive partnership with Mick Lyons, but lost his place to Mark Higgins after a League Cup loss to Ipswich Town just before Christmas.

Some thought Walsh's absence was harsh, and one supporter voiced his concerns to the *Liverpool Echo*: 'Am I alone or are there other Evertonians who are mystified by the continued absence of Mike Walsh from the Everton line-up?' he enquired, 'Certainly my immediate stand season ticket neighbours and I share the view that Walsh is the most effective and polished defender on the books and one of the shrewdest buys Everton have made in seasons.' Mark Higgins had shown great form since replacing Walsh and Kendall – not usually a fan of two left-footed centre-halves[82] – was therefore not keen on breaking up a partnership with either Mick Lyons or Billy Wright. After that, Walsh played only a handful of games at left-back before leaving Goodison for the United States two years after his arrival. A sad ending perhaps for a player who was definitely not a dud.

Number 5 – Alan Ainscow, £250,000, Birmingham City

Keen to add to his midfield, Kendall made enquiries about several players, including Liverpool's Jimmy Case, but Liverpool thwarted any chances of a move when invoking the unwritten rule that players could not move directly between the two clubs. The Bolton-born midfielder had made 300 league appearances for Blackpool and Birmingham City in a decade as a professional when Kendall struck a £250,000 deal. 'Alan is one of the few quality natural right-sided players around who can play in midfield or break wide,' the manager said at his unveiling. The opinion seemed questionable at the time, and that was proved correct. Ainscow, although a hard-worker, was no better than the players Kendall inherited and left two years later after just 28 league appearances.

Number 6 – Mick Ferguson, £280,000, Coventry City

Mention the hirsute forward to Evertonians of a certain generation and they will mention one characteristic: the size of his feet. Contrary to popular belief, the 6ft 2in striker's shoe size was not five-and-a-half – they were a dainty size seven. Whether that differential affected the number of ankle injuries suffered by the

---

82 That is why the Everton manager passed on signing Terry Butcher in the summer of 1986, with Kevin Ratcliffe his central defensive partner.

former Coventry City player is debatable as he later claimed they were due to an incident during a reserve game against Everton, ironically enough, early in his career. Ferguson tangled with centre-half Ken McNaught, who fell awkwardly on the striker and tore his ankle out of the socket.

The Geordie's injuries were a shame, for during his limited career Ferguson looked an effective, if a slightly awkward player, with a terrific record of 67 goals in 164 top-flight games. Some big-name managers expressed an interest in signing the striker, most notably Brian Clough, but a swap deal involving Martin O'Neill collapsed at the last minute in early-1980. Later that season Coventry wanted John Gidman from Everton and offered Ferguson in exchange.

Kendall's move was a surprise, with Ferguson having played just three league games during the previous season. The Everton manager struck when Coventry were waiting for an FA tribunal to decide on the transfer fee for the 26-year-old to Notts County. Having learned of Ferguson's availability, Kendall completed the deal quickly. Valued at £900,000 eighteen months earlier, Kendall acquired Ferguson on the cheap. 'I think the price had something to do with my injury record because Howard Kendall took a gamble on me really,' the forward later told *The Evertonian*. But his boss did not agree at the time. 'Mick Ferguson is a big lad, a target player, one of the best in the business upstairs, I have been looking for someone like this for a while.'

However, despite the sugar-coating, the deal was risky and Ferguson's time at Everton summed up his career perfectly. Winning a first-team place in early October, the striker netted six goals in eight matches but hamstring – not ankle – problems sidelined him. Graeme Sharp took his place and never looked back. Confined to the reserves, Ferguson went on loan to Birmingham City before moving to St Andrews for £60,000 in June 1983.

Number 7 – Jim Arnold, £175,000, Blackburn Rovers

'I have worked with him for two years now and I believe he is one of the top keepers in the country.' Howard Kendall's words when signing the late bloomer, who was 18 when he took up the game. His route to Goodison was similar to the man who ultimately replaced him: Kendall was at Stoke City when he watched Arnold playing for non-league Stafford Rangers and on joining Blackburn bought the then local government accountant for £20,000.

Arnold was a key part of Blackburn's formidable defensive record under

Kendall and at Goodison showed the reliability and maturity his boss expected, but now in his early thirties it was unrealistic for the former England semi-professional to move into the top-bracket. Having said that, there were performances reminiscent of prime Southall, most notably at Old Trafford and Anfield on successive Saturdays in March 1983. The keeper did stay long enough to gain a European Cup Winners' Cup medal, a deserved reward for a fine professional who bought Kendall time while a legend was finding his feet.

The Magnificent One – Bob Latchford

The striker was out of contract at the end of 1980/81 campaign, after failing to recover from a hamstring injury sustained in November. Following three failed attempts at a comeback, Latchford eventually made it on the pitch as a substitute for sixteen minutes of Lee's final game. After speaking with Kendall, the striker, aware that Alan Biley had joined and Graeme Sharp was waiting in the wings, understandably told the new manager he wanted to leave for a new challenge. 'I must say I'm a little disappointed, because he can still do a lot for us,' the Everton boss admitted though. On departure Latchford's 138 goals in 289 appearances were a post-war club record.

With his details circulated to other clubs, during the summer the striker signed for Swansea for £125,000 and joined John Toshack's Merseyside colony. Latchford carried his scoring boots to south Wales, netting an excellent 36 goals in 75 appearances over two seasons. During that period, his mythical status ensured any return to Goodison generated excitement in the home crowd, who celebrated a consolation goal for Swansea in their 3-1 defeat in December 1981 like one of their own. After moving to Coventry City he was made captain for the day on his final visit as a player in September 1984. Since then Latchford has retained a certain amount of mystique, due to living abroad for twenty years, with infrequent trips 'home' attracting the same type of adoration that emanated from the terraces during his glory years. And rightly so, for the striker will always be an Everton legend.

CHAPTER 21

In the starting enclosure

FOUR DAYS BEFORE THE START OF THE 1981/82 SEASON, PHILIP
Carter spoke about the exciting new era at Goodison Park. 'We have had our
difficulties in the past, and we have had our good times,' he remarked. 'But it is
time we carved a new niche for ourselves in the First Division.' The chairman
complimented the new manager on his recruitment. 'The moves have been done
with skill and dexterity,' he said, 'All he now has to do is put the whole thing
together.' Significantly, Carter was speaking at a press event at Goodison Park
promoting the launch of the new executive boxes sited in the Goodison Road
Enclosure, as the game continued to look at new ways of generating income and
meeting the needs of supporters. The club had spent £150,000 on eleven suites
and they had rented all but one at a cost of £5,000 for the season.

Nevertheless, there was still the red shadow across Stanley Park. 'Liverpool's
run of success is like an albatross on the shoulders of Kendall whose predecessors
Gordon Lee and Billy Bingham, wilted under the weight of the same bird,' said
the *Daily Mail*. Encouragingly, the new manager, helped by his previous spell in
the city, wanted to use Liverpool's success as a means to driving ambition, not
torture. 'I'm well aware of the fierce competition across the way, but I don't lose
any sleep over it,' he said, 'Still it's time for Everton to become number one on
Merseyside, and everyone on the staff will be working to that end.' Newspaper
pictures had the Everton boss standing in front of the infamous cabinet that
existed for the European Cup. 'There is no point in having a trophy cabinet if
there's no room for the major prizes,' said the Everton chairman. If the Everton
boss needed an idea of the size of the task ahead, he only had to read the season's
preview in the *Observer*:

A monumental task. A big club which has won nothing since 1970, fans with a great hunger for success and a nostalgic longing for the return of players like 'the golden vision' Alex Young... Kendall's record suggests he can build a good, well-organised side. Whether he can supply the glamour the fans demand is another matter. Kendall won't be allowed time to rebuild slowly, and unless his hopes that Biley and Thomas will blossom out as exciting individuals are fulfilled, he could be in big trouble.

Early issues

Everton opened the 1981/82 campaign – the first to feature three points for a win – against Kendall's former club Birmingham City. At a sunlit Goodison before 33,000 spectators, the home team were victorious 3-1 in an enterprising display. But poor away form plagued Kendall's early months. Even with his best teams, he did not play an expansive game on opposition territory, the usual method was to keep it tight at the back and then open out later in the game. At Blackburn his successful team had averaged less than a goal a game – 38 in 44 league matches – on their travels. On taking up the job, the manager said bluntly, 'I want both an attractive and successful side, but if I had to make a choice I would rather have success.'

Therefore, in his early days, Kendall's side lacked penetration on the road. During a 1-0 loss at Southampton in early September the main tactic appeared to be long kicks from goalkeeper Arnold. 'Everton. Entertainment. The two concepts relate the way that chewing gum relates to rice pudding,' opined Chris Lightbown in the *Sunday Times*. Two weeks later the performance in a 3-0 loss at Spurs was worse. The Everton manager packed the defence with Micky Thomas playing as an auxiliary left-back, his team failing to register a single shot on target. 'Yesterday Howard Kendall brought Everton to White Hart Lane, where they were a disgrace,' wrote Brian Glanville in the same publication, 'How pleasing it was, after their miserably negative performance, to see them beaten by two goals from free-kicks and one from a penalty... they came to kill the game and ridicule the gimcrack new idea of three points for a win.'

By the middle of October, lying fourteenth after a 1-1 draw at West Ham United, the summer signings had largely failed to make an impact. In the previous game – a 3-1 defeat at Stoke City – the line-up had a distinct look of a Gordon Lee side, with seven from that era, including players like Trevor Ross and Eamonn O'Keefe, both of whom should have been in pastures new. 'Poor Bingham, poor Lee and now Howard Kendall,' commented one correspondent to the *Liverpool Echo*, 'Once more it seems we have an average team with average results, watched by average attendances.'

However, then came a game that pointed to better days. Bobby Robson's Ipswich Town arrived at Goodison as league leaders and title favourites, with one defeat in nine games. When Jim Arnold was declared unfit at the last minute, reserve keeper Southall was promoted for his first senior game at the club whilst Gary Stevens was making his home league debut. In the midst of an injury crisis, Kendall's team produced probably their best performance of the campaign, outplaying the visitors for a 2-1 victory that failed to reflect their dominance. 'Everton didn't just beat Ipswich, the pretenders to Liverpool's championship crown. They annihilated them!' proclaimed the *Sunday Mirror*. On two minutes, Mick Ferguson put the home team ahead with a glancing header but the East Anglian outfit equalised with a messy goal not in keeping with Everton's controlled performance. An initially shaky Southall failed to stop Eric Gates' lob and when Ross kicked off the line, the ball found its way back to the striker, who scored easily. Just before the break, Stevens netted the winner, the eighteen-year-old pouncing on a loose ball at the edge of the box to fire home with his left foot.

The home team continued to dictate in the second half, with Steve McMahon imperious in probably the best performance of his Everton career, the youngster completely overshadowing the vaunted Dutch pairing of Arnold Muhren and Frans Thijssen. After missing several chances to extend their lead, when the final whistle blew the players left the pitch to a standing ovation – the disappointingly low crowd of 25,000 a reflection of the prevailing economic conditions. 'The fans were ecstatic by the final whistle, rightly sensing that at last here was a team to challenge the best,' were Simon Inglis' words in the *Guardian*. Sadly, their wishes proved optimistic.

Tied up in Notts

The roots of success are in the most unusual of places. Famously Sir Alex Ferguson's triumphant two decades at Old Trafford followed Mark Robins' goal in an FA Cup third round tie at Nottingham Forest in January 1990. Coincidentally, across the Trent at Notts County's Meadow Lane, the origins of Everton's halcyon days of the mid-1980s are in a midweek league game on a freezing cold evening eight years before. Although they could not realise at the time, the crowd of 7,771 – the lowest in the division that season, reflecting the size of the home club and that Everton were not exactly the hottest ticket in town – saw a tantalising glimpse of the future.

Everton had gone into the encounter on the back of three successive league defeats, after rising to seventh following a first away league victory over Middlesbrough seven days after the Ipswich Town game. Signs were that Kendall's methods were having an impact and looking forward to the forthcoming Merseyside derby, the *Liverpool Echo's* Ian Hargraves talked up Everton's chances, especially as Liverpool were rebuilding themselves:

> *Though there can be little doubt that Liverpool will eventually come good again with a largely unfamiliar side, Everton's process of evolution is currently the more advanced. Without suggesting they are yet capable of the football that graced Goodison in the days of the Golden Vision, they do seem to have hit on a fairly successful, if relatively unambitious, formula based on hard work, with close support and considerable speed, both on and off the ball.*

Seven days before the visit to Anfield, John Bond's Manchester City, not for the first time, took Everton down a peg with a 1-0 win at Goodison when the away team reopened old wounds from the bitterly contested FA Cup tie in March. The bruising encounter managed to do the impossible – there were more fouls than in the quarter-final game and Everton supporters verbally abused Bond as he left the directors' box. 'There is bound to be a bit of crying from the home team because they lost,' he provocatively said afterwards, 'But I saw nothing really wrong with the way we went about it.' Kendall was furious: 'I shouldn't have to blow my top. Even the most uneducated football fan has seen something today that he recognises.' When told of Kendall's comments Bond abruptly ended his press conference, announcing, 'He's a new manager, he's one of those young, up and coming ones... he'll be all right.'

Kendall's managerial education was subject to another harsh lesson across Stanley Park seven days later. Hargraves, so confident about Everton's prospects beforehand, wrote afterwards: 'There is one cruel, inescapable conclusion to be drawn from Saturday's derby match. It is that, for all their spirit and determination, Everton still lag quite a long way behind their neighbours and deadly rivals when it comes to creative ability.' Beaten 3-1 by a vastly more experienced and skilful Liverpool team, the game was men against boys. That did not look the case during a competitive opening period before Bob Paisley's team moved up a gear in the second half and went ahead in the opening minutes with the type of goal good players and teams do not concede. John Bailey's misdirected throw-in back to Arnold went out for a corner, the keeper could not hold Ronnie Whelan's volley and Kenny Dalglish scored easily. The Scot found the net again within minutes and Ian Rush added a third as Stevens' clearance rebounded in off him. But for the gallant Arnold it could have been more, as the frustrated away team lost all discipline with Eamonn O'Keefe sent off for a violent lunge at Whelan.[83] With Lyons pushed up-front like some sort of recurring nightmare, Ferguson's late consolation was merely a footnote. The Kop serenaded the away fans at the Anfield Road end with a chant of 'You'll win f--- all again, Everton, Everton.'

For the first time, after the game people publicly questioned Kendall's rebuilding process. The summer transfer activity had merely added numbers and little else. 'In McMahon, Stevens, McBride and one or two others, manager Howard Kendall has men round whom he can build,' Hargraves wrote. 'But if his team are ever to match those feared rivals he is going to have to find some players of genuine class.' The view was a damning indictment of the absence of real quality in the manager's business. Apart from moving on John Gidman and Bob

---

[83] O'Keefe said, surprisingly, Kendall did not blame him back in the dressing room, the manager pointing out a characteristic missing that his mid-1980s team had in abundance. 'It turned out he was absolutely furious that nobody – not one person – from the Everton team had come over to back me up when the Liverpool lads had surrounded me,' O'Keefe said in his autobiography, 'He laid into them and, pointing at me, finished with: "... at least he showed some feelings whilst that lot took the p--- out of you."'

[84] Varadi was the subject of one of the more outlandish transfer stories of the time. Offered to Fourth Division Halifax Town for £30,000 in August 1980, nine months later a telegram was received at Goodison from a club who wanted the striker – Benfica. Although the Portuguese giants were deadly serious, the move fell through.

[85] Hartford's move was originally signposted in *City!* Granada TV's extraordinary fly-on-the-wall documentary about the Maine Road club largely filmed during the autumn of 1980. After a 3-0 home defeat to Liverpool, chairman Peter Swales suggests to manager Malcolm Allison that they should bring the Scottish midfielder back from Everton. 'Do me a favour,' was Allison's response. His successor John Bond was obviously more enthusiastic.

Latchford, to balance the books Kendall had sold the promising but still raw Imre Varadi to Newcastle (£100,000),[84] Asa Hartford to Manchester City (£375,000)[85] and Garry Stanley to Swansea City (£150,000). Accused of selling players superior to those purchased, Kendall pointed out that he had offered new deals to Latchford and Hartford but they moved elsewhere for more money. The subsequent specious argument that the signing of Southall counterbalanced the failures elsewhere is not correct.

That criticism heightened when a fortnight later came a catastrophic home defeat to bottom-of-the-table Sunderland, managed by Kendall mentor Alan Durban. When Peter Eastoe put the home team ahead on the hour a comfortable victory was on the cards, but Jim Arnold endured a calamitous afternoon, making three handling errors that led to a disallowed effort and two legitimate Sunderland goals that turned the game on its head. 'We threw it away. We made elementary mistakes. We're running out of time – or I am!' a furious Kendall said afterwards.

One of the problems was Kendall had inherited a bloated squad. 'There was so many chop and changes and I think nobody felt settled at that time. It wasn't only me,' Alan Biley later said, 'There must have been at least another ten players in the squad at the time that didn't see the tail end of that season.' By the middle of November, Kendall had used 22 players. 'As he goes back to the drawing board he must consider a twenty-third – himself!' the *Daily Mirror's* Derek Wallis suggested.

The Everton manager had retained his playing registration on joining the club but, having sold Hartford, the midfield was in desperate need of an experienced, creative presence and calls for the manager's return increased, especially with Steve McMahon and Paul Lodge injured for the midweek trip to Notts County. Kendall had already impressed for the reserves, where he had seen a group of promising youngsters at first hand. Graeme Sharp, after a tentative beginning to life at Goodison, had netted seven goals in eleven games for the second string while Kevin Richardson, who had joined the club as an apprentice two years before, was looking another fine prospect.

With injuries and poor form laying waste to the squad, the manager donned his boots for the visit to Nottingham. There was a spare weekend beforehand, due to World Cup qualifiers, and Everton appeared in a testimonial for Rangers defender Colin Jackson at Ibrox. Peter Eastoe had injured a hamstring so Kendall handed the number nine shirt to Sharp. Possibly inspired by appearing at the home of his boyhood club, the youngster played well and scored. Sharp kept his place and equally significantly, there was a recall for Kevin Ratcliffe to the starting line-up where he would largely remain for the next decade. Richardson was on the substitute's bench after a nightmare start to his Everton career against Sunderland, where he unluckily conceded a penalty after Arnold blundered. At Meadow Lane, trailing 2-1 just before the hour mark, Sharp got the break needed to launch his Toffees career. The Scot's speculative 25-yard left-footed strike took a slight deflection off Pedro Rodriguez before goalkeeper Raddy Avramovic allowed the ball to squirm under his body as Everton avoided a fourth successive defeat with a deserved point. The goal gave the striker all the confidence he needed. At Arsenal four days later, Brian Glanville in the *Sunday Times* presciently said, 'Sharp… suggested that with decent support he might be quite an incisive player.' The 21-year-old scored his first goal at Goodison a week later, a header in the 3-1 victory over Swansea.

The trip to Notts County therefore heralded a change in Kendall's selection policy. On the day of the Arsenal game, Richardson scored five goals for the reserves in a 9-1 victory over Blackburn Rovers and within weeks the midfielder, goalkeeper Southall, plus promising Scottish winger Alan Irvine joined Stevens, Ratcliffe and Sharp in the side. For the 2-0 home victory over Aston Villa in mid-December, seven of the starting line-up had started the season in the reserves.

Kendall goes Dutch

The tale is one of the memorable anecdotes from Goodison's greatest night. Bayern Munich's Hans Pfluger injured Peter Reid with the German further incurring the wrath of the Everton player by shouting 'You English pig' as he walked away. Obviously keen to get revenge, when Reid later saw Pfugler approaching, he described in his own words what happened next:

> I smashed him. As he was rolling about in pain, I stood over him to unleash some verbal vengeance on top of the physical retribution. 'Have some of that, you Nazi b******,' I said. I began to walk away, only for my victim's voice to stop me dead in my tracks. 'I'm Danish,' he said... and I went cold. I'd got Soren Lerby instead.

However, it is largely unknown that Lerby could well have been playing for Everton that evening, as Kendall had been in interested in signing the then Ajax midfielder since his early days at Goodison. In November 1981 chief scout Harry Cooke journeyed to Holland and 'A favourable report came out so we could be following it up,' admitted Kendall, who then expressed an interest in signing the player. However, Lerby was in a relationship with a famous Dutch singer, thirteen years his senior, and understandably, the Dane felt that was a more rewarding alternative to playing on Merseyside. Elsewhere, Kendall could not prise AZ67 Alkmaar's gifted Jan Peters and Johnny Metgod away from Holland.

Kendall was also desperate to acquire Manchester City midfielder Nicky Reid. Despite two cash bids – with one involving John Bailey as a makeweight – the young Scot remained at Maine Road, much to the manager's regret: 'Reid is a quality player... for the money I was offering he would have been a tremendous addition to the squad.' Rumoured interest in Aston Villa's Dennis Mortimer also came to nothing as did a bid for Sheffield Wednesday's Terry Curran. 'If Curran is made available he is one I want to talk about,' admitted Kendall.

Although the manager deserved credit in refreshing the first-team when the summer spending spree had clearly failed, these targets did not fire the imagination of supporters. As one wrote to the *Liverpool Echo*: 'Mr Kendall has bought a host of second-rate players... none of them are international stars. Yet in recent months, the following top class players have been available or disillusioned at their present clubs: Shilton, Clemence, [Trevor] Francis, [Kenny] Burns, Stapleton, [Bryan] Robson, [Mark] Lawrenson, Gray not to mention [Justin] Fashanu. Were Everton ever seriously considered in the market for these players?' It was a fair point but Kendall had bid for players of the calibre of Shilton, Robson and Steve Coppell over the summer but there were no deals because, rightly or wrongly, the board would not pay out the mammoth fees. 'It's in our own hands,' chairman Carter said, 'We are completely against these deals. In times of stress, people try to get out of trouble by going into the transfer market at great expense. It lacks a certain professionalism, this attitude that you can buy your way out of trouble. We have made it clear that we are completely against it.'

Supporters may not have welcomed Carter's words but such prudence harked back the refusal to back the move for Trevor Francis. With football's financial struggles reflecting those of wider society, the club operated a strict system of financial control and was not prepared to mortgage its future by spending beyond their means. Although John Moores retained a stake, spending did not compare to the days of the 'Mersey Millionaires'. But such prudence had also allowed a cash reserve of almost £500,000, from the cup runs under Lee, which provided a third of Kendall's initial transfer kitty. The Everton chairman was clearly playing the long game, hoping to ride out the storm and forge ahead in calmer waters. Consequently, compared to their free-spending north-west rivals, Everton's 'break-even' figure at the gate reflected their judiciousness.[86]

Kendall famously later claimed that he tried to use the entire transfer budget on West Brom's Bryan Robson, but the midfielder joined Ron Atkinson at Old Trafford. Even if Robson wanted to come to Everton, the board would not have put up the cash. 'We would have spoken to him [Kendall] about it and attempted to dissuade him about committing himself to one player,' Carter explained. There was no shortage of access to funding – Carter admitted as such – but there appeared to be a limit on what the club were prepared to spend on an individual, as a collapse in the market would devalue their expensive asset, which happened to Manchester City with former Gordon Lee target Steve Daley. Bought for close to £1.5 million in 1979, City sold him for £300,000 less than two years later.

This ran contrary to the strategy of the early 1960s when the Everton board had willingly given Harry Catterick funding to buy the best, to help guarantee success. Yet twenty years later, their approach resulted in the purchase of mid-range or unproven players. Understandable from a financial perspective but it pointed towards a lack of confidence in the manager's judgement in his early days. Yet Kendall, in his first year in the job, was in no real position to challenge the policy. 'The club has taken a firm stand on transfers which I admire,' he said, 'And I'm in full agreement with the chairman and the board.'

There may have been a bunch of youngsters showing promise, but that was only potential. The board's disciplined stance therefore did not necessarily find favour with the success-starved fans, who were conscious that since signing Bob Latchford and Martin Dobson the club had not been in the market for top-class

---

[86] Everton's break-even attendance was 25,000 per home game, against Liverpool (35,000), Manchester City (37,000) and Manchester United (46,000). That said, by 1982 only 54% of the club's income came via the turnstiles, 37% came from lotteries and other commercial activities with 9% contributed by programme sales, executive club subscriptions and television.

players. 'Ten years of second-class buys have produced a mediocre team,' one fan wrote, 'Unless the present policy is changed we'll go the way of clubs such as Newcastle and the Sheffield pair. The board cannot sit lamenting the trends and refusing to take part in the transfer market. The policy is so short-sighted and economically unsound.'

However, on the pitch there were signs of recovery at the end of December 1981. In the worst winter for twenty years, the undersoil heating at Goodison gave Everton a welcome run of home league fixtures. After defeating Swansea City and Aston Villa, the 3-2 Christmas victory over Coventry City saw a return to the back pages for Mark Higgins. England's most-capped schoolboy at the time scored twice, both headers. The 23-year-old had suffered from a number of injuries – amongst them a broken ankle, an ear infection needing an operation and a broken nose – in the preceding three years.

Graeme Sharp also continued to flourish, netting in the victory over Coventry, although supportive words from his manager had a sting in the tail. 'Our young centre forward Graeme Sharp is also doing very well, he scored a fine goal and it will do him a lot of good because I think there have been times when he has lacked a little bit of confidence. He's moving about well, showing good finishing ability and also looking dangerous in the air,' Kendall said, before adding caustically, 'Which, to be honest, has surprised me a bit, because he wasn't all that good in the air when he came here.' The Scot's advancement was also the result of a 'sliding doors' moment. Top of Kendall's shopping list was burly Brighton striker, Michael Robinson, but the Ireland international's minor knee operation delayed the deal by three weeks and when he regained fitness, Sharp's rapid development meant there was no need for a new striker and the focus moved elsewhere.

The Everton manager played in all those games before making his final professional appearance, poignantly, in an unlucky FA Cup defeat at West Ham, the fixture in which he had made Wembley history eighteen years before. 'I was so nervous ahead of the six games I played,' Kendall said in *Love Affairs and Marriage*, 'There was always a fear that I'd go out there and be a laughing stock.' That was not the case and the player-manager was man-of-the match against Swansea. Kendall kindly gave credit for the change to assistant Mick Heaton, who persuaded him to put on his boots again. Heaton expanded on the rationale to the *Liverpool Echo* at the time:

I wanted Howard to play much earlier than he did, because of the organisation he could bring on the pitch. You can work on something week by week and shout on the touchline, but there is nothing like having somebody on the field to put it into practice. This is what he did, and I think the players learned more of what we wanted them to do in the space of the games he played in, than we would have put over to them for the rest of the season, if he hadn't have played.

The players learned those lessons quickly and, in his first game after effectively retiring, Everton arguably got the better of a draw at Old Trafford against the championship hopefuls. Sharp showed the manager both his rising confidence and aerial ability when opening the scoring with a fine header during a vibrant display, although three other wasted opportunities meant Frank Stapleton, typically, snatched a late goal for a 1-1 draw.

Harry Catterick was at the game and afterwards said Everton had their best crop of youngsters since those who became the class of 1970. Drawing on his own experiences at Goodison in the early 1960s, the great manager said that a youth policy usually took five years to come to fruition, but the new incumbent could feel privileged. 'To some extent Howard has been lucky in inheriting so many young players,' Catterick said. 'Our last championship side had a whole lot of young home produced players... and we won the championship very impressively. This lot of youngsters could prove just as good if they get the chance.'

Often forgotten, but the breathtaking speed of transformation in the final six weeks of 1981 provided the groundwork for the halcyon days later on. 'I've made a good many changes and we now have a different team from the one I started with,' Howard Kendall said before the Old Trafford clash. That was true – there were nine players under the age of 23 in the line-up in Manchester, with – for all the summer spending – only three who attracted a fee. Astonishingly eight had appeared in the first reserve game of the season just three months before. As Mick Lyons said, 'The first team and reserves have virtually changed places. We have the situation where the Central League side is now older than the first.'

Everton v Manchester United, 6 January 1982
Southall, Stevens, Lyons, Higgins, Ratcliffe, Irvine, McMahon, Richardson, Lodge, Sharp, Eastoe. Sub: Biley

Everton Reserves v Bolton Wanderers, 29 August 1981
Southall, Borrows, Ratcliffe, Stanley, Higgins, Lodge, McMahon, Sharp, Mullan, Irvine, McBride. Sub: Stevens

Kendall expanded on the enormous change after the trip to Manchester: 'What has happened over the last few months is that the youngsters have started to come through and mature much faster than we expected. I would say we are at least six months ahead of our target at the moment.' For the first occasion, more by accident than design, this felt like a Kendall team and not Gordon Lee's with a few summer signings. That belief gathered further momentum when one of Goodison's favourite sons came to town within 24 hours of the Manchester United trip.

'A big man in a little frame'

Howard Kendall had long been an admirer of Adrian Heath, since their days together when the player was starting out at Stoke City. 'Heath was so good he used to make me look like a novice in practice matches and I never forgot him,' the Everton manager later admitted. With Heath impressing in a poor team, the Blues boss made an official bid in November but, with Aston Villa also interested, the Potteries club rejected the offer. There was another opening in early January and this time Stoke got their asking price: £700,000, an Everton club-record. 'A big man in a little frame,' said Kendall of his latest signing. Intriguingly Michael Robinson's injury freed up the funds for Kendall to buy Heath.

Although Philip Carter had stated the club would never pay seven figures for a player, according to Kendall they were getting their first million-pound star. 'When you're talking of genuine quality you simply have to pay the price,' the manager emphasised, 'I know that Adrian is a great player who can become as big a favourite at Goodison as men like Alan Ball and Colin Harvey.'[87] Interestingly, Heath had become unsettled because of manager Richie Barker's insistence that he played off a big target man in Lee Chapman and his comments after signing were fascinating in the light of later events. 'I'm much happier coming

---

[87] Although within 48 hours the Everton manager said, 'People will go on about the Ball-Kendall-Harvey era, but that's dead and gone now. We can't go on living in the past. Let's think in terms of Heath, Irvine, Sharp, Lyons and company.'

through from midfield,' he explained, 'A good professional obviously plays wherever he's asked, but I hope I'll be able to operate at either right or central midfield with Everton.'

On the pitch, there were further signs of progress at the end of January 1982 in a game against Spurs that produced one of the great Goodison goals, one that firmly put Graeme Sharp on the back pages. After ten minutes Lyons' long ball into the corner of the area was backheaded by Heath and Sharp, striking the ball a good yard above the ground, saw his crunching volley follow a seemingly impossible trajectory into the right-hand corner of the Park End goal. 'It was a fabulous goal by Sharp, one in a million,' opposing keeper Ray Clemence said after the game. The strike was one of those rare efforts that produce a buzz in the crowd afterwards. As the 21-year-old said later, 'I was running round in a daze for several minutes, I couldn't believe it.'

In a marvellous match against a talented Spurs outfit, Everton held their own before Ricky Villa's second-half equaliser earned the visitors a well-earned draw. There were excellent performances that pointed to future success: Sharp's goal, Heath's industry and the clean ball-striking of Kevin Richardson. The young Geordie had taken Howard Kendall's place in the side and impressed with his passing range and ability to intelligently plug gaps when others moved forward, which the team had been missing. 'The Everton revival, in the hands of one of the youngest teams to take the field in the First Division, is in a marvellous embryonic stage,' wrote Rob Hughes in the *Sunday Times*.

Above all his teammates though was Southall, who kept the visitors at bay with a string of fine saves. 'The goalie gave us nothing,' said Spurs boss Keith Burkinshaw afterwards, 'He didn't even fumble a shot or two, so we never had the encouragement we wanted. I haven't seen him before, but he was outstanding.' After the game, the Everton scorer was also a focus of attention. 'I don't think I'll ever score a goal like that one again,' Sharp told Granada TV's Elton Welsby. Thankfully, for Evertonians everywhere, he did.

Easter exits

With so many youngsters in the first team, there were too many senior players draining the wage bill with little chance of meaningful action. Kendall, consequently, showed the ruthlessness of top managers in making headlines on Easter Saturday by putting ten players on the transfer list. 'The League clubs will be circulated next week of one of the biggest sales of talent by an unendangered club in the history of football,' said Nick Hilton in the *Liverpool Daily Post*, 'The players could be valued at £1 million even in a collapsing market.' The out-of-contract Peter Eastoe, Joe McBride, Martin Hodge, Trevor Ross and reserve Dean Kelly all left the club, as did four who were still under contract: Mick Walsh, Paul Lodge, Alan Biley and Mick Ferguson. The exception was John Bailey, who eventually signed a new deal.

The brutal fire sale was not the first time Kendall had shown a hard-nosed edge and seven days after the Easter cull he left a number of players out of the game at Sunderland, one for disciplinary reasons after admitting in a radio interview that finding motivation for the 1-0 defeat at Coventry was difficult 'after playing in big matches against Liverpool and Manchester United'. Kendall was furious afterwards. 'If he said that it's disgraceful,' the manager warned, 'and if he doesn't think the match at Sunderland is a big game – he won't be playing.'

Prior to Easter, understandably some of the early momentum of Kendall's young charges had disappeared. There was only one victory in eight league games over February and March, although four were drawn.[88] There was still plaudits and following a 3-1 defeat at Brighton, old foe Jimmy Case said, 'There's a lot of skill in the side, but at the moment they are not used to each other. Given time they could be some team.' The final two matches in that sequence produced excellent performances that confirmed the burgeoning quality of Kendall's young side. At Maine Road, a 1-1 stalemate witnessed the first signs of the understanding between Sharp and Heath. The new-boy opened the scoring in brilliant fashion, dummying a pass played to him into Sharp's path and then, taking the Scot's touch in his stride, firing home brilliantly from 25 yards out. 'His darting raids on

---

[88] One of these was a goalless draw against West Ham United at Goodison when the usually placid John Motson managed to incur the wrath of both Kendall and Carter. Motson appeared on BBC's *Grandstand* programme after the contest and described it as 'the worst match I have seen this season and an example of what is wrong with the modern game'. With Kendall waiting be interviewed in the dressing room area by the BBC man, an angry Carter watched the comments in the boardroom and stormed down to inform his manager, but it was too late. 'The chairman was incensed and wanted to inform me before I went on,' Kendall said, 'I still got the gist of what Motson was trying to get at and I was astounded. He could have said that it was uncharacteristic of West Ham to play as defensively as they did.' Like Harry Catterick, the Everton boss was not necessarily a fan of televised football, feeling there was too much of it and broadcast highlights set expectations too high. 'People go to a game and expect to see that type of action for ninety minutes,' he said, 'The sooner there is a cut-back on edited soccer the better.'

City's back four, reminiscent in style of a young Kevin Keegan, had a perfect foil in Sharp's hard yet skilful running,' John Keith wrote in the *Daily Express*. Kendall declared afterwards: 'Our front two were brilliant.'

In the Merseyside derby game at Goodison seven days later, the result was the same as at Anfield but the performance completely different. With six players making their derby debuts, the home team went toe-to-toe with their distinguished neighbours, the turning point being Bruce Grobbelaar's astonishing save from Sharp's well-struck shot as Everton trailed 2-1 in the second period. 'Never mind about it being the best save I've seen in a derby I don't think you could see better than that in any match anywhere,' Kendall said about the goalkeeper's acrobatics. There were enormous positives in the defeat. 'A large proportion of Merseyside's first 50,000 gate of the season went home in no doubt at all that in players like Graeme Sharp, Adrian Heath and Steve McMahon, Everton now have men ready to stand comparison with some of the household names at Anfield,' Ian Hargraves encouragingly proclaimed in the *Liverpool Echo*, 'A great many Evertonians must surely have come away from Goodison believing that the gap in sheer footballing quality between the clubs is starting to close at last.'

The chairman reaffirmed the optimistic mood at the shareholders' meeting in the following week. 'We said last year that we were resolved to build for the future on the basis of youth, and that is exactly what we have done,' Carter emphasised, before warning, 'One thing we thought important was that we must not look for instant success. We must be patient.' The Everton manager shared his optimism. 'I believe that we are on the right lines and that we have something to offer. In the near future we will have something to excite you, and we will soon be ready to win a trophy or two.'

One of the features of Howard Kendall's management was an unwillingness to let seasons atrophy. As the campaign entered the final six weeks, the Everton boss warned: 'There is no way this season is going to die for us; it's the time when we can really develop our own style.' Which they did, the players responding with panache, winning seven of their last eleven matches, with two drawn. Once again there were signs of the successful days ahead: a 2-0 victory at St Andrews witnessed a superb display by Southall – 'He defied Birmingham's relegation battlers almost singlehandedly,' remarked David Moore in the *Daily Mirror*. Heath was now featuring in a more forward role and scored after 37 seconds after Sharp played him in. Afterwards the record signing spoke in glowing terms about the young Scot: 'He's strong and puts himself about a bit and isn't afraid to work, all of which helps me a lot. Believe me he's going to develop into a really great player.'

Sharp's goals in the final weeks made the biggest contribution to the strong finish. There were two in the home victory over Nottingham Forest on the day of his call-up to the Scottish under-21 squad then another brace in an impressive 3-1 win at third-place Swansea City in south Wales on the first day of May. Three days later the forward added to his reputation as a scorer of great goals when thumping home spectacularly from thirty yards for a 1-0 win over Leeds United at Goodison. The victory over the Yorkshire club was a major stepping stone, with a rite-of-passage battle with hard-man centre-half Kenny Burns. 'A few other players have tried it on with me because I'm a young lad, new into the side,' Sharp explained afterwards, 'When I first came down here from Scotland, at 19, I tended to go out of the game a bit if people kicked me. Now it helps me. I've started throwing my weight about.'

There was another double on the final day of the campaign, in a 2-1 victory away at eventual European Cup winners Aston Villa, the winning goal struck with rare finesse – put through by Trevor Ross, Sharp deftly chipped the ball over the advancing Jimmy Rimmer. 'People are always excited with goals and he has scored some great ones since coming into the side. They are always hitting the headlines, which he has done with a superb record,' Kendall said at the end of the season, 'Graeme has come through quicker than anyone expected.' Statistics reflected the youngster's progress: during his first full season at the club, Sharp bagged eight goals in 31 reserve team matches, in his second there were fifteen goals in thirty First Division games.

The late run for a European spot ultimately failed, but the Toffees ended a creditable eighth, two points off Southampton who filled the final UEFA Cup place. After the mini-crisis of late autumn, Kendall's team lost just five of their last 26 league matches. The manager also fulfilled one of his stated aims at the start of the season. 'Since I came back,' Kendall told the *Guardian* before the first game, 'I've had loads of letters, even people coming up in the street, saying "Don't worry about a trophy, just entertain us." Well, I can't quite go along with that, but I do think it's important to give the crowd players they can identify with.' More by accident than design, with a team featuring several outstanding young talents the manager had done that. However, after the impressive victory at Swansea, Kendall posted a warning about trophies needing to arrive sooner rather than later. 'We have some young players and the signs for the future are encouraging,' he said, 'But with a club the size of Everton, a successful future must not be too far away.'

CHAPTER 22

Struggling with the Liverpool model

THE BRITISH FILM INSTITUTE RIGHTLY VOTED *BOYS FROM THE Blackstuff* as one of the top ten British television programmes of the twentieth century. Dark and uncompromising, the drama series – the majority of which was written by the Liverpool-born Alan Bleasdale when Labour were in power – presented an uncomfortably realistic view of the devastating impact of the large-scale unemployment on the city, yet with moments of warmth and richly dark humour. During the first episode, Workers Revolutionary Party member 'Snowy' Malone (played by Chris Darwin) irritates colleagues with his extreme left-wing views. Ridiculed by 'Loggo' Logmond (played by Alan Igbon), when Malone claims that 'I've been brought up by me dad to support what's worth supporting', quick as a flash Logmond sarcastically replies, 'I didn't know your dad followed Everton' to the amusement of everybody.

The exchange pretty much reflected prevailing attitudes towards Everton in the city – a bit of a joke, albeit in a light-hearted manner and a world away from the vicious tribalism of today. Yet the peerless drama series also reinforced the significant gap between the two clubs in the public consciousness. During the fourth episode 'Yosser' Hughes (played superbly by Bernard Hill) turns up at a celebrity event featuring Liverpool players Graeme Souness and Sammy Lee, before menacingly confronting the former in a memorable scene. Asked later why no Everton players were involved, Bleasdale casually remarked that the viewing public would not recognise any.

Picking and choosing

But more significantly, the series reflected the desolation felt by a large proportion of the local population. On the same day that the city's big two collided in the FA Cup in January 1981, a *Guardian* article titled 'A time bomb on Merseyside' set out in stark terms the area's decline. 'Liverpool is not just worse off than other cities in the current depression: it was worse off before and it will be worse off after,' the piece opened, 'Some, indeed, say it is a dying city.' Authored by Professor F.F. Ridley of Liverpool University, the usual factors were set out for declining employment levels: the death of the port; the low manufacturing base; the dearth of skilled labour and the large reliance on factories owned by national and international companies where those holding the purse-strings had no personal or emotional connection to the city. Even in a failing national economy, the city was marooned.

However, by the time of the first broadcast of Bleasdale's masterpiece in October 1982 the position had become even worse. During the late-1970s, economist Patrick Minford was at Liverpool University and using the only mainframe computer in the campus, Minford and his research team constructed a mathematical model that tested out various economic scenarios. Minford was a keen believer in the policy of monetarism, a theory that governments could only control inflation by reducing the amount of money in circulation. After he schmoozed the Conservative Party, Margaret Thatcher and her associates were seduced by the concept, especially when his new development – ironically called 'The Liverpool Model' because of where it was conceived, not where it impacted most, although that could also be true – showed monetarism could work. There was one catastrophic error – the model assumed that the subsequent loss of jobs would be hundreds of thousands. The figure was closer to two million. 'To many people, the most obvious sign that Thatcher's economic strategy was misfiring was the rate of unemployment,' Andy Beckett wrote in *Promised You a Miracle*, his magisterial history of early-1980s Britain. When the Conservatives came to power in May 1979, 1.3 million were jobless – three years later the figure exceeded more than 3 million for the first time since the depression of the 1930s.

The effects were equally catastrophic on Merseyside. In May 1979, the rate of unemployment was eleven percent. Six weeks before the broadcast of *Boys from the Blackstuff* it broke the twenty percent mark, or more than one in five of the workforce. In real terms, an increase of almost 60,000 jobless over three years.

'In Liverpool, the effects of monetarism, and of the economic policies that flowed from it, were being graphically demonstrated,' Beckett concluded, 'but not as Minford and his computer model intended.'

Inevitably, the parlous economic position continued to filter through to football. Even Liverpool were feeling the pinch. During 1978/79, an average of more than 46,000 spectators attended every home league game. Three years later, Anfield gates had fallen to 35,000. Tellingly, over the same period, Manchester United's remained around 45,000. The gate of 11,000 at Anfield against Exeter City in the League Cup, in September 1981, was the smallest on the ground in living memory and at the end of the season, Liverpool announced they would be moving from four to three professional teams to reduce costs. Over at Goodison there was a similar slide: 35,000 in 1978/79 to 25,000 in 1981/82. Having said that, the support was there, but fans were picking and choosing their games: in March 1982 just 15,000 watched the home match against Middlesbrough, but a fortnight later more than 52,000 filled the ground for the Merseyside derby.

The sad story of the blues

On the first Saturday of November 1982, the same fixture packed Goodison again. Twenty-four hours later, on the day the BBC broadcast the final episode of Bleasdale's seminal work, the *Sunday Telegraph* published a feature on the impact of the economic slide on football in the area. 'It is some time since the gates were locked regularly at Goodison and Everton's expectations have been scaled down by the inordinately long period of time they have had to spend in Liverpool's overwhelming shadow,' reported Colin Malam, 'Nevertheless, the attendance [8,941, the first four-figure gate on the ground in the post-war era] for the recent Milk [League] Cup second leg against Newport was still a shock... and, as such, must be regarded as a disturbing sign of the times.' To cut costs and help manage an £800,000 overdraft, Jim Greenwood told Malam that Everton would be reducing the number of professionals on the books from thirty to twenty.

However, at least Liverpool's dominance provided some solace for those of the red persuasion suffering from the economic decline. For Everton supporters more than a decade without a trophy only added to their misery. Subsequently, that bleak November afternoon at Goodison summed up life for many Evertonians, both at and away from football. On the morning of the game, whereas Liverpool occupied their usual top spot, Kendall's outfit were eleventh. Seven days before at

The Dell there had been another symbolic reminder of the glory days that now seemed unreachable. Leaving to play in Hong Kong, Alan Ball made his final top-flight appearance, appropriately against the Toffees, twenty years after making his debut as an eighteen-year-old at Anfield for Blackpool. Southampton won 3-2 and could afford the luxury of the World Cup winner missing a penalty. Before the game, Kendall gave his midfield teammate an affectionate embrace in a special ceremony.

While an Everton legend was bowing out on the south coast, at Goodison Park the reserve derby was taking place. Earlier in the week, Kendall had returned to Ewood Park and secured a loan deal for unsettled Glenn Keeley. The Blackburn centre-half had an excellent game in the second string during a dour goalless draw. 'Considering that he hasn't been playing this season, he did very well,' reserve coach Colin Harvey said. As Kendall was unhappy with the first-team defence, the manager gambled before the senior fixture: Mark Higgins was out and the loan star was in. 'I have a high regard for Keeley,' Kendall said beforehand, 'He did a tremendous job for me when I was at Blackburn and once I was sure of his fitness I had no doubts about putting him in for such a big game.'

Kendall made many wise choices in his time at Goodison, but this was not one of them. Keeley had not played for six months and the decision contributed to a one-sided opening period, with the debutant's presence unsettling an already shaky defence, which seemingly had no clue on how to play the offside trap. Early on young right-back Brian Borrows pushed up to the halfway line as Alan Hansen brought the ball out, Ian Rush stayed in the space Borrows left and put away the centre-half's through ball. Liverpool dominated the opening half-hour: Rush struck the woodwork while Kenny Dalglish should have had a hat-trick.

Then came a traumatic moment in Everton derby match history. At the start of the season, in one of their periodic reviews of the application of the laws of the game, the Football League decreed that the so called 'professional foul' used in preventing a goalscoring opportunity was a straight sending-off offence. When Dalglish got on the wrong side of Keeley, the defender cynically held him back and referee Derek Civil had little choice but to dismiss the Everton player. 'Keeley left Everton – already a goal behind, and fortunate that it was not four – with a hopeless task,' said Tom German in *The Times*. Having not featured all season, Keeley admitted later he was unaware of the change in punishment for the foul.

An already difficult mission became impossible, not helped by the manager's baffling decision to retain two players up-front and deploy only three in midfield. Outmanoeuvred in the centre of the park and with youngster Borrows at centre-half, Everton gave Liverpool free rein to play through them at will. After the break Rush scored three times with Mark Lawrenson completing the rout in the visitors' biggest derby victory on the ground. The home team were lucky to escape with just a 5-0 defeat as Liverpool had two goals wrongly disallowed and Southall made several superb saves. 'All Liverpool's superiority over Everton in the past twelve years seemed to be condensed into one dramatic afternoon,' a fawning John Motson proclaimed on *Match of the Day*. 'Catching up with the Joneses, let alone keeping up with them, now seems much more a hazy horizon for Everton than reality,' was Tom German's view.

Although supporters made the hapless Keeley the scapegoat, that is unfair. He was not top-class, but more than competent, and had a lengthy league career that ran to more than 450 appearances, mostly with Blackburn whom he captained to victory in the Full Members Cup final in 1987. Far worse players have appeared for Everton. Instead, the manager was completely at fault. Bringing in a lower-division player without a first-team game for six months was a huge mistake as, even with eleven men on the pitch, the visitors were threatening to run-up a cricket score. Not surprisingly, Keeley never played for Everton again, his half-hour of fame right up there in the annals of nightmare debuts. The Blackburn defender broke his long silence to the *Lancashire Telegraph* in 2015. 'Howard was desperate to change things and we had a practice game on the Monday,' he recalled, 'It went quite well and on the Tuesday he said, "I'm playing you Saturday against Liverpool". And when he said that, I thought, "Don't be silly". It was miles too soon because I wasn't match fit.'

To be fair, the manager was happy to speak about his tactics afterwards. 'Do you go negative at 1-0 down?' Kendall asked, 'I felt it was worth a gamble. We had the added pressure of being down to ten men, but our midfield didn't work hard enough.' Perhaps, but McMahon had moved to right-back after the sending-off, with Borrows playing at centre-half, leaving the midfield short of a ball-winner, while Kevin Richardson was sat on the bench until the score was 4-0. When Keeley walked, Kendall should have taken a forward off, moved McMahon and not Borrows to centre-half and brought Richardson on. Motson may have said Liverpool were majestic, but the home team's naive tactics when a man down certainly helped.

The defeat was something of a watershed. Brian Borrows never played for Everton again, but had an excellent career at Bolton and Coventry City, where he played nearly 500 times in twelve years, unluckily missing the 1987 FA Cup final through injury. Kendall recalled Kevin Ratcliffe, who ironically had a transfer request accepted before the game, in place of John Bailey before the Welshman moved to the centre of defence. Neville Southall, after suffering from a foot infection for a fortnight, failed to usurp Jim Arnold and went on loan to Port Vale.

The following Saturday evening's letters page in the *Liverpool Echo* would have made painful reading for the Goodison hierarchy. 'Howard Kendall aims to close the chasm on the Reds' superiority in this city over the past decade, but on Saturday's showing he is a million light years away,' was one of the more balanced comments. 'Howard Kendall thinks too small for a big club. Come on, Everton, let's have a manager with some charisma, who can make Everton a proud club again,' was another. Yet there were some prescient points within the darkness. One supporter wanted Colin Harvey promoted to first-team coaching duties with immediate effect. That change would have to wait. However, another remarked, 'The midfield needs a general – a schemer to direct play and stamp his influence around him.' A month later Kendall would bring in somebody who, in time, would do exactly that. But on this occasion Alan Bleasdale had done Everton a favour – the great playwright had once been his manager.

CHAPTER 23

Laying the foundations

THE BACK-PAGE OF THE *LIVERPOOL ECHO* DATED 20 APRIL, 1971 HAS an interesting picture from the second leg of the English Trophy final at Goodison between Huyton Boys and Stoke Boys. The photographer catches Huyton's young midfielder – described as 'small of stature, has class' in the match programme – firing over. The significance was that he was a fourteen-year-old Peter Reid. Huyton Boys were victorious 5-1 on aggregate to become the first non-city side in Lancashire to win the competition. After the game the teenager lifted the trophy with his teammates on the ground – a feeling he would get used to.

Huyton Boys were managed by the former Sheffield Wednesday player Eddie Kilshaw and Alan Bleasdale. 'Alan was brilliant at man-management,' Reid told the *Liverpool Echo* in 1988. 'He was a teacher [at St. Columba's], but talked to us as if we were all his mates. His enthusiasm for the game and for life was incredible and you got the feeling that he was always going to do well for himself.' Reid, however, eventually went to Bolton Wanderers. 'Liverpool and Everton were interested, but I held on. In the end I opted for Bolton because they were renowned at that time for blooding young players. The possibility of an early breakthrough swung it for me.'

Reid's career had stalled during the early part of the 1980s, with more injury problems following a broken leg at the start of the 1981/82 season which kept him out until April.[89] Towards the end of 1982, the Burnden Park club needed the cash

---

[89] Interviewed on television 24 hours before a game, Reid was asked about his ambitions. 'Well, I'd like us to beat Barnsley tomorrow, I'm not looking any further than that because I could break a leg or something.' Sadly, he did.

and the midfielder spoke to Jack Charlton at Sheffield Wednesday, but that evening Howard Kendall phoned. This time Reid settled terms quickly and the clubs agreed a fee of £50,000.[90] Reid's former manager was pleased. 'He had great skill and application and tremendous heart. He really was an exceptional boy, never mind footballer... You always felt he had tremendous application,' Alan Bleasdale said about his former charge, 'I just hope coming to Everton he makes up in the next six or seven years for what has happened to him in the last two years with that terrible bad luck he has had.'

Building the blues

The signing of Reid was part of Kendall's attempt to right the wrongs of his first summer. After releasing Micky Thomas, the Everton boss had been looking for a left-sided midfielder all season and went across Stanley Park during the summer to sign Liverpool reserve Kevin Sheedy. After moving from Hereford United for £70,000 in June 1978, the Ireland under-21 international made his first-team debut in February 1981 against Birmingham City at Anfield, when he struck the bar at the Kop end. 'He has a wonderful left foot, he's fit and he's strong and lately he's been scoring goals with his right foot,' reserve-team coach Roy Evans told Granada TV after the game.

With Ronnie Whelan impressing, Sheedy played only twice during the 1981/82 campaign but had scored fifteen goals for the second string. Kendall famously travelled to see him play for Liverpool Reserves at Preston, with Colin Harvey, on the final day of the season, rather than take the first-team squad to Villa Park. In his autobiography, *Love Affairs and Marriage*, the Everton manager recalled the scouting mission:

> *His left foot was like a wand; his technique glorious. But I still didn't think he had what it took. "Superb effort, but I think he's lazy, Col," I said. "Take him," he said. Colin was only ever forthright about the very best players. It was an important part of our partnership; me appreciating his opinions and knowing when he was right, even if doubts crossed my mind. "All right," I said, "We'll take him."*

---

[90] Not £60,000 as generally reported, that was Bolton's original asking price. Everton famously had to change banks to get hands on the cash.

Liverpool were keen on invoking the unwritten rule forbidding transfers between the clubs, but the fact Sheedy was nearing the end of his deal weakened their hand. As a free agent, the player could now move where he wanted, subject to the clubs agreeing a fee.

There were some complications. With Portsmouth and Swansea City circling, Sheedy initially wanted a house as part of the deal – 'A house! He was a good player, but he was still just a Liverpool reserve; he wasn't exactly a star signing,' Kendall later recalled – which Everton understandably rejected. With the transfer on ice, the Liverpool player saw sense and changed his mind. A tribunal set a fee of £100,000, making Sheedy the first player since Johnny Morrissey twenty years before, to cross the great divide. 'Looking back, he was worth a house, a car and whatever else he wanted. He was one of the best signings I – and Everton – ever made,' Kendall recalled.

Kendall also raided the Anfield dressing room for his former teammate David Johnson who, like Sheedy, had spent most of the previous season in the reserves. Johnson had made his Everton debut in 1971 before moving to Ipswich Town and in 1976 went to Anfield for £200,000. During a trophy-laden six years, the striker accumulated 78 goals. Whereas the deal for the promising Sheedy made sense, the signing of the thirty-year-old Johnson was odd. The striker had been a playing contemporary of the Everton manager previously, which surely made the relationship a strange one – at one stage Johnson was threatening legal action against his former teammate.[91] In addition, the player had clearly left his best years behind. Five goals in 45 appearances in a second spell told its own tale. 'I'm not saying he was a failure,' Kendall later admitted. 'But he disappointed a little bit.'

The Everton manager's third signing of the summer was more welcome. Andy King's career had been drifting since leaving Merseyside. Following a year in London with QPR the midfielder had spent a disappointing season with West Brom. The Midlands side had tried to buy Peter Eastoe in the previous campaign and when the opportunity came for a swap deal during the summer, things moved

---

91 Over remarks attributed to the manager concerning the player's unwillingness to play at West Ham in the League Cup in December 1983. A war of words followed. 'I want him away from here as soon as possible,' Kendall remarked, 'David Johnson has not produced the form or the goals in the games he has played since he came here.' Johnson left for Manchester City shortly after the Oxford game in January 1984.

quickly. The returning midfielder breathed a sigh of relief over an unexpected opportunity. 'I lost myself, not realising when you leave Everton you leave a love, and I lost something. When I left this city I left something you can't buy with money. Now I have a second chance to get it back, and I realise it is a great chance.' At the end of a pre-season friendly against Bruges, supporters carried the popular midfielder on their shoulders.

On the threshold

'He can be satisfied with his first season at Everton, the kind of football we played on many occasions was especially heartening... we feel we are on the threshold of great things.' Chairman Philip Carter's words when he delivered the club's annual report in the summer of 1982. Consequently, there was real optimism that, following a strong end to the previous campaign plus some decent recruitment, the team would progress. But an opening day 2-0 defeat at newly-promoted Watford acted as a reality check. 'There is every reason, on the basis of what we saw yesterday, to suppose that Everton have another thoroughly mediocre season in front of them,' remarked Brian Glanville in the *Sunday Times*, 'Everton were so sterile, negative and poor.' Disappointingly, Glanville had said exactly the same thing twelve months earlier, following the 3-0 loss at Spurs.

But inconsistency characterised defined Kendall's early years. Three days later Everton annihilated European Cup holders Aston Villa 5-0 at Goodison, in a scintillating showcase of attacking football. 'It was an authoritative display by Howard Kendall's young and developing side,' wrote Patrick Barclay in the *Guardian*. One man who looked at home was Kevin Sheedy, who provided width on the left and his crisp and accurate passing over distance gave Everton an extra dimension, reminding those watching why Liverpool made it so hard for him to leave. Adrian Heath was also outstanding as a striker, buzzing purposefully around the penalty box and showing the quickness of thought and quality finishing that characterised his play two years later. Spurs were beaten 3-1 on the following Saturday, with Sheedy scoring the first of 97 goals for the club. Everton reverted to type in the following week, losing narrowly at Manchester United and Notts County.

Nevertheless, in the opening weeks of the season, it was the Everton defence causing Kendall angst. After a 4-2 loss at Coventry City had left his team with just one point from four league games, the manager complained that 'Some of the goals we have conceded have amazed me. In football terms my players are sitting their eleven-plus rather than their A-levels.' Everton's unpredictably continued. There were four straight victories in October, followed by the defeat at Southampton and then the derby humiliation.

Curran lifts a weight off Kendall

Like twelve months before, a difficult afternoon with the neighbours took time to remove from the system. A further six games followed without a victory, with only two goals scored, including a 3-0 defeat at Arsenal in the League Cup. The goal-drought affecting Heath and Sharp reflected the lack of firepower, the pair having scored just three goals in three months by the end of November, when Kendall's team stood fifteenth.

The first Saturday in December brought a dour goalless draw against Birmingham City at Goodison, despite the home team winning 23 corners.[92] 'Victims of rigor mortis might be expected to show more life and get-up-and-go than these dead-end kids,' commented the *Sunday Mirror*. In a familiar story, just 13,707 spectators watched the game, the lowest top-flight attendance at Goodison in the post-war era. They saw no goals and very little in the way of goalmouth action, but the manager's comments showed the growing disconnect between the professional game and supporters. 'We showed great character and professionalism under a lot of pressure and did well enough on the breakaway to have stolen a win,' Kendall claimed. 'Our young players are beginning to build up their confidence and can only get better.' But others thought differently. 'It merely emphasised that, improvement or not, time is beginning to run out for Everton,' said Ian Hargraves in the *Liverpool Echo*.

To make matters worse, there was an extraordinary development on the following Friday with significant ramifications. Twenty-four hours before a difficult trip to Ipswich Town, Kendall left out skipper Billy Wright for unusual reasons. 'Wright was given a warning about his weight two weeks ago when it was seen to be affecting his fitness,' Kendall declared, 'I am sorry to say that he was found to be overweight when he got on the scales today, and so he has been omitted from the squad to travel to Ipswich... a decision about the club captaincy

---

92 A little bit of history was made though, Birmingham's Mick Ferguson became the first Everton player to appear against the club while on loan to another.

will be made later.' Wright responded by claiming, 'As far as I'm concerned it's not been affecting my game, but the boss reckons I'm about eight pounds overweight.' Although Kendall used the old quip to a local radio station of Wright failing a 'fatness test' in truth, possibly due to his own inexperience, he hung his skipper out to dry. The Everton manager had a cruel streak on occasions – witness his treatment of Alan Biley – and should have kept the matter in-house. By making it public he was causing irreparable damage to his skipper's reputation and Wright left for Birmingham on a free at the end of the season.

Kendall had shown himself capable of making tough decisions before, often to his own detriment. Wright was his only natural right-sided central defender and they were facing Alan Brazil and Paul Mariner, two of the best strikers in the division. With nine games without a victory, the pragmatic option would have been to put Wright in the squad and deal with the disciplinary issue afterwards. The Everton manager bravely stuck to his managerial principles, but his captain's irresponsibility left Kendall with an enormous headache. There were two options to partner Mark Higgins in the centre of defence: new £30,000 signing from Tranmere Rovers, Derek Mountfield – and the transfer listed-Kevin Ratcliffe, dropped again for the Birmingham game. The Everton manager went with Ratcliffe in the middle and, thankfully, the gamble paid off.

Also in the party travelling to East Anglia was winger Terry Curran. The perm-haired, moustachioed Yorkshireman was one of the last of the 1970s mavericks who had lit up the English game, and frustrated their managers in equal turn. Curran had started with Doncaster Rovers but had later played for some of the biggest names in the game: Brian Clough, Lawrie McMenemy and Jack Charlton. As well as being a productive winger, the extrovert Yorkshireman could also play as a centre-forward but an erratic nature meant his immense talent was unfulfilled. Twelve months before both Manchester United and Everton were interested, but doubts over his character prevailed. 'He's an idiot,' said one his former bosses, 'He's had four or five managers who have all finished up using the same word that I used at some stage.' But Lawrie McMenemy said that 'On his day he was the best outside-right in British football.'

Having moved across the city during the summer, Curran was treading water in Sheffield United reserves and, with Alan Irvine injured, Kendall arranged a one-month loan deal. The much-travelled forward reacted in typical style, confidently proclaiming 'I've no fear about playing in the First Division – it's the easiest in the world.' 'He's a very exciting player,' Kendall said, 'He can go past people, he's got tremendous pace... He's got good quality when he gets in the final third. He's proved he can score goals.' At Portman Road, the talented frontman was inspired. 'It is always a pleasure to watch Curran when he is at all in form,' Brian Glanville wrote in the *Sunday Times*. The on-loan winger was certainly that, runs from deep troubled the home defence and his crossing caused chaos. In Everton's best performance for three months, the visitors dominated, reflected in a corner-count 10-1 in their favour.

However, they had to wait for an hour to open the scoring, through Sheedy, and doubled their lead in the final minute, with Curran heading Heath's centre back across goal for Richardson to tap in on the line. Although Curran was the shining star, the middle of the defence was the basis for the superb victory. Higgins took the dropped skipper's place on the right hand side and defended like a colossus while Ratcliffe, after an uneasy start, grew into the game magnificently. 'The enforced absence of Billy Wright led to employment of a central defensive partnership that looked the best Everton have fielded since the days of Labone and Hurst,' claimed Ian Hargraves, 'it is to be hoped that the significance of this fine victory is properly appreciated.' Four decades on, it still is. Seven days later, Kendall's team massacred Luton Town 5-0 at Goodison, with Curran outstanding, scoring once and setting up another for Heath.

Inevitably, Kendall wanted to make the move permanent. Trevor Ross had gone on loan to Bramall Lane and the deal rumoured to be on the table was £100,000 in cash with the midfielder as a makeweight. Indications were that United were amenable but they changed their minds at the eleventh hour, now valuing Curran significantly higher. 'United have gone back on their word and as far as I'm concerned the deal is off,' Kendall raged. The failure to land a target brought into focus the club's decline. 'Terry Curran is staying at Sheffield United because, Everton, once one of the country's richest clubs, cannot afford £250,000,' said *The Times*. Although Curran would return, a second spell was not as influential as the first, when his characteristic brand of skill and personality reinvigorated the squad, one that impressed Peter Reid. 'It was a shock to find so many excellent players here and not in the first team,' the new signing said, 'It's given me quite a shock.' With league form inconsistent, as in most of the previous seasons Everton's hope of a trophy rested with the FA Cup.

CHAPTER 24

Last tango at Goodison

THE TOFFEES' REVIVAL STALLED SOMEWHAT IN EARLY 1983 WITH only a single point taken from two away games at West Brom and Spurs, leaving Kendall's team thirteenth. In the FA Cup third round, Everton reprised their League Cup encounter with Newport County earlier in the season, which they won 4-2 on aggregate. Although in the Third Division, Newport paired two of the most prolific goalscorers of their generation in attack. John Aldridge and Tommy Tynan accumulated close to 800 career goals between them and their substantial threat meant the journey to Somerton Park had all the potential of a classic cup shock.

That looked the case for 22 minutes during a dark January afternoon, after the veteran 34-year-old substitute David Gwyther put the underdogs ahead midway through the second half. But, with three minutes remaining, the visitors got a deserved lifeline. Kevin Ratcliffe's high ball into the box was headed back out to Kevin Sheedy, who did something he would make a habit of – rescuing Everton with a piece of magic. From fully thirty yards out, the Irishman's tremendous low drive skidded across the turf and past keeper Mark Kendall. The two teams regrouped at Goodison three days later. Everton went ahead against the run of play through Sharp but Aldridge equalised just after the break with a marvellous overhead kick. However, the Welsh team switched off at the restart and allowed Andy King to head home Gary Stevens' cross. Against a third tier team showing no little quality, the Toffees hung on for an undeserved victory and a home draw against Shrewsbury Town. 'It was a battle,' Kendall admitted in a huge understatement and their brave opponents thoroughly deserved a standing ovation at the end. 'Shrewsbury Town will be delighted that they will be meeting

Everton in the FA Cup,' wrote Paul Fitzpatrick in the *Guardian*. 'On the evidence of last night's replay at Goodison Park they would have had more cause for concern if they had been meeting Newport County.'

Shrewsbury Town, FA Cup fourth round (h)

The FA were now freely allowing clubs to play on a Sunday and with Liverpool drawn at home against Stoke City, to avoid congestion Everton moved the tie back 24 hours. Like the only previous Sabbath fixture, against West Brom nine years before, there was a bumper attendance – more than 35,000 in bitterly cold wind and sleet, twice that for the Newport encounter. Graham Turner, the visiting manager, was well prepared. 'I noticed that they use an Adidas Tango ball at Goodison. We are used to a Mitre and it does make a difference,' he said, 'We went out and paid £37 for a Tango. It certainly swings about in the air and bounces higher than normal.'

Kevin Sheedy was already proving to be a master of manipulating any ball and ten minutes before the break he put the home team ahead. The midfielder, who had already been criticised for his (lack of) tackling, won a 50-50 in the centre of the park and was upended at the edge of the box. Sheedy then bulleted the free-kick into the net high to the right of goalkeeper, Steve Ogrizovic, who had also left Liverpool during the summer. In a poor game, the wind caused havoc, although on the hour, a prone Sheedy crossed to Heath from the byline and the diminutive striker finished easily. Backed by a vocal travelling army of 6,000 spectators, the Shropshire side remained competitive and pulled a consolation goal back through Steve Cross. It was not pretty, but Kendall's side hung on for a hard-earned victory. There was no doubt who was man-of-the-match. 'Kevin Sheedy was superb in his all-round play,' Kendall said. 'We have been working on the defensive side of his game and he showed great determination.'

The reward was a home draw against Spurs, who were aiming for a third successive final appearance. That was a good omen for Everton supporters: two years before Arsenal had been the last team on a similar run, before coming to grief at Goodison.

Tottenham Hotspur, FA Cup fifth round (h)

With Liverpool again drawn at home, Spurs manager Keith Burkinshaw refused Everton's offer to play the tie on a Sunday. Instead, Liverpool moved their game against Brighton. Kendall's team were on a decent run, moving to fifth following a 3-0 victory over Notts County after just two defeats in thirteen matches.

Two weeks later the Everton manager had the opportunity to remove the holders, who were unbeaten in the competition since a 1-0 home defeat to Liverpool three years before. On a glorious afternoon, the home team duly took advantage of a weakened north London outfit, with Osvaldo Ardiles injured and Glenn Hoddle only fit enough for the substitutes' bench. In front of a crowd of more than 42,000 and after a goalless opening period of several half-chances, the Toffees went ahead just after the break. Sheedy picked up a clearance and, as the Spurs defence pushed out, the midfielder's clever ball found Heath on the right-hand side of the area and Andy King smoothly converted the striker's cross at the near-post. A second goal fifteen minutes later was similar in construction. Sheedy's floated free-kick from the same position fell into no-man's land at the edge of the six-yard box and, as King, Ray Clemence and Gary Mabbutt challenged, the ball squirmed free before Sharp smashed home on the line, although possibly from an offside position. With the home defence standing firm Spurs had little chance of reducing the deficit.

The 2-0 victory took Everton to the quarter-finals for the third time in four seasons. Burkinshaw was typically gracious about the victors in defeat. 'They were ultra keen, young and enthusiastic,' he said, 'And gave it everything they had got, and probably deserved it.' Kendall let the victory speak for itself. Asked on the Saturday evening who he fancied next, the victorious manager smiled and quipped, 'Brighton would be nice.'

Manchester United, FA Cup sixth round (a)

There was good and bad news for the Everton boss 48 hours later. The good was that Brighton had shocked Liverpool 2-1 but the draw had also brought an away game at 7-4 favourites Manchester United. 'To win the cup you have got to be prepared to beat the best,' said a defiant Kendall.

His team though were still worryingly inconsistent and unable to convert territorial domination into points through erratic finishing. The three league games between the two FA Cup fixtures brought just two points against Manchester City and Swansea, clubs eventually relegated, and a 2-1 defeat at Sunderland featuring a woeful display of refereeing by Colin Seel, a name familiar to all Evertonians. The 1980 semi-final official awarded the home team a ridiculous penalty when the strong wind blew the ball onto John Bailey's arm. At 1-1, the hapless Seel disallowed Kevin Sheedy's brilliant volley because David Johnson was offside, although obviously not interfering with play on the other side of the pitch. On the hour came the worst decision, Iain Munro's appalling challenge on Andy King was a potential career-ending one: studs up and knee high it left the club's top-scorer with serious ligament damage that ended his season. Seel ludicrously only booked the player. King was top scorer with thirteen goals in 32 matches and his absence was a bad blow.

Steve McMahon returned from injury to replace King at Old Trafford for the biggest game of Kendall's reign. 'We are not just going for the ride. We are going there to win,' the Everton boss proclaimed. But the statistics were against the visitors. United had lost one of fourteen games in 1983, while Everton had not won at a top-flight side in the competition since a victory ironically at Old Trafford in 1969. But the Toffees took a remarkable record into the game, they had scored at least one goal in each of their previous 52 cup ties (including replays) going back nine years.

The match was an epic, played out in front of 58,198 spectators, the biggest domestic gate on an English club ground in the final two decades of the century. Beforehand, there may have been a bit of gamesmanship by Kendall. David Johnson had been included in the original starting line-up but withdrawn at the last-minute. Unusually, such was the game's importance Granada TV had cameras in the bowels of Old Trafford beforehand for their *Match Night* programme and the Everton manager, somewhat sheepishly, explained Johnson had been suffering all week with a 'neck injury', with Alan Irvine stepping in. The cameras then showed Ron Atkinson receiving the Everton team-sheet. 'I think Irvine will be a straight match for Arthur [Albiston] and Arthur usually deals quite well with him,' the United boss told his coaching staff. That was not necessarily the case, as Irvine had caused the home team problems in the past.

Everton, backed by a huge travelling army of 14,000 massed at the Scoreboard End, realised that sitting deep in defence was footballing suicide and were positive from the start. Indeed, to the general astonishment of those watching, the visitors threatened to overrun the home team in the opening half-hour. 'Instead of crossing Lancashire to play safe and take United back to Goodison, the underdogs elected to try to win it first time,' wrote Colin Malam in the *Sunday Telegraph.*

Irvine was outstanding in the early stages and on sixteen minutes, he pulled the ball back invitingly to the prowling Heath who, seven yards out and with the whole goal to aim at, snapped at his shot and screwed the ball wide. United stopper Gary Bailey then did well to save Heath's deflected shot three minutes later before diving bravely at the feet of the onrushing Sharp. With McMahon and Richardson controlling a frantic – and frighteningly physical – centre of the park, little was seen of United and only in the last fifteen minutes of the half did the home team gain a foothold with Jim Arnold saving well from Arnold Muhren and Gordon McQueen. 'Everton's blue shirts dominated midfield and their speed and incisiveness gave United as embarrassing a first half as they have suffered at Old Trafford for a very long time,' recorded Ronald Atkin in the *Observer*.

United had not conceded a goal in the competition but in the second period the visitors continued to threaten that record. In the opening fifteen minutes both Sharp and Heath could have put Everton ahead. The Scot's chance was beautifully constructed. Sheedy's perfectly weighted ball from the left was headed back by Heath to the onrushing striker who, slightly stretching on his left foot, sliced agonisingly just wide in front of the travelling army of fans. Heath then saw his shot across goal pushed away desperately by Bailey. Sharp also shot weakly with his left foot straight at Bailey when well placed. 'They dominated the second half… just as convincingly as they had controlled the first,' noted Atkin.

Nevertheless, like in the opening period, the balance of power shifted in the final fifteen minutes. Whether by accident or design, Everton fell further back into the final third, allowing United to launch wave after wave of desperate attacks towards the Stretford End. Arnold thwarted Norman Whiteside twice and then Steve Coppell from close range – although the shots were straight at the keeper, that was down to his excellent positional sense and not luck. The excitement built to such a crescendo that the noise damaged the sound equipment used by Granada TV. However, after this classic encounter passed ninety minutes of breathless and relentless drama, it looked odds-on that United would be playing again at Goodison three days later.

On the bench for United was the veteran Scottish midfielder, Lou Macari, who was nearing the end of a distinguished career. With the game in stoppage time – or as one writer said 'heart-stoppage time' – the United boss had one last card to play. 'The substitution was a desperate gamble,' Atkinson admitted afterwards, 'We had a corner so I thought I'd throw Macari on.' From the cross, two United players appeared to foul Arnold and although the Everton defence cleared the ball to the halfway-line, Ray Wilkins's long pass into the heart of the box found Macari and his well-directed header back towards Frank Stapleton fell perfectly. What happened next was heart-breaking. The Irishman volleyed with the outside of his right foot and, as time appeared to stand still, the Everton players watched on agonisingly as the ball took an age to reach the top left-hand corner of Arnold's net.

As the United hordes swept down the terraces of the Stretford End, the immediate thoughts of those present were about the brave visitors. 'We did not know whether to cheer Stapleton or cry for Everton,' said Patrick Barclay in the *Guardian*. 'It was 4.50 pm on a Saturday, a time and a day worth noting, for this was an occasion to remember,' recorded *The Times'* Stuart Jones, whose choice of words could have been spoken by his eloquent father, the great radio broadcaster Peter Jones.

Poor finishing had cost the visitors dearly. 'We created so many good chances, good chances, and we didn't finish them,' a frustrated Andy King told the television cameras. However, asked if he had any sympathy for the visitors, Ron Atkinson said 'no'.[93] The crestfallen Everton boss later voiced his frustrations. 'It was disappointing to lose after playing so well, but I was proud of the team,' Kendall said, 'we are trying to build something big at Goodison, and in the process we want to win friends and win matches. We are certainly winning friends with our football – even the United fans applauded our coach away from Old Trafford – and now we have to start winning our matches.' The Everton then issued his annual refrain. 'Anyone who thinks the season is over won't stay in our team,' he promised.

The players heeded those instructions seven days later at Anfield in a gritty goalless draw against the champions. Jim Arnold put in another man-of-the-match display, an impressive achievement for somebody who lost three teeth after being kicked in the mouth. The game was another tale of missed opportunities. In the opening period, a rare mistake by Mark Lawrenson allowed

---

93 These things can come back to haunt you. In September 1986 Everton defeated United, then in the bottom three, 3-1 at Goodison in a game broadcast live by the BBC. With Atkinson's job under threat, Kendall was asked whether he had any sympathy for the United boss. The response indicated the Everton manager had a long memory.

Heath a clear run at goal at the Kop end, but frustratingly the striker's shot ended up closer to the corner flag.

Although the team had woken from their pre-Christmas torpor, there was still frustration with the lack of firepower up-front and their Scottish striker in particular. 'Sharp should be transferred as he is just not good enough,' said one correspondent to the *Liverpool Echo*. Another complained about 'the vastly over-rated Graeme Sharp, who continues to look an expensive luxury and should have been replaced months ago.' The young striker was certainly suffering second (full) season syndrome, displaying a lack of self-assurance and frustration which was reflected in attempting the impossible on occasions. Consequently, his poor goal return – just ten in 42 matches by the start of the April – frustrated his manager. 'I have tried everything with Graeme,' said Kendall, 'I've left him out to give him a break from the pressures, I've given him a kick up the backside, I've praised him through the bad times… It's now down to the player to come through this difficult period – and I'm sure he will. He's got the ability. It's all about confidence.' The club's post-war record goalscorer responded in style, as did the rest of the team. The final eight games of the season witnessed six victories and a draw, with Sharp scoring seven times, to finish top-scorer with seventeen goals.

Player of the 1982/83 season though was Kevin Sheedy. The only squad member not dropped at some point during the campaign, the midfielder won eleven *Liverpool Echo* man-of-the-match awards, six more than any teammate. The campaign brought thirteen goals, many of them spectacular and several crucial. The memorable away game at relegation-threatened Brighton in early April saw the Irishman at his best. A combination of Clive Thomas and *Match of the Day* usually guaranteed controversy and the crucial encounter was no exception. Sheedy put the visitors ahead, a lead they held until sixty seconds from time. Thomas then awarded Brighton a disputed penalty, which Arnold saved brilliantly from Gordon Smith. The Welshman ordered a retake, claiming that the Everton keeper had moved. Smith coolly scored from his second attempt. With seconds of injury-time remaining, Thomas then harshly chalked off another goal for the striker following a Steve Foster foul and from the resulting free-kick a phalanx of Everton players broke the offside trap. After Heath's shot was saved, Higgins headed back into the box where Sheedy coolly killed the ball with one touch and then tucked it into the corner of the net. Thomas allowed the kick-off and blew for full time. 'What an extraordinary end,' was Barry Davies' understated commentary.

That good run brought a seventh-place finish, one higher than Kendall's first season – still outside the European qualification places, but with ten more goals scored. However, after two years in charge, there was still question marks hanging over key positions and whether the young squad could fulfil their potential. 'You are kidded to a certain extent by some individuals,' the manager confessed to the *Liverpool Daily Post*. 'They aren't capable of consistency... some players have let themselves down this season. It is a situation which can't be tolerated for very long.'

Nevertheless, there was still room for optimism. 'We are a young side, capable of playing good football,' the manager also said. 'I am looking to improve my squad, but only with a couple of players. This is because I know we are in the right lines.' Kendall believed that but supporters knew time was ticking after thirteen years without a trophy.

CHAPTER 25

'Yes, this is still a big club'

CONTRARY TO POPULAR BELIEF, FOOTBALL DID NOT BEGIN IN 1992. The roots of the modern game actually originate in the events of nine years earlier after the FA and Football League commissioned Sir Norman Chester to produce a follow-up to his 1968 report, looking for recommendations on changing the league structure and finance. The subsequent findings show that 2020's provocative 'Project Big Picture' was hardly original. Chester made eighteen recommendations, mainly aimed at enhancing the powerbase of the biggest clubs, as well as reducing the number of top-flight sides and the regionalisation of lower leagues.

Controversially, the 75-year-old's principal argument was that the game should support the interests of those richer clubs best-placed to survive the economic downturn, claiming that the equal sharing of pools and television money was a waste because it directed cash towards those further down the league who were poorly run. The cross-subsidisation irked the former Oxford Don, who recommended a redistribution of revenues to ensure the biggest and richest received a larger portion. Furthermore, Chester also recommended that the sharing of gate money – at the time thirty pence per spectator went to the away team, meaning Everton lost £35,000 net per year – should end, with the home side keeping all the revenue, thus depriving their smaller rivals of much needed cash. Club secretary Jim Greenwood particularly welcomed that move. 'We believe that the answer, in general terms, is to leave clubs as much freedom as possible to be masters of their own fate,' he admitted. 'If clubs are free to keep their own receipts, negotiate their own terms and manage their own affairs, then the best clubs will get to the top, which is just as it should be. The thing is, the leading clubs have got to stop subsidising the smaller and less efficient ones.'

Greenwood's views were broadly representative of the historically larger clubs. Publication of the report was against a backdrop of perennial veiled threats from the so-called 'big five' – Manchester United, Liverpool, Everton, Arsenal and Tottenham – about forming a 'Super League', with selected others, including the two Glasgow giants. The latest had been early in 1983 when the *Daily Mirror* exclusively revealed, under the banner headline 'Blackmail by the big Boys', that up to twelve clubs had already secretly discussed a clean break, with Bob Russell reporting:

Back us – or we will go it alone. That is the ultimatum from the top soccer clubs to the lesser lights of the Football League. For if the other clubs don't accept the new Chester report, due out this week, the threatened Super League almost certainly will kick-off next year.

Most club chairmen unsurprisingly voted against virtually all the Chester recommendations.[94] However, with the 'super league' threat, predictably two were accepted. 'In view of the threatened breakaway, it was foreseeable, too, that the chairmen should accept that home clubs should keep all the receipts from League games and that those covered more frequently on television should receive a larger share of proceeds,' reported Stuart Jones in *The Times*.

That summer's negotiations over a new television deal displayed the heightening influence of the league's elite. Appetite for screening football highlights had fallen dramatically – eight million lost viewers in four years – with television companies keen to show live games, something that clubs opposed. After two proposed deals had previously collapsed, the big clubs, alarmed at their

---

94 The archaic voting structure gave each club in the top two divisions a vote apiece, with the bottom two having four collectively. The 'three quarters' majority rule in the Football League meant that of 48 votes available, 36 were needed to instigate change. In echoes of the modern Premier League, the smaller clubs usually block-voted to protect their own interests whilst scuppering the ambitions of the elite. The outmoded model had infuriated John Moores more than twenty years earlier. 'We are at the mercy of clubs who cannot compete with us, but can veto our progress,' the Everton chairman once complained.

lack of representation, co-opted Liverpool's Peter Robinson and Philip Carter onto the negotiating committee. Although both were live football refuseniks, they had previously led the fight against the ban on shirt advertising on television. Four years before Carter had said, 'the fact that shirt advertising is not allowed on television is, I think, quite wrong, and, ultimately clubs should band together to re-negotiate with the TV companies.' The Everton chairman, plus Robinson, therefore sensed an opportunity and a mutually beneficial deal was agreed. For the princely sum of £2.6m a year the networks could broadcast ten live league games a season (they had asked for 62 originally) while the clubs were allowed shirt advertising in televised matches – effectively meaning more money from their sponsors. For Carter (and Everton) it was the beginning of a period of significant influence at the top of the English game.

The genie of live football was well and truly out of the bottle. The first live league fixture, under the new television deal, was broadcast by ITV on the first Sunday afternoon of October 1983. Millions of armchair viewers saw Spurs defeat Nottingham Forest 2-1 at White Hart Lane, but events off the pitch symbolised the way ahead. Pre-match entertainment included skydivers and cockney singing duo Chas and Dave. To pay off debts for their new Main Stand, Spurs had also made plans to become the first club to float on the Stock Exchange and they used the event to distribute their glossy 35-page prospectus. As it happened all 3.8 million shares sold quickly, valuing the club at a princely £9m. With paid directors also now permitted,[95] football clubs were taking the first steps towards becoming commercial enterprises. As for the game itself, Spurs manager Keith Burkinshaw remarked 'it was a little item down at the bottom of the bill'.[96] With the FA doing likewise with cup matches, BBC and ITV broadcast seventeen domestic games live during 1983/84. All but six featured Liverpool or Manchester United, proving once again that, in football as in life, the more things change the more they stay the same.

---

[95] The FA's Rule 34 prohibited paid directors and restricted dividends to shareholders, thereby ensuring owners could not exploit clubs financially. Bafflingly, the FA allowed Spurs to evade these conditions by forming a holding company, a practice that new owners have followed ever since, meaning clubs can be bought and sold like any other business, to the detriment of the game itself.

[96] Frustrated by the boardroom's commercial priorities, Burkinshaw left Spurs in 1984. His famous lament on leaving White Hart Lane for the final time, attributed to him by the journalist Ken Jones, of 'there used to be a football club over there' remains one of the game's most famous and oft-used quotes.

Macca can... leave

On the same day as the announcement of the ground-breaking television contract, there was further evidence of the game moving into a new era when the Football League announced a sponsorship deal with Japanese electronics giants Canon. English football received £1.1m per season over the next three years and an appalling phallus of a First Division trophy, a smaller version of which would not have looked out of place in the seedy back-street shops of Soho.

The trophy may have been a gaudy, golden monument to eroticism, but Everton's chances of getting their hands on it seemed as distant as ever in the summer of 1983. The Toffees, like others, were still feeling the effects of the financial crisis within the game. Through the trimming of the wage bill, Everton actually showed a small profit for the previous campaign but the gap to their close rivals was growing. Whereas the Goodison club had one employee earning more than £40,000, there were fourteen at Anfield. The recent activities in the transfer market also reflected the divide. 'Everton have avoided the big names and been content with far less spectacular investments,' Ian Hargraves said in the *Liverpool Echo*, 'And in so doing, they have given their supporters the impression, rightly or wrongly, that they have opted out of the big time and are now content to play a supporting role.'

With that in mind, the *Liverpool Daily Post* asked Kendall whether Everton should still be classed as a big club, given they did not have the financial muscle to buy the coveted Alan Brazil and Charlie Nicholas, who had both moved to north London. The Everton manager responded:

Yes, this is still a big club. We just aren't in a position to go for highly valued players. We aren't prepared to go overboard and spend money we haven't got. Those clubs which do, take a gamble which could backfire. [About Brazil] I couldn't go after him, although I would have liked him in my side. He was too expensive... I am very limited. I am fully aware of the financial situation at the club. Times are still hard.

Club finances were in sharper focus when Steve McMahon's contract was up for renewal at the end of July. Kendall had dropped the midfielder for the final game of the season after word leaked out that he had spoken to another club. McMahon subsequently rejected a better contract, to Kendall's apparent dismay.

'He is a good player and I would much rather have him than the money we would get for him,' the manager admitted. McMahon had spoken with Aston Villa and Liverpool, but the Midlands outfit got in first and Everton accepted their bid of £250,000.

The midfielder gave his version of events in his 1990 book *Macca Can!* 'The parting of the ways between Howard and myself was not the most amicable,' he recalled. 'Howard insisted that he had made every effort to persuade me to stay and suggested he had made the biggest contract offer ever made by the club. I was puzzled because that simply was not the case.' McMahon pointed to Everton offering others better deals and felt that they just wanted to sell. 'I got the impression that the final decision to let me go was not taken solely by the manager. I just had the feeling that maybe the Board of Directors wanted to cash in on my transfer,' he wrote. The lifelong Evertonian was probably correct about being a pawn in a bigger game – despite the manager's platitudes, if he really wanted McMahon he could have found the money. In truth, the player had enjoyed an inconsistent campaign as he later admitted: 'My performances for Everton were getting a bit stale towards the end.' Kendall believed the midfielder was too ill-disciplined, preferring the more restrained Kevin Richardson as the season ended. 'I was never entirely convinced by Steve McMahon,' Kendall wrote in *Love Affairs and Marriage*, 'There was a determination to him which was good, but a 'professionalism' too. He was no Johnny Morrissey, but I was never a believer in or a fan of those players that boasted a nasty streak. I didn't think a player needed that.'

That said there were some eyebrows raised in the dressing room. 'I was surprised when Howard Kendall let him go – very surprised,' Kevin Ratcliffe told the *Daily Mirror* before the 1989 FA Cup final, 'A lot of lads could see he was going to be a good player.' Kendall may have, perhaps unfairly, forced McMahon into a corner, because he knew exactly what he was doing with the money.

Feast of Steven

In early 1982 *Kick-Off*, Granada TV's Friday night magazine programme, broadcast a profile of a promising Burnley midfielder. Although outside of his control, the feature annoyed Kendall. Believing he was the only manager on the trail of the talented eighteen-year-old, the Everton boss was convinced the piece would bring the delicate skills of the spindly youngster to a wider audience.

He was wrong. The *Guardian's* Patrick Barclay had earlier watched Burnley against Altrincham in an FA Cup tie, and came away suitably impressed by a number of young players, but saying that 'The most impressive was the eighteen-year-old Trevor Steven, whose skill, pace and balance made light of a pitch that was anything but. He looks a quite exceptional talent.'

'I almost had a season ticket at Burnley when I was tracking Trevor Steven,' Kendall told the *Liverpool Echo* two decades later, 'And it was only after we had signed him that I learned Bob Paisley had been just as frequent a visitor to Turf Moor, standing unnoticed behind the goal with his cap on!' There was also interest from both Manchester clubs. On one occasion, conscious that he had not seen the starlet play away from home, Kendall travelled to Lincoln of all places. A 300-mile round trip one Wednesday evening in March 1982 required just twenty minutes in Paisley's preferred location. 'Trevor was majestic and I'd seen all I wanted by then. I thought he'll do, and left,' the Everton boss later admitted. The chase for the youngster had echoes of Harry Catterick's pursuit of Kendall at Preston sixteen years before.[97]

Kendall's time in Lancashire proved well spent. With Paisley's interest waning – feeling the youngster lacked stamina, having seen him substituted on a number of occasions – the Everton manager moved into pole position during the summer of 1983, with the two clubs eventually agreeing a fee of £300,000.[98] 'I think Trevor's an Everton type of player and that our fans will like him,' he said. That was certainly true, Steven's aristocratic manner was apparent even in a struggling team. But there was as much substance to the midfield wide-man as undoubted style and grace. Equally significant off the pitch, Steven was a strong, intelligent character who knew his own mind. There was also an interesting by-product from the deal. Kendall had been talking to Stoke City's Paul Bracewell about a move to Goodison, but with limited funds could not afford both. The midfielder eventually joined Sunderland, but twelve months later Kendall would come calling again.

---

97 Kendall's words about watching Steven were virtually identical to Catterick's about scouting the future Everton manager in 1967: 'I have had practically a season ticket for Preston's games in the last twelve months.' Like Kendall with Steven, Catterick would watch from the terraces on occasions.

98 Kendall later recalled in the *Liverpool Echo* that he was in the boardroom at Goodison and the now former Liverpool manager approached him. 'Bob said: "You've done well with young Steven. You were right all along about him." It was very satisfying and humbling that Bob paid me such a compliment.'

The ghosts of the past

Kendall was halfway through his four-year contract at the start of the 1983/84 season. Beforehand this was clearly the make-or-break campaign. In other cities taking a club that had finished fifteenth and seventeenth to eighth and seventh constituted progress. But the Everton board and supporters judged Kendall by completely different standards. Being top dogs on Merseyside meant becoming the best team in Europe.

Kendall told the *Daily Mirror* about the frustrating nature of matching the red machine, even with Joe Fagan replacing Bob Paisley. 'You look for signs that Liverpool are on the decline, you see them, and get kicked in the face,' he declared, 'I thought when Ray Clemence left, it was our chance, I was wrong. Now Bob Paisley has stepped aside, Manchester United have beaten them in the Charity Shield, and you wonder again. But they had £2 million worth of players on the sidelines.' For all that, Kendall admitted that 'I wouldn't say we've made it if we finished halfway and they were two places below us, if I'm top and they are two places back that would be success.'

His two predecessors had found surpassing the Anfield club too much of a challenge and, for all his public aspirations, after two years there was no evidence that Kendall was up to it. With money in short supply, the only hope was that his young players could convert their undoubted talent into something more tangible. But even Kendall did not share that belief. 'I've found since I came here from Blackburn two years ago that certain players can't cope with the past,' he claimed at the time. 'They look round this ground and it's too much for them. But they had better believe the only thing that will bring fans back here is a side that wins something, and wins it in the Everton tradition.'

On the basis that imitation is the best form of flattery, Kendall added another Anfield reserve, full-back Alan Harper, to the playing staff over the summer. His main priority had been a striker, with Sunderland's Stan Cummins reportedly turning down a move, until Kendall landed a familiar name – Terry Curran, for a knockdown £95,000. Six months earlier, after his successful loan spell, the Everton manager had tried to sign the gifted winger before the transfer deadline. After agreeing a £120,000 fee with Sheffield United, there were dramatic scenes when the two men met to register the deal. 'The first thing that struck me when he arrived at Lytham yesterday afternoon was that he had his agent with him,' Kendall said later. 'You would expect a player who was desperate to play for you to turn up with an overnight bag and his boots.' Curran explained that he wanted more money and an angry Kendall pulled out of the deal: 'I am a much more wiser man than I was 24 hours ago and I feel that I know a lot more about Terry Curran.' It says something about Kendall's perilous position that six months later he was prepared to forgive and forget.

Both chairman and manager were under pressure at the start of the crucial 1983/84 season and feeling the weight of the past on their shoulders. As one fan put it in the pages of the *Liverpool Echo*: 'Everton's history since 1970 is one of speedily extinguishing genuine talent, never going for the winner-type manager and being ruled by a board which many fans see as the biggest obstacle to success.' To be fair both men fully understood the demands of followers. 'I still get letters from people who talk about Ted Sagar and Dixie Dean,' Philip Carter admitted, 'Of course it's frustrating for our supporters. There is constant pressure from Liverpool. But we don't just want to win something. We want to have some success, and sustain it.' His manager spoke in similar vein. 'I accept this is a club where they are crying out for new heroes,' Kendall accepted, 'In five years' time, if they are talking about Kevin Sheedy, Adrian Heath and Trevor Steven, then we'll be a club of the present – not a lot of ghosts from the past.'

CHAPTER 26

The edge of darkness

THERE WAS ABSOLUTELY NO INDICATION AT THE START OF THE 1983/84 campaign that it was to become such a tumultuous season. The start was certainly odd. Kendall had some quirky beliefs and one was a dislike of back-to-back home games. The manager certainly did not approve of the ridiculous scheduling of the opening Bank Holiday weekend: matches at Goodison against Stoke City and West Ham United within the space of 48 hours. The Potteries outfit were dutifully despatched 1-0 on the opening Saturday thanks to a Graeme Sharp goal. But the game attracted a measly 22,658 spectators, the lowest for the home opener for seventy years and a sad sign of the times. On the Monday, a dreadful mistake by Jim Arnold allowed a Steve Walford cross to drop over his head and inside the far post as the Hammers stole three points.

The die was cast for the first four months of the season in those opening weeks. Everton drew 1-1 at Coventry City before a 3-0 midweek defeat at Ipswich where Kendall, perhaps due to the building pressure, publicly criticised one of his players. With the game goalless, Paul Mariner intercepted John Bailey's ill-judged back-pass and buried the chance. The manager substituted the left-back six minutes later. 'It was the one thing that turned the game… it was fairly even until that point,' Kendall said afterwards, 'That was the worst mistake by a defender in the First Division for a long, long time. It was a schoolboy error that let them in. You can't accept that at this level and while John was dejected, you must get through to the players.' The substitution left the team a defender short when still in the game and two late goals rubbed salt in the wounds. As one supporter wrote in the *Liverpool Echo*: 'Although Bailey's error cost Everton the first goal, Mr Kendall's emotional reaction cost Everton the match. I also strongly disapprove of the way Mr Kendall publicly condemned Bailey's error, as this does not improve team morale. Also, if the Everton boss is going to be consistent why did he not criticise Jim Arnold for his error against West Ham?' Sadly, this type of comment was merely the tip of a large iceberg of discontent.

'30,000 stay at home fans can't be wrong'

Before the start of the season Kendall wanted an improvement in Everton's away record – 'relegation form' he called it – and one of the ironies of the troubled start was vastly improved results on the road, with two victories and a draw in the opening four matches. One win had been at Spurs in mid-September when, with Kendall wanting more midfield bite, Peter Reid stepped in for the difficult trip. The fixture was a make-or-break appearance for the Huyton-born player, having featured just ten times since joining. Reid was excellent, opening the scoring in a 2-1 victory – the first time a Kendall team had won away at one of the traditional big clubs. 'I thought Peter had a superb game,' said his manager afterwards, 'It was probably his best display since he arrived at the club.' Two weeks later the midfielder scored the only goal of a trip to Notts County, when Neville Southall replaced Jim Arnold to become the club's established number one.

But the backdrop to improved away form was a series of drab, characterless performances at Goodison against moderate opposition. A goalless draw against West Brom preceded a lucky 1-1 stalemate against Birmingham City, thanks to a fortunate penalty and a Mick Harford goal wrongly disallowed. Nick Hilton, in the *Liverpool Daily Post*, pointed fingers at the board after the game. Noting the recently announced profit, he wrote, 'Have these gentlemen forgotten they are in the entertainment business… I don't believe there is a single customer on the Gwladys Street terraces who rejoices in seeing a neat set of accounts and his club in profit each year. He just wants to be entertained, to be excited and impressed.'

There was no chance of that in the mid-October game against Luton Town, a calamitous defeat thanks to Paul Walsh's late winner in front of just 14,325 spectators. 'Gates are dwindling and near empty stands make Goodison an eerie, near-silent mausoleum,' said Chris James in the *Daily Mirror*, 'The most noise was at the end – boos, jeers and catcalls.' The defeat meant Everton had accrued just one victory, and two goals, from their first five home games. 'The dressing room corridor to the pitch has become a tunnel of fear to the Everton players,' claimed James. 'Anxiety is creeping in,' Kendall said in agreement.

The defeat left Everton fifteenth in the table, with three victories from nine games. The defence had conceded just eight goals (the third lowest in the division) so there was no doubt where the problems lay – a powder-puff attack that had scored just six times. A year before Sheedy and Heath had scored goals from midfield, while Andy King's good form had disguised the lack of firepower within the forward line until late in the campaign. However, the 27-year-old was not the same player after his injury and was out the side. Replacement David Johnson had not impressed and when Adrian Heath stepped in, the team clearly were not playing to his strengths by knocking balls in from deep. Also Sharp had lost all confidence, exemplified by a strange choice in the win at Spurs. Graham Roberts' mistake left the Scot with a clear run, but rather than draw Ray Clemence from goal for a one-on-one, the striker took an early shot from twenty yards out that went wide. 'If I am honest with myself looking back, I was not going anywhere as a player,' Sharp recalled of this period when interviewed by Chris Bascombe in the *Sunday Telegraph* in 2020. In the middle of the park, the manager had randomly shifted players around. 'What I would like to see at the moment is more Peter Reids,' Kendall said at the beginning of October, 'There is not even a thought of leaving him out.' Three weeks later, he did.

Uncharacteristically Kendall fell out with some of the media too. The manager cancelled his Friday press conference before the Spurs away game, 'That was only our sixth game of the season but I had already had enough of the sniping and criticism,' he said in his 1991 book *Only the Best is Good Enough*. 'I don't know whether or not certain individuals were actively trying to get me out of the job but I began to suspect that they were not simply reflecting public opinion, but fuelling it.' Pressure building, after the victory at White Hart Lane neither Kendall nor his chairman spoke to the newspapers, with Carter criticised for not talking about his manager. In the strained environment following the Luton defeat, the chairman did just that, in a famous statement, delivered exclusively to John Keith of the *Daily Express*. Reprinted here are Carter's words in full:

The rumours, accusations and criticisms currently circulating about Everton Football Club demand an answer. And that is why I am taking the opportunity to present our case factually and honestly, to try to correct some of the misconceptions. The areas of concern – to us as well as our supporters I must stress – cover home performances and attendances, finance and transfers.

The first point I want to underline is that we are not complacent about our present problems. We are most concerned. But let me state equally unequivocally that our manager Howard Kendall has the fullest and absolute support of the board. He is a little more than halfway through a four-year contract and the board have not and are not exerting any pressure on him. If there is any pressure on Howard it is self-induced because he is a professional and like all good professionals wants the team to do well. We are right behind him.

There has been some misinformed comment recently that we are not in a position to support him in the transfer market… yet the facts are hardly mentioned. In just a few months since the end of last season we have spent £500,000 signing Trevor Steven from Burnley, Alan Harper from Liverpool and Terry Curran from Sheffield United. Before that we paid £700,000 for Adrian Heath from Stoke. It is true we did not make an attempt to sign Charlie Nicholas but, then, most other clubs also decided that the price was out of reach.

Howard Kendall is constantly searching for new talent but he has to be satisfied it would be right for Everton. If he does find a player he considers is the right type, he knows he can put the matter to the board and we will consider it. But suggestions that we imposed some kind of ban on buying players are nonsense.

As regards Goodison Park attendances and performances I think the two are inter-linked… and the figures tell a strange story. Compared with the attendances for our first five home games last season we are 25 per cent down – yet we are more than fifteen per cent up on last season's fixtures with same clubs, Stoke, West Ham, West Brom, Birmingham and Luton.

On the field there has been almost a complete reversal of our early-season fortunes between this year and last year. While we opened our home programme last season with spectacular wins against Aston Villa and Tottenham and shortly after beat Manchester City, our first away League point did not come until our win at Swansea in mid-October. This year we have won two, drawn one and lost one of our four opening away First Division games. But the fact that we have had disappointing home results *means our supporters were happier at this stage last season than they are now.*

We are concerned about our home attendances. Our average this season is now slightly below 18,000 and our financial break-even figure is 20,000, taking into account our other fund-raising activities. So we look forward to seeing an upturn in our attendances coupled with improved Goodison results.

We have every confidence the team will achieve that under Howard Kendall. That is just not a club chairman trotting out a hackneyed phrase – I am stating that categorically.

They were brave words indeed, from a chairman who was under pressure himself to deliver. After terrace criticism during the Luton game, Nick Hilton wrote that 'the common thread linking the jibes suggests the club as a whole is at fault, not particular players or the manager.' The press and supporters frequently made this type of comment in the previous decade or so. Amongst the criticism was the reasonable point that the board was distant and too domineering, a by-product of the days when John Moores ruled the roost. As one fan wrote in the pages of the *Liverpool Echo*: 'Everton's plight has been brought upon by the directors who over the years have consistently refused to appoint "big name" managers. We have had a long-line of "quiet" managers who seemingly would not say "boo" to the directors.' That was true to a point, but the board did go after big-name managers, but they would not come to Goodison because of the club's reputation.

The consensus was that unless the board got it right then there no chance of success. To counter that, Carter, who was a hugely clever man, defended his and the board's role to the *Daily Express* whilst cleverly placing distance between themselves and the manager. However, in supporting Kendall, Carter was also putting his own credibility on the line, having backed Gordon Lee for far too long. Nevertheless, if the chairman thought the supportive words would assuage fans, he was wrong.

Going off at Goodison
A week later Everton faced Chesterfield in the second leg of their League Cup tie, defending a single-goal lead from the game at Saltergate. In front of a new post-

war low attendance of just 8,067 supporters, the home team clumsily allowed a two-goal lead to slip against the Fourth Division outfit. At the end of the 2-2 draw an angry section of fans distributed leaflets 'expressing disgust at the way the club is being run' according to one observer. As the players made their way off the field to a blanket of boos, photocopies of the hand-written note were thrown into the air.

The leaflet read: *'30,000 stay at home fans can't be wrong. Bring back attractive winning football to Goodison Park. Kendall and Carter out!'* Understandable sentiments perhaps from a frustrated group, but something that upset the manager. 'I don't like that. It hurts,' he remarked on being shown the document, 'But we must keep going the way we are, because we think it's the right way.' Asked about his future, Kendall was adamant: 'I do not intend to go; I have no intention whatsoever of resigning and I am sure that Mr Carter feels the same way.' A week later, the *Liverpool Daily Post* spoke to the organiser of the protest, who confirmed a group of twelve had been responsible for circulating the 1,400 leaflets:

We needed to do something positive, rather than stop going to games like so many have done... we want the club to be aware that its supporters are not happy. We believe something drastic needs to be done because we fear for Everton's future as a First Division club... We support the club in itself and we believe there are a lot of people who support the stand we are making. Hardly anyone in the ground took exception to the leaflets we handed out at the Chesterfield game... Either the chairman should change his attitude or resign. We want someone who is interested in Everton and what goes on on the pitch, like John Moores did. We have a tremendous respect for Howard Kendall as a past player but we do not rate him highly as the manager of Everton Football Club.

Although Everton Supporters' Club were critical – 'It's a disgrace that some people will stoop so low' they said – if the actual method of communication is set aside then there was nothing controversial in the statement. The general impression amongst fans was that Everton were a club in crisis with a massive question mark over the manager. Other than buying a new striker, Kendall appeared to have run out of options, and money. The manager had bought trusted professionals, spent big on young talent, brought back old favourites and promoted several promising players from the reserves. He had retained the best players from the Lee era and moved on those who were not good enough or possessed the wrong attitude. But after two-and-a-half years, the 37-year-old had produced a defensively sound team that could barely find the net whilst playing in front of the lowest attendances at Goodison since before the First World War. Although Kendall argued that low gates were largely down to the recession – only 9,000 were at Anfield on the night before the Chesterfield contest – the large numbers of absent fans in league games compared to Liverpool (in 1982/83 the Anfield average was 35,000 against 20,000 at Goodison) told the true story. However, Carter still had faith in his manager, as he explained to Colin Malam in the *Sunday Telegraph* two years later:

> *It wasn't a question of sticking with Howard, but of giving continued support to the man I had selected in the first place. When we appointed him we knew he had limited experience, but a lot of potential. We realised we were going to have a period of rebuilding and consolidation, and what we said, in effect, was: "We believe in you and your judgement – now go out and get it right."*

When the dust had settled, the Everton boss reflected on the season so far. 'I admit that I have made mistakes, I have probably been changing the side around too much in recent weeks. I am doing this job to the very best of my abilities. I don't believe that anyone could do it better,' he claimed. The manager needed evidence to back that assertion up in the away game at Leicester, three days after leaflet-gate. The Foxes were bottom of the table having not won a league game all season and, tellingly, they were the only club in England with fewer league goals than Everton's seven. But the travelling fans saw a pitiful display by the visitors, with only Adrian Heath emerging with any credit from a costly 2-0 defeat. 'The fans gunning for Kendall's head were given plenty more ammunition,' wrote Peter Edwards in the *Daily Express*, 'Everton were passionless and predictable and could have been beaten by double the margin.' It was not a great day off the pitch either: whilst visiting supporters fought in the main stand, others chanted for Kendall's head both inside and outside the ground. Badly needing a break, the Everton manager now faced the most difficult fixture in English football.

A grey Sunday

Then, as now, the Merseyside derby was a big attraction and unsurprisingly the first of the season, scheduled for Bonfire night, was put back 24 hours for the benefit of ITV. Beforehand Kendall was optimistic. 'In ninety minutes they can give us a new start and show what they can do,' the Everton boss said, 'We are the underdogs and I want our lot so wound up that they have got to do something special.' The live television coverage meant both clubs were playing their first-ever league game on the Sabbath and on the Saturday evening those Evertonians soothing their pre-match nerves in the city's pubs could read Johnny Morrissey also talking up their chances in the *Liverpool Echo's* football pink edition. Kendall's title-winning teammate proclaimed: 'I know they are the underdogs but this is where Everton's fighting spirit will come out.' The visitors needed more against a team who, in the previous week, had crushed Luton 6-0 and produced one of their finest European results: a 1-0 victory at Athletic Bilbao in the European Cup after a goalless draw at Anfield.

Ominously for the 6-1 outsiders, the omens were not good. The fixture took place one year to the day after the 5-0 hammering at Goodison and, sadly for Kendall, the contest was similarly one-sided. For all the talk of doing something special, the Everton manager picked the wrong side. Sharp was a lone striker and Kendall packed the midfield. Alan Irvine and Kevin Sheedy played out wide but the central trio of Andy King, Adrian Heath and the inexperienced Trevor Steven were hardly natural middle-men or ball-winners. In contrast, Liverpool had Graeme Souness, Ronnie Whelan and a deep-lying Kenny Dalglish in the centre. The injured Kevin Richardson hampered Kendall's selection but substitute Peter Reid should have started. 'I admit to making a quite dreadful managerial blunder by leaving out Peter Reid,' he said later, 'Subconsciously, I possibly opted for an exercise in damage limitation.'

In front of a national television audience, the visitors faded after a reasonably bright start, falling behind when Southall failed to grasp Steve Nicol's cross and Rush pounced. In the second period one-time target Michael Robinson and Nicol completed the rout. 'Howard Kendall, Howard Kendall, there's a taxi at the gate,' chanted the delighted Kop in reference to the infamous sacking of Johnny Carey two decades before. In the television gantry the watching Jimmy Greaves found it all a bit one-sided. 'Liverpool aren't boring, but it is boring to talk about the game,' he said. Sidekick Ian St John summed up the thoughts of many: 'It was men against boys.'[99] Although they did not know at the time, the most hurtful aspect for Everton supporters would have been the response of the Liverpool manager. In his diary of the season, uncovered thirty years later, Joe Fagan expressed disappointment with the Everton performance and their lack of fight. 'It wasn't like a derby game,' he wrote, 'It was too easy for us so there wasn't much excitement.'

Now seventeenth in the table, Kendall was surprisingly sanguine. 'I'm not that down. We have probably turned on our best and they produced what they are capable of,' he said, 'But at the end you have to hold up your hands to the opposition and I can't fault one player on my side in terms of effort.' They were fair points as Liverpool put in a superb display, but the result reinforced the gap between the two clubs.

Three days later the manager took an important step in bridging that divide when he promoted highly respected reserve-team coach, Colin Harvey, to first-team duties. The second string had rampaged through the Central League during the campaign, winning all eight games, scoring 21 goals without conceding. The Everton boss explained to the *Liverpool Echo*'s Ken Rogers why Harvey was joining Mick Heaton on the senior coaching staff:

We have worked as a threesome since I came here, but now we want Colin to be even more involved. We think it's a positive move and one that will give us an important boost. I have the highest respect for Colin. When I was at Blackburn I offered him a coaching job. That emphasises the way I feel about him. He's been doing a tremendous job with the reserves and just wants the best for Everton. He is happy to step up and if some of the success he has had with the Central League side can rub off on the first team then we will all be delighted.

The permanent appointment made sense. Kendall had promoted a significant proportion of the first-team after they had played for Harvey's reserve side,

---

99 St John was involved in a moment of high comedy after the game. Hosting his excellent *World of Soccer* show on Radio City that evening, the Saint received a call from somebody complaining that Peter Reid should have been playing. As the caller continued to rant, the former Liverpool player sensed something was up. 'Can I ask who is calling?' he enquired. 'I'm Mick, Peter Reid's brother,' was the sheepish response.

so there was some continuity. Harvey's experience of the campaign had also been different, knowing nothing but victory. As Kendall remarked, he was looking for a morale boost in the short-term as much as anything else: 'Colin just wants the best for Everton and if he can help in any way to bring results then he will be delighted to do it.' The 'promotion' certainly came with the approval of the players. 'Colin was the man,' Kevin Ratcliffe wrote in the *Blues and I*. 'I've never met anyone like him. He should have been promoted at the start of the season, or even before.'

The first opportunity to change fortunes came that evening, in a fourth-round League Cup tie against Coventry City, a side that had won their previous three away games. Fears about the gate proved well-founded as only 9,080 loyal supporters turned up on a cold, bleak evening. Understandably, having witnessed just two 1-0 victories at home all season, there was a funereal atmosphere during the opening period when the home side had Neville Southall to thank for keeping the game goalless with three good saves. With rumours circulating all day that Kendall had to win the game to remain in the job, the manager's prospects looked bleak when beanpole striker Dave Bamber scored for Bobby Gould's side with a towering header early in the second half. With twenty minutes left, there had been little chance of an equaliser and when Mike Reid finally got his wish with brother Peter replacing Trevor Steven, the substitution was greeted by whistles and booing. However, the changeover had a dramatic impact as the home players were now imbued with previously hidden energy. Goalkeeper Perry Suckling saved superbly from Heath and Sharp before Mark Higgins' header struck the post. With Coventry sitting deeper and deeper Heath finally equalised after Higgins and King had shots blocked.

The home team smelt blood but when Micky Gynn broke five minutes from time, Southall saved crucially with his feet. With the Park End scoreboard saying normal time had ended, both sides were preparing for a replay but, with ninety seconds of stoppage-time played, Heath's cross from the byline ballooned into the air towards Sharp at the far post. The hobbling Scot headed home and the 9,000 long-suffering fans could not have celebrated with more elation than if the goal had won the final itself. A relieved Everton manager said afterwards: 'The attitude of the players after a goal down was absolutely superb... I'm delighted for everyone here and for the fans most of all.' Two months later Adrian Heath outlined to the *Liverpool Echo* the importance of the victory. 'The 9,000 who turned up were obviously the die-hards, the way they rallied round to inspire us that night was incredible and we responded to come back from the death. That win was a bit of a turning point for us in many ways.' As many have reflected since that was definitely the case, but sadly was not apparent at the time.

A Gray week

Interviewed by the *Liverpool Echo* early in the 1983/84 season, Alan Ball spoke about the challenges facing his former teammate, Kendall. The points he made were prophetic. 'The only way an Everton manager can go about wresting back the power on Merseyside is not by copying Liverpool. In other words Howard Kendall must build a character side rather than a machine,' the World Cup winner surmised, 'He needs a quality player that the Everton fans can worship. He needs a top man to lift the rest of the team and the crowd.' Regarding the latter suggestion, Kendall had made it known during the troubled times that he was after an experienced striker. 'Last season the goals were shared out... what we didn't have was a consistent performer alongside Sharp. That is something we are determined to solve,' he said. There were several potential targets. The Everton boss made an unsuccessful approach for Tottenham's unsettled striker Alan Brazil, whilst he considered Ipswich's Paul Mariner, at £600,000, too expensive. Kendall wanted Lincoln City's Glenn Cockerill but pulled out when the Third Division club upped their price to £200,000, which he considered too much for somebody with no top-flight experience. Bob Latchford was very much on the radar, as he was available on a free transfer, however he was ruled out. 'Bob didn't feel like the right move,' Kendall wrote in *Love Affairs and Marriage.* 'Time is beginning to run out for Everton,' Ian Hargraves warned in the *Liverpool Echo*, 'Unless public support is dramatically stimulated, the club who used to boast that nothing but the best would do, will have to choose between spending money they haven't got and accepting that they are no longer one of the British game's pacemakers.'

As well as time, options were running out too but there was an opportunity for one of the more entertaining tales of the Kendall era. Twenty-four hours before the Anfield derby, following a tip-off from a South American agent, Everton were reportedly preparing a deal to bring striker Joao Batista Nunes over to England, initially on loan. The 29-year-old Brazilian international had pedigree, two years before scoring twice for Flamengo in their 3-0 victory over Liverpool in the World

Club Championship in Tokyo. 'I have asked for a tape of one of his recent games,' said Kendall, 'We don't want to meet his plane and find his brother on it, instead of him!' The Brazilian was certainly enthusiastic: 'Imagine the headlines – from the Brazilian Backlands to the country of the Queen,' he proclaimed, 'I'm ready to be a success in Liverpool, the land of The Beatles. I would like to send the Everton fans a message – in my first game I promise to score a goal in their memory, and in memory of John Lennon, one of my heroes.' Delays in obtaining a work permit sadly resulted in the deal collapsing three months later as the flamboyant striker had become frustrated and changed his mind.[100] 'I am glad the uncertainty is over because things have changed considerably since November,' Kendall said. The Everton manager was talking about an inspired piece of business.

If Everton thought they were in crisis during the autumn of 1983, then Wolves were in a far worse state. Bottom of the league, the Molineux club were in dire straits financially and desperate to offload British record signing Andy Gray. Manchester United's Ron Atkinson was an interested party, watching the Scot several times. 'I've heard nothing, but if United are interested in me then I'm flattered,' Gray said. Wolves valued Gray at £400,000 but United felt he was overpriced. With Atkinson prevaricating due to doubts over the striker's fitness, Kendall had also been looking at the striker and when the board agreed to free up funds the manager struck.[101] Wolves boss Graham Hawkins was coincidentally at the Coventry game and within 24 hours the two clubs agreed a knockdown fee of £250,000.[102] However, the narrative is that to make Gray available for the Saturday, the clubs agreed an initial loan deal. However, that was only half the story as the Everton striker wanted to keep his options open. 'I knew Everton had some great players and fine potential – but I still wanted time to think over the move,' Gray

---

100 This is not the generally accepted version of events – which consists of Kendall rejecting the deal because he saw the Brazilian wearing gloves in the South American sun(!) The wearing of gloves may have been true but Everton still wanted Nunes until the player backed away.

101 The United manager knew Gray's knee specialist, Freddie Griffiths, who was Manchester-based. Atkinson asked him, 'If I sign Andy will he play me thirty-five games a season?' to which Griffiths replied, 'You'll be lucky if he plays you fifteen.'

102 The Liverpool Echo were famously first to the story thanks to a vigilant member of the public, as Ken Rogers recalled in his book *Born Not Manufactured*: 'Suddenly the phone rang and a Scouse voice at the other end of the line asked: "Are we signing Andy Gray?"' Rogers recalled, 'I asked the caller why he was posing the question and he said: "Because I've just seen him in a newsagent's opposite Goodison Park!"'

told the *Daily Mirror* eighteen months later, 'So I would only sign for one month.'

When the Scot finally put pen to paper, the cut-price deal was for two reasons: Gray was out-of-contract the following summer plus the 27-year-old's faltering knees. 'Andy is an outstanding player and it has just been a case of getting a goalscorer,' Kendall said. The manager was also relaxed about Gray's fitness. 'He has had a lot of injuries because he is so brave, but I don't want him to change,' he said after the Scot passed a medical. That said, the striker may have been a bit economical with the truth when checked over by the club doctor. Hawkins had handed over his medical file the day before and its size shocked Gray. 'I took one look at it and thought to myself, "Bloody hell, if I show them this there's no way they'll sign me,"' he confessed in his book *Gray Matters*. 'I had a big open fire in my house and that night I sat in front of it sifting through this folder and chucking documents into the flames. The next day when I travelled up to Merseyside I appeared to be a good deal healthier than I had been the day before.'

CHAPTER 27

New year, new belief

'THE END WAS CONTAINED IN THE BEGINNING,' GEORGE ORWELL wrote in *1984* but as 1983 drew to a close there was little sign of Kendall's fortunes changing for the better. Although Gray's debut produced a spirited 1-0 victory over Nottingham Forest, two weeks later there was a demoralising 2-0 home loss to Norwich City. In front of 14,106 fans, a moment of black comedy for the visitors' second goal summed up the depressing afternoon. Goalkeeper Chris Woods' long clearance arced towards the home penalty area but John Bailey failed to see Southall rushing out and only succeeded in heading into an empty net. 'That wouldn't have been conceded on a local park,' a furious Kendall said afterwards, 'For senior professionals to do that makes it one of the worst own goals you will ever see.' After the previous Everton manager lost 2-0 at home to Norwich, Philip Carter effectively gave Gordon Lee notice of execution,[103] this time the Everton chairman was holding his nerve – for now.

Festive fear

By Christmas, Kendall's team were sixteenth in the table, six points above the relegation zone, but having scored a paltry eleven goals in eighteen matches. Everton had provided tantalising glimpses of improvement. The first Saturday in December witnessed a 1-0 victory at third-placed Manchester United and there was progression in the League Cup at the expense of second-placed West Ham

---

103 History repeating itself in 2019 when Marco Silva was sacked less than a fortnight after another 2-0 home loss to the Canaries.

United. The Toffees played superbly in a 2-2 draw at Upton Park when a late equaliser deprived them of a deserved victory. Seven days later, they earned a quarter-final tie against Oxford United with a 2-0 win, after extra time, which was Mark Higgins' final appearance in an Everton shirt. The centre-half had been struggling with a pelvic problem, as he recalled twelve months later. 'That extra time really finished me off,' Higgins said, 'I could hardly walk down the tunnel at the end and I was rushed straight to hospital. It turned out that I had ripped my stomach muscles as well as aggravating the pelvic problem and I was confined to bed for a week. I'd carried the injury for years, but all the problems started from there.' Despite the Herculean efforts of both player and medical staff, the injury forced Higgins to retire, although after further surgery the burly defender made a brief comeback with Manchester United two years later before moving to Bury.

The renaissance was short-lived. A dreadful 2-0 loss at QPR on the weekend before Christmas re-opened old wounds. Everton's first appearance on a plastic pitch resulted in their players 'finding the ball about as hard to control as a blob of mercury' according to Stuart Jones of *The Times*. 'King had a penalty saved and Sheedy contrived to hit two shots which went for throw-ins. That just about summed up Everton,' Jones concluded. The feel-good factor following the purchase of Gray had now disappeared. 'Buying Andy Gray, in the belief that two heads are better than one for fielding the barrage of park-life punts up-field will not bring spectators back,' was one view to the *Liverpool Echo*. The Everton manager's insistence on using full-backs as a substitute – Gary Stevens had come on for Adrian Heath during the Norwich defeat – was bemusing, given the team had one of the best defensive records in the division. The supporters' frustrations drew sympathy from David Lacey in the *Guardian*: 'Watching Everton can be rather like watching celery grow – but without the dramatic impact.'

Christmas brought three crucial games against teams who were also struggling. Boxing Day witnessed a dour goalless draw against Sunderland in front of a disappointing home crowd of 18,683, but the nadir of Kendall's reign arrived 24 hours later. Everton travelled to bottom-placed Wolves who had won once in nineteen games with no league victory at Molineux in eight months. The die was cast when David Johnson pulled a hamstring getting up from his seat at the team dinner on the previous evening. The visitors fell away after a bright opening twenty minutes, conceding three goals with none in reply. Southall at fault for two. Afterwards an ashen-faced Kendall faced the press. Plummeting towards the drop-zone and with his future uncertain, Kendall said he was 'only prepared to discuss the ninety minutes of football – nothing else'. However, he did add mysteriously: 'Things are not going well on and off the pitch.' The off-the-pitch issues were unknown, but the Everton manager felt the end was nigh and on his return went to see the chairman to proffer his resignation. In *Only the Best is Good Enough*, he revealed, 'What I needed to know from Mr Carter was whether or not he still had faith in my abilities. I decided that if he gave the impression of no longer having confidence in me, I would resign on the spot.' When Kendall made his offer, Carter replied, 'No, I am not accepting that at all.' Reassuringly, the chairman then said he and the board had full confidence in the manager's abilities.

With the club suffering an injury crisis – 'This is quite simply the worst situation of its kind I have ever experienced...even the club dog Yogi is limping,' joked Kendall – Everton faced Coventry City on New Year's Eve. Before the game there was a strange incident on the training ground that indicated Kendall, for all his bonhomie, was in some turmoil. In his autobiography, *The Binman Chronicles*, Neville Southall recalled the odd encounter. Kendall approached the Welshman and asked if he could guarantee a clean sheet against the Midlands side. 'No I can't,' said Southall. 'And the answer was true. I couldn't. I really couldn't,' he wrote, 'I couldn't guarantee that even if – as we were not long after – we were the best team in the world... Yet Howard wasn't happy with my answer one little bit. So he called Jim Arnold over.' When Arnold gave the same answer – 'He was selfless and honest and he looked out for me,' Southall said – Kendall 'stomped off'.

Southall remained for a dreadful goalless draw before the *Match of the Day* cameras. The final moments at a windswept Goodison were painful. To background chants of 'what a load of rubbish', the referee blew for full time and widespread booing from the terraces followed. 'Everton have got difficult times ahead,' said local-born commentator Alan Parry, 'sad to see a team like Everton struggling in this manner and receiving this type of treatment from their own supporters.' The home manager's post-match press conference lasted all of thirty seconds. Kendall 'summed up his side's current plight in two succinct sentences, extended an all-embracing New Year greeting and walked on' according to the *Liverpool Daily Post's* Ian Ross. 'He was right to do so because there was quite simply nothing to be said. All those present at Goodison Park on Saturday had endured a spectacle which in many ways defies description. The only applicable words are boring, predictable and sad.' At the game – and standing in the shadows behind Kendall when the latter entered the directors' box – was Welsh national team manager Mike England. After the match BBC Radio 2 announced that, following an emergency meeting, Kendall would be relieved of his duties with England installed as manager. Carter angrily denied the claim as 'absolute nonsense from start to finish... The situation regarding Howard Kendall is exactly the same as I stated earlier this season. He has our full support and we are looking forward to a change in fortunes in 1984.'

Although injuries certainly had an impact – the only time Sharp and Gray had played together in two months was at Old Trafford in early December – there was little confidence up front due to a lack of service from midfield, where Kendall continually chopped and changed the personnel. Like Lee before him, Kendall appeared to have no idea of his best team and the lack of goals pointed towards his failings and managerial inexperience. The Everton boss could efficiently organise and solidify a defence but there had been little evidence during his four-and-a-half year managerial career that his teams could play consistent attacking football. Although some of his signings – Heath, Sheedy and Steven – could produce flair, they needed time to gel. Even in the match against Coventry at Goodison, Everton's best player was Peter Reid, who at least tried to provide a sense of purpose and direction.

With the walls closing in, on the second day of the new year Everton travelled to St Andrews for a vital clash against Birmingham City, having not scored a league goal for four games. Beforehand the manager spoke candidly with the players, as Andy Gray recalled in *Gray Matters*:

> *Howard sat us all down in the team hotel and gave us a long and at times blistering team talk. He said, "This is it. This is your last chance." He accused some players in the side of not pulling their weight and said that if we didn't get a result that was the lot of us finished. He would bring in reserves and kids from the youth team instead.*

The dressing down worked. In awful conditions Everton, who had to wear the Birmingham away shirts because of a colour clash, ground out a hard-fought 2-0 victory. Gary Stevens, only recently recalled, opened the scoring and Andy King wrapped up the game in the closing moments. The visitors had to thank Neville Southall for two breathtaking saves, the first at full-stretch from Billy Wright described as one of the best seen on the ground. 'It was all about character and determination and the fact that our lads came through to win said a lot for them,' a relieved Kendall admitted. The victory lifted the pressure a little, but the biggest game of his managerial career was on the following Saturday.

FA Cup third round, Stoke City (a)

The trip to the Potteries on the first Saturday of 1984 is enshrined within the fabric of the club. For Kendall the omens were good: earlier in the week, the Everton boss had won at one of his former clubs, and now he was facing another, managerless Stoke who had just one league victory in three months. Kendall was not fazed about the trip, declaring: 'Two of our best victories this season have been at Spurs and United and really we have played better away than we have at home.'

Kendall finally had Graeme Sharp available after missing six matches and the return of the Scot made a big difference. He replaced Andy King, who typically sat in the front row of the away stand. Backed by a vociferous travelling army of 5,000 supporters, in dreadful pitch conditions the visiting team survived one scare early in the second half as Brendan O'Callaghan struck Southall's legs when put clean through. However, on 66 minutes, the important breakthrough arrived. Andy Gray met Kevin Sheedy's looping cross from the left with a perfect diving header that flew in off the underside of the bar. 'It was a header of the highest class,' reported Ken Rogers in the *Liverpool Echo*, 'a superb exhibition of centre-forward play that brought a deafening salute from the giant army of Evertonians who had out-sung and out-shouted the home fans all afternoon.' Alan Irvine had probably his best game for the club and the winger moved in from the right six minutes from time and smashed a left-footed drive into the roof of the net.

The visitors deserved their 2-0 victory, but fans remember the game for Kendall's immediate post-match comments that have entered Everton folklore. 'In the dressing room beforehand we could hear the noise our fans were making,' he told the press. 'And opening the window gave the players more of a boost than anything I could have said. These fans are the people I feel good for now.'

FA Cup fourth round, Gillingham (h)

Everton's league form continued to improve, with four points from two games in the middle of the month, including an excellent 2-1 victory at Goodison over highly-fancied Spurs. On the final Saturday of January, the Toffees hosted the Third Division side at a sunlit Goodison Park. In the visitors' line-up were centre-half Steve Bruce and striker Tony Cascarino, who would play a key role in the tie. At Goodison, Bruce was excellent, showing all the defensive nous and leadership qualities that later brought huge success at Manchester United and he came closest to scoring for the visitors, when Alan Harper cleared his powerful header off the line.

The home team, with the Gray-Sharp axis on show for the first time on the ground, created little in response apart from a Gray effort cleared off the line, and in a return to the dark pre-Christmas days the bulk of the 22,380 crowd roundly booed the players from the pitch. 'To be an Everton follower must be like riding some crazy fairground machine that shoots you high into the sky before dumping you rudely on your backside,' John Keith wrote in the *Daily Express*. Three days later the replay at the 16,000 capacity Priestfield Stadium was as difficult as it seemed on paper, with the big news beforehand that Kendall had dropped Gray, a decision relayed during the pre-match meal. The decision angered the striker hugely, as he recalled in *Shades of Gray*:

> *To say I was devastated is an understatement. I was totally amazed at his decision. I'd been playing as well as any of the others and my surprise or shock at being left out soon turned to anger. I was just about to tell Howard Kendall to shove it and walk out of the team's headquarters when I managed for once to control my emotions... Howard Kendall turned to go back into the dining room and I paused. Shall I go back in or shall I just clear out now? That was the decision. I only had a couple of seconds to decide and thankfully someone up there guided me through the doors to rejoin the Everton team. Heaven knows what would have happened if I'd staged my one man walk-out.*

On the night Neville Southall came of age as an Everton goalkeeper, the underdogs tore into the visitors from the start. The Welshman pulled off two fine saves from John Leslie in the opening minute, with the players engaging in a personal duel afterwards. When Leslie did beat Southall, the recalled John Bailey kicked off the line. The goalkeeper was beaten again just after the break, but Terry Cochrane's shot hit the inside of the post. Kevin Richardson and Reid eventually got a grip but Everton had only two serious attempts on goal by full time.

With extra time a war of attrition as legs tired on the heavy pitch, the biggest opportunity to break the deadlock came five minutes from the end. The visitors left nobody at the back and a defensive clearance left a tired Cascarino with a clear run on Southall from his own half. In his entertaining 2000 memoir, *Full Time: The Secret Life of Tony Cascarino*, the Ireland international described his thoughts on the journey to the penalty area:

Any striker worth his salt will put this ball in the net.
Yeah but...
This is your big chance.
It's not as easy as it looks, you know.
You're shitting yourself, aren't you?
No, I...
You're going to miss.

And he did. An inspired Southall moved out and blocked the shot with his legs. Sixty seconds later Everton had a chance to perform daylight robbery but Sheedy's shot bounced back from the underside of the bar. After two hours of enthralling combat the game ended goalless and there was a question of the venue for the third game. 'We were in the dressing room when Philip Carter was tossing up,' Kendall recalled in *Three Sides of the Mersey*, 'He came in and said, "We're back here again." We went, "Aww, no. Oh dearie me," because it was a tight little ground and a difficult place to go.' Gillingham boss Keith Peacock summed up the thoughts of all those watching when asked about the man-of-the-match. 'That goalkeeper is something special,' he responded.

When the two teams reconvened, like many cup sagas the ending was swift and merciless. The second replay took place in farcical gale-force conditions, the ferocious wind ripping the roof off a nearby church and threatening to overturn coaches parked nearby. Kendall recalled Andy Gray and the striker's clever and powerful performance resulted in the visitors ending four hours of scoreless deadlock with three first-half goals inside eleven minutes. The first came from

Sheedy when Gray nodded down Reid's high, hanging cross. Heath added a second when he nipped between defender and goalkeeper to head home Gray's clever ball. The third goal was the best of the night, Sheedy rifling home a tremendous shot into the roof of the net from a tight angle after another pass from the striker. With Everton wisely keeping the ball on the ground, Gillingham found it difficult to gain headway in the second half. 'It was a tremendous performance,' a jubilant Kendall proclaimed after the 3-0 win, 'I don't think I've ever seen a game played in a stronger gale.' Asked about Wembley aspirations, the Everton manager replied: 'I don't talk about finals. I have lost too many semi-finals as a player.'

FA Cup fifth round, Shrewsbury Town (h)

The good news for Kendall was that the draw again produced a home tie against the Shropshire side. In the previous round, history had also repeated itself with Brighton removing Liverpool again. With Manchester United also out, there was a big opportunity should Everton win.

In front of a crowd of 27,106 – 8,000 less than twelve months before – the visitors posed fewer problems against a far superior Everton team. There was an early scare when Steve Cross – a scorer the year before – struck the angle of bar and post after Southall flapped at a cross but the Blues quickly got into their rhythm. On 27 minutes, Gray found Reid inside the penalty box but with the midfielder's route to goal blocked, he simply fed the speeding Irvine who thumped the ball past Steve Ogrizovic. The Scottish winger returned the compliment on the hour, moving inside and feeding the onrushing Reid, who timed his run to perfection and finished first-time at the Gwladys Street End. 'Peter Reid has not been one of football's luckier players,' wrote Derek Wallis in the *Daily Mirror* about the man-of-the match, 'Most of the bonuses he has earned have come in the form of handfuls of games uninterrupted by some horrendous injuries. Now 27, Reid has at last rid himself of the jinx that once threatened his career after, as a young player with Bolton, looking destined to win the game's highest honours.'

Everton wasted enough chances to bury the visitors, but had to settle for only one more goal, when the unlucky Colin Griffin deflected in Andy Gray's shot. The quarter-final took Everton to relegation-threatened Notts County, where they won 1-0 earlier in the season. The beneficial draw meant the Toffees were also 4-1 second-favourites to lift the trophy, after Southampton. The bookmakers thought differently to the *Guardian's* Simon Inglis, who said after the game that Everton were 'not convincing enough to suggest that the club can win its first major honour since 1970.' But Kendall's side were now hoping to challenge that theory across two fronts and prove that the Orwellian end to 1983 had indeed been part of the beginning.

CHAPTER 28

Oxford blue

THE MANOR GROUND, HOME OF OXFORD UNITED UNTIL 2001, IS now a hospital. If the medical profession had reported on Everton's condition in the middle of January 1984, they may have said that the patient was showing signs of recovery after multiple organ failure.

However, when the draw took the Toffees there to face Jim Smith's side in the League Cup quarter-final there was every chance of a relapse. Kendall was not joking when he claimed beforehand 'We are the First Division side who are underdogs'. Smith had fashioned a skilful and exciting team that stood second in the Third Division, but more relevantly had shocked Newcastle, Leeds and Manchester United after replays. Worryingly for Kendall, they had dominated Ron Atkinson's high-flyers in a second replay on the ground after going behind.

The main issue for the manager was Andy Gray being cup-tied, so the Everton manager recalled David Johnson. In front of a full-house of 14,000 – Everton sold all their allocation in fifteen minutes, including 200 stand tickets priced at an exorbitant £8 – the home team started on the front foot and Everton had Southall to thank for several fine saves, including one from a point-blank George Lawrence effort described as 'amazing' by John Motson on BBC's *Sportsnight*. Teams had previously failed to outplay Oxford so Everton went long, but sitting too deep meant the visitors created little and midway through the second half, Oxford got their deserved breakthrough. Kevin Brock's free-kick was headed back across the six-yard box and Bobby McDonald steered the ball home. Three years earlier the Scottish full-back's two goals in a quarter-final replay had done for Gordon Lee, now he had quite possibly finished off Kendall's Everton career too.

The Everton manager took off Johnson after his final appearance in an Everton shirt and pushed Adrian Heath up front. But there appeared to be no way back in the final fifteen minutes. Everton had rejected Kevin Brock as a teenager and the skilful midfielder had eyes on revenge when he picked up the ball midway in his own half, nine minutes from time. But pressed towards his own goal by Peter Reid, Brock's scuffed back-pass with his wrong foot was seized upon by Heath, who had cleverly anticipated a mistake, and the Everton player rounded keeper Steve Hardwick before equalising. The usual camera view made it look straightforward, but from behind the goal the angle was frighteningly tight and the club record-signing had produced a brilliant finish under immense pressure on a bumpy and icy pitch. The visitors managed to hold out for the reminder of the game for a draw which they barely deserved, having created only two chances all evening. Speaking to the *Independent* eight years later the Everton hero described the goal: 'I'd been pushed up front from midfield to try and save the game. Gary Briggs was marking me, but I nipped in and nicked it past the keeper. That end of the pitch was icy and hard, and I remember thinking "Keep your feet" before putting it in from an acute angle. People may think now that drawing at Oxford was no big deal, but they were a very strong side.'

Afterwards Oxford boss Jim Smith – who had prowled the touchline in a camel coat and flat cap, looking like he had stepped off the set of *Only Fools and Horses* – bitterly complained that justice had not been served. 'Everton had two shots and one went in. Their way of stopping us playing was to keep the ball in the air and they treated it like the cup tie it was.' Meanwhile Kendall was a relieved man. 'We are delighted we are still in the competition. That was the object of the exercise and now our players know what they are up against from this Oxford team,' he revealed. The players certainly used their Oxford education effectively: at Goodison a week later the reinvigorated home side ran out easy 4-1 winners, in a match played in a blizzard at times. Encouragingly, the attendance of more than 31,000 was the best on the ground for eleven months.

There has been speculation since whether a defeat at Oxford would have resulted in Kendall's sacking. Heath himself said that 'the feeling in the club was that he'd have to go if that happened' but alternatively the manager was safe as long as Everton remained in the FA Cup and maintained their improved league form. As Kendall told the *Sunday Express'* James Mossop later in the season, the club could only have been in crisis if they were out of both cup competitions and in the bottom-half of the table.

However, the equalising goal undoubtedly prefaced a golden period for the club's record signing. Heath had sporadically displayed his undoubted potential during two years at the club and like others had struggled before Christmas. 'My form was pretty awful and the team were poor,' he admitted, 'People were wondering why he'd paid so much for me.' Three days later, he scored twice in the victory over Spurs, followed up by a further goal in the replay victory over Oxford. On the first Saturday in February, Heath netted a hat-trick in the 4-1 home win over Notts County, taking his tally to nine goals in eight matches. By then Everton were continuing their pincer movement on Wembley.

League Cup semi-final (first leg), Aston Villa (h)

In 1971, Harry Catterick spoke about the challenges of taking over Everton ten years before. 'The club were becoming a bit like Villa, trophies were antique,' he said, 'This is wrong. You want modern trophies and this club simply has not had them.' Thirteen years later only one half of that statement remained valid. Whereas Everton were suffering a prolonged trophy drought, over the previous decade the Midlands club had garnered two League Cups, the League Championship in 1981 and European Cup twelve months later.

By the time the two clubs clashed in the semi-final, although Villa had retained a strong element of their title-winning team there were new additions like winger Mark Walters, plus Steve McMahon. With the opening leg at Goodison, Everton could take heart from their opponents' poor away form that had resulted in only one league win all season. The Gillingham second replay had delayed the tie, so unusually for a two-legged semi-final the teams already knew their opponents at Wembley – holders Liverpool. For Everton, after fourteen years in the wilderness, the stakes could not have been higher. 'Thankfully I can say that we could not be better prepared,' Kendall confidently admitted, 'We are at full strength and have enjoyed a good run of success to give ourselves confidence.'

A frantic opening half at Goodison tested that buoyancy, when the only tactic appeared to be kicking the ball as far as possible whilst squandering possession in embarrassing fashion. After almost half-an-hour of shapeless action there had been one half-chance, when Heath fired over the bar. 'The ball at times seemed an irrelevancy as bodies collided, tackles crackled and tempers frayed,' said Stuart Jones in *The Times*. Then out of nowhere, the home team scored via a messy goal in keeping with the occasion. Sheedy broke clear on the left and his deflected cross veered towards the near post where Dennis Mortimer, Gary Williams and goalkeeper Nigel Spink appeared to have any danger covered but, with Heath prowling, all three left it to each other and the ball dribbled over the line.

Kevin Richardson had enjoyed a fine game in a defensive midfield role but bizarrely both arms of the 21-year-old became the game's major talking point. The Geordie both fractured and dislocated his right wrist in the opening half, which needed a heavy strapping on the lower arm during the break. Thereafter chances and coherent football were in short supply before a second Villa defensive error with eight minutes left had disastrous consequences. Des Bremner's weak header went straight to Richardson at the edge of the box and the midfielder – always a wonderfully crisp ball striker – fired home clinically to the right of Spink. The Everton player waved away any celebrating teammates for fear of causing further damage. Villa immediately launched a counter-offensive and ninety seconds from time, to most of the 40,006 spectators, earned a penalty. Withe's header from Alan Curbishley's corner crashed down from the bar and after Southall desperately scrambled to gather the ball, Richardson's left arm appeared to turn away Gary Shaw's flick from the line. Amazingly, referee Alan Saunders appeared to be the only person in the ground who missed the handball.

With Kendall happy to take a single-goal lead to Villa Park, Richardson's late involvement at both ends was a bonus. The midfielder was coy when asked about the handball. 'I don't remember too much about it at all, because things were a bit hectic then,' he explained, 'I'm sure I didn't handle. I just moved across the goal and the ball went past me and on towards the corner flag.' The Toffees may now have been strong favourites but the *Guardian's* Charles Burgess was not impressed: 'On the basis of the appalling football played by both teams at Goodison Park, the holders, already through to Wembley, would have little difficulty in beating both teams together.'

League Cup semi-final (second leg), Aston Villa (a)

In front of more than 42,000 fans – including 12,000 who had travelled down the M6 – the second leg was a far more attractive affair, although still feisty. When the PA announced the attendance some wag asked if it was the number of fouls. Unbeaten in fourteen games, during the opening half Kendall's team, probably for the first time, showed that they had now turned undoubted promise into the enduring characteristics of a very good side. Solid at the back, the midfield pressed and harried Villa while Heath and Sharp remained a constant menace.

Both strikers came close to finishing off the home side, with Heath providing the individual highlight of the tie. Exhibiting marvellous acceleration to beat Bremner to a long pass, the striker lifted the ball over the Scot's head but saw his fabulous shot come back from the underside of the bar. Sharp then saw a header strike the inside of a post. By the hour mark, the game was meandering but Andy King, playing in place of Richardson, fashioned a suicidal back-pass and Villa substitute Paul Rideout gratefully fired past Southall. For the long-suffering away supporters, the final thirty minutes were tortuous, but displaying the resilience that was to become their trademark, Everton stood firm.

The scenes after the game were memorable. Alan Irvine could not escape the playing area and Everton fans carried him shoulder-high. Ten minutes later the players returned to the pitch for an encore. 'It was a night to remember, particularly for our supporters, who were quite unbelievable,' Kendall said later, 'It was the proudest moment of my managerial career and when it was over, I felt ecstatic... My only regret is that we have to play Liverpool on what is virtually their own ground.' Kendall's job was on the line at the start of January, seven weeks later his team was 12-1 for a domestic cup double.

Liverpool, League Cup final, Wembley

So the date was set for the historic occasion. The final Sunday in March would witness the first Merseyside derby at Wembley but thankfully for ticketless fans ITV televised the final live, for the first time ever. Intriguingly, there was a warm-up in the league at Goodison three weeks before when, after being a goal down at the break having not really competed, in the second period Everton were unrecognisable. Inspired by Reid they compressed the play in midfield and shook the Anfield side out of their aristocratic stride. 'Everton swarmed forward in such numbers that Liverpool lost control of the midfield – and very nearly themselves,' said Derek Wallis in the *Daily Mirror*. The home team had a chance to equalise from the spot after Alan Kennedy fouled Andy Gray in the box,[104] but Bruce Grobbelaar saved Sharp's weak kick. Six minutes from time, Kendall's side got their reward. A series of headers eventually led to the ball reaching an unmarked Alan Harper in the box and the substitute's beautifully struck shot left the

---

[104] Curiously the second time it had happened that season, at Molineux on the opening day Wolves were awarded a penalty when Kennedy fouled Gray there as well.

Liverpool keeper with no chance. The deserved draw was a huge psychological boost and for the first time in a while, Everton had fought back in a derby match to gain a share of the spoils.

Before the final, the focus was on how Everton had turned fortunes around in less than three months. There had been an obvious change in the style of play. The arrival of Gray had only accentuated the ineffective reliance on the long-ball, but there was a definite movement from January onwards into a more methodical, possession-based game. Many suspected that the arrival of Colin Harvey on the coaching staff was behind the change. In training, Harvey's approach led to more competitive, intense sessions. 'He led by example,' Neville Southall recalled in *The Binman Chronicles,* 'He trained and trained and trained. Players looked at him and were inspired by what he did.'

Kendall was seeing the benefits of a settled goalkeeper and defence. Southall, after a rocky spell at the end of December when the Everton manager seriously considered recalling Jim Arnold, was developing into a keeper of the highest class. At full-back, a more mature Gary Stevens had regained his place from Alan Harper. In the centre Derek Mountfield had replaced the stricken Mark Higgins. Signed from Tranmere Rovers in the summer of 1982, the centre-half had featured in only a handful of games before Higgins' injury but afterwards showed that he was probably the most improved player at the club. Strong in the air and deceptively quick, the 21-year-old gave Kendall the right-foot/left-foot central defensive partnership he craved. Having skippered the team in place of Higgins, Kevin Ratcliffe was also developing as a lightning-quick centre-half who read the game superbly. The Welsh international also possessed the mean streak and slyness required of all the best defenders – a favourite trick early on would be to push the ball a yard further than required to draw in the opposition centre-forward, who would then be clattered with little chance of receiving a yellow card.

Elsewhere, apart from Adrian Heath's goals, the two biggest influences were, famously, Peter Reid and Andy Gray. On the pitch, Reid had the greater impact in the opening months of 1984. After a career riddled with injuries the midfielder had adapted his style, now relying on cunning and experience to nick the ball off opponents, rather than engage in constant physical combat. Reid set the tempo for the team, rarely lost possession and would often drive forward from a central position towards the box. Kendall later paid tribute to the midfielder: 'He came into the side and said "I will do it. Give it to me." That was the important factor when the confidence was low. I had too many players at the time leaving it to each other.' In a memorable piece in *The Times* after the game against Shrewsbury, David Powell wrote that 'Watching Peter Reid on Saturday was like trying to follow an ex-convict on his first few hours out of jail. Determined to make up for lost opportunity, Reid could not stay still for a minute... several years of hard labour have left his fingers itching for silverware.'

Gray's impact was less quantifiable. The Scot was a naturally ebullient and confident personality, as much a contributor in the dressing room and at Bellefield as on the pitch. 'He has had a marvellous influence on everyone,' Kendall said, 'Every time he has joined a new club, that club has won something in his first season, so that has to be a good omen.' Peter Reid also spoke about Gray's influence to the *Liverpool Echo*. 'It's a different team since earlier in the season,' he confided, 'Confidence is half the battle and Andy Gray's arrival has made a big difference to us. Things like this help put things together – you can't put a finger on it, but it all combines to make us into a decent side.' Asked if he was similar to Gray, the midfielder replied 'We both like to get stuck in. I like winning.'

On a damp Sabbath the midfielder had a chance to do both. Upwards of 70,000 fans left the city and the authorities wisely allowed pubs around the stadium to remain open,[105] but at £1 a pint the price was significantly greater than at home. The scenes in and around Wembley are almost clichés now: the cars and coaches filled with blue and red scarves plus the lack of segregation. Kendall's only selection problem was Kevin Sheedy, who had missed the preceding three games with an ankle injury. But the Ireland international was fit and Everton's line-up (4-4-2) for the historic occasion was: *Southall; Stevens, Ratcliffe, Mountfield, Bailey; Irvine, Reid, Richardson, Sheedy; Heath, Sharp. Sub: Harper.* The bookmakers made Liverpool heavy favourites: 5/6 on, with Everton 11/4.

'We didn't think they'd give us much trouble again that season,' Kenny Dalglish later wrote about Liverpool's 3-0 derby win five months before but that is what Everton did at Wembley. The atmosphere at the start was electrically-charged, as indeed was the underdogs' performance in the opening period as

---

[105] Amongst the other requests that the authorities refused was a trip round the ground by the Toffee Lady and a sponsored streak.

their midfield, plus Heath, disturbed the favourites' smooth rhythm. Ironically, the moment in the game that still resonates with Evertonians occurred early on. Heath and Grobbelaar both went for Sharp's flick-on, the striker wrestled the ball away from the goalkeeper and hooked it towards goal. The galloping Alan Hansen was covering and the centre-half lifted both arm and leg to stop the ball, which quite clearly struck the former. Amazingly, referee Alan Robinson and his assistant failed to see the contact and allowed play to continue. Brian Clough was bemused on television. Asked by legendary commentator Brian Moore whether it was handball, he replied 'From where I'm sitting, definitely.'

While making Liverpool look lethargic and unnerved, the team in blue showed they had more in the locker than just hard work. 'What was surprising was the imaginative quality of their play once they had gained possession,' David Lacey noted in the *Guardian*, 'Some excellent interchanges of position, assured first-time passing and intuitive running... at times found Liverpool's defenders falling over one another in their anxiety to clear the danger.' There were further chances, Richardson's fierce left-footed shot went inches wide while Sheedy, who was clean through, surprisingly shot early at Grobbelaar rather than take extra steps. That said, Phil Neal had just clattered the Irishman from behind, a tackle that led to the Irishman's early departure. After the game, opposition manager Joe Fagan said the holders could have been three down at half-time. Unsurprisingly, Liverpool came on strong in the second half, as Everton legs tired due to the heavy pitch. Ian Rush – kept quiet by the opposition defence, with Ratcliffe outstanding – missed the best chance of the game, hopelessly miscuing from three yards out and firing over. After a sparkling, but goalless, ninety minutes the final went into extra time for the fourth successive year. Four minutes into the additional period came the save of the match, Southall producing a blinding stop from Rush's crunching volley. Fittingly though Everton had the last word, when confusion in the Liverpool defence nearly resulted in Neal putting through his own net.

After two hours of breathless and dramatic action, there was nothing between the teams, who both walked up to the Royal Box to meet the Queen Mother. On returning to pitch level the players walked round the ground to the strains of 'Merseyside, Merseyside' from the 100,000 spectators, who had witnessed the right result in the circumstances. Kendall's side had done the Everton contingent proud – 'How many people could come here and handle that,' he said. Brian

Clough agreed, 'I think they will regard it as a moral victory.' The two clubs now had to resume hostilities at Maine Road three days later.

Liverpool, League Cup final replay, Maine Road

The fall-out from Wembley focussed on the penalty incident. 'I could have understood it if the linesman had been on the other side, but he had a clear view,' said a frustrated Kendall, 'It was disappointing because we had started well and it's important to take the lead if you have a good spell.' Hansen for his part admitted to handling the ball, but claimed it was unintentional, although his response looked a quite deliberate attempt to get both leg and arm in the way of the shot. Although, for balance, supporters forget Liverpool had two goals disallowed for, at best, marginal calls.

With Sheedy out, Kendall drafted Harper into the team with Andy King, the sole Everton survivor from the 1977 semi-final, named as substitute. The consensus was Everton would struggle to contain Liverpool again with a repeat of seven years earlier a possibility, when the Toffees similarly felt hard-done by after the first game. Underdogs seldom made the most of a second opportunity.

However, Everton immediately disproved that theory, settling into the same Wembley groove in a frantic encounter before 52,089 spectators, who created an even better atmosphere. 'It took Liverpool an hour to adjust to the difference last Sunday,' commented Stuart Jones in *The Times*, 'Now they were ready. They had to be.' If Sunday was about the occasion then Wednesday was about winning. Consequently, the replay was contested in a far more raucous spirit in keeping with a local derby – 'the pace of the game is white hot' said an admiring Clough – although Kendall's side again had much the better of the opening twenty minutes. Then against the run of play, Liverpool ended the stalemate. Graeme Souness received the ball twenty yards from goal and, whether by accident or design, it rolled over the Scot's right foot. Swivelling round instantly the midfielder's left-footed strike rocketed into the corner past a startled Southall. There were a few observers – Clough and Andy Gray included – who thought the Welshman was partially at fault in not being at the edge of his six-yard box, although Gray did qualify his statement by saying he was judging Southall by the keeper's own high standards. The Welshman was also unsighted in fairness.

Everton remained in contention, Grobbelaar stopped Heath at the near post and Neal cleared off the line from Richardson. Whereas the two Everton forwards remained a constant threat, Ian Rush was having a quiet game again, superbly marshalled by his Welsh international colleague. Brian Clough remarked that the striker 'Doesn't look happy at all. If I was to give him any advice, I'd tell him to get away from his mate because his mate has got him in his pocket.' In the second half Everton continued to have plenty of possession but wasted their one great opportunity to equalise. Sharp directed a header towards the unmarked Heath and Reid at the far post but they blocked each other and the midfielder's shot went wastefully wide. Kendall played his last card by bringing on Andy King for the ineffective Alan Irvine, but the Toffees ran out of steam and Grobbelaar collected a constant stream of crosses with unusual assurance. In the end Liverpool had enough quality and experience to win the trophy for the fourth successive season, but as Souness charitably admitted afterwards, 'Evertonians will go home crying but they shouldn't – they should be very proud of their team. They never stopped trying and they are such a difficult team to beat.' The match-winner also defended the Welsh international: 'When I hit the ball it dipped and that probably deceived Neville Southall, who is playing better than any 'keeper in the country at the moment.' Kendall's reaction in the immediate aftermath mixed anger, defiance and optimism in equal measure. The Everton manager was not happy with referee Robinson, accusing him of not penalising centre-backs in the area when being happy to award fouls for the same offences elsewhere. 'I don't think we were kindly treated by the officials,' he complained. Yet this works both ways, Everton were the beneficiaries of a crucial refereeing blunder against Villa in the semi-final. Nevertheless, the Everton manager left Maine Road with a call to arms: 'Most people regard Liverpool as the best. We have played them for 300 minutes in recent weeks and that Graeme Souness goal is the only thing separating the sides. That shows our progress and how much nearer we are to achieving something... we've still got the chance to reach another final.' There was a good omen too. The two previous beaten finalists – Tottenham and Manchester United – had gone on to lift the FA Cup.

CHAPTER 29

'Fourteen years'

IN THE DARK DAYS, KENDALL WAS BRAVE ENOUGH TO ATTEND A question-and-answer evening in one of those nicotine-filled venues that were very much a feature of working-class Britain. The Everton boss made the oft-quoted statement that managers live and die by their results. Immediately from the back, a gruff voice boomed through the smoke, 'In that case Kendall, you've got a week to live.'

Thankfully, by spring 1984 any rumours of the manager's demise were greatly exaggerated. In March, Everton had gone the distance with their Merseyside rivals three times and travelled to Notts County for their quarter-final FA Cup tie, played in sporadic torrential downpours that turned an already muddy pitch into a boating lake. The visiting army of more than 10,000 outnumbered the apathetic home fans in a 19,534 crowd. With Adrian Heath ruled out, Kevin Richardson was back in the team after his injury, but only after the referee had cleared the plaster-cast on his wrist at the eleventh hour. It took only six minutes for the returning midfielder to make his presence felt. Everybody missed Gary Stevens' long throw and Richardson ghosted in to head home in front of the ecstatic away supporters.

Yet County stayed in the game and got their reward on nineteen minutes, Southall saved brilliantly from Trevor Christie's header but John Chiedozie thumped home the rebound. The home side forced Southall into excellent saves from Aki Lahtinen and Iain McCulloch but Everton restored their lead in the second half with a headed goal that summed up Andy Gray. Sheedy's free-kick landed about nine yards from goal and the Scot reflected on what happened next in *Gray Matters*: 'I knew instinctively that if I went for it with either foot I'd be stretching and I'd put it over the bar so, instead, I launched myself at it at full length. It was about eight inches off the ground when I made contact, practically a half-volley, but it went into the net.'

Thereafter Everton dominated, as the home team rarely threatened and the visitors were good value for their victory. Those fans who could swim invaded the pitch at the final whistle, prompting BBC commentator John Motson to proclaim: 'A match memorable really for the incredible away support that proves Everton are still a great club.' Whereas the game at Stoke was the first awkward meeting after a trial separation between players and fans, the victory on the banks of the Trent was different. For the first time in the Kendall era, the feeling was one of communion between the two parties, a bond that remained for the rest of his first spell. 'It is no exaggeration to suggest that this sixth-round triumph belonged to supporters more than to the team,' said Derek Wallis in the *Daily Mirror*. Kendall himself declared: 'They were simply magnificent as they have been all season. They urged us on all the way and the lads were overwhelmed at the reception.' However, at a function in the Town Hall 48 hours later celebrating the all-Merseyside League Cup final, they found out their semi-final opponents. It was the worst-case scenario.

FA Cup semi-final, Southampton (Highbury)

Of the three remaining semi-finalists the Saints were the toughest draw. Lawrie McMenemy's outfit possessed a fine balance between youth and experience and were favourites going into the game at 5/4, with Everton 15/8, a surprising price given their performance in the League Cup final and a sequence of just three defeats – all by the odd goal – in 26 games. Having said that, the Saints were good enough to finish runners-up at the end of the season. Two weeks before the semi-final Everton had defeated Southampton 1-0 in the league at Goodison, when McMenemy controversially rested four players who were risking suspensions for the semi-final.

Alan Ball had played for both clubs and surprised Kendall by tipping the south-coast side to triumph. 'Bally knows as well as I that semi-finals are one-off affairs,' he retorted, 'We've got players like Andy Gray who can make things happen and the whole side is full of confidence.' That self-assurance was apparent in the tunnel beforehand. McMenemy later told the Scottish striker that when he looked at their relaxed rivals oozing self-belief, he knew there was probably going to be one winner.

There were two changes from the League Cup final. The coaching staff believed that Alan Irvine's temperament was suspect on the big occasion and consequently Kendall dropped the Scot. Trevor Steven had returned to the team and performed reasonably well. Terry Curran was also back from his prolonged thigh injury and selected instead of Graeme Sharp, who was substitute after a goalless streak of nine games.

A crowd of more than 46,000 packed Highbury on a beautifully sunny spring day, greeting the teams with balloons and a sea of colour. However, a goalless ninety minutes was typical semi-final fare, frantic and edgy. Ironically, Everton had more possession and territorial advantage but the south coast side had the better chances, with speedy winger Danny Wallace a constant menace. Even when Southampton broke through they found Southall in unstoppable form. 'He made death-defying saves from Moran, Wallace twice and Worthington,' wrote Clive White in *The Times*, 'that were brilliant enough to earn him a place in any national team, let alone that of Wales.'

But with skipper Steve Williams clearly not fit, an initially tentative Everton gained the ascendancy after Southampton made all the early running. Nevertheless, the absence of a natural left-sided player hampered them, with Steven having a quiet game. On the other wing, Curran also lacked match-fitness. The two best chances fell to Heath: first Gray's header appeared to catch the striker by surprise, but Peter Shilton narrowed the angle and he screwed his left-footed shot wide. Then Mick Mills brilliantly cleared the forward's mishit shot off the line. Everton forced no fewer than nine corners in one nine-minute spell but an hour-and-a-half of goalless endeavour ended with referee George Courtney's whistle, with the underdogs fancying their chances in extra time.

With four minutes of the additional half-hour remaining, the Blues were given one final opportunity when Reuben Agboola foolishly handballed near the byline. Peter Reid went over to take the free-kick in front of the mass of Everton fans on the North Bank, who prayed for a winner.[106] Clive Tyldesley, commentating on Radio City, described what happened next:

---

[106] One fan literally was. A supporter standing behind Reid before the midfielder takes the kick is clearly making the sign of the cross and looking to the heavens for divine inspiration. Maybe that made all the difference.

A free kick. On the byline. Reid takes it. Mountfield. HEATH! HE'S SCORED! ADRIAN HEATH HAS SCORED FOR EVERTON! A pitch invasion... memorable scenes... as the Everton fans stream out to congratulate Adrian Heath, because with just four minutes of extra time to go he has scored the goal which will take them back to Wembley and an FA Cup final for the first time since 1968. Surely that's going to be enough!

It was a great header by the striker as Mountfield's knock-on gave him no pace to work with so the finish was all about placement. Heath did brilliantly to put the ball in the corner to Shilton's left: 'I didn't think I was going to get to the ball because it bounced awkwardly, but I managed to bend my neck to it,' the striker said later. Time stood still for those on the North Bank and the ball took an age to ripple the net. There were chaotic, but largely good-natured, scenes immediately after the goal that took Everton to Wembley.[107]

Heath's goal was actually the product of some clever management. Kendall had noted that Southampton's Frank Worthington rarely came back for set-pieces or if he did seldom picked up anyone. 'Try and hit his area,' was the manager's instruction, and that is exactly what happened as Mountfield was unmarked. 'It's down to a little bit of planning or a little bit of luck on the day. Who knows?' the manager said in *Three Sides of the Mersey*. Everton thoroughly deserved the victory and a final appearance against Watford.

Kendall was naturally ecstatic afterwards. 'Getting to the Milk Cup Final was a tremendous achievement but this is a little bit more special, it is a showpiece at the end of the season,' the manager said of days sadly long gone. The manager also paid tribute to the match-winner: 'He really has done well for us after a difficult start when he was trying to justify his price tag.' 'We even threw the doc in the bath at Highbury,' Heath would recall of the post-match celebrations, 'The dressing room window looks out on the street, but it must be about 25 feet high. After the game we were pouring champagne out of the window to the cheering supporters.'

---

107 There were no fences at Highbury and on the final whistle the initial pitch invasion was similarly good natured, but when Everton fans taunted their Southampton counterparts there was a pitch-battle, leading to more than eighty arrests and 100 injured, with mounted police taking fifteen minutes to clear the playing area.

The focus after the game was on the man at the other end of the pitch. For some the semi-final was a battle of goalkeepers. Shilton versus Southall. Sorcerer versus apprentice. The Welshman came out on top after a superb performance while Shilton was shaky. 'Neville has proved by his performances this year that there is no finer keeper in Britain,' proclaimed Kendall, of a man who kept 27 clean sheets in 52 games by the end of the campaign. Informed they were cup favourites, Kendall replied, 'At last the bookies have got it right.'

FA Cup final, Watford

Like the two previous seasons, Everton finished the league campaign on a high, with four victories and two draws in the final six fixtures. Kendall wisely used the remaining matches to refine the playing style of the team. The strategy was to push as high up the pitch as possible, pressing and squeezing the play into a congested area twenty yards either side of the halfway line. Ratcliffe and Stevens, in particular, would use their pace to pick up any ball played over the top. In the middle of the park, the alert and industrious Reid would use his experience and know-how to break up play and use the ball simply.

In retrospect, there was also a blessing in disguise for Kendall when the unlucky Terry Curran pulled a hamstring two weeks after the semi-final. This necessitated a reshuffle in the centre: Trevor Steven moved out right and Richardson went left, giving the best balance to the midfield since Sheedy's injury. There was also a bonus when Heath's suspension meant a recall for Sharp in the home game against Manchester United. The Scot played well, scored his first goal for fourteen games in the 2-0 victory at Aston Villa and followed up with a brace against QPR at Goodison. With a vacancy in midfield, Heath moved back to his preferred position at the time. The net impact was more penetration through the middle and better service from out wide for the Sharp-Gray axis.

An interested spectator at Villa Park was the great Gordon Banks, who was scouting Neville Southall for the *Daily Mail*, and his comments provided an interesting insight into the rapidly-improving Welshman:

There is no doubt in my mind that Neville Southall has been the most consistent goalkeeper in the First Division this season... It wasn't a difficult match for him, but it allowed me to see a vital strength – his superb concentration... Southall spends his time organising his defence and keeping them on his toes. He is prepared to venture to the edge and that's not a bad thing. It also helps in his positioning, which I noted was of excellent standard... I have not seen Southall fail to look secure and dependable on crosses. He rarely looks like making a mistake. His reflexes are of the highest order too, undoubtedly enhanced by his positioning because he gets himself properly placed to make shot-stopping more comfortable.

Commendably there was no slacking off. Five days before the cup final Everton travelled to Upton Park for Trevor Brooking's final game in a Hammers jersey. With nothing at stake, the visitors' play was a world apart from their early-season struggles. Kevin Richardson scored the only goal that secured seventh place for the second successive season. In contrast, Watford's run-in included two heavy defeats, 6-1 at Norwich and 5-1 at Nottingham Forest. 'When a team gets to a final it's easy for their form to dip,' said Kendall, 'But it's a compliment to the professionalism of the players that we have finished our league programme so well.' That form made the Toffees 8/11 before the game, against the Hornets' 11/10.

Graham Taylor's side, like Everton, had struggled early on but recovered to finish eleventh. John Barnes was one of the most promising and dynamic young players in the country, while one-time Everton target Maurice Johnston had scored twenty goals in 29 league games. The big Scottish striker George Reilly posed a physical presence to Ratcliffe and Mountfield – the top-flight's most consistent centre-back partnership, according to the *Guardian's* David Lacey. The unfortunate suspension for veteran captain and full-back Wilf Rostron left Taylor's team with a hugely inexperienced defence.

Jimmy Hill interviewed both managers on the eve of the game when they expressed their widely differing hopes for the day. 'People are saying the most important thing is to get to Wembley but I honestly believe that once you're there you've got to try and win it,' admitted Kendall, 'The winning of it is really important for us as it would mean European qualification and also mean a return to Wembley to play Liverpool in the Charity Shield. Those two things will take care of itself if we win tomorrow and that is the aim.' In contrast, Graham Taylor responded, 'I want to see Everton and Watford supporters with their arms around one another both before and after the game and I want in years to come people to think back, whoever won the game, and say "What a hell of a game that was, what a cup final that was." Then at the end of the day, I will be very happy and very satisfied.' Whether Watford were there only to 'enjoy the occasion' was not relevant – if Everton played to their potential then they had enough to lift the cup, regardless of how the opposition performed. 'We must learn to be winners again, then the flair might come. The game is about winning trophies, and this is our priority,' Kendall told the *Sunday Telegraph's* John Moynihan. Everton supporters matched the Everton manager's desire to end the trophy drought dating back to 1970. Famously one at the back of the queue for final tickets at Goodison was asked how long he had been waiting. 'Fourteen years' came the response.

The respective club chairmen also had widely differing preparations on the night before the game. Whereas Philip Carter attended a dinner dance at Everton's hotel with fellow directors, Elton John was performing a concert in Berlin. The pop superstar was a memorable and welcome presence at Wembley for a day that dawned warm and sunny. Television coverage on both BBC and ITV commenced at 11am, 'comedy' on the former came from respective celebrity fans Freddie Starr and Michael Barrymore, while the latter channel featured Jimmy Tarbuck, the omnipresent Kenny Lynch... and Status Quo. With Kendall managing a depleted squad of only thirteen players, then the starting XI picked itself: *Southall, Stevens, Bailey, Ratcliffe, Mountfield, Reid, Steven, Heath, Sharp, Gray, Richardson. Sub: Harper.* Watford's novice defence included two teenagers, a twenty-year-old, with Steve Terry (at 21) the most experienced. 'Most of the team Watford sent out at Wembley could be used as ringers in a schoolboy competition,' commented Hugh McIlvanney in the *Observer*. Referee was John Hunting, who eight years earlier had allowed the notorious dog-assisted goal against Everton at The Hawthorns. For possibly the last time, no player had appeared previously in the final. However, Peter Reid later pointed to the importance of the Wembley encounter against Liverpool as being crucial. 'It was an occasion when we proved we were not far off the best,' he explained, 'Most of the lads were playing at Wembley for the first time. I didn't know how I was going to react, but it gave us a tremendous lift.'

An ITV clairvoyant rejected Reid's claims, predicting a first goal after seven minutes followed by a Watford victory. The underdogs set out to prove the latter correct, creating the best early chance when Southall blocked Barnes' shot and Les Taylor's follow-up went wide, although John Bailey looked to have touched the ball. Southall then saved bravely at Johnston's feet. Nevertheless, on 38 minutes Everton went ahead in typical fashion. The Toffees' midfield broke up some untidy play by the halfway line, Richardson exchanged passes with Reid and defender Lee Sinnott headed his cross towards Stevens. As the Watford defence pushed out, the full-back's miscued shot fell to Sharp, who swivelled quickly and fired home off goalkeeper Steve Sherwood's right-hand post. Although there were calls for offside, Kenny Jackett had been playing the Scot on.

The game's biggest talking point came six minutes after the break. When Trevor Steven put in a hanging cross there appeared to be little danger, however Watford keeper Sherwood had looked uncomfortable collecting balls and misjudged its flight. Hampered by Steve Terry, Sherwood back-pedalled awkwardly, the combative Gray leapt and appeared to connect with the ball or keeper's hand – perhaps both – and headed into the net. Many referees would have disallowed the goal but Hunting was happy for it to stand.[108] Graham Taylor was furious afterwards: 'Nine times out of 10 or 99 times out of 100 that goal would have been disallowed.' As the scorer himself said later, 'I don't think I actually made contact with the ball, I thought I wasn't going to get there and the keeper did quite well to get his hand to it. The only thing I could think of doing was heading the back of his hand.' Although Gray changed his story on the day – claiming to head both ball and hand – the television replays indicated that Hunting made the right call. There was no dangerous play and the ball was never under the keeper's control. Asked if Gray had headed the ball, Kendall replied, 'You try taking it off him.'

In *The Times* 48 hours later, David Miller wrote: 'I am convinced it was the uncertain Sherwood's bad luck in a legitimate challenge… whether Sherwood was knocked, or the ball came off Gray's head or shoulder, is debateable [sic], yet I am convinced that Gray was attempting to play the ball within his rights.' In the years that followed Watford attitudes softened. Talking to the *Daily Mail* in 2019, Les Taylor said about the goal: 'Steve Sherwood was 6ft 4in and in hindsight he should've just come and smashed Andy Gray. It was quite a soft goal from our point of view.'

The Everton striker deserved greater credit for his clever header and quick-

---

108 Sherwood may have realised it was not going to be his day when he saw David Coleman introducing the BBC's coverage. Commentating on Great Britain's David Hemery's famous 400m hurdles victory in the Mexico Olympics sixteen years before, Coleman said 'who cares who finished third'. It was John Sherwood, the Watford goalkeeper's brother.

thinking, with the goal a typical example of Gray's flair for the unorthodox and bending events to his will. As the Scot wheeled away, the Hornets knew the game was up. The remaining forty minutes were an anti-climax, which is exactly what the Everton bench required. Ian Ross in the *Liverpool Daily Post* summed up those rather surreal final moments:

> *Time stood still for three precious minutes at Wembley on Saturday. Shortly after 4.30 pm as the 1984 FA Cup final moved inexorably towards its climax, an unnerving silence swept across the terraces to the rear of Everton goalkeeper Neville Southall's goal. Howie's Army, the most resolute and long-suffering supporters in the business, stood, enraptured, as they prepared to vociferously signal the end of a fourteen-year period in the wilderness. It was if, with just seven minutes remaining, they had suddenly realised to a man that Watford were dead and buried. There could be no coming back. The Cup was won. Their action was perfectly understandable. Who could blame them for wishing to savour a magical and historic moment in a purely personal and very private manner?*

Supporters exhaled fourteen years of frustration at the final whistle before Kevin Ratcliffe climbed the Wembley steps to become the fourth Everton skipper to lift the famous trophy. Down below the television cameras caught a proud Kendall looking up at his players, who finally received deserved reward for their efforts since the turn of the year. 'We didn't get hold of the midfield early on but after Andy Gray's goal we were always in command,' the Everton manager said before admitting, 'What I have to be thankful for is that my chairman and directors felt I was doing a job. They knew I was doing all I possibly could to turn the tide. They stood by me.'

On the following Sunday more than 200,000 supporters welcomed the victors back in Liverpool, when for a change it was a team in blue with the trophy. The dark days now seemed in the distant past as the Everton manager set out the future. 'We must go for the championship now – I want us to be a threat to Liverpool,' proclaimed Kendall. 'Success is what you do over a season not weeks or months and although we've won the FA Cup after reaching the Milk Cup final the championship is the big one, the Blue Riband.'

CHAPTER 30

The Blue Tendency

THE KINDEST DESCRIPTION OF THE CITY'S POLITICS DURING THE first half of the 1980s is 'colourful'. During the end of the previous decade, the local Labour Party lost not only members but strong leadership, ceding control to a group called Militant Tendency, a Trotskyist offshoot with roots two decades before. With a Liberal-Conservative coalition ruling the city following the 1979 election, four years later, on the back of a manifesto targeting the regeneration of the housing stock and preserving public-sector jobs, Labour won its first overall majority in the city for more than a decade.

The city council immediately requested an extra £30m from central government on the basis that previous incumbents had been forced to hold down rates, thereby reducing the central grant, with the broad threat that if the money was not forthcoming, then they would set an illegal budget. By the spring of 1984 the deadline for setting a budget had gone but in July of that year a settlement of £20m was agreed between the council and Patrick Jenkin, the Environment Secretary. But even that amount was disputed between the two parties: the council claimed it was 'new money' but Jenkin was adamant that only £2.5m was additional funding, with the balance coming from fiscal opportunities arising from the lifting of penalties for overspending and such like. Either way it as a pyrrhic victory for the council. '... political exploitation of the victory by the Militant Tendency and Derek Hatton in particular convinced the Conservative government that it was pointless trying to help the city,' Michael Parkinson suggested in *Liverpool: Beyond the Brink*. Rightly or wrongly – and however valid the motives – the whole local financial and political saga, which dragged on a further three years, did not exactly enhance the city's already broken reputation.

Ironically, positive moves to improve the area's image came to fruition during the same summer. In the wake of the Toxteth riots three years before, Tory grandee, Michael Heseltine was appointed 'Minister for Liverpool'. It proved an unlikely but hugely progressive partnership. 'Heseltine got, spoke for and lobbied for Liverpool, at a time when few other national – certainly Tory – politicians could or would,' Michael Parkinson wrote. As somebody who understood the value of property, the Tory minister formed the Urban Development Corporation to redevelop the Albert Dock and make it the centrepiece of the rebirth of the city centre.

One of the first major initiatives was an idea Heseltine took from Germany: using derelict and polluted land to host garden festivals, as a means of attracting tourism. In Liverpool's case the area selected was a 100-acre landfill site in Otterspool. Opened by the Queen on 2 May, 1984, the location featured, amongst other attractions, sixty ornamental gardens as the venue of the UK's first International Garden Festival. Billed as 'a five month pageant of horticultural excellence and spectacular entertainment' the hugely successful event closed in October, having attracted more than 3 million visitors. With the Tate Gallery planning a home in the city, for a change there was some positive press.

Elsewhere there were further signs of recovery: the docks made a record profit of £6m in 1983, with some of the old terminals converted to handle other goods like grain and timber. The port handled just 520 tons of scrap metal in 1982 but twelve months later shipped 700,000 tons to the Far East for the car industry. Tourism then – as now – was hugely important, providing 10,000 jobs to the city and in 1982 there were 1.3 million visitors who spent £38m (£135m today) rising to £75m (£266m) in 1983 and £90m (£320m) twelve months later.

Rhythm and blues

However, the one thing the city did better than virtually anybody else was, of course, music. That said the disappearance of any songsmiths of note matched the area's economic decline from the mid-1960s. The city's acts rarely infiltrated the singles charts during the first half of the 1970s until The Real Thing – the country's biggest-selling black group of the decade – filled that gap.

But the opening of the legendary Eric's nightclub on Mathew Street in

October 1976 gave the city a window on the wider music scene and, in the following three-and-a-half years, the club hosted virtually every group worth seeing at the time. Nearly all the city's performers who found fame over the next decade had their roots in the venue and such was the renaissance in musical creativity that at the end of January 1984, seven of the top twenty best-selling singles in the country were Liverpool acts.

But popular music and football in the city continued to be mutually exclusive. The football clubs' only contribution to the wider music scene during the decade was Pink Floyd's baffling use of the Kop singing 'You'll Never Walk Alone' on their 1971 song 'Meddle'. Local musicians largely regarded football as uncool. As Pete Wylie told Paul du Noyer for his marvellous journey through the city's musical heritage, *Liverpool - Wondrous Place*: 'No one at Eric's talked about football... You would have been seen as a part-timer if you could also like football. The idea of being able to like two things at once was bizarre! To some extent we rebelled against that football culture – but then we rebelled against everything.' In the early 1980s, of the city's most prominent musicians, only Echo and the Bunnymen's Ian McCulloch ever displayed a public interest in the sport – in his case Liverpool FC and even then speaking about football seemed anachronistic in the music press. It would be ten years or more before there was an acknowledged relationship between the two parties.

While Eric's was redefining the city's affiliation with music, another aspect of youth culture was developing in tandem that did owe much to football. The local 'scally' scene had developed in the late-1970s, against a backdrop of expensive trainers – originally 'sourced' from abroad – and casual leisurewear. By the start of the following decade the look had transferred to mainstream and a *New Musical Express* article in early 1982, submitted by Phil Jones, co-founder of the cult local fanzine *The End*, painted an accurate picture of the city's younger male population:

The younger scals tend to have flicks, wear their jeans too tight and too long. Short-collared shirt, Slazenger jumpers and trainers 'zapped' from Europe. Also if it's cold they either wear sheepskin coats or anoraks (nearly always green) and maybe sheepskin mittens, borrowed off their sister. The older scals are different. They dress very 'sensible'. Short, sensible haircuts, tweed or corduroy jackets, short-collared checked shirts. Either jeans or just normal kecks. And shoes, so they can quite easily get into the poshest of clubs in Liverpool... They represent the REAL youth of Liverpool in these terrible, Thatcherised times...

With playwrights like Alan Bleasdale and Willy Russell also enjoying huge success and having hoovered up all the major football trophies, the city's wider cultural impact stood higher than at any point since the mid-1960s. However, the feeling remained that it was only a welcome distraction from the real issues of the day. Subsequent claims therefore that strong links existed between the political situation in the city and its football have been overblown – people went the game as a refuge from their problems, not to be reminded of them.

Nevertheless, the horrific tales within the city more than outweighed the good news stories. The jobless rate remained at twenty percent, but in soulless council estates the rate for the young nudged 70 percent with second generation unemployment common. Mercedo, the economic unit of Merseyside City Council, claimed to have brought in 10,000 new jobs but even they said, 'The number of losses is unbelievable. It's very much a feeling of one step forwards and three backwards.' The dire economic position in turn led to urban deprivation and a rise in crime, fuelled by a heroin epidemic amongst younger people – in one area surveyed at the time 87 percent of users were unemployed and most likely to be aged nineteen. With a daily habit for addicts at £70, small wonder street crime went through the roof. 'It is a cosmetic kind of success,' Alan Bleasdale told *The Times* in 1985 about the city's cultural rebirth, 'I don't want the cosmetic success that I or Willy Russell have had to suggest the city is better for it.'

After lifting the FA Cup, Howard Kendall spoke about the importance of football. 'We have real problems in this city and success is important to our fans,' he said, 'It has been very difficult living on the doorstep of Liverpool. We are neighbours really and our fans have taken a great deal of abuse over the years and now they feel they can stick their chests out.'

Two Tribes go to score

By the summer of 1984, musically, the big story was the dramatic rise of local group Frankie Goes to Hollywood to the top of the charts. Their reissued first single 'Relax' – infamously banned by the BBC – was number one for five weeks early in the year and the thunderous follow-up, 'Two Tribes', appropriately topped the charts for the two months prior to the city's blue and red rivals reconvening at Wembley Stadium for the Charity Shield in August.

The Everton manager had a relatively quiet summer after adding one quality signing. Paul Bracewell had started at Stoke City and was a seventeen-year-old captain of their youth team when making his full debut at Anfield in April 1980. Steady progress followed and three years later the midfielder, who had spoken with Kendall but was out of financial reach at the time, joined Sunderland for £250,000. Twelve months later the FA Cup winning manager was back to acquire the only ever-present member of England's under-21 European champions. Everton clinched the deal in the week before the cup final, with Bracewell keen to move after being unsettled over the sacking of Kendall guru, Alan Durban, who gave the player a ringing endorsement: 'Everyone loves playing when their own side is in possession, but not a lot have the same appetite to go back and do the hard part. Bracewell thrives on that.' Kendall was delighted: 'In this day and age you talk about attacking and defensive midfield players. He can do both and will be a tremendous asset to our squad.' There was a smooth pre-season with the highlight being a 3-0 victory over Olympiakos in Athens, a performance that brought the admiring 25,000 crowd to their feet at the end. Everton 'played some fantastic stuff,' Colin Harvey later recalled, 'And you felt something's going to happen here.'

Meanwhile, 48 hours before the curtain-raiser, virtually everybody ridiculed the government's latest attempts to tackle the hooliganism problem. One idea to create a league table to rank the worst clubs was mocked by Chelsea's Ken Bates. 'Will the hooligan final be at Wembley?' the combative chairman remarked. The report 'merely echoes the hopelessness of the situation and the helplessness of those unfortunate enough to become caught up in it,' said David Lacey in the *Guardian*. That gave context to the neutral's sense of wonder at the largely unsegregated (and well-behaved) crowds for Merseyside Wembley derbies. There was a paradox in how a city, very much regarded as troubled and troublesome, could demonstrate the required behaviour at football grounds to the rest of the country. To rubber-stamp that view, for the first time ever at Wembley, the Charity Shield attracted a full-house of 100,000.

New signing Bracewell made his debut and the midfield partnership with Peter Reid immediately looked natural. His smooth passing over distance from the middle of the park gave the team an added dimension. 'Sunderland were the ones who had their locks if not their pockets picked when they lost this talented 22-year-old,' said Clive White in *The Times*, 'He and the contrasting Reid, his grey hair a reminder of the years the First Division spent without him, had too much bite and nous for Liverpool's silent quartet.' In blazing sunshine, like the Milk Cup final, the Toffees had the better of the game and pleasing for Everton supporters was the sight of hitherto peerless central defenders Mark Lawrenson and Alan Hansen bickering at the back.

The game remained goalless at the break, but at the start of the second half came the first derby goal at Wembley after almost three hours' play – from an unusual source. Sharp broke through the middle and after Grobbelaar saved his first attempt, the Scot saw Hansen stop his second before the ball rebounded in off the Zimbabwean keeper. Throughout Everton had looked a half-a-yard sharper, from the confidence that comes from winning trophies, and thereafter the game became largely one-sided. For their long-suffering supporters, the final two minutes of olé football was joyous. 'The Blues outplayed, outfought and finally out-manoeuvred their great rivals on the day,' wrote Ken Rogers in the *Liverpool Echo*. Kenny Dalglish admitted, 'We deserved what we got.'

As the great Brian Moore said on ITV when Kevin Ratcliffe climbed the Wembley steps, for all the progress over the previous six months this was the biggest prize of all. If the victory over Watford was about drawing a line under the past, the derby win under the twin towers was the first chapter of the future. With the departure of Graeme Souness leaving a gargantuan hole, the Anfield side were vulnerable. 'We've beaten the best and deserved to,' a delighted Kendall said afterwards.

'The fans are already beginning to desert Goodison in their droves'

There was one group not particularly impressed by the dominant Wembley victory: the bookmakers. The departure of Souness had left a more open field than usual in the title stakes, but surprisingly Everton (14/1) were still only sixth favourites, behind Liverpool (7/4), Manchester United (3/1), Arsenal (9/1), Spurs (10/1) and Nottingham Forest (12/1). Yet the odds proved that the power in English football, reinforced by the Chester Report changes twelve months before, was increasingly with the 'big five', as Stuart Jones claimed in *The Times*: 'The dawn of the so-called super-league has broken, whether the authorities like it or not... Not only do they threaten this season; their omnipotence stretches far into the foreseeable future. No-one else can hope to compete with those five, whose roads are paved with gold.'

Ominously, Jones also noted about Everton that 'there remains a nagging suspicion that they will not sustain their run.' That sadly proved to be the case on a sunlit opening day against Spurs when there was an air of triumphalism at Goodison, with the FA Cup and FA Youth Cup[109] on parade. In front of 35,630 fans – the best opening day gate for six years – it was business as usual for more than thirty minutes, Everton fluent in attack before Adrian Heath scored from the spot. Then from nowhere, the home team dramatically crumbled. Six minutes before the break, Neville Southall failed to grab Micky Hazard's through ball and Mark Falco pounced for the equaliser. Everton had lost just five times in 36 games, conceding only 24 goals but, within ten minutes of the restart, uncharacteristically shambolic defending had contributed to three further strikes, with Spurs easing to a surprising 4-1 victory.

With a visit to West Brom 48 hours later, a shell-shocked Kendall gruffly told reporters 'Our season starts on Monday' although there was more frustration at The Hawthorns when loose defending allowed Albion in twice before Heath's late consolation penalty. With a tough-looking fixture live at promoted Chelsea on the Friday evening, broadcast live on the BBC, there was a possibility of bottom-place in the embryonic table.

What had gone wrong? There had been injuries: Kevin Sheedy had not played, while Bracewell was out at West Brom with a sore foot. The side was missing the injured Gray's personality and ability to bring others into play. At the back it was a mystery. Mountfield had done well while Stevens looked international class at Wembley. There was also a suspicion that more goals were needed from the strikers. 'The fact that we have scored only two penalties in two games and conceded six goals concerns me. But that is all it is... a concern,' Kendall admitted.

---

109 Everton had lifted the trophy for the second time after defeating Stoke City 4-2 on aggregate in a two-legged final. Ironically the team that had reached the final twelve months before was vastly superior, including a formidable attacking trident of Stuart Rimmer (who later became Chester's all-time record scorer), Robbie Wakenshaw (who scored on debut against Manchester United in May 1984) and Mark Farrington. After destroying Spurs 5-0 and then Sheffield Wednesday 7-0 in the semi-final, they ran into a similarly strong Norwich in the final. After both teams won their home legs 3-2, Norwich won a third game at Goodison 1-0 in front of 20,000 spectators, which matched Everton's average league attendance for the campaign. Ian Bishop and Ian Marshall both played for the Toffees and went on to have lengthy careers. The team also featured Jimmy Coyle, one of Goodison's great lost talents.

At Stamford Bridge against a team unbeaten in nineteen league games, the visiting manager told his players 'whatever happens we're not losing tonight' in the dressing room beforehand. Consequently, the nation witnessed a typical away performance, tight at the back with the high-line producing constant offsides – eleven alone in the first-half for the London club. Wearing the classic all-grey away strip, the visitors created little and escaped when Kerry Dixon's volley struck the angle of post and crossbar. The Everton manager rollicked the players at the break – 'He didn't think we were competing hard enough,' Adrian Heath admitted later – and there was a big improvement in the second half. After 53 minutes came one of the key goals of the campaign. Bracewell's sweeping pass went out to the Everton left and Kevin Richardson nipped in to score underneath Eddie Niedzwiecki. Kendall's team dictated the tempo of the rest of the game, retaining possession and allowing Chelsea few openings for a vital win.

Yet the moderate offering on show and the odd 7.15 pm kick-off time to fit in with TV schedules reopened the debate over the relationship between television and the sport. The contest attracted a disappointing gate of just 17,000, probably 15,000 less than on a Saturday afternoon, undoubtedly affecting the match as a spectacle. As Kendall argued previously, highlights packages did not provide a true picture and there was always a danger that a poor live game was probably going to do more harm than good. 'As a live TV advert for the new season this match was about as profitable as trying to sell a Goodison season ticket to a Kopite,' Steve Curry pondered in the *Daily Express*, 'I trust the gate figure will alert all Football League chairmen to the obvious dangers of over-exposure on TV.' Robert Armstrong in the *Guardian* came at the problem from a different but familiar angle, suggesting that rescheduling the kick-off to meet the demands of television unnecessarily burdened the players with three games in six days. Nearly forty years later, striking a balance on this matter remains an enormous problem.

The first league victory failed to have the desired effect. On the following Tuesday Ipswich Town proved obdurate opponents at Goodison, taking the lead through Eric Gates before Heath equalised twelve minutes from time. Nevertheless, the crowd was 13,000 fewer than the opening day and only 20,000 turned up four days later for the visit of Coventry City. The home fans witnessed another uninspired display as Everton stole a late victory through two scrappy goals. 'It was a success of sorts, but a display which reeked of uncertainty and near-poverty bodes ill for the future,' Peter Welbourn wrote in the *Sunday Express*, 'With the campaign only three weeks old, the fans are already beginning to desert Goodison in their droves. And who can blame them?' The absence of Sheedy was proving a big problem. At the end of the previous season when Richardson deputised, Heath had joined Reid in the centre so there was still the right midfield balance between attack and defence. However, following the signing of Paul Bracewell, the feeling was that the new midfield duo and Richardson were too similar in style. Combining that issue with a forward line short on confidence reduced the goal potential.

On the following weekend, Everton's main issue was selection when they travelled to newly-promoted Newcastle United. Terry Curran had helped turn the tide as a substitute in the previous two games but was left out of the trip to the north-east and the furious winger handed in a transfer request. With Andy Gray fit, Kendall had to perm any two strikers from three and he did not exactly endear himself to the trio when explaining selection depended on the opposition. With Gray and Sharp the most similar pairing, the likely permutation remained one of the two with Heath. So it proved at Newcastle, Gray was back in place of his fellow Scot. Although in his enjoyable autobiography *Sharpy*, the younger man explained he saw things differently, when following Curran into the manager's lair:

> When I asked why I had been axed despite the fact that I had scored against Coventry, Howard replied, totally unexpectedly, that it "wasn't a proper goal." I asked him to expand his bizarre remark. "It came from a set-piece, so I don't consider it to be a proper goal." I couldn't believe what I was hearing and we had a right argument about it. I felt that Howard wasn't being honest with me. I'd never ever heard him describe a goal from any sort of set-piece as not being "proper" – this from the man who had encouraged me to take penalty kicks to increase my goal tally!

However, Kendall was justified in changing things. Sharp had been off-form and, apart from a brief flurry at the end of the previous campaign, this appeared to be a worrying long-term issue, with just eight goals in 41 appearances. Kevin Sheedy was back and, for the first time, the manager's favoured midfield quartet was on the pitch with the team immediately looking far more fluid. The visitors had to be, as Ratcliffe gave away a soft penalty for a foul on Chris Waddle after thirteen minutes. Peter Beardsley converted but Sheedy responded with a crunching first-time shot. Level at the break, again the visitors shot themselves in the foot within seconds of the restart when Kenny Wharton scored after intercepting Mountfield's weak back-pass. Steven equalised six minutes later and the game was slipping to a hard-earned draw in injury time before, not for the last occasion, Gray had the final word. Sheedy's corner from the right went to the heart of the six-yard box and the newly dyed blond-haired striker powered home a point-blank header.

Even at an early stage of the season, the win seemed crucial, taking a largely below-par Everton sixth with ten points from six games. Having said that, one man was impressed. 'Everton had all of the things that I like in the game,' said Newcastle boss Jack Charlton, 'They hustle you, play the ball early and are probably the best balanced side in the First Division at the moment, without having anyone who is brilliant.' Forty-eight hours later Sharp visited Kendall's office to hand over a transfer request, which the manager rejected. The likes of Alex Ferguson's Aberdeen had previously shown an interest but, with Gray out for up to six weeks with a broken foot, it was a wise move by the Everton boss. Typical of the rather stop-start nature of the campaign at that stage, Kendall's side threw away a two-goal lead against Southampton at Goodison in a 2-2 draw seven days later.

The Toffees travelled to Watford for a rematch of the FA Cup final at Vicarage Road on the final weekend of September. The previous February the two teams had drawn after an eight-goal bonanza, the visitors equalising in stoppage time. There was a chance of goals but unbelievably the two sides went one better in front of a sun-drenched crowd. The crazy tale of the tape was as follows:

15 mins – Bulky centre-forward George Reilly nets with a close-range header from a Nigel Callaghan cross (1-0)

33 mins – A glorious goal from Trevor Steven, who exchanged passes with Adrian Heath before scoring with his left-foot past Watford debutant keeper Tony Coton (1-1)

35 mins – After Kenny Jackett loses the ball in the area Adrian Heath scores into the far corner (1-2)

44 mins – Slack defending in the home penalty area from a John Bailey throw ends up with Heath firing home following a Sharp lay-off (1-3)

56 mins – Derek Mountfield heads into his own net from a John Barnes free-kick (2-3)

61 mins – Dreadful defending again from the home team following a corner allows the Everton central-defender to atone straightaway with his left-foot (2-4)

70 mins – Nigel Callaghan reduces the deficit with a header from another Barnes cross (3-4)

72 mins – Sharp chases Southall's quick long clearance and cleverly lifts the ball over the advancing Coton to restore the two-goal margin (3-5)

87 mins – Barnes ensures a frantic finish with another header (4-5)

The Toffees may have been unbeaten in six league games and stood sixth, but the bookmakers were still not convinced. Liverpool (6/1 after a difficult start) had drifted with unbeaten Manchester United the new 13/8 favourites. Kendall's side were now out to 20/1. One of the concerns had been the porous defence: sixteen goals conceded in eight games, the fourth highest in the top-flight. A fortnight earlier the Everton manager, keen to tighten-up the backline, secured the services of Birmingham City defender Pat Van Den Hauwe for £100,000. The Belgian-born player had broken through as a centre-half but made the left-back berth his own over the previous eighteen months. It says much for the reputation of the St Andrews dressing room that Van Den Hauwe, who was to attract a fearsome standing himself, was not even part of the infamous 'Birmingham Six',[110] one the biggest group of troublemakers ever housed in a single squad. Indeed, with the left-back, less was more. Charles Lambert, who had moved to BBC Radio Merseyside by this time, later recalled briefly interviewing the new signing when he arrived. 'And that was it. I didn't speak to him again in the five years he was here.' The Belgian read the game well, had pace, was strong in the air and used the ball effectively.

John Bailey's place was under-threat as Kendall felt that he was suspect defensively and the manager had previously dropped him after costly errors, as

---

110   For the record: Mick Harford, Mark Dennis, Noel Blake, Howard Gayle, Tony Coton and Robert Hopkins.

well as transfer-listing him as part of the infamous 1982 Easter cull. For the difficult away game at table-toppers Arsenal on the first Saturday in October, Bailey was out with a hamstring injury and Van Den Hauwe stepped in. The game, in front of more than 37,000 spectators, was a real war of attrition. Everton, as per normal, compressed the play into a narrow corridor either side of the halfway line, which disrupted the flow of the game, as the visitors showed enough skill and fluidity to promise a fourth away win. Four weeks before Arsenal had gone ahead against Liverpool in first-half added time after being second-best, before emerging victorious. History sadly repeated itself, with an enormously controversial moment after 47 minutes of the opening period. Referee Mr Hedges gave a throw-in after Ratcliffe and Charlie Nicholas jostled for a ball however, linesman George Prevett, much further away, flagged for an offence. After consulting Prevett, the referee awarded a ludicrous penalty. Nicholas claimed that Ratcliffe cut across him afterwards. 'I'm not saying it was a definite penalty, but it was one of those which sometimes you get and sometimes you don't.' In other words, he was very lucky. To rub salt in the wounds, Nicholas himself scored and the controversial spot-kick decided the game, despite the visitors' battling performance.

The unlucky Blues departed Highbury feeling a sense of injustice. They also had little idea that they were on the cusp of one of the most remarkable periods in the club's long history.

CHAPTER 31

Bringing back Mr Beggs

A TWO-LEGGED LEAGUE CUP SECOND-ROUND TIE AGAINST Sheffield United during the autumn of 1984 warrants merely a footnote to the Kendall era. The Yorkshire team were mid-table in the Second Division but regarded, at the time, as being the sort of hard-working, combative team that could cause an upset.

The first leg at Bramall Lane was hard-fought, Everton escaping with a 2-2 draw after falling behind twice. However the second game at Goodison, three days after the Highbury defeat, was the biggest sign yet of where Kendall's team were heading. The blue-shirted dynamos tore into the Blades, who had a player booked after just 35 seconds. Mountfield opened the scoring after five minutes – his fourth in six matches – and Everton surgically dismantled their opponents with some magnificent football. Bracewell added his first club goal after the break and then there were superb strikes by Sharp, delightfully set up by Heath, and the latter who scored with a snap header after fantastic work on the byline by Trevor Steven. 'Everton's brilliance shone so brightly last night that manager Howard Kendall was almost lost for words,' wrote John Keith in the *Daily Express*.

The vast majority of the healthy gate of 18,740 left Goodison having witnessed a quality not seen on the ground for many years. 'This performance brought into sharp focus a horizon now glowing with possibilities,' mused Ian Ross in the *Liverpool Daily Post*. 'Everton destroyed Sheffield United in a manner which suggest their loyal fans will not have to endure another fourteen-year wait for a trophy.'

Whether that prize was the League Championship was questionable. Everton were eighth going into the weekend's vital clash at Goodison against a dangerous Aston Villa side who had ended Manchester United's unbeaten start on the previous Saturday. After a scrappy beginning, the Toffees went ahead on 25 minutes with a superbly crafted goal. Peter Reid picked the ball up in the right-back position, immediately showed (surprising) speed and rode the tackles of Didier Six and Steve McMahon in front of the Main Stand. The midfielder fed Heath on the right flank and Sharp met the striker's perfectly-weighted cross with a powerful header.

After Peter Withe equalised, the second period witnessed a siege of Mervyn Day's goal at the Gwladys Street end. The final half-hour was the Toffees' finest passage of football all season, thirty minutes of bewildering interplay at pace in and around the Villa box, usually involving Reid, Steven and the glorious forward pairing of Heath and Sharp. 'You won't see a better example of front players working together than that,' Kendall said afterwards. Chances came and went. Sharp missed from six yards and struck one shot with such ferocity that his boot followed the ball's trajectory. Heath had one effort kicked off the line before Day saved his penalty. Then on 72 minutes came the winner of unusual beauty. Reid moved the ball to Heath on the halfway line and the striker turned brilliantly, taking two Villa players out of the game. 'Inchy' back-heeled the ball to Reid, who had now moved wide right while the forward headed towards the box. Reid's left-footed cross sped towards Sharp at the edge of the area before the striker's beautifully weighted and cleverly directed chest-down took out three defenders. Heath had anticipated the 'pass' and strode forward to volley home in a typically joyous manner. 'We could have lost by four or five,' said Villa boss Graham Turner. At the end of a week where Everton had played the best football seen at Goodison since 1970, the possibilities were endless.

Inchy and Sharpy

By the end of 1983, Graeme Sharp and Adrian Heath were largely unfulfilled talents. The latter had shown signs of being a top-quality acquisition, but there were concerns whether the record-signing was too lightweight to shine in his preferred position as an attacking midfielder. However, Heath had not shown the instincts of a natural predator either as a striker, with his finishing best described as 'erratic'. A constant shifting of positions followed, something not helped by Kendall signing Andy King, a player who filled the same role.

But that started to change at the beginning of 1984. Inspired by the presence of Andy Gray, the 5ft 6in striker embarked on a hot-streak that produced eighteen goals by the end of the campaign. Heath had scored only once from open play in the first ten matches of 1984/85 but the brace at Watford acted a springboard for a spell of inspired form, establishing the Potteries-born star as one of the best players in the top-flight. But Heath was more than a goalscorer. The striker was a creator and the perfect foil for a target-man. 'Adrian is like one of those toys you see advertised at Christmas,' said Kendall, 'Stick a key in his back, wind him up and he runs all over the place and pops up in the most unexpected positions.' Kevin Sheedy certainly appreciated his qualities. 'I had a great understanding with him,' he wrote in *So Good I Did It Twice*. 'When I received the ball I knew exactly where he was going and whether he wanted the ball played short, in behind him or wherever he wanted it. Inchy... just had such great movement and I was on exactly the same wavelength as him.' Like all the best players Heath possessed a nasty streak and was not afraid to leave his foot in. His brilliant performances brought this tribute from Ian Hargraves in the *Liverpool Echo* after the Villa game, who started by looking back to the turn of the year:

> Somewhere along the line the real Adrian Heath emerged, a gifted individual who, like Alan Ball before him, refused to fit any conventional mould. As he reminded us against Aston Villa on Saturday, great players make their own rules. His swift, darting runs, his ability to pinch possession in the twinkling of an eye, and his awareness of the slightest opening mark him as a real original.

Striking partner Sharp had been more inconsistent over the previous two years. The Scot's reputation for being a scorer of great goals, rather than a forward who would accrue tap-ins, had counted against him. Nevertheless, even to the untrained observer here was a player of great potential, one who possessed all of the gifts needed for a top-class striker. Mobile, strong in the air, intelligent and, like his partner, Sharp was quite happy to let the opposition know he was on the pitch. However, there were puzzling periods of poor form and Kendall dropped him on several occasions. 'In truth, we had never seen eye to eye completely and when I analyse my Everton career I maintain that I would never have been given the opportunity to develop and progress had it not been for Colin Harvey,' the Scot said in his autobiography, 'I was never fully convinced that Howard rated me as a player but knew that Colin did and that he always defended my corner.'

When the manager dropped Sharp for the Newcastle away game, Coventry's Bobby Gould was rumoured to be preparing a bid and watched the striker in the match at Sheffield United. After Gould registered an interest with the Everton boss afterwards, Kendall responded with one of his best lines: 'I am not selling, but I'll give you a season ticket so you can come and watch him scoring goals for us every Saturday.' Sharp was one of Goodison's great survivors and, after the recall, the goal against Villa was his sixth in seven matches. Even if Sharp felt the manager did not rate him, Kendall was complimentary after the win over the Midlands outfit. 'You will never see a better performance from a striker than you saw from Graeme today,' he proclaimed, 'He did everything right and scored a superb goal, which was a credit to the people who made it.'

Fit-again Andy Gray was the only person at Goodison with anything to lose from the forward partnership's sparkling form. Typically, the senior pro was gushing in his praise to the *Liverpool Echo*: 'They make an ideal combination because Inchy is so quick and clever while Graeme is big and strong and willing to put himself about a bit... if there are a better pair anywhere in England I haven't seen them.' However, Gray was still competitive. 'But make no mistake. I am not going to make it easy for them. Andy Gray wants to play First Division football and I certainly don't envisage languishing in the reserves! But competition for places can only be good for the club.'

The out-of-favour striker then spoke about the prevailing feel-good factor. 'Everyone feels this is the place to be at the moment,' Gray admitted, 'Things are certainly happening and the whole place is buzzing. We are in Europe and well positioned in the league.' But the two biggest tests of the season so far awaited – the Anfield derby followed by the visit of title-favourites Manchester United.

Shifting the balance

Although Everton were very much on the rise, across Stanley Park there was still turbulence following Graeme Souness' departure. With Ian Rush injured, Joe Fagan's men had struggled in the opening months of the campaign and the Liverpool manager, unbelievably, dropped Kenny Dalglish for the televised defeat at Spurs, a sixth league game without a victory, leaving the Anfield side unusually languishing in sixteenth.

With just one defeat in twelve matches, Kendall had no such worries. Twenty-four hours beforehand the Everton boss spoke about the changing perspectives towards their illustrious rivals. 'Most clubs still fear going there, but we no longer do,' he said, before explaining that the 1-1 draw at Goodison was a turning point. 'We didn't pay much attention to them during the build-up. We played well, missed a penalty, and deserved a point. Perhaps in the past we have paid them too much respect. We approached the two Milk Cup final games and Charity Shield in a particular manner and have repeated it this time.' With no Anfield victory since 1970, the bookmakers did not share his optimism, amazingly making the form team 3-1 to win a two-horse race.

The injured Sheedy and Richardson were out so the versatile Alan Harper came in on the right of midfield, with Steven moving to the left. The former Liverpool player provided invaluable service during the campaign, making thirteen league appearances when stepping up. The feeling amongst Evertonians was this was their moment – reflected by the huge number of away fans inhabiting the left-hand side of the Kop. From the start, the blue shirts tore into their red rivals, with the opening half witnessing panicky and desperate defending by the home team and even more erratic goalkeeping from Grobbelaar. With Reid and Bracewell first to every loose ball, Kendall would have been disappointed that the dominant visitors had not turned their territorial advantage into goals with Grobbelaar's marvellous save from Gary Stevens' free-kick the closest.

However, precisely 147 seconds after the break, Evertonians finally got their moment to savour. 'It would be easy to dwell on the awesome Graeme Sharp goal after 48 minutes which settled the game,' wrote the *Daily Mirror's* Chris James. 'A 25-yard right-foot volley after neat control with his left which exploded into the net after dipping over Bruce Grobbelaar.' But supporters have dwelt on it ever since, and quite rightly too – the Scot producing a perfect strike that combined technique and power in equal measure. The photograph of Sharp volleying the ball, against the backdrop of a packed Kop in the distance, is one of the club's defining images. 'It was a bloody good goal,' admitted a sporting Joe Fagan, 'Worth winning any game. It would almost have been a shame if we had scored after that.'

With the visitors retaining their composure, Reid and Heath both wasted chances to increase the lead before referee Neil Midgley ended fourteen years of hurt by blowing for full time. 'The balance of power may be shifting on Merseyside and Everton needed this result to prove it,' were John Motson's words on *Match of the Day* as the players sprinted from the pitch. Afterwards Kendall was delighted: 'It was a simply tremendous performance particularly when you bear in mind Liverpool's record against us over the years.' But James put some perspective on the performance in the *Daily Mirror*:

> *In the space of ten months Everton have emerged from the depths in which Liverpool are now floundering and have lost one of the five derbies at Goodison, Anfield, Wembley and Maine Road in 1984. More important is that since the turn of the year their results and form have been so impressive that the long forgotten words 'League Championship' are again being whispered in the Goodison corridors.*

The victory was really for the fans however. There had been provocative chants of 'going down' from delighted Everton supporters to their rivals on the Kop and a young lad wearing a blue scarf perfectly captured the joyous mood around Anfield. Asked about his team's championship credentials after the game, he replied: 'Well if we're gonna win the league we've got to beat these bottom-of-the-table teams.'

1-2, 1-2-3, 1-2-3-4, 5-0!

In the aftermath of the derby win Kendall told the waiting press: 'I hope you don't start writing about their [Liverpool] problems, but instead say how well we played.' Yet the *Guardian's* Patrick Barclay, as was his right, went against Kendall's wishes, ending his piece by saying 'Everton may or may not be championship material – Manchester United's visit should provide a clue.'

Before Ron Atkinson's expensively assembled side came to Goodison on the final Saturday in October, the Toffees had travelled to Czechoslovakia for the first leg of the second-round Cup Winners' Cup tie against Inter Bratislava. The opening round against Irish part-timers UCD proved more difficult than expected. The university team from Dublin were slightly eccentric. Manager and lifelong Evertonian Theo Dunne was always happy to show off his uncashed cheque for £1.85 from the club for scouting services, while the team took to the field for home games behind a four-year old Labrador mascot called Henry. However, their deep defensive set-up in the first leg at Tolka Park produced a dour goalless draw and the return at Goodison was equally mind-numbing, settled by a Sharp strike after eleven minutes. Although there was never a danger of the Irish amateurs equalising and proceeding on away goals, the restless fans in a poor

16,277 crowd booed the home team off.[111] The game in Bratislava was a far more comfortable experience, a single-goal victory via an early Paul Bracewell header.

Three days later Manchester United came to Goodison for a game in which both teams were putting their championships credentials on the line. Both had twenty points from eleven games, five behind leaders Arsenal, but United's record of just one defeat and a goal difference of +11 (against Everton's moderate +1) looked far more representative of a team with title aspirations. Astonishingly by 4.45 pm on the Saturday evening, Everton had wiped-out the ten-goal gap as, under a symbolic blue sky, the 40,769 spectators witnessed a footballing masterclass from Kendall's team. Two weeks before United had overrun West Ham 5-1 at Old Trafford, leading Ron Atkinson to suggest that no other side would play better all season. Everton ensured that the claim was redundant a fortnight later. As Kendall admitted after the game: 'I don't think adjectives have been invented to describe that team performance. It was the finest you could wish to see from the first whistle to last.'

Seldom in the 92-year-old history of the ground had supporters witnessed a team full of class players, such as England skipper Bryan Robson, reduced to the role of helpless bystanders, as Everton ground the visitors into the Goodison dust. 'In every department Everton's superiority was astonishing,' Nick Pitt wrote in the *Sunday Times*, 'Faster of thought and action throughout the team, they gripped United from the first whistle, shook them and shook them, and never let go.' The Toffees won the ball straight back from the United kick-off and after five minutes of frightening intensity went ahead from an unusual source. Mountfield crossed from the right and a surprisingly spring-heeled Kevin Sheedy beat his Ireland teammate Kevin Moran to the ball and saw his header loop over Gary Bailey into the far corner at the Park End. It was 2-0 after 22 minutes. Remi Moses gave the ball away to Heath, and the forward fed the onrushing Sheedy in the inside-left channel who beat Bailey with a perfectly placed finish. Twelve minutes later it was 3-0 when Heath swept home Steven's low cross. 'United soon discovered, as Liverpool had last week, what a horrible side Everton are to play against,' Pitt remarked. Atkinson could argue he had no fit right-back and had to

---

[111] There is an urban myth surrounding this game that has grown over the years. Joe Hanrahan was the one UCD player of note and the story goes that in the final minutes he struck the bar (or post) and that fine margin kept Everton in the competition. That is simply not true. Keith Lambert had the visitors only shot in the game, midway through the second half, which skied way over Neville Southall's bar.

reshuffle the defence when Moran, after clashing heads with Sheedy for the first goal, had to go off, but that made little difference.

The home team's appetite for destruction did not diminish in the second period. Sharp twice went close while Heath saw his header kicked off the line by Arthur Albiston. It was 81 minutes before the visitors had their first shot on goal but by that stage, Kendall's team had scored their fourth when Gary Stevens fired home from outside the box. There is a difference between the perception of 4-0 and 5-0 victories – the narrative moving from a heavy defeat to a proper thrashing – so when Sharp headed a fifth four minutes from time the result finally reflected Everton's complete dominance. Twelve months before Everton had scored five goals in their opening eleven home league games. They had matched that tally in ninety minutes against the title favourites.

After the game, Kendall reflected on the blue hurricane that had struck United in such devastating fashion and was candid when asked about comparisons with 1970. 'There's no way even we could have matched this performance,' he admitted, before adding, 'If we can keep that up, it's obviously enough to win titles.' Watching the edited highlights on Rob Sloman's brilliant film, *Howard's Way*, the most noticeable aspect of the performance is the almost manic, but disciplined, way Everton pressurise United when they have the ball, forcing them into mistakes. Even with the score at 5-0, five home players press Remi Moses in the right-back position. Peter Reid was obviously one and Kendall picked out the midfield powerhouse for special praise. 'His was a tremendous individual performance,' the manager commented, 'Do you think he's trying to get a cap?' Meanwhile Ron Atkinson, when asked about where it started to go wrong for United, replied 'When Everton started scoring goals'.

The banner headline after the rout belonged to Everton legend Joe Mercer. The 1939 title-winner had seen it all in his six decades in the game, but when the great man remarked afterwards that he had not witnessed an Everton side play better, journalists had their intro. 'Everything about them was right, from the goalkeeper right through the team. It was a fabulous display,' Joe said.

Pleased as punch

On the Saturday following the 2-2 leaflet-strewn draw against Chesterfield in October 1983, a 72-year-old season-ticket holder called John Beggs, who had watched Dixie Dean at his peak, wrote a scathing letter to the *Liverpool Echo*.

'Since the age of eight I have never missed a home game except through illness and war service overseas,' he explained, 'Following the Chesterfield Milk Cup match, I shall not be at the derby or the Coventry cup-tie. In my opinion, the teams that are being selected to represent Everton are the worst I have known.'

But the startling victory over Manchester United only reinforced the miraculous turnaround in the team's fortunes. Nick Pitt of the *Sunday Times* interviewed the Everton manager a few weeks later, and afterwards outlined Kendall's strategy: 'He wanted every Everton player to adapt to his pattern of play; to be able to support his teammates without question; to be able to run anyone into the ground; to be able to deny any man space on the ball, and then having won it, to be able to use it.' Adapting to this rigid system of playing was always going to take time but as Pitt remarked, 'Then, sometime early this year, the young mostly unknown, recruits began to believe. Suddenly, they got it.' Kendall admitted he could not understand why the pieces of the jigsaw had fallen into place: 'I don't know whether it was through playing together, or through their own intelligence, but at last they knew what I wanted.'

However, the transformative role of Colin Harvey cannot be underestimated. As Andy Gray remarked in 1997: 'Howard's strength is man management. He gets you going, builds you up and sends you out 10 feet tall. But he needs a tactician alongside him. In my day it was Colin Harvey. He was the one who pulled you aside on Monday morning and went through mistakes you had made or talked through new ideas.'

The Everton manager had constantly preached that results came first, flair afterwards. Kendall was now implementing the second phase of the battle-plan, as witnessed against United. Consequently, Mr Beggs had now returned to Goodison after his self-imposed exile. The pensioner described the performance in the 5-0 victory as the best he had seen in fifty years. In fact, he was as 'pleased as punch'.

Back to the top

The football gods had worked their magic and deigned that the League Cup draw should feature Everton travelling to Old Trafford three days after performing their public execution at Goodison. 'There were two good sides at Goodison – but only one of them played,' said Atkinson on the morning of the game, 'It will be very different tonight.' Remarkably, the bookmakers agreed. Everton were at 3-1 to defeat United for a second time, with Atkinson's team 5-1 to lift the trophy.

As expected, the encounter was a far tighter affair than on the Saturday. The blue skies over Merseyside also gave way to a horrible, damp Mancunian evening. United, conscious that Everton had wrested the initiative in the opening seconds at Goodison, tore into Kendall's team and got their deserved break on 23 minutes, when Alan Brazil fortunately deflected Kevin Moran's shot past Southall. Atkinson had told Bryan Robson to keep Peter Reid in check and this led to Bracewell becoming the game's most influential player as the midfield duo began to dominate, with the Toffees equalising from Sharp's spot-kick after Graeme Hogg felled Heath in the box. The second period brought more of the same fierce physical combat: 'This was not the night either for delicacy or for decoration,' wrote Stuart Jones in *The Times*. But just as the 50,918 spectators were bracing themselves for a replay, Reid drove into the final third and his chip towards the middle of the box took an awkward deflection, Trevor Steven and United full-back John Gidman went for the ball and the former Toffees defender unluckily headed over the onrushing Bailey. Appropriately, an incoherent game had seen three messy goals but even more typically, Kendall's team had shown the necessary resilience to drag out a result. Asked by Granada TV's Elton Welsby for the fundamental difference between the teams in the two games, Peter Reid responded, 'On the two days, we've wanted it a bit more than them.'

'Already the most consistent side in the country over the last ten months, they are emerging as unforeseen favourites for the championship,' were Stuart Jones words after the game. When leaders Arsenal lost, ironically enough, at Old Trafford on the Friday, Kendall's side had the opportunity to go top by defeating Leicester City at Goodison 24 hours later. After a dour first half, three goals after the break were enough to put Everton at the summit for the first time since February 1979. Then the spell on top lasted three days. Supporters were hoping for something more permanent on this occasion. Four days later Kendall's table-toppers comfortably defeated Inter Bratislava 3-0 at Goodison to move smoothly into the last eight of the Cup Winners' Cup.

Countering the southern press

Even during the mid-1980s, there was a divide between the northern and southern press. So when Everton travelled to West Ham for their first game in London since going top, there was an ideal opportunity to demonstrate their championship credentials to Fleet Street's finest. Upton Park was an ideal place for Kendall's young team to showcase their varied talents and so it proved. On an afternoon of incisive football, the visitors scored the only goal twelve minutes from time when Sharp set Heath free and after West Ham keeper Tom McAlister saved his initial shot, the in-form striker score from the rebound. Jeff Powell of the *Daily Mail* was certainly impressed. 'Everton are startled to find themselves besieged by admirers of the sparkling qualities which win most of the glittering prizes,' he wrote, 'Efficiency, competitiveness, professionalism, application... such virtues have been ascribed to Everton ever since they began their drive towards last season's FA Cup Final victory at Wembley. Genuine recognition is coming only now, couched in terms like classy... exciting... varied.' Bryon Butler had commented on the game for radio and speaking on BBC Radio 2's legendary *Sports Report*, he was equally effusive: 'Other sides may have bigger stars, or better players, but Everton are the best team.'

West Ham boss John Lyall also praised the way Everton mixed solid organisation with spells of intelligent passing at pace, before adding: 'They're a very good side. They've got a lot of variety in their game. The four players in midfield have all got their own particular talents. They're all comfortable on the ball and that is difficult to play against when there are two who work hard and run hard up front... They'll be in there or around there when the championship is decided.' Howard Kendall was almost embarrassed about the compliments. 'Listening to this, we must be a good side,' he admitted.

When Stoke were vanquished 4-0 a week later, Everton had recorded ten successive victories in all competitions, scoring 26 goals and conceding just two. During 1984 they had played 58 matches, won 34 and lost just eight. There was a warm glow to the campaign. Speaking after the West Ham game, Kevin Ratcliffe was in confident mood. 'Unlike some other teams, we don't have star individuals,' the skipper said, 'We're just a bunch of lads who work for each other. The difference is the confidence we've drawn from winning the FA Cup. As a team, we actually believe we're good enough to stay at the top.' Three weeks later those hopes took a huge blow.

Wednesday's side is full of woe

The image is sadly an abiding one. On the opening day of December, Everton faced Sheffield Wednesday at a rain-sodden Goodison and after seventeen

345

minutes Adrian Heath is carried off the pitch by Everton physio John Clinkard. The game against the Yorkshire side, promoted at the end of the previous campaign, had already developed a nasty, niggling edge. Even in a division known for harsh physicality, the Yorkshire side's uncompromising approach broke new ground. Fielding three tough central defenders, one being Mick Lyons, they adopted a tactic that involved kicking the ball as far up the pitch as possible and giving chase.

Nevertheless, they possessed some dangerous players, like former Toffees striker Imre Varadi and winger Brian Marwood. Ironically, the latter was involved in the incident sadly synonymous with this soggy, bad-tempered encounter. Marwood and Heath both challenged for a loose ball, however the Wednesday man lunged at pace and left Everton's player of the year in a motionless heap on the ground. The prognosis did not look good as the stricken forward left the pitch and Sharp's penalty twelve minutes later was merely an afterthought. For the rest of the half, some Everton players clearly wanted retribution and in a second ugly incident, Reid clattered Marwood with a reckless, pre-meditated challenge that could have caused serious injury. In terms of intent, the challenge was far worse than the victim's tackle, but referee Trevor Jones unbelievably allowed the Everton player to remain on the pitch. To exacerbate the unpleasantness, the home crowd shamefully jeered Marwood as he left the pitch on a stretcher. Patrick Barclay called it 'the ugly and unacceptable face of football' in the *Guardian,* 'A disgraceful pseudotackle, greeted by equally disgraceful cheers from the crowd.' Both were undeniably true but Reid was hardly contrite after the game. 'If people want to say it was an eye for an eye, they can,' he said. However, regarding Reid's tackle as something symbolising the camaraderie amongst the team is not right, on another day it could have ended Marwood's career. The game finished 1-1, Everton's struggles showing how much they missed Heath's instinctive play and darting runs around the box, but most of all his goals.[112]

A dreadful game, the disappointing result and Heath's injury came at the end of a rotten fortnight for Kendall's side. In the League Cup, Grimsby had made a mockery of a one-sided game at Goodison to triumph 1-0 in the last minute while

---

[112] Despite missing the last month, Heath's 28 goals in 1984 were the highest by an Everton player in a calendar year between Bob Latchford's 29 in 1978 and Romelu Lukaku's thirty in 2015.

Norwich ended the unbeaten run in the league with a 4-2 victory at Carrow Road. There was confirmation within 48 hours of the Sheffield Wednesday game that Heath had suffered cruciate ligament damage and was likely to miss the rest of the season. However, Kendall accepted that Marwood was blameless. 'I've seen it again on TV. The lad came in at 100 miles per hour I don't think for a minute that it was intentional,' the manager said.[113] Kendall also reflected on the striker's cruel misfortune: 'It is a terrible blow for us but even more so for Adrian... It comes at a time when he is playing possibly the best football of his career. At the moment he is one of the finest front players in the country. He will be missed and so will his goals.' The manager was losing half of the top-flight's most productive partnership. The 23-year-old had scored thirteen times, the same as Graeme Sharp with the pair accounting for half the team's goals. In the marvellous ten-game winning run, at least one of the pair scored in nine. Sadly for the striker he was also very much in Bobby Robson's plans. 'I knew all about Heath and what a marvellous season he was having,' the England manager said later, 'His injury was a cruel blow, extremely disappointing for everyone concerned.'

But the injury opened the door for the reserve team centre-forward, an option Kendall was content with. 'I just feel very, very fortunate at having Andy Gray available,' he admitted, 'He has been waiting patiently and now he has got his chance. He is not a squad player – he is a first-class quality player.' Gray, as ever, was prepared: 'It is not the way I would have wanted it but it is now up to me.'

Gray was back for the trip to QPR and a goalless draw on the dreaded plastic pitch. However, there was nothing artificial about the mass brawl which made all the headlines. Tempers initially frayed following a dreadful challenge by Terry Fenwick on Trevor Steven, which led to an ugly altercation between them. Moments later, when an aerial challenge by Gray flattened Gary Waddock, following an earlier skirmish, Simon Stainrod ran over and pushed the striker but then took two punches to the head and ended up on the floor. Meanwhile Fenwick waded in throwing his own haymakers. With sixteen players engaged in a proper old-school free for all, one not involved was Kevin Sheedy, who stood in the centre circle 'directing operations like General Montgomery' according to his colleagues. When the dust settled referee John Deakin dismissed Stainrod and

---

[113] Kendall had tried to sign Marwood, who was at Hull City, when at Ewood Park but the two clubs could not agree a fee.

Pat Van Den Hauwe, but Gray was lucky to stay on the pitch as was Fenwick. The referee also missed a looping right-hook from Rangers' Gary O'Neill that sent Van Den Hauwe crashing to the floor. 'A disgraceful brawl on the 36th minute disfigured this match, led to two players being sent off,' Brian Glanville wrote in the *Sunday Times,* 'quite why at least a dozen others were not expelled was obscure.' The draw left Everton a single point ahead of Spurs at the top, with the leading five teams covered by three points.

Seven days later, for the third successive Saturday the league leaders were embroiled in controversy. Searching for a first win in five games, Everton faced Nottingham Forest at Goodison and rediscovered the sparkling form of the golden autumn, romping to a 5-0 victory. 'Everton, incisive, intelligent and immeasurably superior to a sorely-depleted Forest... confirmed to the 22,487 spectators that they were not watching pretenders, but probable champions elect,' was Derek Hodgson's verdict in the *Observer.* The home team displayed both silk and steel but, according to their opponents, far too much of the latter. After ten minutes Sharp's challenge on Gary Mills left the defender with a broken leg, although it appeared purely accidental and the striker apologised immediately. With Everton already two goals ahead by the hour-half mark, Forest's young defender Chris Fairclough was sent off for a crude tackle on the Scot.

Several Forest players came out on the offensive about Kendall's side, especially as young forward David Riley left the pitch injured. 'We still feel angry about Everton's tactics,' claimed one unnamed player. 'There were a lot of things going on which have no place on a football field. I saw several over-the-top tackles.' Another said, 'Everton might win the title this way though I doubt they'll win any friends.' The stricken Mills said: 'My injury was caused by Graeme Sharp's tackle early on in the game. Perhaps I'd better limit my remarks to just that.' Kendall refused to be drawn on the allegations afterwards, other than saying, 'the crowd saw a tremendous performance, we did everything right.' Peter Reid did however come to the team's defence. 'You can't look at our team and honestly pick out one hatchet man,' the midfielder argued, 'A hard tackler maybe, nothing more.' However, he did admit 'Some of our tackles in the last three games have been wrong and the referees have punished them.'

There was another possible by-product from the game. Kendall had tried to buy Forest's Birkenhead-born Peter Davenport – once an Everton junior – after

Heath's injury but Brian Clough rejected any deal, possibly because he was upset by the home team's aggression at Goodison where he spent most of the game stood up pointing at the Everton bench, with Mick Heaton the unfortunate target. The Forest boss publicly accused his counterpart of leaking interest in the player, which Kendall naturally denied. When the Toffees made a further £400,000 bid in February 1985, Clough told the press. 'I must admit I was rather surprised by Brian's statement about our offer,' Kendall responded, 'I don't know why he has shown resentment about our interest.' Perhaps it was the events at Goodison.

Christmas on the road

Chelsea were the closest Everton had to a bogey team during the mid-1980s. Promoted during the summer of 1984, John Neal's side had made a solid start but had not won away. That changed on the final Saturday before Christmas when a display of clinical finishing – they created five chances all afternoon and scored four – produced a stunning 4-3 victory. Their hero was underrated Welsh striker Gordon Davies, who netted a hat-trick. Worryingly for Kendall, for the fourth time in twenty league games the defence had shipped four goals and it was noticeable that the suspended Van Den Hauwe had not played in three of them. Afterwards Kendall gave his Chelsea counterpart a Christmas card, joking that it was from his goalkeeper and back-four.

Paradoxically, the Toffees were in title contention having conceded four more goals than at the same stage twelve months before, when a 3-0 defeat at Wolves had left them in crisis. The difference was at the other end of the pitch, but equally concerning was that the loss of Heath robbed Everton of imagination and speed of both thought and movement. Instead there was a seemingly endless salvo of high balls to Sharp and Gray.

To make matters worse, Everton had fallen to third in the table, two points behind leaders Spurs with Manchester United sandwiched in-between. 'I don't think that losing the leadership will prove to be a real psychological blow,' Kendall said reassuringly, 'we have slipped up in the past and come back.' Nevertheless, the Christmas fixture-list gifted two geographically awkward away matches: Sunderland on Boxing Day then Ipswich. At Roker Park, Kendall deployed the usual tactics when requiring a result: squeeze the life out of the opposition in midfield and take it from there. After some early alarms, the players did just that with Bracewell outstanding. The unlikely hero was Derek Mountfield, who scored twice in the opening twenty minutes and, although the home team pulled a goal back, the visitors remained in control to seal a vital victory. Yet the display was unconvincing in a varied season for all the top teams, characterised by plenty of Christmas presents on the same day from Everton's rivals. Liverpool, Arsenal and Manchester United all lost while Spurs drew against West Ham United after throwing away a two-goal lead. 'The game amply illustrated why the First Division is so open this season; there are no consistently good teams, as the results over Christmas have shown,' said Charles Burgess in the *Guardian* at Roker Park. The win took Everton joint-top, behind Spurs on goal difference.

Three days later, there was more of the same in a frozen East Anglia. An injury-hit Everton kept it tight and allowed the home team few opportunities before striking in devastating fashion during the second period. The hero was Graeme Sharp, who netted with a header following a burst of speed and cross from Sheedy on the right and just before the end the striker pirouetted beautifully on a difficult surface to nudge the ball past Paul Cooper in the Ipswich goal. Sharp may have felt unappreciated by Kendall, but the manager was generous in his praise: 'He has hit a rich vein of form in recent weeks and is playing quite beautifully. He is brave, good in the air and has good control. He has most of the things you look for in a top striker.'

The result kept Everton level with Spurs but confirmed them as undoubtedly the team of the year: 81 points from 43 league games was seven higher than anyone else (and eleven more than Liverpool) with an FA Cup, Charity Shield and FA Youth Cup thrown in for good measure. But there were still doubts. Then the national press usually only had away games to pass judgement on northern teams and, of the seven away victories thus far, Ipswich was the first by more than a single goal. Asked by an unimpressed reporter after the game whether his team's performance was of championship quality, Kendall replied 'Why not?'

That press cynicism existed because, on their travels, Everton undoubtedly played with less flamboyance than title rivals Spurs and Manchester United. Clive White of *The Times* was at Ipswich and suggested, 'If the title is to be won by qualities of more physical than artistic merit then Everton would be front runners.' There was an element of truth in the comment. However, White then claimed that 'the title is going to be won by lesser mortals than the old Liverpool.' But Fagan's team were champions after winning only one of their last nine away matches, scoring just six goals.[114] Comparisons were probably unfair, given Kendall's side were still developing and the *Daily Mail's* Jeff Powell provided a more balanced assessment: 'Everton's efficiency needs more time yet to develop the precision ball-work and fluent movement of Liverpool.' Ironically, away from home Everton were largely employing a template their local rivals learned from Europe: play a high-line and take the sting out of the contest early on by liberal use of the back-pass, then grow into the game.

Consequently, Everton supporters felt the side was not receiving their dues. 'It is ridiculous that the national press should disregard the essential elements of the Everton team,' said one letter to the *Liverpool Echo*, 'Skill allied to teamwork and strength… I believe this side has the ability to better that team of 1970. They are much more tenacious and have the ability to kill off sides. Perhaps the championship will be the only thing to silence the carping critics.' The question as 1984 ended was, could Kendall's team do that?

---

[114] In 1976/77 Liverpool won the title despite winning only one away league game from early November onwards.

CHAPTER 32

Spur for success

THE TOFFEES OPENED THE NEW YEAR WITH A 2-1 VICTORY OVER Luton Town at Goodison following two goals from Trevor Steven, taking his tally to eight, one more than Kevin Sheedy on the opposite flank. Although nominally wide players, neither were orthodox wingers, a role Kendall mistrusted. Steven had played virtually all his games with the Lancashire club in the middle, but the Everton boss convinced him that his future lay out wide where natural discipline, when combined with his grace and technique, made him such an accomplished performer.[115] As the season progressed the 21-year-old would also display invaluable versatility, playing as a striker – it would soon become apparent that he was one of the best, if not the best, header of the ball at the club. The burgeoning relationship with Gary Stevens was a huge asset, the two complementing each other perfectly: the elegance and style of Steven combined with the muscular physicality of the right-back, although both possessed huge endurance. Twelve months before Everton were in a relegation fight, now they were a key partnership in a team heading back to the top.

Shout to the top

With Spurs victorious in the north London derby on New Year's Day, they were still top when Newcastle came to Goodison in mid-January. The perfect display banished any doubts over Everton's title credentials as the Geordies were overrun

---

[115] Brian Glanville once described Steven in the *Sunday Times* as a 'Stakhanovite'. Puzzled readers were put straight by the Everton match-day programme: '*Noun* a worker in the former Soviet Union who was exceptionally hard-working and productive.'

4-0. 'It was a measured, almost magisterial, performance from a side which used Christmas to accelerate away at the top of the league,' said Malcolm Winton in the *Sunday Times*. Pat Van Den Hauwe's left-footed cross lead to the opening goal after seventeen minutes, Graeme Sharp leaping high to put a looping header over Kevin Carr. Derek Mountfield effectively killed off the away team with a second on the half-hour, following a scramble in the six-yard box. With the midfield quartet purring, the second period was a procession. The third goal after 62 minutes was a beauty. Paul Bracewell's sublime reverse pass to Sheedy took out three Newcastle players and the Irishman finished into the corner, before adding a second three minutes from time. Afterwards Kendall was delighted. 'When you can sit back, relax and enjoy what is happening on the field you make the most of it,' he declared, 'It was a great team performance. They all deserve praise. I sensed a determination to get back to the top after the defeat to Chelsea.'

Jack Charlton told waiting journalists in the Goodison corridor that it was men against boys. 'They confused our lads to a degree that was embarrassing. They are a hell of a good side.' The rout took Everton to 53 league goals, the highest in England, and restored them to top spot after Spurs could only draw 2-2 at QPR. Exactly twelve months before they were eighteenth. With Manchester United losing a second successive home game, suddenly what looked a three-horse race now looked like a shoot-out with Spurs, who were six ahead of Atkinson's outfit.

Frank Sibley was QPR caretaker manager and he made some interesting comments after facing Spurs. 'My money would be on Everton for the title,' he declared, 'they are becoming a good Liverpool type of side. I don't think they've the outstanding individuals that Tottenham have got but collectively they're very, very difficult to beat.' Sadly, the frozen wasteland meant the two teams could not test out Sibley's comments at White Hart Lane seven days later, when the Pools Panel predicted a home win for Spurs. Understandably, by then Kendall cut a frustrated figure.

'My players are just not appreciated'

In early January 1985, Bobby Robson announced a 23-man England squad for a get-together at Bisham Abbey. More than half came from Arsenal, Spurs and Manchester United. There was precisely zero from table-topping Everton. West

Brom's Steve Hunt was in ahead of Peter Reid and Paul Bracewell. Mark Chamberlain from bottom-of-the table Stoke City was in the queue before Trevor Steven. The only Gary Stevens in the squad was the Spurs midfielder. But the selection was not necessarily a surprise as Kendall's team were largely on the periphery. A newspaper article about 'anonymous Everton' had all the squad's faces blanked out while *Match of the Day* had not visited Goodison once. Eight days after the squad announcement, Kendall attended a lunch in London where he received the Sportswriters' Association's Guinness Cup. Having claimed that 'My players are just not appreciated,' the Everton manager used the event to promote the gifts of his team:

> *I know the talent that I've got because it delights me and excites me every day of the week. Some of our present team are as skilful and exciting as I've ever seen. Trevor Steven is the nearest I've seen to Alex Young in terms of graceful movement. He's not a winger or a midfield player but a combination of both... Peter Reid is a rare player who can take a game by the scruff of the neck and say "Give it to me, I'll run it."... Reid and Bracewell would have kept me out of the side had I been playing for Everton now.*

Unsurprisingly, Kendall went on to say Andy Gray was one of his most important signings before giving the first public outing to the famous story about the striker's first training session. 'John Bailey put the ball over and Andy Gray put a bullet of a header into the back of the net. Andy said "John, that's the first quality ball I've had for two years." John replied "That's the first time I've had anyone on the end of a cross for two years."' Asked about their biggest threat, Kendall was complimentary about Spurs. 'They have a strong squad and seem to have the advantage of knowing what their strongest team is,' he said, 'Continuity is essential – but winning the title is our objective.'

A week later Bobby Robson stepped into the 'Everton for England' debate. 'Everton have a good team, but they have not achieved their success because of any one particular player. The side has superb shape and balance and their strength lies in teamwork... what I am saying is that in my own opinion they don't have anyone who stands head and shoulders above the rest.' There was no logic to Robson's argument – the question was whether their individuals were better on current form than players in his own squad, which was certainly the case.

The two most likely to be called up, Gary Stevens and Trevor Steven, gave Robson a nudge by scoring in the regulation 2-0 home win over Doncaster Rovers in the FA Cup fourth round.[116]

'With Andy back in that form, it's going to put us in overdrive'

Everton were on a six-game winning streak at the end of January, with fourteen goals scored. There was one name missing from the list of scorers: Andy Gray, who had not found the net in seven appearances since Adrian Heath's injury. Although largely performing well, the chances had not been coming. However, apart from the bid for Peter Davenport, Kendall had shown little inclination for moving into the market. The manager made an inquiry to Ipswich about Eric Gates, but the £500,000 quoted was considered too high for a 29-year-old. The Everton manager also watched Leicester City's Gary Lineker a number of times, but when pressed the Everton boss retorted: 'We are the leading scorers in the country, so who would I leave out if I brought someone else here?'

Gray drew another blank in the home victory over Watford at the beginning of February, when Kendall's team again showed the ruthlessness of champions. Goalless just before the hour-mark, Graham Taylor's dangerous side were in the game, yet within twenty minutes they trailed 4-0. The former Wolves striker was thwarted by a brilliant Tony Coton save, but also played a part in a brilliant third goal. Following Bracewell's brilliant turn, the midfielder's cross was heading towards Gray, who ducked after a Sheedy shout, and the Irishman struck with a brilliant volley. After the game Kendall explained, 'It doesn't worry me that Andy hasn't been scoring. He's brilliant at taking the weight off other people and making space.' With Spurs drawing again, Everton were now four points clear.

In the FA Cup fifth round fourteen days later, it was the same again at Goodison when non-league Telford United proved obdurate and frustrated their illustrious opponents for more than an hour. Then Gary Stevens looked like he had netted for a third successive home game but Peter Reid had flicked his drive in. A Sheedy penalty and a sumptuous left-footed Trevor Steven strike wrapped up the scoring. Sadly, the visitors left the pitch to a chorus of boos from the majority of the 47,000 crowd as their strong-arm tactics left five Everton

---

116 Steven won his first cap in the World Cup qualifier against Northern Ireland at the end of February. Stevens, Reid and Bracewell made their England debuts in the summer tour of Mexico.

players needing treatment on the Sunday.

Gray by now had not found the net for five months. 'Unfortunately I'd also got to the point where I felt I was never going to score,' he confessed in *Gray Matters*, 'I was playing well enough, making a real contribution to the team, but as the weeks went by my confidence started to go.' The striker reflected about two missed chances in the Telford game: 'The nearer I got to scoring the more desperate I started to feel. I began to wonder if I'd lost my touch altogether.'

A week later a weakened Everton travelled to Leicester City for their first away league game since Christmas. Sharp was out – 'we have 22 goals between us this season' Gray quipped – with Steven playing up front as the 29-year-old wore the number nine shirt for the first time since Newcastle away. Before the game Gray's future Sky sparring partner Martin Tyler entered the dressing room and informed the Scot he required two goals to reach 100 in English league football. 'I'll be lucky to reach my century by the end of the year,' he joked. The Everton goal led a charmed life in the opening period, with Southall saving well from Lineker and Steve Lynex. However, on 66 minutes Gray's found his missing killer touch. Bracewell flicked on Sheedy's cross from the byline and the forward stole in to score with a header, immediately crashing into the post. The goal was his second in seventeen matches.

However, on 82 minutes a suspiciously offside Lynex broke through and fired an equaliser past the onrushing Southall. With Everton looking to have thrown away a vital two points, Gray proved once again why he had been worth taking a punt on. Steven's head skilfully glanced on a Van Den Hauwe long ball and the Scot moved forward to fire home from the edge of the box. Gray immediately ran towards the linesman who had flagged Lynex onside and using a bit of finger-pointing, politely suggested the goal may have been payback for his poor decision. The hugely significant goal secured a priceless 2-1 victory that retained the four-point lead. 'The great football machine called Everton grinds relentlessly onwards,' Alec Johnson wrote in the *Daily Mirror*. After the game, Peter Reid paid tribute to the match-winner. 'Andy has been playing well, but was snatching at chances,' the midfielder remarked, 'but he is a great battler and showed here he is the best finisher in the business. It was a magic goal that won the game. With Andy back in that form, it's going to put us in overdrive.'

Despite their blip over the turn of the year, Manchester United were still in the hunt by the time Everton travelled to Old Trafford on the first Saturday in

March. Atkinson's team were seven points behind, having played a game more, but on the previous weekend had won at Highbury. Although the home team were missing Bryan Robson, the visitors were without the forward duo who had run riot at Goodison. Everton were remarkably aiming to equal the post-war club record of ten successive wins set earlier in the campaign.

Such was the interest, the two clubs turned down more than 20,000 ticket applications for one of the matches of the season. The encounter was just that, a marvellous game of ebbs and flows that displayed the contrast between the teams: United's ability to run with the ball as individuals against the passing, positional play and movement of Everton's midfield quartet. The tense afternoon started with a penalty but Gordon Strachan fluffed his lines and Southall saved easily. Then United went ahead when Jesper Olsen's shot deflected in off Stevens. But Kendall's outfit showed their usual resilience and were behind for only five minutes: Terry Curran flicked on Trevor Steven's corner and Mountfield headed downwards into the roof of the net for an eighth goal of the season. Gray had enjoyed an excellent game but wasted his best chance. Unmarked from a free-kick in the second half, the Scot headed over from eight yards out as the cameras captured him mouthing apologies to the Everton fans massed at the Scoreboard End. After Alan Brazil's shot crashed down off the bar, eight minutes from time the visitors wasted an opportunity to bury their opponents' title hopes. Arthur Albiston pushed Steven over at the byline but Gary Bailey palmed Sheedy's penalty away. The turbocharged 1-1 draw suited the Toffees but in a season when the debate over live football continued, the *Guardian's* David Lacey pulled both subjects together perfectly: 'It would have made enthralling television covered live but thank goodness the game was spared that. These occasions belong in front of a packed house on a Saturday afternoon and not in the nation's armchairs on a Friday night.' After the game, Ron Atkinson singled out the Scottish striker as his man of the match. 'Gray was superb. He gave a tremendous performance and was always causing us problems.' Spurs won 1-0 at Stoke City, cutting the lead to two points, with Liverpool moving menacingly one behind Manchester United.

Four days later Kendall's men faced Fortuna Sittard at Goodison in the quarter-final of the European Cup Winners' Cup. The Dutch side were mostly semi-professionals although they did feature Frans Thijssen, one of the stars of Bobby Robson's superb Ipswich team. On a freezing March evening, they put up a defensive blanket which a visibly hesitant Everton initially failed to breach. 'We are novices as a team in Europe and I felt it showed in the first half,' Kendall said after the game. However, Gray showed the ability to win a match single-handedly that had once made him Britain's most expensive footballer. Three minutes after the break goalkeeper André van Gerven failed to hold Reid's shot and the Scot stabbed the ball home. On 74 minutes Gray scored the type of goal that defined him. Terry Curran's clever cross went towards the far post and the striker poked his head between the trailing boot of Wim Koevermans and the approaching van Gerven to dive full length for his second. 'Some people think that's brave but I just think it's stupid,' Gray said afterwards when shown the goal on ITV's *Midweek Sports Special*. The crowd had barely caught their breath when Koevermans misjudged Sheedy's cross and Gray nipped in to power an unstoppable half-volley into the roof of the net. The Scot's first hat-trick for seven years gave the Toffees a very handy lead for the return. 'I am delighted for Andy Gray,' said a delighted Kendall afterwards, 'He has been playing well but has had no luck.' By the strength of his own personality, the Everton striker had played himself back into form with five crucial goals in three games. There was talk of Heath's injury damaging ambitions, but with Gray now firing on all cylinders, the treble was on.

Irish magic

Everton were also aiming to successfully defend the FA Cup. Four days after the Sittard game, they entertained struggling Ipswich Town in the quarter-final at Goodison Park, with the *Match of the Day* cameras in attendance for the first time since the infamous Coventry City game on the final day of 1983. Their brilliant play in the opening fifteen minutes showed how far Kendall's side had travelled in that time. Although Everton's opening goal remains one of the most memorable of the era, the build-up was equally remarkable. The ball was played into Reid fifteen yards from the left-hand touchline and the midfielder's first-time return pass out wide into the space in front of Bracewell (who was not in his line of sight) betrayed a sixth sense, his partner producing a perfect left-footed cross, which swerved away, forcing the onrushing Paul Cooper to handle outside the area.

Kevin Sheedy had developed the reputation as a dead-ball expert, but there was far more to the Irishman's game than that. His passing – both short and long – was exemplary and imaginative, plus Sheedy had that natural patience and vision on the ball to take the tempo out of the game. Although there were certain trademarks – the far-post volley for one – what set him apart from Everton players of any era was a flair for the unorthodox or unexpected: the 'how did he do that' moment. If every Toffees star had to produce a five-minute highlights' reel of their career, his would undoubtedly be the best: a decade of goals ranging from delicate chips to thirty-yard missiles, of crunching volleys and swerving free-kicks. Mixed in with some outrageous assists.

But probably the highlight of Sheedy's career came following the award of the free-kick. The Ireland international's first attempt was fired into the roof of the net to Cooper's right, but referee Alan Robinson, having already controversially chalked off an Andy Gray header for handball from Bracewell, disallowed it as he was moving the ball back. 'Now it was a little bit of a mind game between me and the keeper,' the midfielder wrote in the aptly-named *So Good I Did It Twice*, 'I could see Paul edging over towards the side I'd put the original kick, obviously feeling I was going to do the same again. But in doing so he left a little bit of a gap to his left.'

The second effort brought the house down, Sheedy taking advantage of the gap and delicately chipping the ball over the wall and low into the opposite corner. The midfielder wheeled away in front of the ecstatic crowd, who knew they had witnessed something unique, as did Barry Davies on commentary: 'What a lesson in taking free kicks by Kevin Sheedy... he almost said to Mr Robinson "I don't mind if you don't allow me to put it one corner, I'll put it in the other."' Perversely, by the break the visitors were 2-1 ahead. Neville Southall allowed a Kevin Wilson shot to squirm underneath him and then Romeo Zondervan put the visitors ahead with a snap volley. The second half was all one-way traffic towards the Gwladys Street end. Uncharacteristically, Kevin Ratcliffe found himself with only Cooper to beat but chipped tamely into the keeper's hands. Referee Robinson unbelievably then failed to award a penalty after Trevor Putney twice felled Trevor Steven within seconds and when Gray headed over with the goal at his mercy, the Toffees' ten-year unbeaten home run in the competition appeared over. But five minutes from the end of a pulsating contest Everton, like all the best teams, found a way back. Pat Van Den Hauwe cleverly controlled Reid's chipped forward pass and Mountfield stabbed home the defender's volleyed cross in front of the relieved supporters to secure a replay.

After the game, Kendall paid tribute to his team's fighting qualities. 'In the end we got a left-back on the right side of the box showing great skill to get in a cross – and a centre-half getting on the end of it to equalise.' The manager was indirectly paying tribute to Van Den Hauwe's under-appreciated footballing intelligence: knowing that Ipswich left-back Steve McCall had earlier been red-carded, the defender just occupied the space he had left.

The afternoon, however, is sadly also remembered for the death of Harry Catterick, who collapsed with a heart attack towards the end. 'He was the man who gave us what we wanted at Goodison – a successful team playing the attractive soccer our fans demand,' said Sir John Moores, 'Our present manager Howard must have learned a lot under Harry as did Colin Harvey.' They certainly had, Brian Labone's statement that he 'produced effective teams that had flair' applied to the class of 1985. 'In many ways his influence is still here,' Moores added.

The replay on a freezing evening in East Anglia was less dramatic but red-blooded. The key moment came fifteen minutes from time. Sharp's cross bounced awkwardly and Russell Osman unluckily handled in the area. The returning striker fired home from the spot and although the home team struck the woodwork twice, the visitors held on for a semi-final berth.[117] That was the second piece of good news in twenty-four hours, on the previous evening there was a beneficial twist in the title race. Spurs seemingly possessed a huge advantage in having ten of their last fifteen matches at home – one crucially against Everton – but Manchester United immediately scuppered that theory by winning 2-1 at White Hart Lane. The Toffees were now two points ahead with a game in hand.

But Kendall's side squandered the advantage on the Saturday, drawing 1-1 at Aston Villa following a tired and uninspired performance. With Sheedy injured and Reid suspended, Alan Harper and Kevin Richardson deputised and the latter's goal looked enough for an undeserved three points until Allan Evans' late penalty levelled matters. When a journalist suggested to Kendall afterwards that the champions-elect looked jaded and under pressure the manager replied curtly, 'Jaded, you must be joking.'

News of the result at Anfield may have contributed to Kendall's mood. Usually a Liverpool defeat was a cause for celebration, but not this time. Even when

---

[117] Against Luton Town, whose home victory against Millwall on the same night was marred by rioting away supporters in some of the worst spectator violence seen in this country.

football used statistics sparingly, it was widely known that Spurs had last won on the ground in the year the Titanic sank. With a fair proportion of Evertonians hoping for a Liverpool victory, a Garth Crooks goal ended 73 years of hurt and took Spurs level with Everton at the top, having played a game more. But 48 hours after the uninspiring draw there was more criticism of Kendall's side. 'The trouble with being the best in the country is that you are vulnerable to instant impressions,' John Wragg wrote in the *Daily Express*, 'It is all right at home where opinions are built soundly over a succession of performances, but away you are only as good as the show you put on. And you will not get anyone in Birmingham to say that Everton are worthy of the title after digging out a dull 1-1 draw against Villa… it was dreadful.'

In midweek Everton travelled to Sittard for the second leg of their European tie. With a history of trouble at Dutch grounds, the club did not take a ticket allocation, although many ended up on Merseyside via British servicemen based just across the border. That said, the several hundred fans who made the journey were well-behaved and watched the team record an excellent 2-0 victory. On a freezing evening, the main highlight was a male streaker risking more than his liberty in escaping from two police dogs via a barbed wire fence. In a surreal development, the two dogs then started fighting each other.[118]

The semi-final draw produced the biggest challenge remaining: Bundesliga giants Bayern Munich. 'It's going to be a big game for us. It has got a ring to it,' admitted Kendall. His counterpart Udo Lattek said, 'Bayern against Everton – that's really the final. Whoever wins this semi-final will also win the Cup.' That may have been true, but there was a title to contest. On the following weekend, Everton defeated Arsenal 2-0 at Goodison while Spurs thrashed Southampton 5-1, to set up a week that could effectively decide the championship.

---

118 There was a rare error of judgement by Kendall – he selected too few players and had only four substitutes. Fortunately, Andy Gray had been taken 'for the ride' so Kendall told him he was needed despite the striker spending the entire trip enjoying Dutch hospitality. 'You canna make me sub Howard, I was having a few drinks,' the Scot protested. 'We'll stick you on the bench, don't say anything to anybody,' the Everton boss replied. Much to the amusement of his teammates, a worse for wear Gray spent the night freezing as a substitute.

CHAPTER 33

Witnessing a miracle

ON THE MORNING OF THE FINAL SATURDAY OF MARCH 1985, THE *Guardian's* David Lacey previewed the following week. 'The next five days will not settle the League Championship,' he predicted, 'but there is a strong possibility that after Wednesday night the lines for the final run-in will be established once and for all.'

The peerless football writer was referring to Everton's trip to Tottenham four days later, a fixture originally scheduled for January but postponed due to freezing weather. Then Everton led Spurs by two points, now the pair were level and because the two teams had remained within touching distance there was further intrigue. 'The ten-and-a-half week delay has merely heightened the significance of the confrontation,' Lacey said.

Beforehand Everton had a tough fixture at The Dell, having not won there since Kendall was a player in April 1972 and with a run of seven successive league defeats on the South Coast. Spurs meanwhile had an easier fixture versus Aston Villa at White Hart Lane. 'Tottenham must be quietly fancying their chances of regaining the league leadership today for the first time since early January,' was Lacey's take. The afternoon proved to be more significant than expected.

We need to talk about Kevins

There was a noteworthy new presence on the south coast. Kevin Sheedy was still injured with Kevin Richardson covering on the left. Unfairly labelled a 'utility' player and overshadowed by the marvellous Toffees midfield quartet, the Geordie was never a reserve but a formidable operator in his own right and he went on to enjoy a hugely successful career after leaving Goodison, winning the title with

Arsenal in 1989 and captaining Aston Villa to the League Cup at Wembley five years later.[119] A strong-willed, battle-hardened leader, it speaks volumes that Richardson was still playing top-flight football near the end of the 1990s, ironically having outlasted his midfield colleagues on both Merseyside and in north London. 'He's a winner,' was Andy Gray's verdict when Ron Atkinson took him to Villa in 1991.

Richardson came from stage-left to play the lead role during a soggy afternoon on the south coast, as the muddy surface produced a strange contest riddled with errors. In the opening period, he struck the bar with a header and fired over when well-placed after Graeme Sharp played him in. The Scottish striker himself struck the post after David Armstrong's back-pass got stuck in the mud. Goalless at half-time, spirits lifted in the away dressing room with news that Paul Rideout's goal had given Villa the lead at White Hart Lane. The first five minutes after the break were pivotal in the championship chase. Trevor Steven skipped inside from the right flank and when Peter Shilton could only parry Graeme Sharp's shot, Richardson was on hand to knock in the rebound. Two minutes later it was 2-0. Gray nodded on Gary Stevens' cross, veteran defender Mick Mills allowed the ball to run on and Richardson nipped in round the back to slide the ball past Shilton. After Southall saved Armstrong's penalty and Joe Jordan scored an injury-time consolation for the home team, the visitors held on for a crucial victory. With Mark Walters adding a second goal for Villa, the shock 2-0 defeat left Spurs three points behind having played a game more. A delighted Kendall paid tribute to the match-winner after the game: 'He poached both goals and the second in particular was a real striker's effort, one that any front man would have been proud of, let alone a midfielder.' The 2-1 victory showed that if championships were awarded for winning efficiently and clinically, then Kendall's team would be runaway leaders. However, some felt that they should be displaying more class. Robert Armstrong reopened the debate in the *Guardian* after the victory at The Dell:

> *Yet they remain a peculiarly charmless side, picking up points for the most part in the metronomic style of a committed base-liner. Rather like a tennis player who makes a good living from his sport, Howard Kendall's side*

---

119 Making him the first player to win the three major domestic honours with three different clubs.

concede nothing and venture next to nothing, shrewdly covering the angles and capitalising on their opponents' defensive errors...while Everton continue to score a fair number of goals, one often has a feeling that all work and no play is making their games a dull experience for the fans. Winning is not quite everything.

There was a degree of truth in that. Everton's pressing style existed to force their opponents into errors, now universally recognised as a vital part of the modern game. However, critics regarded pressing – or 'closing down' to use the contemporary term – with a bit of stuffiness as they largely judged teams by what they did with the ball. Liverpool pressed as much as any team, but more than a decade at the top had given them the opportunity, and riches, to also develop a style of passing and movement that featured imagination and flair.

That really was Everton's problem – the team had not been together long enough to fully develop all those attributes, particularly away from home when it was difficult to press opponents in numbers and give yourself space to play an expansive game. The injury to Heath and introduction of Gray had produced a change in style, more direct but certainly not long ball. Kendall had obviously tightened up the team defensively after leaking goals before Christmas, at the expense of reducing the attacking threat. That was sound management. Elsewhere, Sheedy's absence affected the team more than anybody else, as they missed the one player who could create time and space on the ball, to give better shape, width and variety. The treacherous surfaces of the winter months and early spring also worked against flowing football.

Consequently, after Christmas the team certainly played with less freedom and away games could become wars of attrition, with Everton giving nothing away. 'Southampton often struggled for periods of ten or fifteen minutes to deliver a shot on target simply because they were not allowed to get out of second gear around the centre circle,' Armstrong wrote. Since January, away goals had largely arrived through set-pieces or errors: Richardson's three in a fortnight had come from an errant back-pass at Villa and two mistakes at The Dell. But forcing the opposition into blunders and taking full advantage is an art-form in itself. As Southampton boss Lawrie McMenemy said after the game: 'Everton are the best team in the country at the moment...They don't create many chances, but they take them when they do. That's the hallmark of a good team.' The former guardsman also outlined the difficulties in facing Kendall's team. 'They pack very well around the man with the ball,' he said, 'if one of your players has it there are always two or three blue shirts in a very close area. They make you change the play.'

However, in Everton's case, Armstrong was wrong to say winning was not everything. Given the lack of success since 1970 and Liverpool's primacy, Kendall made it clear from the start that supporters – and himself – desired winning football above anything. Spurs and Manchester United may have been inherently more attractive but a glance at the championship odds showed whom the bookmakers thought were the most effective: Everton were 8-13, with Spurs 15-8 and Manchester United 8-1. 'Big Mal' also agreed. 'Resting' between jobs, Allison claimed: 'Liverpool and United have the best players, Spurs have the best fixtures…but Everton have the best team.'

White Heart Lane

'Don't count the players, count the hearts.' The words of Harry Storer, the Liverpool-born goalkeeper and club boss whose idiosyncratic management style was replicated by protégé Brian Clough. Had he been in north London, Storer – who also scouted for Harry Catterick – would have counted a full complement as the Everton squad stepped down from the team coach for their title showdown at White Hart Lane.

Kendall sensed this was the moment to kill off their rivals. 'Spurs will see it as an opportunity to bounce back,' he said at The Dell, 'We will see it as a chance to push further ahead.' The Everton manager's biggest problem was one of selection, now Kevin Sheedy was available. Including the midfielder was the easy bit, the harder part was leaving out his deputy, as Kendall admitted: 'I don't think I've ever been in a situation where I've had to leave someone out after they have just scored a winning double, Kevin Richardson has done an outstanding job.' The players matched their manager's determination. 'It is probably in importance the most important league game that I've played in a ten-year career in England certainly and I think it's probably Everton's most important league game since they clinched the championship [in 1970],' Andy Gray told Martin Tyler, 'We feel if we can get a result tonight we can go and complete the season nicely.' When Tyler asked 'by a result do you mean a win or will a draw satisfy?' Gray responded 'No, only wins satisfy this team.'

More than 48,000 spectators were shoehorned into White Hart Lane on a windy, drizzly evening, including several thousand in an unbelievably packed away end. With the wind at his back, Southall's long clearances caused the home defence difficulty and after ten minutes Paul Miller misjudged the Welshman's goal kick, headed square across the edge of the area and Gray was on hand to thrash the ball home with a right-footed half-volley. With the visitors taking the sting out of the game – there were 22 back-passes to Southall in the first half and nearly forty in all – Spurs were restricted to one goalscoring opportunity when the well-placed Hoddle fired wide. But the most crucial goal in the entire league campaign arrived on the hour. Spurs' full-back Mark Bowen appeared to have Sharp's long clearance under control but Trevor Steven dispossessed the young Welshman. Moving into the area, the winger rounded Ray Clemence and passed the ball into the net in front of the delirious away fans; the sight of an Everton player leaving behind a player associated with Liverpool dominance was hugely symbolic.

In the biggest league game of the campaign, the performance was one of disciplined intensity from Kendall's side. 'They outplayed Spurs by virtue of their ability to oppose every Tottenham player with at least two challengers and so deny him the chance to do anything with the ball,' wrote Ian Hargraves in the *Liverpool Echo*. Shortly after the second goal, four Everton players surrounded Osvaldo Ardiles in his own area and forced the Spurs star to literally pass the ball into touch for a corner. However, when Graham Roberts pulled a goal back with twenty minutes left following a typically powerful strike from distance, Spurs came alive. With the home team building up the pressure, near the end came a moment firmly woven into the fabric of the club, best summed up by Steve Curry in the *Daily Express*:

> *Everton should put the League championship trophy in the safe hands of goalkeeper Neville Southall when they collect it from neighbours Liverpool next month. Not since the steamy Mexican afternoon when Gordon Banks kept out a header from Pele in the 1970 World Cup has a goalkeeper produced quite such an astonishing save as Southall conjured at White Hart Lane last night. There were three minutes left, the score delicately poised at 2-1 in Everton's favour when Mark Falco met a centre with the force of a hammerhead driving in a nail. Yet like some kind of contortionist, Welshman Southall*

managed to turn the ball over the bar leaving Falco looking as if he had witnessed a miracle.

Southall's heroics preserved the points, with the manager paying tribute afterwards: 'He's been doing it all season but that one was something special.' But Falco himself spoke for everybody in the ground. 'I thought it was in,' the striker said, 'So did our players and even Everton thought we had equalised. No one on the pitch could believe it.' Spurs' boss Peter Shreeves was equally effusive: 'The talking point in our dressing room was that save. Southall is world class. Clearly it takes something special to beat this man.' As for the great goalkeeper himself, it was just another day at the office. 'It was a bit of a fluke,' he remarked, 'The ball just hit me.' The miraculous save came on the night when the Toffees convinced the southern press of their mettle. Harry Miller of the *Daily Mirror* recognised 'The calm competence and all-round control they displayed throughout their performance – some of the many qualities which will make them worthy champions.' Twenty-four hours later Kendall was still playing it cautiously over a team enjoying a seventeen-game unbeaten run which had taken them four points clear at the top, with a game in hand over Manchester United, now in second. 'There will be no talk of the championship at Goodison,' he declared, 'We have learned from Liverpool over the years and we will know we are on top when we lead everyone else by four points with one game to play.'

On Easter Saturday they faced relegation-threatened Sunderland at Goodison. It was a strange encounter in many ways, in front of the *Match of the Day* cameras, televising a league game at Goodison for the only time during the campaign. Ian Wallace opened the scoring for the visitors after just 81 seconds and later Clive Walker had two goals chalked off for marginal offside decisions and had one effort miraculously cleared off the line by Stevens.

But supporters remember three marvellous goals by the home team after the shock opener. The first on 34 minutes was beautifully constructed. Bracewell's clever hooked pass on the Bullens Road touchline fed Reid and the newly-crowned PFA Footballer of the Year slipped the ball past Peter Daniel and his inviting, driven cross was met by the diving figure of Gray who scored with a magnificent header, which he later described as 'straightforward'. Three minutes later Gray scored with an even better diving header via Steven's cross from the other wing. The Scot went off at the break to a standing ovation, showing again that there was nobody better at changing the atmosphere and direction of a game through sheer force of personality. 'Everyone at the club loves the man. The fans think the world of him, which is hardly surprising,' said Kendall afterwards. The third goal on fifty minutes was magnificent. Bracewell's first-time volleyed pass travelled the full width of the pitch to Steven on the right and the winger's first touch took him past Nick Pickering before his venomous left-footed strike arrowed into the roof of the net. The eventual 4-1 win showed the nation for the first time that Kendall's players could be as daring and as imaginative as their rivals. 'The one criticism of Everton this season has been that their overwhelming efficiency has forced a blanket over any individuality trying to get out,' wrote David Powell in *The Times*, 'The blanket has been shaken this past week to reveal a hotbed of individualism.' Next up were a couple of big semi-finals.

Bayern Munich (a), European Cup Winners' Cup semi-final (first leg)

The final seven weeks of the campaign was a massive test of Everton's individual talent and resilience. A patched-up squad travelled to Munich for the midweek semi-final against the Bundesliga leaders, who were chasing the same treble having already scored 100 goals during the campaign. Bayern were an exceptionally talented team with a strong spine, starting with Belgian World Cup star Jean-Marie Pfaff in goal. At centre-half was the Rolls Royce, Klaus Augenthaler, a worthy successor to Franz Beckenbauer. In the centre was Lothar Matthaus, who would later become one of the greatest midfielders of all-time. The gifted Soren Lerby, who Kendall had tried to sign four years before, joined Matthaus and on the left was Ludwig Kogl, a speedy old-fashioned winger. Up front was the gangly, but effective, 6ft 2in Dieter Hoeness. Bayern boss Udo Lattek had pedigree as the only man to have won all three major European trophies as a manager.

With Gray and Sheedy out injured, Harper and Richardson played out wide with Steven moving up to support Sharp. In front of 67,000 spectators, as expected the home team opened up with an assault on the visitors' goal but, apart from a Michael Rummenigge shot kicked off the line by Kevin Richardson, Everton kept Bayern at arm's length. It was the same after the break, a number of harmless long-range efforts from Lerby reflecting the home team's frustrations. 'Everton proved conclusively that the transformation from eager youngsters to seasoned professionals is complete,' Ian Ross concluded in the *Liverpool*

Daily Post. With Mountfield having one of the games of his life, Dieter Hoeness was rarely seen but with Reid also quiet, Everton failed to pose any sort of threat. The goalless draw certainly pleased a jubilant Kendall: 'This is a tremendous result for us because Bayern are a very good side. The important thing is that this is only the halfway stage… This result will make people all sit up and take notice of us.'

Luton Town, FA Cup semi-final

When asked about his team's treble chances, Kendall was uncharacteristically bullish before the game at Villa Park. 'I think it is possible to win three trophies – why not?' he said, 'Liverpool have set the standard in recent years, they have shown it can be done, so why can't we do it?' With Luton in one semi-final and Liverpool facing Manchester United at Goodison in the other, ominously Old Moore's Almanac had forecast an FA Cup final involving two teams beginning with a letter 'L'.

Everton were at full strength against an improving team that had lost just three times in thirteen league games, although any difference in quality disappeared because of the physical impact of playing in Munich less than 72 hours earlier. David Pleat's team must also take enormous credit, Mick Harford, Brian Stein and Emeka Nwajiobi caused the Everton defence no end of problems while Ricky Hill – Bingham's initial target when he bought Andy King from Luton a decade before – controlled the midfield. After Nwajiobi had missed two good chances and forced Stevens into a desperate goal-line clearance, the 6-1 outsiders went ahead. Stein appeared to foul Stevens at the edge of the box and the ball ran loose to Hill, who fired home off the post. Kendall later admitted that his side were lucky to go into the break only a goal down after an appalling display, admitting 'nobody has played that well against us for a while.'

The Everton manager added: 'I didn't have to say a lot in the dressing room. They knew they hadn't played well but we have a tremendous spirit, a tremendous attitude and the will to succeed.' Ronald Atkin in the *Observer* commented, 'That will was evident in a second half which developed from an enthralling match into a classic semi-final.' Nevertheless, with ten minutes left, the closest to an equaliser had been when Bracewell's shot cannoned back from the upright. At that point, Kendall moved Mountfield up front and five minutes from time referee John Martin awarded a soft free-kick at the edge of the box following

Steve Foster's challenge on the centre-half. Although ideal territory for Kevin Sheedy, unusually the Irishman's shot was a real pea-shooter but, via a very slight deflection off Brian Stein, the ball arced away from Les Sealey's desperate clutches into the bottom corner.

With the game at 1-1 following ninety breathless minutes, when extra time commenced the question was whether the favourites could summon enough strength to drag out a winner. After Gray had an effort kicked off the line and Sealey saved at point-blank range from Reid, Everton, like the best teams, found the killer punch at the death. Sheedy's free-kick from the left was arrowed towards the six-yard box and Mountfield powered home the header for a tenth goal of the campaign. At the end there was sympathy for losers but much admiration for the victors' resilience. 'Once Everton had that whiff of victory they were a different team,' said Pleat. Having criticized the team a fortnight before, the *Guardian's* Robert Armstrong summed up the strengths of the cup favourites perfectly:

> *Howard Kendall's splendidly balanced side have the priceless habit of scoring late goals which simultaneously destroy their opponent's morale and revive their own spirits... Such timing suggests Everton possess that will to win without which no club can lay claim to greatness.*

Forty-eight hours later Kendall again spoke about whether the treble was on. 'It has to be when you look at the position we are in and the way we are playing,' he admitted. Bookmakers agreed. Some were offering 100-30 for the Toffees to win three trophies, although effectively the odds were for the double, as most were no longer taking bets on the title. Favourites for the FA Cup and Cup Winners' Cup, the most famous game of the Kendall era provided the biggest test.

Bayern Munich (h), European Cup Winners' Cup semi-final (second leg)

Everybody who was there quite correctly claims that the breathless game against the German giants is Goodison's greatest. But it is not because of the result on its own, the encounter reigns supreme because the semi-final captures a huge number of Everton archetypes: Celtic spirit, passionate support, triumph following adversity, Goodison under lights, rampaging centre-forward(s), homegrown players and local boys making good, plus the obligatory humour.

More than 140 years of Everton history condensed into ninety minutes. Ironically, the only missing characteristic is School of Science which, as Kendall later admitted, was not the type of football needed.

The Toffees went into the semi-final on a fabulous unbeaten run of 23 matches, with nineteen won. Just as significantly, they had scored 51 goals with just twelve conceded, figures associated with the petro-funded super-clubs of today. The returning Sheedy and Gray buoyed Everton with Kendall simply saying: 'Everyone knows what to expect and we are ready.' When told that the Germans feared Gray's aerial menace, the Everton manager prophetically responded: 'A lot is being made of Andy's role, but it should be noted that Graeme Sharp has grabbed 28 goals this season and so must be a threat.' If Kendall wanted a good omen, Bayern had gone out to British opposition in the four previous seasons.

More than 49,000 privileged spectators packed into Goodison Park where they witnessed 'A night to savour, a magical combination of fervent excitement and naked aggression' according to Ian Ross of the *Liverpool Daily Post*. Yet for all the drama associated with the game, the first thirty minutes or so was tight and over-physical with Trevor Steven – who was to endure a largely frustrating first eighty minutes – missing the best chance when the wide-man, standing at the far post, screwed his shot nervously across the goal.

The Toffees had set a British record in Europe with their seventh successive clean sheet in the first leg but that lasted only a further 37 minutes. Ludwig Kugl breached the Everton back-line following an exchange of passes with Lothar Matthaus and, after Southall blocked the winger's first effort, Dieter Hoeness followed up to score. During the days of little travelling support for European ties, stunned silence greeted the away goal everybody at Goodison feared.

With Kendall happy with the first-half performance, the home team maintained their high tempo and got an immediate reward. Gray flicked on Stevens' long throw and Sharp's glancing header nestled in the far corner of the Gwladys Street goal. In front of a baying home crowd, the game came close to slipping out of control on occasions, thanks to some indulgent refereeing from Erik Fredriksson. Hans Pfugler had twice floored Graeme Sharp and when he targeted Gray, the pumped-up Scot responded with a wild kick and was lucky to escape with just a booking. The home team then got their break seventeen minutes from time, although there was a sense of absurdity about the goal. Jean-Marie Pfaff had not played since the first leg due to a worrying thigh injury and the goalkeeper needed a pain-killing injection to appear. 'Our chances are going to depend very much on how Pfaff performs – we will be under a lot of pressure, especially as Gray is playing,' Lattek said beforehand. However, a troublesome injury combined with the pressure of the game can do strange things.

Therefore, only Pfaff knows why he attempted to try and catch another Stevens' long throw, rather than let it pass out for a goal kick. The experienced Belgian could claim two teammates buffeted him but poor handling allowed the ball to slip from his grasp into Gray's path, with the Scot joyfully sweeping home. Norbert Eder was off the pitch, having suffered a broken nose following an altercation with Gray, and perhaps his absence influenced Pfaff's intervention. With the Germans waving the white flag, a third goal memorably scored by Steven, set up by Sheedy and Gray, completed an evening enshrined in the memories of everyone present.

Kendall explained his team's tactics afterwards: 'We decided before the game to bomb them. We felt the best way to approach the tie was to put them under immediate pressure and not get involved in the patient, slow build-up routine... It was a case of cashing in on our strengths and it paid off all night.' The game therefore showcased some of the simple, but hugely effective attributes of Kendall's team. Strong tackling high up the pitch. Accurate passing combined with support for the man on the ball. Most of all, clearly apparent in both semi-finals, carrying a huge danger from set pieces. 'The Germans were never happy, never able to settle, with our strikers challenging for everything,' Kendall added, 'With the tackles flying in Bayern were never going to clear balls decisively around the box and the key factor was picking up the second ball. What else can I say except that it was a superb team display.'

Yet there was an undercurrent that Everton's vigorous approach crossed the line. Bayern manager Udo Lattek famously told the home bench during the game that 'Kendall – this is not football' while in the tunnel, general manager Uli Hoeness informed Gray: 'That was not football, it was war, you are crazy men.' The Germans feared the Scottish striker and had mistakenly tried to fight fire with fire. As ever Gray was keen to have the last word. 'They dished it out but were not happy when they got some stick back. It was a physical game, but at the end of it we have beaten one of the best teams in Europe.' After the game, it was noticeable that the striker was the only player from either team to shake hands with the match officials. That said, Stuart Jones in *The Times* remarked that the result was 'Fitting justice after the cynical attitude of the West German team throughout this tie.'

For some though Everton did cross the line. Patrick Barclay in the *Guardian*, noted Bayern accused Gray of breaking Eder's nose with blows from the head and fist, leading to Lattek claiming the striker 'should be playing rugby, not football'. Furthermore, Barclay commented that the Scot's response that football was 'a man's game' did not necessarily answer their argument and even Kendall said that 'Andy was a little bit naughty'. Whilst Barclay pointed out that Bayern were hardly saints, he added: 'The question of bangs on the head did leave a nasty taste in mouths other than Eder's.' To be fair he put the incidents in the context of a worrying trend in the wider game that needed addressing – Mountfield had taken an elbow in the face from Mick Harford at Villa Park, leading to a black eye. The team's undoubted physical streak clouded judgement on their overall ability. Brian Glanville, whilst acknowledging Everton's consistency, felt Manchester United were capable of reaching a higher level of performance. For all his aggression, the Scot was the key man. When somebody asked Peter Reid what was the difference at Goodison, the midfielder replied: 'They hadn't seen Andy Gray in the first leg.'

However, everybody involved forgot those valid points about over-aggression, as even Lattek gracefully acknowledged after the game: 'On this showing Everton are the best team in Europe. They put us under pressure and, in the final analysis, were simply too strong for us.' But the final word on the passionate, truly memorable evening goes to Howard Kendall. 'It was a privilege to be present that night, let alone be the manager. I've never ever known an atmosphere like it. Nobody at Goodison will ever forget it.'

CHAPTER 34

League of their own

ON THE FIRST SATURDAY IN MAY THE *MATCH OF THE DAY* CAMERAS were at Hillsborough for Everton's visit. Since defeating Sunderland on Easter Saturday, apart from reaching two cup finals, Kendall's side had beaten West Brom, Stoke City and Norwich City in the league. However, on a cold, wet afternoon in south Yorkshire, according to commentator Barry Davies a fourth-placed Sheffield Wednesday was one of their toughest fixtures.

Unusually the cameras caught the players leaving the dressing room area and marching down the tunnel. Captain Ratcliffe is first, then Southall, Stevens,[120] a deep-breathing Andy Gray, Mountfield, Van Den Hauwe, Sheedy, substitute Alan Harper, Trevor Steven, Graeme Sharp, Bracewell before Peter Reid brings up the rear. Each player appears lost in his own thoughts, making for a hugely imposing entrance. The collective will-to-win from a teak-tough outfit is palpable. 'Unquestionably deserving of the title of the team of the season,' says Davies as they enter the arena. In the opening period they showed exactly why.

For the first thirty minutes, the visitors were on a completely different level, out-running and out-passing Wednesday. A superb break and cross from Steven resulted in Gray having a header kicked off the line before the Scot produced one of the passes of the campaign – a first-time volleyed effort that took out the Wednesday defence to put Bracewell in. After 25 minutes the striker put the visitors ahead, an untidy scuffed effort from Sharp's mishit cross. All this to a backdrop of boos aimed at Peter Reid, for his part in Brian Marwood's injury at

---

[120] An example of how even the strongest players have superstitions, early in his career Stevens enjoyed a good game after being third out onto the pitch, and retained that position.

Goodison. One challenge from Lawrie Madden on the midfielder was particularly brutal, with Reid just standing up without any shred of emotion. Later Davies commented, 'Peter Reid is so hyped-up it's not true!'

But the game remains in the memory for the five minutes before half-time when Everton, to quote David Lacey in the *Guardian*, 'showed why they are where they are and they did so, moreover, on their own goalline.' The incredible passage of play began when Southall made a stupendous save from Varadi, parrying the former Everton player's volley round the post, after having to change direction. That forced the first of six corners in 120 seconds. At the height of the barrage, Southall pulled off a wonderful point-blank stop from Mark Smith's header before Marwood's volley from the rebound crashed down off the underside of the bar. 'Brilliant save again and then one off the crossbar,' roars Davies, 'Unbelievable stuff! I don't think I've ever seen such intense pressure applied by a football team and Everton are really suffering at the moment... Southall has made two remarkable saves and was helped out by the crossbar, what an end to this first half!' But the champions-elect showed their resolve, before the referee blew for the break and a standing ovation for both teams. 'Listen to the applause,' Davies says, above the noise. 'An unrelenting first half. Hugely demanding physically. So determined in style.'

Knowing that victory would provide an opportunity to clinch the title on the Bank Holiday Monday, the visitors comfortably survived the second half to make it 26 games unbeaten and equal the club record set in 1969/70 of twelve away victories in a league campaign. 'Everton again demonstrated that rare gift of exceptional resilience,' wrote Clive White in *The Times*, 'The ability to absorb pressure while on the ropes yet seldom seem in trouble, à la Muhammad Ali.' White also paid tribute to a previously unheralded member of the team: Derek Mountfield, who was magnificent. 'He has developed from an ugly duckling of a centre back from Tranmere Rovers into, if not exactly the most graceful of defenders, certainly one of the most consistently successful.' Afterwards the press asked Kendall about the treble. 'We're only three matches away from three titles,' he replied.

Bank Holiday vault of memories

Potentially the first of those was 48 hours later, when a crowd of 50,514 packed Goodison Park for QPR's visit. There was a carnival atmosphere with the home crowd acclaiming every player's name equally beforehand, reflecting that one of the strengths of the squad was collective unity. Enhancing the mood was the news that Neville Southall was the new Football Writers' Player of the Year while Kendall received his April Manager of the Month reward. On the morning of the game, Kendall spoke about the team and a golden future. 'It is very difficult to compare this side with the 1970 one,' he said, 'But any team which takes the League title is a very good one... I would like to think that this is just the start of things. I believe this side is good enough and young enough to get even better.'

The fact every press photographer was behind the QPR goal at the Park End indicated where the action was expected. They were not wrong as Rangers struggled to get out of their own half but for all Everton's pressure there was just one goal – on 27 minutes when Mountfield's close range volley found the back of the net via the underside of the crossbar and goalkeeper Peter Hucker's back. The second period was a much more even contest, Rangers going close to equalising when Gary Bannister's header cannoned back off the post. The scare injected new life into Everton and eight minutes from time came a typical goal. Bracewell received the ball from Stevens, moved it to Van Den Hauwe and Sharp met the left-back's cross with a perfect header. When referee John Hough blew for full time at 4.49 pm Kendall had got the title he (and supporters) prized above anything else.[121] The balance of power of football on Merseyside had shifted for the first time since the FA Cup semi-final defeat of 1971. 'The object of the exercise was to catch them and eventually overtake them,' the Everton manager said. Everybody knew who 'them' were.

There were emotional scenes at the final whistle. Kendall leapt onto the pitch to congratulate his team. The ludicrous stage-managed laps of honour of today feature all sorts of hangers-on, and largely exist as a monument to vanity. Then they were performed properly: only the victors accompanied by a gaggle of photographers. The circuit of the pitch cemented the connection between players and supporters, rather than serve as an opportunity for self-indulgence. As the supporters chanted 'Hand it over Liverpool' elsewhere there was hardly a dry eye in the house. Mrs Rita Carter – wife of Philip – wept openly in the directors' box.

---

[121] The victory over QPR meant Everton had beaten all 21 rivals at least once in the league during the season. Only two teams achieved this when the top-flight featured 22 clubs from 1919-1995: the other being Everton in 1969/70.

Sir John Moores was joyous: 'I never thought that I'd live to see another League championship come to Goodison. It's great to feel free of the domination of Liverpool.' A supporter symbolically tied a scarf around the former chairman's neck. Kendall understandably was a happy man. When Bob Paisley had congratulated him on the train home from the FA Cup final, he replied: 'Thanks Bob, but it's the League next season.' Kendall had got his wish. 'What a day. We got the win we wanted and got it at Goodison Park, which is great,' he said, 'The champagne tastes very sweet. It's been a hard slog, but we've proved we are the best.' In his collaboration with Ken Rogers for *Everton's Z-Stars*, the Everton boss admitted that he drifted back fifteen years:

> *And so as I stood on the Everton pitch at the end of that season with our title dream unfolding before us if we beat QPR, I took great satisfaction from the fact we had moved forward in a big way. My thoughts flashed back to the day in 69/70 when I was an Everton player and we clinched the title on home soil... There was so much confidence in the team, a trait I could also sense in my Eighties Championship side... It was nice for everybody that it was settled at Goodison, just as it was in 1970. To have been part of both of those occasions just added it for me.*

Inevitably, the manager also reflected on the dark days of 1983 when fans wanted him out. 'It was understandable and I was aware of what was demanded here,' he explained, 'The two previous managers had been given three seasons. I was in my third season and we hadn't won anything so I knew all about pressure.' With supporters now cheering him, the irony was not lost on the *Daily Mail's* John Roberts: 'Many of those who yesterday so easily declared "There's only one Howard Kendall" considered that this was one too many a couple of seasons ago.'

However, the press paid tribute to the new champions. 'Everton are a team of the 80s – not in their tactics... but in their attitude,' said David Lacey, 'they are a blue overall side who have given work rate a better name. Earlier this season someone described Everton as an anonymous team. Presumably this view has been modified.' Steve Curry of the *Daily Express* had known Kendall since his days as a cub reporter in Preston. 'His team reflect his own personality,' he wrote, 'Dependable, determined, diligent and, when the occasion demands it, dour. Everton work prodigiously for each other and for the team.' Ken Rogers in the

Liverpool Echo wrote, 'The FA Cup Final and the European Cup Winners Final are still to come, but this was the prize that Howard Kendall and his outstanding young side wanted most of all.' Speaking to Stuart Jones of *The Times*, Colin Harvey was typically modest. 'It is all down to one man, Howard Kendall. He brought in a few players, Gray in particular, Reid came back into the side and the youngsters started performing to their potential and, in some cases, above it.'

The championship trophy dully made its way to Goodison 48 hours later, presented to the team before a comprehensive 3-0 victory over West Ham. There were two further goals for Derek Mountfield, taking the centre-half's tally to a ridiculous fourteen. The local-born player had been a schoolboy striker and several goals displayed those centre-forward instincts. 'The boss gave me five goals as a target before the start of the season,' Mountfield admitted after the QPR game, 'But then he doubled it to 10!'

What a marvellous Philip

Inevitably, there was praise for the way Philip Carter had held his nerve in the dark months of late-1983. Yet there were others behind the scenes who also deserved credit. Club secretary – in reality de facto chief executive – Jim Greenwood was the great facilitator, handling the logistics of a complex campaign with the coolness of one of the shrewdest operators in the game. Greenwood had joined a decade before and commanded huge respect. Normally the handing over of the championship trophy was on the final home game but as that was against Liverpool on 23 May, Greenwood persuaded the Football League to bring it forward, feeling a presentation three weeks after clinching the title would be an anti-climax. Carter, Greenwood and Kendall therefore formed a hugely powerful triumvirate. One of the greatest Evertonians and club servants, Greenwood passed away in 2017. 'He was one of football's great administrators,' said Bill Kenwright at his funeral, 'And his legacy of helping steer Everton through its greatest years will never be forgotten in Goodison history.'

Understandably, the focus off the pitch was on the club chairman. In a profile of Carter, Julie Welch of the *Observer* noted how during the title celebrations he had not accompanied the players on the pitch nor tried to share the glory in the directors' box. The Everton chairman 'Would not know a high profile if it shinned over an electric fence and ran towards him waving a broken bottle,' she claimed. That said, he was becoming a more influential figure within the game.

Carter also told Welch about the importance of a chairman keeping a cool head during the dark days. 'I think it involves a lot of restraint by the people involved,' he asserted, 'The fans want success and everything less than success will provoke a reaction. You can't blame them, but it's the prime duty of a chairman to be a calming influence.' In late-1983 that was certainly the case, Carter keeping his head amidst the growing discontent and both he and his manager reaped the rewards.

The chairman had also retired as Littlewoods group managing director fifteen months before and the remarkable transformation in fortunes followed. When the *Sunday Telegraph* asked Carter in May 1985 whether this was just a coincidence, the chairman just smiled. 'I'd hate to claim the credit for it,' he told Colin Malam, 'Perhaps my added interest has helped – but no more than that.'

The closeness of the Carter-Kendall relationship was apparent when the BBC interviewed the pair for a memorable *Sportsnight* feature broadcast on the night of the West Ham home game. 'When Howard came here we said both of us at the time that certainly it would take three/four years before he could remould the team, reshape it and hopefully bring some trophies,' Carter admitted. When asked whether he had considered sacking the manager, the chairman became more animated:

I can honestly say that was not the case. I have been asked this question before and one can say it is simple to sit here today with the improved success that we are getting that it didn't cross our minds. But truthfully at no stage did we consider the manager's position other than to support him. And as you well know, at that time, I went out publicly [in the Daily Express] and supported both the manager and coaching staff because I felt that was the right thing to do.

Carter was putting his reputation on the line supporting the manager but, on a personal level, he also liked Kendall as an individual and revealed 'They talk a lot – I'm not interfering, he's needed a sounding board.' This led to an almost paternal relationship, reflected in the way he spoke about the manager to Welch. 'I was prepared to back him, and now it's nice to see a younger man coming through and reaping the reward of his endeavours.'

Now it was for the Cup Winners' Cup final in Rotterdam, with an FA Cup final to follow against Manchester United three days later. Beforehand Carter was quite happy to give credit elsewhere: 'Naturally I get tremendous personal satisfaction from our achievements but everything that has happened is due to a complete team operation throughout the club.'

CHAPTER 35

'You're still the best'

MORE THAN 20,000 EVERTON SUPPORTERS HEADED TO HOLLAND for the game against Rapid Vienna. The Austrians had ridden their luck in getting to the final, most notably in the second round against Celtic. After the Glaswegians lost 3-1 in Vienna they won the return at Parkhead 3-0 to go through on aggregate, however UEFA upheld the Austrian camp's debatable complaint that a bottle had struck their keeper. Rapid won a third game 1-0 at Old Trafford.[122]

Fortunately for Everton their two most well-known players, prolific striker Hans Krankl and Antonin Panenka (of penalty fame), were way past their best. Their other threat was 25-year-old Peter Pacult, who had shown a rare turn of speed to net against Celtic at Old Trafford. Rapid had created a siege mentality following the criticism of their behaviour, but Everton had some unexpected support with letters from fans of the Glaswegian side wishing them well. Although strong favourites, Kendall was still cautious: 'We have checked out the Austrians very carefully. They have a number of players who can be a threat and are a side to respect.' However, his midfield commander was more confident. 'We have adapted to European football very quickly, which I think has surprised many

---

[122] In those primitive days, one of Kendall's main sources of information on the Austrians was a videotape with Russian commentary.

people,' Peter Reid explained, 'The continental game suits our style; we don't give the opposition time or space.' In previewing the two forthcoming finals in the *Sunday Times*, Brian Glanville wrote that Kendall 'Has put together, with immense skill and shrewdness, a team at once skilful, combative and resilient.' The esteemed journalist added:

> *While I'd hardly agree with Udo Lattek, Bayern's manager, that Everton are the best team in Europe, they have learned wonderfully fast. The midfield of Trevor Steven, Bracewell, Reid and Sheedy is outstanding, Ratcliffe and Southall are two of the best defenders in Europe and if Gray tends to duplicate rather than compliment his fellow Scot Sharp, his courage sows terror in defences. Everton must start favourites in Rotterdam. Wembley is another matter.*

There was a call-to-arms from Kendall before the game. 'We are looking forward to the challenge,' he asserted, 'I am delighted that all my players are fit and that we go into the game injury-free. Now we want to complete the job. I am very proud to be here. We want to bring the club's first European trophy back home to Merseyside.' His opposite number, Otto Baric, feared one man: 'Everton play a lot of high balls and Gray always seems to be around. He is very brave, but sometimes goes too far... but even so we are ready for Gray.'

A relaxed Everton squad were staying at the same hotel used by Aston Villa when they won the European Cup three years before. 'Not that we're superstitious,' quipped Kendall to ITV's Brian Moore, before informing the great commentator 'I'll be wearing my lucky suit'. Such was their confidence, Everton arrived on the Tuesday evening, did not train in Holland nor inspect the pitch. However, there were problems within the Rapid camp, with wrangling over the crucial defeat by Austria Vienna in a league game on the previous Friday.

The supporters from both teams behaved impeccably on a lovely spring day in the Dutch city, staging football games with the police, including chief officer Patrick Verwer, who later became managing director of the Merseyrail franchise. 'I was in charge of the police operation in Rotterdam when Everton played there and when the police played football with the fans in the town square. They were great,' Verwer said on his appointment. Clearly apparent was that Everton's following outnumbered their Viennese counterparts 2:1, creating a blue wall of noise at their end. 'Our supporters have proved to everyone today what we already know – they are brilliant,' skipper Kevin Ratcliffe said after the game.

A half-fit Panenka could only make the bench while tough midfielder Petar Brucic was suspended, which helped Everton's cause. Following kick-off, the chasm in quality between the teams reflected the gap in their support. 'Everton took the game to the Austrians right from the start and Rapid were forced to throw up a desperate defensive curtain,' Alec Johnson reported in the *Daily Mirror*. Trevor Steven and both full-backs were outstanding in the opening period but Rapid gave Everton so much space on the wings their tendency was for too many crosses, which their opponents handled.

Although Kendall's side forced Rapid into countless errors, picked up every loose ball and continually probed around the opposition box, the best legitimate chance of the half came as early as the twelfth minute. Kevin Sheedy exchanged passes with Gray at the edge of the box and goalkeeper Michael Konsel pushed away his right-footed shot. It was 31 minutes before the incongruously red-shirted Southall saw sight of an opponent but despite territorial domination, the favourites created few genuine chances. Indeed the closest they came to scoring was on 37 minutes. In 2003, Kendall told Ken Rogers for their book *Everton's Z-Stars*: 'I noticed that they often failed to cover at the far post when defending free-kicks. In Kevin Sheedy, we had someone who could exploit that with his accurate crosses.' The Everton bench thought their homework had paid off when his free-kick speared towards the unmarked Mountfield at the back who headed across goal for Andy Gray to scoop in. The goal was beautifully and intelligently constructed but, thanks to an errant linesman, incorrectly chalked off for offside against the Everton centre-half. 'I am afraid it is just a case of when the dam is breached and then it will collapse,' said Brian Clough on co-commentary duties on ITV, but there was frustration for the English champions at half-time, in that such a vibrant performance had brought no tangible reward. 'Everton came in at the interval wondering how on earth they were not ahead,' David Lacey said in the *Guardian*. 'Keep it going, the game will be yours,' Kendall told the players at half-time.

Although Rapid showed more ambition on the resumption, the long-awaited breakthrough arrived twelve minutes in. Sharp intercepted Leo Lainer's suicidal back-pass, stayed on his feet when rounding Konsel before intelligently pulling the ball back to the predatory Gray, who used his trusted left foot to volley home.

'I do realise it was a bad back-pass but Sharp does absolutely magnificently here,' said Clough, 'He could have gone down there for a start, he even finds time to look up and puts it through the goalkeeper's hands. I think he did and Gray puts it away beautifully.' The scorer later wrote in *Gray Matters*: 'People will say it is a simple goal, but believe me when you've got to hit one on the volley to give your side the lead in a cup final it is never easy. Luckily I caught it nice and crisply and in it went.'

On 65 minutes came the move of the match and perhaps the season: a bewildering passage of play that swept down and across the pitch, involving every Everton outfielder apart from the two centre-halves. The wonderful exchange ended with a cute chip by Bracewell to Steven at the edge of the box, the wide-man swivelling beautifully before Konsel blocked his fierce right-footed shot. Seven minutes later there were further rewards when Sheedy's corner ran through to an unmarked Steven at the far post – Kendall's pre-match intuition proving correct – who fired home from inside the six-yard box. It took 82 minutes for Southall to touch the ball directly from a Rapid player, when saving from Johann Gröss, the substitute who had looked their only threat. But three minutes later, the lifeless Austrians undeservedly pulled a goal back when an offside-looking Krankl rounded the Welshman to slide the ball home. But in typical fashion within fifty seconds, Sharp set up Sheedy and the Irishman produced a typically precise finish to make the game safe. 'You've seen something special tonight, that was an unbelievable performance that, tremendous,' Kendall told ITV's pitch-side reporter Elton Welsby. 'I thought every one of our players was magnificent, as a team performance you won't see any better.'

After Kevin Ratcliffe received the trophy from UEFA president Jacques Georges, the tributes to a special team started. 'If there were any doubts whatsoever remaining about the qualities Howard Kendall has coaxed to fruition,' Jeff Powell wrote in the *Daily Mail*, 'They were dispelled by a performance of collective cohesion and individual excellence which establishes Everton among Britain's outstanding post-war teams.' Rapid's skipper also paid a big compliment. 'It's been a very long time since I've played against a team as good, over the years English sides always give you a chance. But not Everton, they were brilliant,' Hans Krankl admitted. Rapid manager Otto Baric was also fulsome in praising the victors. 'Everton were the better team and we could not cope with their speed and aggression... even on our best form we could not have lived with Everton tonight.' As the team arrived back at Speke airport in the early hours after the most memorable day in the club's history, thoughts turned towards the weekend. 'This tremendous performance can only boost our confidence for Saturday's clash with Manchester United,' said Kendall.

A game too far

'Everton covered themselves in glory here last night, enhanced the esteem in which English football is held in Europe and restored some respect for Britain's fans abroad,' wrote Jeff Powell in the *Daily Mail*, 'That is a treble of such towering merit it will not be surpassed even if they win at Wembley on Saturday.' Wise and important words, especially after the effervescent performance and the exemplary behaviour of supporters. But, quite rightly, the Everton party focused only on the FA Cup final and the chance of an unprecedented treble.

United had endured a completely different midweek, hammered 5-1 at Watford, when Ron Atkinson trialled a new defensive high-line for use in the final. 'I did not want Gray and Sharp to spend all afternoon under our crossbar. I needed to keep them at bay,' he later said. John Barnes ran riot and Atkinson went into the dressing room and said, 'I have to tell you, lads, we won't be playing that way on Saturday.' However, Kendall knew it was a tough task. 'We are well aware of the quality within the United side,' he said, 'It is crammed with skilful players... But, having said that, we too have players of immense quality, players who can score goals and swing games.' Ironically, in the weeks before the game stories linked both managers with the Real Madrid job, Kendall being the choice of one of the presidential candidates. 'There are men at the club who consider him a bright, progressive thinker and a wise spender of money,' one Madrid insider claimed.

The Saturday morning previews pointed towards a close contest. United had proved too powerful for Liverpool in the semi-final and consequently the meeting between the country's two best teams was a 50:50 call. 'The popular feeling seems to be that United will win and thwart Everton dreams of a treble just as they foiled Liverpool's threefold ambitions in 1977,' wrote David Lacey in the *Guardian*, 'But for every individual strength they have Everton have the ability to match it.' The experienced David Miller in *The Times* forecast 'I take Kendall's team to achieve a rare and distinguished treble,' but colleague Stuart Jones said,

'If United recapture the spirit and the aggression with which they attacked Liverpool in the semi-final… Even Everton in all their glory would be hard pressed to withstand an unremitting force.' However, Brian Clough in the *Daily Mail* was as insightful as ever and his comments on the Everton team are well worth revisiting and reprinted in full, with a sting in the tail:

Neville Southall

If he was English I would have no hesitation nominating him as Peter Shilton's No. 2 – he's that good. Over the past couple of years he has progressed enormously and has obviously learned his trade well.

Gary Stevens

For my money the best – most improved – right back in the country. If there is such a thing as a 'cert' for Mexico he would be it – and I don't say that lightly because everyone knows how much I admire Viv Anderson.

Pat Van Den Hauwe

He's as aggressive as any defender in the English League. There aren't many quality left backs about and I can well understand Bobby Robson having shown an interest. Thought it was a cheek the Welsh moaning we were trying to poach an Englishman born in Belgium.

Kevin Ratcliffe

Yet another quality member of one of the best defences in the country. Think of the fastest central defender around – and you automatically think of him.

Derek Mountfield

He looks like one of Al Capone's henchmen – and he acts like a hit-man when he gets sight of the opposition goal. Apart from being a darned good defender, he's scored plenty of times for Everton this season and it certainly helps when you've got a secret weapon like him in your armoury.

Peter Reid

Whoever was responsible for buying him for £60,000 from Bolton deserves a medal for showing more astuteness than most people in football management. Reid is a tremendous asset to the club after battling back from injury. There's no more aggressive or competitive side in the country than Everton – and he is its heartbeat. By some divine intervention he was around at Goodison at precisely the right time with the experience to complement the young talents of Bracewell and Sheedy.

Trevor Steven

At 21 years of age he finds himself not only playing in the best team in the land, but a full international. Coming less than two years after his £300,000 transfer from Burnley, that's staggering progress.

Paul Bracewell

A comparative unknown to me. He bounced around at Stoke and Sunderland before joining Everton. A competent midfielder who fits perfectly into Kendall's overall scheme.

Kevin Sheedy

He must be enjoying the sweetest experience in the world. Sold by that club across the road, he's now winning the League and Cups with rivals Everton and Liverpool going through a period of transformation. I've never known Liverpool sell a good player before.

Andy Gray

… or should I say Roy of the Rovers. Andy's resurgence this season has been pure story book stuff. Back in a young side he's revelling in the pursuit of more honours. It's rose blossoms all the way. He's as brave as they come, a superb header of the ball – but he does rabbit on to referees.

Graeme Sharp

I really don't want to talk about this young man. He's not my favourite player since Forest went to Everton earlier this season. He was involved in a tackle in which Gary Mills suffered a broken leg and an incident which resulted in a sending off for Chris Fairclough.

Clough had kept his powder dry about the Everton striker after the game at Goodison, but December was still obviously on his mind. The Forest boss had been nothing less than complimentary about Sharp in Rotterdam and the newspaper comments sum up his contrary nature perfectly – as well as his unmatched flair for controversy.[123] Elsewhere it is hard to disagree with his views, although previous loyalty to Shilton masked the fact that by then Southall was the best goalkeeper in the country. Also, Bracewell was obviously a hidden gem.

The crowd of 100,000 made the final the first £1 million fixture in English football history, with £25 stand tickets changing hands at £250. Both Coral and William Hill had United as narrow favourites at 4-5, with Everton evens. In a statisticians' paradise, Everton could complete the treble[124] while becoming only the third team to complete a domestic double in the twentieth century and the fourth to defend the FA Cup at Wembley. Yet for all the attacking and creative talent on show in the first half, like so many games of that era (even the better ones) for long periods *nothing happens*. Watching again, there are a constant stream of fouls, countless offside decisions and unnecessary back-passes to the goalkeeper. The endless stoppages stultified the atmosphere and the crowd who, on a humid and occasionally sunny afternoon, seemed largely comatose. Atkinson was obviously conscious of the threat from set-pieces and ensured that Paul McGrath, who played brilliantly, stayed touch-tight to Gray while from corners United crowded their six yard box: 'We believe that Robson and Stapleton are the best sealers-off at the near post,' Atkinson said beforehand. Goalkeeper Gary Bailey's instructions were to come out for Gary Stevens' long-throws and in the tenth minute his weak punch fell to Peter Reid and the midfielder's first-time volley appeared to be heading in, before the studs of the diving former Everton full-back John Gidman intervened and deflected the ball onto the post and out for a corner.

The theory that Wembley was a graveyard for wide-men, because of the size

---

[123] Sharp was injured at the City Ground in early May, but in his autobiography the Scot recalled that Clough said to him in the dugout, 'I'm just sorry you're not playing, I won't forget what happened at Goodison Park.' Clough then told Sharp that he had asked son Nigel to 'give you a hard time.' When Sharp reminded the Forest boss he was playing in a European final four days later, Clough shook hands and responded: 'I know you are, young man, and all the very best for it.' However, four months later Everton made an official complaint to the Football Association over Clough's outspoken views about the striker, which ended with the Forest manager making a written apology.

[124] Achieved previously only by Celtic (1967) and Ajax (1972) who both won the domestic double and the European Cup plus IFK Gothenburg (1982) who did the double with the UEFA Cup – the Swedes managed by a certain Sven-Goran Eriksson.

of the pitch and the heavy turf, also came to fruition. Both pairs saw little of the ball and ended up moving inside – where significantly United had Bryan Robson and Norman Whiteside facing Reid and Bracewell for the first time – which resulted in an ugly morass of skirmishes across a narrow avenue of grass. 'The discrepancy between what the contest had promised and what was happening out on the field was indicated by the struggles of [Gordon] Strachan and Sheedy,' opined Hugh McIlvanney in the *Observer*. 'Throughout the first half both were negative to the point of anonymity.' With no pace up-front, Kendall's team could hardly knock the ball over the top and ended up falling into the trap of hitting it long to the isolated front pairing. Any width was on the Everton right where Gary Stevens was the best player on the pitch in the opening half. Apart from Reid's effort and a couple of half-chances (at best) for United that was about it.

After an initial burst of energy in the second period the pattern of play continued, with only two chances. Gray fired wastefully over with his right foot when given a clean shot on goal and then Whiteside forced the only meaningful save either goalkeeper had to make in normal time. Put through by Hughes and with Southall to beat, the young Irishman, according to McIlvanney, 'Could hardly believe what he was seeing as Southall sprawled to his right and not only intercepted the ball but held it.'

Then thirteen minutes from time came the game's major talking point. Reid intercepted a loose ball from McGrath and, with Gray free to his left, United centre-half Kevin Moran took the only realistic option and stopped the Everton player with a badly-timed challenge. With most observers expecting a booking there was widespread amazement when referee Peter Willis, in his final game, dismissed the Irish international. 'Oh he's sent him off,' says an incredulous Brian Moore on ITV while Ian St John accused Willis of being 'One-hundred percent out of order'. Although Moran had given Willis, who received £43 for refereeing the final, a decision to make over whether the tackle constituted serious foul play, the consensus was that the United player was unlucky. 'Moran was the victim of an unnecessarily harsh reaction by referee Peter Willis,' said Ken Jones in the *Sunday Mirror*. Emlyn Hughes surprisingly made a good point on the BBC that if Moran had intended to clear out Reid then he would have taken him out much higher. Typically, the sending-off galvanised both Manchester United and the game itself as Atkinson's men ended the ninety minutes the stronger of the two teams.

United's ascendancy continued in extra time for three reasons. Everton tired visibly and clearly had no energy to make their numerical advantage count. Also, two years earlier United had seen Moran carried off against Liverpool in the League Cup final and Atkinson pulled Frank Stapleton back into defence, but then sat back and lost 2-1. Against Everton, Stapleton performed the same role superbly but the tactics were different. 'We may have learnt from that,' Atkinson admitted, 'This time instead of sitting back, we went at the game.' Finally, Everton looked one-dimensional in attack and missed the energy and ingenuity of the stricken Adrian Heath. As Brian Glanville said in the *Sunday Times* the missing striker gave 'Everton so many alternatives in attack with his darting runs, his turns, his quick intelligence.' No other player possessed those characteristics and his presence, on a heavy pitch against tired opponents, could have made all the difference.

For all that, the chances of a replay five days later became almost a certainty, especially when Bryan Robson misjudged Steven's corner and his headed clearance bounced back off Bailey's crossbar. But then in the 113th minute came the goal. Mark Hughes turned in his own half and, with Bracewell seemingly too tired to even commit a tactical foul, the Welshman's pass out wide found Whiteside ('Whiteside's onside' announced Brian Moore, a line he was probably praying to use) and there appeared to be little danger as the Irish youngster moved in from United's right. Two things happened. Firstly, Van Den Hauwe, knowing that left-footed Whiteside was not the fastest in the parish, should have showed the United player down the outside. However, the left-back stood off and allowed Whiteside an opportunity to use him as a screen. Secondly, Southall, perhaps anticipating that the United player may be forced towards the byline, was too close to his near post. Consequently, both actions meant that when Whiteside produced a beautiful left-footed curler into the far corner, Southall was not far enough across to cover the shot. 'Wembley has rarely seen a more vital or less forgettable goal,' Hugh McIlvanney wrote.

At the end of the game as United celebrated a deserved victory, the Everton players tread warily up the 39 steps with Van Den Hauwe noticeably the most affected for obvious reasons. Kendall blamed neither player in the aftermath and rightly so – the hugely gifted Whiteside deserved enormous credit for a quite brilliant goal – but Southall was typically candid in his autobiography: 'I thought it was my fault, but no one blamed me and I haven't looked at it since.'

Full context Everton

More than a few people have said since that the cup final defeat was an anti-climax. In *Gray Matters*, the Everton striker wrote: 'The FA Cup final was a missed opportunity that rankled with me for years and I know Peter Reid, for one, felt the same.' That narrative is perfectly understandable. But it ignores several relevant facts.

Firstly, the defeat should not overshadow what was – and remains – one of the greatest and most dominant campaigns by any side in domestic football history, their 43 victories in all competitions a record for a single season that stood until 2009. Everton were the first English team to be one game from completing a treble of league, FA Cup and a European trophy. Since then only Manchester United, in 1999, have been in the same position – and by that time the financial advantages afforded to the biggest clubs were already taking effect. Worth noting that whereas United won the title by effectively a single goal, Everton crossed the line with five games to spare.

The rarity of such an achievement stands out even more when considering the records of some of the greatest teams in the previous quarter-of-a-century. Neither Bill Shankly's Liverpool nor Matt Busby's Manchester United had got within even one game of a domestic double, never mind a treble. Don Revie's Leeds United side came close to the former once, in 1972, but lost their final league game at Wolves 48 hours after lifting the FA Cup. Two years before, their pursuit of the double and European Cup had floundered under the weight of a congested fixture list, as did Ipswich's quest for the double and the UEFA Cup in 1981. Liverpool's hugely successful 1976/77 season was like Everton's, Bob Paisley's team wrapping up the league title in their penultimate game seven days before losing the FA Cup final to Manchester United. Four days later Liverpool won the European Cup for the first time in Rome to put the finishing touches to their most historic season. However, although the European Cup enjoys a higher status, Everton's 1984/85 season sits easily in comparison: Kendall's team were domestic champions in a more comprehensive fashion, finishing thirteen points clear, despite losing three of their last four league games when fielding weakened teams.[125] In their respective European finals, although Liverpool faced German

---

[125] The sole victory ironically a 1-0 win over Liverpool at Goodison to complete their first derby double for twenty years.

giants Borussia Monchengladbach and Everton took on an inferior Rapid Vienna, in the last four the Anfield side had only to overcome the moderate FC Zurich while Kendall's team had to contend with Bayern Munich. Everton were also facing a considerably stronger Manchester United side in the FA Cup final. 'Everton, in their great success and relative failure, join some distinguished company,' wrote Brian Glanville.

The schedule did not help Everton either. Five years before Arsenal had been the only other English side to reach an FA Cup and Cup Winners' Cup final in the same season, but on that occasion the European fixture was on the Wednesday after the climax to the domestic campaign, meaning the Gunners had four days to prepare.[126] Paisley's side enjoyed the same benefits in 1977. However, for Kendall's team the reverse happened: the shifting of the Cup Winners' Cup final meant they played both games within 72 hours whilst having to return from the continent and travel down south during that time.

The scheduling obviously does not excuse the FA Cup final defeat – although it probably did contribute – but shows how the fixture schedule can influence the quest for glory. That said, Manchester United were a very strong team full of talent and, with Atkinson's management style always better suited to one-off fixtures, a more convenient final date may not have significantly improved Everton's chances. The manager, unwittingly or otherwise, acknowledged all this history, when he spoke to the players in the dressing room afterwards, as he recalled in *Love Affairs and Marriage*:

> *It was a disappointment, but not a crushing one like the time we'd been defeated in the 1968 final when I was a player. In the context of a wonderful season, it was a slight slip-up, I was still able to leave the Wembley pitch with my head held high and enter the dressing room in the bowels of the stadium where I delivered my four-word post-match team-talk: 'You're still the best.'*

---

[126] As it happened, they lost both games to West Ham United and Valencia respectively.

CHAPTER 36

Making sense of 1984/85

THE SEASON REMAINS UNDOUBTEDLY THE GREATEST AND MOST successful in Everton's history – one that has sustained supporters (and the club) during the fallow years that followed. Such a multi-dimensional campaign raised more questions than answers. Like who should take the credit.

Howard's way? Or Howard and Colin's way?

In Tony Pawson's excellent 1973 book on the trade, *The Football Managers*, an Annex reproduces the job description of Plymouth Argyle's Tony Waiters. His role is 'The overall responsibility for Team affairs including the preparation, selection and recruitment/termination of all staff.' Meanwhile, the most important duties are: i) Preparation and selection of First Team; ii) Recruitment and development of Senior Professional players; and iii) Press and TV relations.

The first comment is that fifty years later the core duties have, surprisingly, largely remained unchanged. In late-1983 the board's assessment of Kendall against those parameters would have been interesting. For (iii) the manager had no issues, the Everton boss was a confident presence in front of the press and TV cameras, witness his mature *Match of the Day* interview after the 2-1 win at Brighton in April 1983.[127] A nice line in humorous quips helped his cause. Yes, there was the occasional awkward moment in the dark days, but Kendall's

---

[127] The victory severely dented Brighton's hopes of staying up. Afterwards Barry Davies asked the Everton boss if he had sympathy for the home team. Kendall said no and referenced Ron Atkinson's statement after the quarter-final defeat a few weeks before, but then wished the south-coast side well for the following week's semi-final.

aptitude for media relations belied his age and managerial experience. 'Howard was only a young manager but he was so wise,' Peter Reid wrote in *Cheer Up Peter Reid.*

For 'preparation and selection of First Team', the proof is in results. The finishes in Kendall's first two seasons of eighth and seventh were a vast improvement over the final years of Gordon Lee. But there had been periods of worrying form. Brian Glanville used to say – rightly or wrongly – that good fortune favoured Kendall. 'Napoleon wanted all his generals to be lucky,' he once wrote, 'He'd have liked Everton.' There was some truth in that, Kendall's first campaign was saved by the promising youngsters in the reserves he promoted ahead of schedule. That said, Kendall was brave to quickly change things as well as getting the team to gel.

The Everton boss was an inherently cautious manager who demanded a tight defence. Although were some painful away performances in the early days, the turning point was the creation of the Ratcliffe-Higgins axis at the end of 1982 and from then on Kendall's team conceded fewer league goals than games played. In golfing parlance being under par in that metric gave the manager a platform to work with, like at Blackburn.

Kendall's main problem was therefore getting the midfield balance right and developing a penetrative attack. The first point here is the experience of the players involved: in the epic FA Cup quarter-final game at Old Trafford in March 1983 the average age of the Everton outfield was just 22 years. The only players with any sort of career were defenders John Bailey (25) and Mark Higgins (24). Naturally, there was inconsistency and a loss of confidence in a young and inexperienced team which was apparent in 1983/84 but the defeat at Old Trafford showed their potential.

For 'Recruitment and development of Senior Professional players' there are two elements and, for the first, by the end of 1983 Kendall's performance can best be described as 'moderate'. The feeling was the manager brought his Blackburn methods to the club, without acknowledging that working with better quality players would need a different style – ultimately one of the reasons why Billy Bingham failed. The players purchased in the disastrous summer of 1981 were collectively journeymen who Blackburn would have targeted if given £1.5m to spend. There was an improvement in the following two years: Adrian Heath and Kevin Sheedy, particularly, looked very good signings. David Johnson was a badly-judged acquisition and, although Andy King had a certain amount of sentimental value, he could still do a job. By the late autumn of 1983, the signings of Derek Mountfield, Trevor Steven, Alan Harper and Andy Gray were in the not proven category. Even Howard Kendall admitted then that signing Peter Reid was a mistake. 'I started to think that it might not happen for me at Everton,' Reid acknowledged in his autobiography.

The 'development of Senior Professional players' is the key to how the team subsequently progressed. It is easy to forget how inexperienced Kendall was when taking the job in comparison to, say, Harry Catterick. The latter had been a manager for a decade when he walked into Goodison, having done the hard yards at Crewe and Rochdale and moved up the ladder to successfully manage Sheffield Wednesday – a big club – for three years. Catterick was a fully-rounded manager when he returned in 1961 – Kendall in 1981-83 was anything but. Although Kendall was firm and ruthless with players – see Alan Biley, Micky Thomas and Billy Wright – the management and coaching staff were probably not as forceful as they needed to be. Kendall's coach Mick Heaton was nicknamed 'Easy' because of his relaxed nature, somebody who would not deliver a fierce rollicking, but who would convey criticism in a nice way. With Kendall's lack of managerial experience and having a not too-dissimilar personality to Heaton, the club lacked the classic 'good cop, bad cop' coaching set-up. In a strange way, the light-touch approach was the opposite of the overbearing intensity Gordon Lee had with Eric Harrison, which caused so much dissention after Steve Burtenshaw departed. The young squad needed something between those two methods.

Kendall addressed this issue when appointing Colin Harvey to the coaching staff. However, the way he broadcast that change to the squad displayed a lack of confidence and too-much sensitivity, particularly towards Heaton. Kendall took both into the dressing room and announced to the squad: 'I know the respect you have for Colin. I'm making him first team coach with Mick. Three heads are better than two.' Everybody knew the implication. 'That was the worst moment for both of them,' Kevin Ratcliffe said, 'You never saw two professionals look more embarrassed.' The promotion of Harvey brought a harder edge. 'Colin is a rough type. He snarls at you, winds you up,' Ratcliffe remarked in his autobiography, 'He would give it straight between the eyes. He's one of the breed who will get another ten per cent out of you even if you haven't got it to give.' Being a brilliant player in his own right also brought a certain amount of cachet and, as several players have noted since, watching Harvey give everything in training, despite chronic hip pain, acted as a reminder of the commitment needed to succeed. The 1970 championship-winner demanded the highest standards, worked the players hard and his enormous will-to-win rubbed off. 'Colin would kick you in training if he felt that a game needed livening up,' Graeme Sharp said, 'He pushed us exceptionally hard and it was often quite easy to resent him for it.' Kevin Richardson told Simon Hart in *Here We Go: Everton in the 1980s* that, 'He'd train with the lads but if you were on his side and he was getting beaten, he was the most horrible man you'd ever met in your life. We'd stay out and play the game until we were winning and then he'd stop the game because that was his mentality. He hated getting beaten. I thought, "To have that mentality is what it takes."'

Within three months of Harvey's ascension, the team was unrecognisable. The exceptional high-standards and scientific approach Harvey brought to Bellefield and away from the training ground – there would be video sessions with the players on a Monday – combined with the burgeoning influence of Peter Reid and Andy Gray, ultimately brought rewards. The question, therefore, is whether the success of 1984 and 1985 would have happened if Kendall had not promoted Harvey during the dark days. When the *Sunday Times'* Nick Pitt asked the Everton manager in November 1984 why, earlier in the year, his players suddenly understood what he required of them, Kendall replied, 'I don't know whether it was through playing together, or through their own intelligence.' That came into it but the promotion of Harvey was not a coincidence, although the previously young squad was maturing anyway and may have got there eventually. However, based on the testimony of the players since, there is an argument that had the Kendall-Heaton axis continued then there may have been, at best, a deferring of success.

The secondary question is if Harvey's promotion was the catalyst, does that diminish Kendall's reputation? No – the move enhances it. The Everton boss recognised the problem and acted. All great managers need strong support teams. Shankly and Paisley had the fabled Anfield boot-room while Sir Alex Ferguson took great pains in appointing his immediate assistant. 'I'm not equipped to manage successfully without Peter Taylor,' Brian Clough said once, 'I am the shop window, and he is the goods in the back.' There was a bit of Clough and Taylor about the Goodison duo. Andy Gray's statement that Kendall needed a strategist beside him was undoubtedly true and in late-1983 the Everton boss was carrying too much on his shoulders. Harvey's coaching excellence lifted that burden and allowed Kendall to do exactly what he was brilliant at: team management in the broadest sense. Waiters' job description began with 'The overall responsibility for Team affairs' and the buck stopped with Kendall. From the start of 1984, he carried out that task brilliantly so it was 'Howard's Way' in the end – with the help of a few others.

Copying the reds

Alan Ball's point that Kendall should not copy Liverpool but find another route-map to success by building 'a character side rather than a machine,' had several different angles. The first is the Liverpool machine had taken more than a decade to develop, via the years of passing and movement finely-tuned over countless games of five-a-side at Melwood. Also, success provided the wealth to buy the best players to execute that strategy. Time and money for Kendall were both in short supply so Ball was correct, the Everton manager had to do something different.

But Kendall did that by taking other characteristics from Anfield. The first was hard work. Nobody worked with more intensity off the ball or ran further than Liverpool, particularly their 1972/73 title-winners, whom David Lacey namechecked in relation to Everton on at least one occasion. Lacey's colleague at the *Guardian*, Eric Todd noted then that 'consistency rather than skill and erratic brilliance' won titles before adding, 'Nobody could call Liverpool a brilliant side; but very few could equal them for the consistency which won them the championship.' They were saying the same things about Everton twelve years later. But whereas Liverpool based their 1973 title victory on a formidable home record in a campaign that saw them score 72 goals in total, Everton recorded twelve away wins and netted sixteen more. Kendall's team also had greater individual quality. 'Between about 1972 and 1974 Everton made the mistake of trying to become another Liverpool through fitness alone; it was run, run, run,' Joe Royle told the *Sunday Telegraph* in April 1985, 'Now, they've got that and the players who can put into effect the sort of teamwork and organisation Liverpool are famous for.'

The other attribute both teams had in common was their away tactics. Liverpool's defeat to Red Star Belgrade in their 1973 European Cup tie famously led to a change of style at Anfield. Bob Paisley wanted to play a more restrained and patient game, especially on their travels. 'Denying the opposition scoring opportunities would also quieten the home fans and put home sides under pressure,' Ian Herbert wrote in his biography of Paisley, *Quiet Genius*, 'That, in turn, would force them to take chances and open up spaces.' Herbert quotes Paisley's instructions to Tommy Smith before a European game, 'the quickest way forward is to push the ball back and frustrate your opponents into making mistakes.' In the opening period of away games, Liverpool would reduce the opposition threat by knocking the ball from deep into their forwards, as a means of getting up the pitch. 'Make plenty of passes. Deny them scoring chances in the first half and their fans will get fidgety,' Paisley told Phil Neal. Once Liverpool had established a bridgehead then the team could play.

That was pretty much Kendall's approach, particularly away from home, and especially in the big matches during the final months of the 1984/85 season: in the first half rack up the back-passes and hit the ball long to Gray and Sharp. After the break come out and play a bit more and take advantage of opposition errors. The champions therefore gained the reputation as a second-half team. Those tactics worked to perfection, for example, in the crucial victories at Southampton and Spurs in April.[128] On the road Everton were superbly efficient: only two of their twelve away league victories were by more than one goal, although this in turn led to criticism. Brian Glanville, for one, felt that Everton played far too much within themselves away from home. That was true but for Kendall the season was about being champions, anything else was a bonus.

The key to the team was balance, but not necessarily in a diverse way. Kendall had a simple approach as he discussed with Nick Pitt: plenty of energy, deny the opposition space to play in and then use the ball well. Having players with similar characteristics provided a chance of performing the basics of the game far better than opponents. There would have been a waste of Gary Stevens' drive and endurance had Trevor Steven been a mercurial, old-fashioned winger who drifted in and out of games. Gray and Sharp had similar qualities and in crunch games late in the season if Kendall wanted to play long or bombard the opposition – like against Bayern Munich – then he had twice the firepower. When Paul Bracewell joined, there were concerns that he and Reid were too alike but, although they

---

[128] From March 1985 until the end of the season, fourteen of Everton's sixteen goals in cup matches came after the break.

had some different attributes, what they had in common was discipline, superb reading of the game and pressing in the same manner. Those shared characteristics gave Kendall extra intensity in the centre of the park. 'We were both tacklers, getting the ball and giving it, engine-room players,' Reid said, 'But it worked.' The strategy worked because it gave the Everton manager free rein to put two attacking players on the flanks in Sheedy and Steven. The result was one of English football's greatest quartets, one that possessed all the attributes a truly great midfield needs, as Rob Smyth recalled in the *Guardian* in 2009:

> *Everton were simply unstoppable, and their midfield showed a desire that verged on the rabid. The erudite passing of Bracewell and the ceaseless energy of Reid - often patronised but the PFA Player of the Year that season - gave them control of central midfield, and on the wings Steven, all direct dribbles and pinpoint crosses, and Sheedy, with a left foot so educated it could have been to Harvard, scored an absurd 33 goals between them.*

Aside from the balance of the team, Ball's point about character was correct. One of the fascinating aspects of the 1984/85 squad was the rich diversity and back-stories of the individuals involved. Apart from youth-products Stevens and Ratcliffe, the 1985 Cup Winners' Cup final side started off their league careers at Bury, Tranmere, Birmingham City, Bolton, Stoke, Hereford, Burnley, Dundee United and Dumbarton. The hazardous and lengthy path from those roots to a European final undoubtedly helped trigger a huge level of mental toughness. There was Neville Southall, the former hod-carrier and binman who became the best goalkeeper in the world. Andy Gray had once been Britain's most expensive player but at Wolves injuries meant he was fighting the dying of the light. Peter Reid had been a candidate for the soccer scrapheap a couple of years before. Pat Van Den Hauwe had learnt his trade in possibly the most troublesome dressing room in English football history. In a parallel universe, Kevin Ratcliffe and Kevin Sheedy could have been playing at Ipswich and Portsmouth in 1984/85. Derek Mountfield was the classic, local-born player who was a life-long supporter of the club. Gary Stevens and Graeme Sharp had overcome teething problems having endured difficult times in Kendall's first few years. Trevor Steven, Adrian Heath and Paul Bracewell were all talented but had to do the difficult work further down. Most had been Everton players while the best team in Europe played across

Stanley Park, which added an extra level of pressure – plus a harder edge. 'Perhaps the humiliation of living in the shadow of Liverpool, constantly mocked by years of Anfield success, has injected steel into Everton's soul,' the *Guardian's* Robert Armstrong concluded after the cup victory over Luton.

Such a wide variety of character-building experiences, both on and off the pitch, created a collective resilience that all champion teams require, but even Kendall's squad appeared to have a level above that. When combined with an equally diverse set of individual talents, superb coaching plus top-drawer man-management and organisation, then it is no surprise that Kendall 'Created one of the outstanding teams of the late twentieth century' according to the *Independent* after his death in 2015.

In retrospect

But how outstanding were Everton? And why do supporters think their achievements largely sit at the margins of English football? In terms of how they ranked in Europe, Brian Glanville wrote before the trip to Rotterdam that he did not rate Everton as the continent's best team. The question then, who was?

Given the Toffees won the First Division by a landslide then safe to assume they were the best in England. Bayern Munich were German champions, but Udo Lattek thought their semi-final opponents were the best in Europe. The Italian champions were unheralded Verona, but eventual European Cup winners Juventus only finished sixth that season. The Turin club, with a line-up including Michel Platini, Zbigniew Boniek and Paolo Rossi were a very good team but they won only eleven Serie A games and scraped through their European Cup semi-final against Bordeaux. In Spain, Real Madrid won the UEFA Cup but finished fifth in La Liga, with eleven league defeats during the season. Champions were Terry Venables' Barcelona, who lost only twice. However, the Spanish side could have played Everton in Rotterdam but for going out 6-5 on aggregate to French side Metz in the first round, including a 4-1 loss in the Nou Camp. That would seem to rule Venables' side out of the conversation. Indeed twelve months later Glanville was saying that Everton and Liverpool were the two best teams in Europe and when comparing the title-holders to Barcelona and that season's other European Cup finalist, Steaua Bucharest, he wrote that, 'I've a strong feeling that Everton, the current English champions, could have beaten either of them.' None of those teams had a dominant campaign like Kendall's side, who were therefore clearly Europe's best in the spring of 1985. *France Football* made them Team of the Year later in 1985 and readers of *World Soccer* did likewise: Everton received 42 percent of all votes cast, with Juventus second with just nine percent.

Where the best team in Europe in 1985 sits within the context of English football is more complex. Although supporters understandably argue that people have ignored Kendall's side or left them in the shadows, there are many reasons for that. Firstly, in the mid-1980s the popularity of the English game was at an all-time low. The scourge of hooliganism, rotten and empty stadiums, plus the lack of national team success, left the reputation of the sport in tatters. The best known sportsmen at the time were probably cricketers, athletes – and snooker players. Any successful English team in that context was always going to have limited publicity. Within that is how the critics regarded Everton during the campaign itself. Up until the end of March there were mixed reviews, a begrudging acknowledgement that Kendall's side had the metronomic consistency and work-ethic of champions, but there was criticism of away performances, especially by those who may have seen Everton only once or twice. That all changed in the first week of April with the victory at Spurs, when they showed their resilience, and then the brilliant televised performance against Sunderland three days later, that provided so many moments of individual skill. From then on people knew the team was special. Jeff Powell's assessment in the *Daily Mail* that they were one of the best post-war British teams was well put.

Secondly, Kendall's finest hour was in May 1985, the darkest month in English football history. The 1984/85 season had already seen hooliganism but, on the Saturday before Everton travelled to Rotterdam, 56 supporters were killed when the main stand burned down at Bradford. A fourteen-year-old boy was crushed to death under a collapsed wall as Leeds United fans rioted at Birmingham City on the same day. Three weeks later came Heysel. Although there always has to be perspective, as Scott Murray wrote in *The Title: The Story of the First Division*: 'One of the great campaigns was soured by the grimmest denouement to any season...English football had reached its painful nadir.' Mention May 1985 about football and Everton's achievements are way down the list, quite correctly.

Also, not many domestic clubs or teams are actually remembered. Only those who create a dynasty or an identity tend to resonate: Busby's Manchester United, Liverpool of the 1970s/80s, Don Revie's Leeds. Otherwise, there has to be something charismatic, like Brian Clough's Nottingham Forest or Bobby Robson's

Ipswich. Aston Villa won the league title and European Cup in the early-1980s – have they remained in the public consciousness?

Finally, probably the most important factor is one of timing. By the advent of the Premier League in 1992, Everton's achievements were too recent for recognition within the history books and culture of the game. By the time they were, the Premier League had become entrenched and a new way of recording history had started, meaning anything that happened in the years immediately before 1992 fell through the floorboards. This omission affected not only Everton but George Graham's Arsenal also (particularly their superb 1991 title-triumph when they lost just one game). Leeds United's League Championship winners of 1992 and Blackburn's Premier League triumph are three years apart but may as well have been light years in the amount of subsequent coverage.

That was all in the future though in the spring of 1985. Kendall and his great team had restored pride – and trophies – to Goodison. 'Liverpool, these days, is Everton's city,' Mihir Bose wrote in the *Sunday Times* after the 3-0 home victory over Norwich at the end of April, 'From shop assistant to taxi driver, everyone seems to have rediscovered their ancient loyalty.' That loyalty was on display when Everton returned to Liverpool on Sunday 19 May, 1985, with memories of the Wembley defeat already forgotten. There was a lovely symmetry to the day. Twelve years before, any Everton fan brave enough had watched on with jealousy as their Anfield rivals travelled round the city celebrating an eighth league title and first European trophy, having rubber-stamped their superiority on Merseyside. Everton supporters were now watching their own team doing exactly the same. History had repeated itself in the most glorious and satisfying manner imaginable.

Acknowledgements

I WOULD LIKE TO THANK ALL THOSE AT THE LIVERPOOL CENTRAL Library, the Manchester Central Library and the staff at the British Library in London. Also to Jim Malone for use of his photographs, Thomas Regan of Milkyone Creative for the cover design and Leslie Priestley for the typesetting. The esteemed John Keith's recollections were invaluable, particularly over the failure to land Bobby Robson in 1977. A big thank you to Rob Sawyer and Liam Fogarty for their assistance at various points, as well as Steve Johnson, whose *evertonresults* website is the ultimate statistics resource about the club. Finally my heartiest thanks to James Corbett, without whom this book would not have been possible.

Bibliography

Billy: A Biography of Billy Bingham, Robert Allen (Viking, 1986)

Everton v Liverpool: A Celebration of the Merseyside Derby,
Brian Barwick/Gerald Sinstadt (BBC Books, 1988)

Promised You A Miracle: Why 1980-82 Made Modern Britain,
Andy Beckett (Penguin, 2016)

Money Can't Buy Us Love: Everton in the 1960s, Gavin Buckland
(deCoubertin, 2019)

The Official Everton Autobiography, compiled by James Cleary
(Sport Media 2012)

Everton: The School of Science, James Corbett (Macmillan, 2003)

Faith of our Families, James Corbett (deCoubertin, 2017)

The Everton Encyclopedia, James Corbett (deCoubertin, 2012)

Never Say Dai, Dai Davies, (Siop y Siswrn, 1986)

Me and My Big Mouth: When Cloughie Sounded Off in TV Times,
Graham Denton (Pitch Publishing Ltd, 2019)

Liverpool - Wondrous Place, Paul Du Noyer (Virgin Books, 2002)

***I Don't Know What It Is But I Love It: Liverpool's Unforgettable
1983-84 Season,*** Tony Evans (Penguin, 2015)

Gray Matters, Andy Gray *(MacMillan, 2004)*

Shades of Gray, Andy Gray (Queen Anne Press, 1986)

King Joey: Joe Harper Upfront and Personal, Joe Harper (Birlinn Ltd, 2008)

Here We Go: Everton in the 1980s, Simon Hart (deCoubertin, 2016)

The Great Derby Matches: Liverpool versus Everton,
Michael Heatley/Ian Welch (Dial House, 1996)

Quiet Genius: Bob Paisley, British football's greatest manager,

Ian Herbert (Bloomsbury Sport, 2017)

Everton, The Official Complete Record, Steve Johnson (deCoubertin, 2010)

2008 Reasons Why Merseyside Is the Capital of Football,

John Keith/Gavin Buckland (Robson Books, 2007)

Colin Harvey's Everton Secrets,

John Keith/Colin Harvey (Trinity Mirror Sport Media 2005)

It's Much More Important Than That: Bill Shankly, The biography,

Stephen F. Kelly (Virgin Books, 1997)

Love Affairs and Marriage, My Life in Football,

Howard Kendall (deCoubertin, 2013)

Only the Best is Good Enough,

Howard Kendall/Ian Ross (Mainstream Publishing, 1991)

A Different Road, Bob Latchford (deCoubertin, 2013)

30: The Story of Bob Latchford's 1977/78 Season,

Bob Latchford/Martin O'Boyle (OB Media, 2006)

The Last Fancy Dan, Duncan McKenzie/David Saffer (Vertical Editions, 2009)

Macca Can! The Steve McMahon Story,

Steve McMahon/Harry Harris (Michael Joseph, 1990)

The Title: The Story of the First Division,

Scott Murray (Bloomsbury Sport, 2017)

I Only Wanted to Play Football,

Eamonn O'Keefe (Strategic Book Publishing & Rights Agency, 2010)

Everton in Europe 1962 - 2005: Der Ball Ist Rund,

Mike Owen (Countyvise Ltd, 2005)

Liverpool Beyond the Brink: The Remaking of a Post Imperial City,

Michael Parkinson (Liverpool University Press, 2019)

The Football Managers, Tony Pawson (Eyre Methuen, 1973)

Everton Player by Player, Ivan Ponting (Hamlyn, 1998)

The Blues and I, Kevin Ratcliffe (Arthur Barker, 1988)

Cheer Up Peter Reid: My Autobiography,

Peter Reid (Trinity Mirror Sport Media, 2017)

Everton, The Official Centenary History,

John Roberts (Granada Publishing/Mayflower Books, 1978)

Shankly – My Story, John Roberts (Arthur Barker Limited, 1976)

Born Not Manufactured, Ken Rogers, (Trinity Mirror Sport Media, 2016)

Goodison Glory, Ken Rogers (Breedon Books, 2000)

Everton's Z-Stars: The Men Who Made History 1984-1987,
Ken Rogers/Howard Kendall (Trinity Mirror Sport Media, 2004)

Joe Royle – The Autobiography, Joe Royle (BBC Books, 2007)

Harry Catterick, The Untold Story of a Football Great,
Rob Sawyer (deCoubertin, 2014)

Sharpy: My Story, Graeme Sharp (Mainstream Publishing, 2006)

So Good I Did it Twice, Kevin Sheedy (Trinity Mirror Sport Media, 2014)

The Binman Chronicles, Neville Southall (deCoubertin, 2012)

With Clough, By Taylor, Peter Taylor (Sidgwick & Jackson, 1980)

Three Sides of the Mersey,
Rogan Taylor/John Williams/Andrew Ward (Robson Books, 1993)

By the Book, Clive Thomas (HarperCollins, 1984)

Toddy, Colin Todd/Jim Brown (Breedon Books, 2008)

Looking for the Toffees, Brian Viner (Simon & Schuster, 2014)

Rothmans Football Yearbooks, various (Queen Anne Press, 1970-85)

Everton's FA Cup 100 (Trinity Mirror Sport Media, 2006)

Index

www.decoubertin.co.uk